Jahrbuch für Wirtschaftsgeschichte BEIHEFT 3

Im Auftrag der Herausgeber
des Jahrbuchs für Wirtschaftsgeschichte
herausgegeben von Reinhard Spree

Herman J. de Jong

Catching up twice

The nature of Dutch industrial growth during the 20th century in a comparative perspective

Akademie Verlag

ISBN 3-05-003697-4

Das eingesetzte Papier ist alterungsbeständig nach DIN/ISO 9706.

Satz: Werksatz Schmidt & Schulz, Gräfenhainichen
Einbandgestaltung: Ingo Ostermaier, Berlin
Druck und Bindung: Druckhaus „Thomas Müntzer“, Bad Langensalza

Gedruckt in Deutschland

Contents

Tables

Figures

Acknowledgements

This book analyses the development of Dutch industry between the 1910s and 1960s in an international comparative perspective. It is based on own research in primary sources on manufacturing output, employment and related items in the official Statistics of Production. The result of this project was accepted as a thesis at the University of Groningen, in the Faculty of Economics.

Several chapters of the book draw upon articles I wrote together with Antoon Soete, Ronald Albers, Peter Solar and Bart van Ark. Parts of the results were presented at conferences and workshops in Oxford, Lund, Madrid, Lisbon and Louvain. Many referees and scholars gave thoughtful comments and suggestions, of which I would like to mention Albrecht Ritschl, Leandro Prados de la Escosura, Jaime Reis, Lars Svensson, Lennart Schön, Olle Krantz, Jonas Ljungberg and Erik Buyst.

Statistical sources were kindly made available by Gert den Bakker, Steve Broadberry, Jan Pieter Smits and Antoon Soete. Many colleagues helped me to clarify my ideas in the field of historical national accounts: Jan Luiten van Zanden, Riita Hjerppe, Isabelle Cassiers, Herman van der Wee, Peter Vikström, Ola Grytten and Steve Broadberry.

I am indebted to my colleagues of the Groningen Growth and Development Centre at the Faculty of Economics. They encouraged me and gave me lots of advice: Bart van Ark, Angus Maddison, Jan Pieter Smits, Simon Kuipers, Jaap Sleifer, Ludger Lindlar, Marcel Timmer and Ben Gales. I have accumulated many obligations to my supervisor Rainer Fremdling, who supported me in exploring the field of historical comparisons and gave detailed criticisms on the draft chapters, displaying his expert knowledge.

I benefited from financial support of the Netherlands Organisation for Scientific Research (NWO). Ian Cressie translated the text into English. Assistance was furthermore given by Ewout Frankema and by the editors of the Jahrbuch für Wirtschaftsgeschichte.

Herman de Jong,
Groningen, April 2003

Chapter 1: The development of Dutch manufacturing in an international perspective 1913–1965

1.1. Introduction

New evidence on 19th and 20th century manufacturing performance shows that there are wide and sustained differences in productivity levels between the advanced industrial countries. In *The Productivity Race* Stephen Broadberry documented a persistent manufacturing productivity gap between the U.S. and Europe, which has existed for already 150 years. According to Broadberry this transatlantic productivity gap can be explained by differences in accumulation strategies and in diverging demand patterns between the economies of the U.S. and the European countries. However, within the European context comparative levels of manufacturing productivity (that is between Germany and the U.K.) were found to be on a par. One important conclusion of this analysis is that during the 20th century the transfer of technology in manufacturing cannot explain convergence of GDP per worker across European countries. Convergence was rather driven by the shift of employment out of agriculture and by changes in comparative productivity performance in services.[1]

This book fills up the picture by presenting evidence on the comparative productivity performance in manufacturing in four industrial countries: the United Kingdom, Germany, Belgium and the Netherlands. Within this comparison the Dutch manufacturing sector is the central point of reference. Taking the industrial performance of the Netherlands as a starting point it will be shown that during much of the twentieth century the manufacturing sector was the most rapidly growing sector of the Dutch economy.

The present study examines the development of the Dutch manufacturing industry between 1913 and 1965. This period includes the two world wars, the depression of the 1930s and the period of reconstruction after 1945. The two wars are generally regarded – and not only in economic history – as external shocks that caused breaks in the country's long-term development. But many studies fail to give an adequate analysis of the effects of the two wars on the long-term development of the economy, because of lack of data on economic performance.[2] The starting point for this study is therefore to include the periods of the wars, and to bridge these years with consistent data for industrial output and employment. The most important statistical source in this study is the Statistics

1 Broadberry, Manufacturing, p. 772–795. Ibid., *The Productivity Race*.

2 A number of studies that explicitly sought to bridge the war periods in quantitative terms were published only recently. See Knibbe, *Agriculture*; De Jong & Albers, Industrial ouput; Van der Bie, *Economische*; Klemann, niederländische Wirtschaft, Van Ark & De Jong, Accounting.

of Production produced by the Central Statistical Office (CBS, or 'Statistics Netherlands'). This source, which has still not been subject to much systematic study, brings together a large amount of quantitative data on industrial output and the associated inputs such as raw materials, intermediate products and labour. From 1913, the Statistics of Production include economic data from about 30 percent of all manufacturing industries. Estimates of the output and employment levels in each year have been drawn up on the basis of this source, continuing through to 1965. Around this year the continuity of the production and price series for the diverse industries became steadily more complicated, because of changes in the reporting of source data. These statistical limitations are in part due to real changes in Dutch industry. In the mid-1960s, industrial development reached a turning point. Already before 1960 post-war reconstruction had been completed. General wage increases in the early 1960s changed the international competitive position, which in turn transformed industrial investment. The discovery of natural gas amplified the changes, because of the availability of cheap fuel. This set in motion structural changes, resulting in a rapid transformation of industry. This complex process requires a separate study.[3]

The period covered by my study follows on from the period that J.A. de Jonge examined in his work on industrialisation in the Netherlands from 1850 and 1914.[4] In this work, which is still considered authoritative, De Jonge claims that the process of industrialisation in the Netherlands only accelerated just before the turn of the century. Thus industrialisation took place later than in the surrounding countries. Since then, studies as part of the 'Reconstruction of the Dutch National Accounts' project of Van Zanden, Smits and Horlings have shown that the Dutch industrialisation process had already taken shape by about the 1860s.

To place the 1913–1965 period in a somewhat longer perspective, Figure 1.1 shows the output of manufacturing industries in the Netherlands in constant prices between 1880 and 1990, as compared to the long-term movement in the real gross domestic product (GDP).

The vertical axis has a logarithmic scale; the slope of the lines indicates the rate of growth. The two variables are shown in index numbers, with the value for 1938 being set at 100. The figure shows that the industrial growth was clearly faster than that of the economy as a whole, especially between 1913 and 1970. However the two curves reveal the same turning points. In both world wars there was an absolute decline in GDP and industrial value added. The turbulent period between 1914 and 1945 is striking. In addition to declining output during both wars, it is also notable that in the early 1930s the GDP declined for five successive years, while industrial production fell less markedly and for a shorter period. Between 1945 and 1973 the rate of growth in GDP was very high, although the first half of this period was characterised by rather marked cyclical fluctuations. Growth after 1973 was much more modest, with industrial production growing more slowly than GDP until about 1980. This means that in the 1970s, industry's

[3] See for example Van Zanden, *Economic history*; CPB (1970), *Nederlandse economie*; Ibid. (1976), *Nederlandse economie*.

[4] J.A. de Jonge, *De industrialisatie van Nederland tussen 1850 en 1914*.

Figure 1.1. Gross domestic product for the total economy and industrial value added in the Netherlands in constant prices 1880–1990

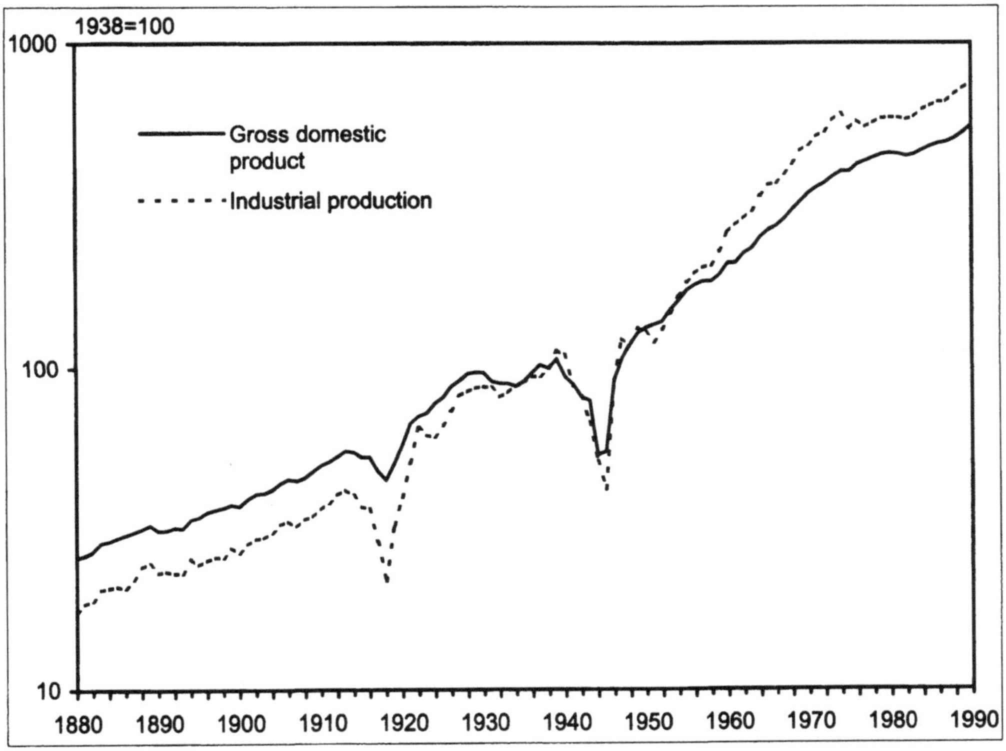

Sources: Total economy: 1880–1913: Smits, Horlings & Van Zanden, *Dutch GNP*, 219–221; 1913–1921: Van der Bie, *Economische*, 86 and the revision by J. P. Smits; 1921–1990: Van Ark & De Jong, Accounting, Appendix C, based in part on Van Bochove & Huitker, National accounting, and CBS, *Nationale Rekeningen (National Accounts)*.

Industry: 1880–1913: Smits, Horlings & Van Zanden, *Dutch GNP*, 157–159; 1913–1921: Van der Bie, *Economische*, 86 and the revision by J. P. Smits; 1921–1939 kindly made available by Gert den Bakker of the CBS; 1945–1990: CBS, *Nationale Rekeningen (National Accounts)*. Note: The figures from 1921 refer to manufacturing industry; figures before 1921 refer to total industry (including the construction industry, mining and utilities).

share of the total economy declined. Nevertheless over the period 1900–1990 industrial production grew at an average 3.78 percent per year, as compared to 2.95 percent for the economy as a whole. Table 1.1 shows the growth rates for a number of periods.

In the period that we are focusing on here, 1913–1965, there was an even greater difference between the growth rates of the two variables, with GDP growing at a calculated 3.1 percent and industry at 4.3 percent. In terms of total volumes, the result of this was that GDP in 1965 was almost five times the volume of 1913, while industrial production grew by a factor of almost ten.

The exceptional growth of industry can also be clearly seen in the development of the structure of the Dutch economy. The share of the manufacturing industry (i.e. excluding mining, construction and utilities) increased markedly from 1913.

Table 1.1. Annual growth rates for GDP and industrial value added in constant prices, 1900–1990

	GDP	Industry
1900–1913	2.28	3.52
1913–1929	3.66	4.68
1929–1938	0.33	1.60
1938–1950	2.41	2.15
1950–1960	4.61	7.24
1960–1973	4.83	6.30
1973–1990	2.19	1.58
Long periods		
1900–1950	2.39	3.21
1950–1990	3.64	4.50
1900–1990	2.95	3.78
1913–1965	3.07	4.25

Sources: See Figure 1.1.

Table 1.2. Share of manufacturing industry in GDP and in total employment, 1913–1965

	% GDP	% employment
1913	21.4	24.2 (1909)
1921	21.1	24.8 (1920)
1938	28.1	24.2
1950	27.3	27.9
1965	38.6	29.2 (1960)

Sources: See Figure 1.1 and CBS (1984), *Productiestructuur*, 39ff.

In the table, the real value added of industry is expressed as a percentage of the real gross domestic product, so that both values are adjusted for price movements. The greatest rise in industrial production took place in the period 1921–1938 and between 1950 and 1965. The total rise was more than 17 percentage points. The share of manufacturing in employment also increased from 1913 to 1965, but the increase, from about 24 percent to 29 percent, is much less.

In 1913 the relative productivity of industry was still below the average for the whole economy; the percentage of the workforce working in manufacturing in 1913 was greater than the proportion of value added produced in this sector. By 1965 this relationship had been reversed: the productivity level in manufacturing was then apparently higher than in the total economy, since the percentage of the working population who were in industry was lower than the proportion of GDP attributable to the value added of industry. In short, the average labour productivity in manufacturing at the beginning of this period was lower than that of the sectors (agriculture, industry and services) combined, and at the end of this period it was higher.

A comparison with industrial development in neighbouring countries reveals the exceptional character of the Dutch industrial expansion. Because the populations of the four countries did not grow at the same rate, a correction has been made: the industrial production has been divided by the total population to give industrial production per head of population, which is not the same as the average labour productivity. Table 1.3 shows industrial production per capita for the four countries, with the level for 1913 being set at 100.

Table 1.3. Industrial production per capita in the Netherlands, the United Kingdom, Germany and Belgium, 1913–1965 (1913 = 100)

Year	Netherlands	U.K.	Germany	Belgium
1913	100	100	100	100
1921	114	80	59	66
1938	189	151	163	95
1950	207	196	130	115
1965	485	376	415	198

Sources: Industrial production: the Netherlands, See Figure 1.1. United Kingdom 1913–1950, Feinstein, *Statistical*, T 112–T 113; 1950–1965 Broadberry. Manufacturing 788–790. Germany 1913–1950: Hoffmann, *Wachstum*, 392–395; 1950–1965 Broadberry, Manufacturing, 788–790. Belgium 1913–1938: Cassiers, *Croissance*, 233; 1938–1965 Soete, *Evolution*.
Population figures from Maddison, *Dynamic*, Appendix B.

The table shows that the growth in industrial production per capita in the three neighbouring countries clearly lagged behind the Dutch growth rate. In contrast to the other three countries, there was no decline in production per capita after the First World War. Dutch industry apparently profited from the country's neutrality. Dutch industry also enjoyed strong growth after the Second World War.[5]

To obtain a more accurate picture of the industrial performances of the four countries, Figure 1.2 compares the average production per worker in Dutch industry, year by year for the period 1913–1965, with production per industrial worker in the United Kingdom, Germany and Belgium. The time series of comparative productivity are based on the extensive comparisons of industries dealt with in Chapters 2 and 3. The figure shows that Dutch industrial productivity has not caught up in a steady, linear process; rather there were alternate periods of high and low comparative levels. Prior to 1921 we have only one observation, that for 1913. Changes in the comparative productivity in the intervening years cannot be calculated. We can see that in 1913 Dutch productivity was very low in comparison to British and German levels, reached a higher comparative level in the inter-war period, but after the Second World War it was again substantially lower. This lost ground was largely made up during the 1950s and 1960s. What factors deter-

[5] The scant growth of industry in Belgium is striking. Nevertheless, in 1938 Belgium still had a much larger industrial sector than the Netherlands, with industry accounting for 33% of employment. De Jong and Soete, Comparative, 29.

mined the changes in industrial labour productivity, and how can we explain differences in levels between the countries? Much of this book is devoted to determining the nature of this development process.

Figure 1.2. Comparative labour productivity in manufacturing in the U.K., Germany and Belgium, 1913–1965 (Netherlands = 100)

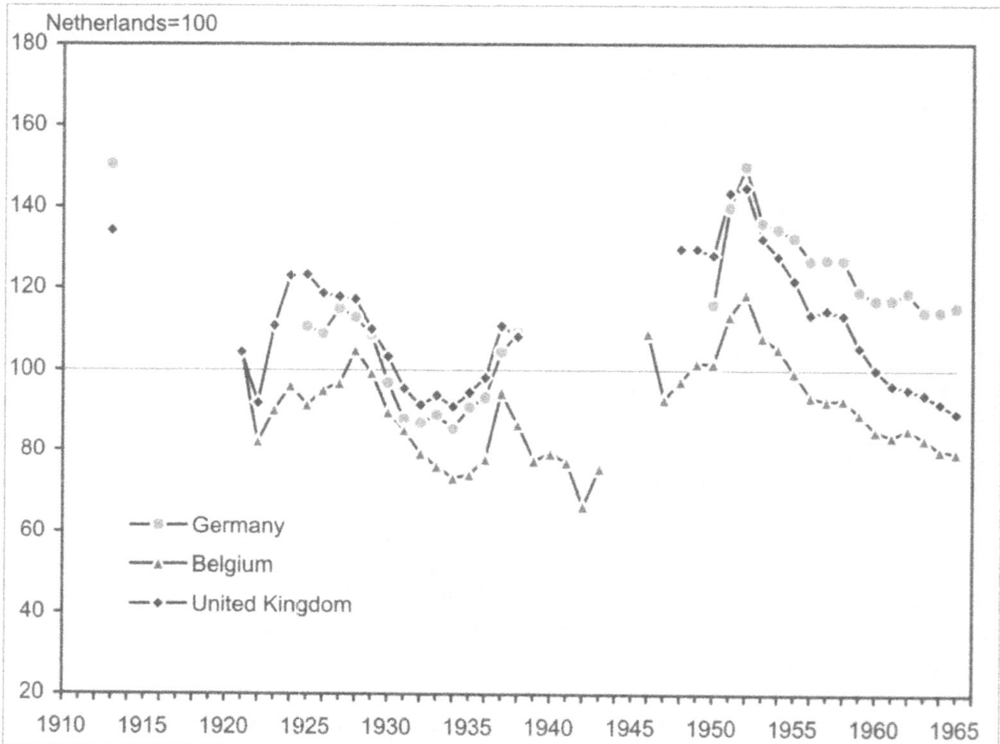

Sources: Netherlands: Appendix C. United Kingdom 1913–1950 Feinstein, *Statistical,* T112–T113 and T129–T130; 1950–1965 Broadberry, Manufacturing, 789–790. Germany 1913–1950: Hoffmann, *Wachstum*, Part 2, Tables 15 and 76; 1950–1965 Broadberry, Manufacturing, 788–790. Belgium 1921–1965: De Jong and Soete, Comparative, 48.

Average labour productivity is used in this study as an indicator of industrial performance and of changes in the structure of industrial production. However it is not synonymous with production efficiency or the competitive position of a country, sector or industry. Labour productivity is the production expressed in comparison to the input factor 'labour'. High labour productivity may indicate high efficiency in production, but may also be an effect of disproportionately large inputs of other factors of production such as capital goods, especially the use of labour-saving machines. The high productivity is then mainly the result of using larger amounts of capital (in the form of machines, buildings and vehicles) in the production process and of differences in labour input.

Productivity should also not be confused with competitiveness, which refers to the degree to which a country or industry is able to sell its products at a competitive price on the world market. Competitiveness depends among other things on factors such as exchange rates, but also on cost of inputs such as raw materials and labour.[6] However in the long term one would expect to see a relationship between the degree of competitiveness and the level of labour productivity.[7]

1.2. The structure of the study

The structure of this study is as follows. The remainder of this chapter shows how the various industrial sectors developed between 1913 and 1965, using figures originating from the national accounts (i.e., the CBS's *Nationale Rekeningen*). I explore how the data in the principal source used in this study, the Statistics of Production, relates to the figures in the national accounts.

The second, third and fourth chapters focus on international comparisons. Chapter 2 presents detailed comparisons of industries, focusing on the period just before the Second World War. The comparisons provide a picture of the average labour productivity in the diverse industries of the four countries, and of differences in their industrial structures. In the following chapter (3) the synchronic comparisons are extended backward and forward using time series on industrial productivity. This puts the industrial performances of these countries in a dynamic perspective, giving a picture of similarities and differences in their long-term development. Chapter 4 analyses the causes of differences in productivity by relating cross-sections of variations between industries in the Netherlands and in the three neighbouring countries to comparative levels of possible explanatory factors such as wages, capital intensity, market size and plant size.

Chapters 5, 6 and 7 focus on explaining changes in productivity in Dutch industry. Chapter 5 examines the extent to which the development of productivity in manufacturing industry as a whole can be attributed to growth within the diverse industries or to structural shifts between industries. Chapters 6 and 7 look at the influence of the amount and quality of two factors of production, labour and capital, respectively. Diverse indicators are used, such as wage rates, categories of labour, installed machinery capacities, electrification rates, and the capital stock. Once again, the approach used considers both synchronic perspectives and changes over the long-term. Chapter 7 concludes with an examination of the extent to which shifts in the relative prices of the factors of production has had demonstrable effects on changes in labour productivity.

Chapters 8 and 9 provide a chronological overview of industrial developments in the period covered by our study, which is divided into two periods: 1913–1938 and

6 For example, low wage levels can temporarily improve the competitive position, and compensate for other factors such as low labour productivity. At the same time, in an open economy low wages cannot provide a lasting basis for retaining competitiveness, because increasing productivity also raises living standards. See for example Rostas, *Comparative*, 6.

7 Broadberry and Crafts have shown that for the United Kingdom in the 1930s the comparative productivity per industry is closely related to export performance. Broadberry and Crafts, Britain's, 542.

1938–1965. The analysis focusses on the impact of the two world wars and the Depression on manufacturing performance and on the effects of government policies. Finally, Chapter 10 summarises the most important conclusions of the study.

1.3. Industrial development by sector between 1913 and 1965

Production data for industry as a whole is provided in the Dutch national accounts drawn up by the Central Statistical Office (CBS). The national accounts provide a quantitative record of all economic activities in the country during a particular period (generally a calendar year). National record-keeping systems describe the formation, distribution and spending of national production and national income in a country. Income and production can be measured in various ways. Here we are interested only in industrial production. In the Dutch national accounts, the manufacturing industry is divided into a number of industrial sectors. These are listed in Table 1.4.

Table 1.4. Gross value added shares (%) in manufacturing in current prices, 1913–1965

SBI classification*		1913†	1921	1938	1950	1960	1965
20/21	Food and beverages	35.0	24.2	35.9	21.2	20.8	20.1
22	Textiles	11.1	10.5	7.8	11.8	6.2	4.8
23	Clothing	9.5	12.8	8.3	5.5	3.4	3.0
24	Leather and footwear	3.7	2.9	2.5	3.2	2.3	1.9
25	Wood and furniture	6.2	5.6	3.2	4.0	3.1	3.2
26	Paper	1.5	1.2	2.5	2.6	3.1	3.1
27	Printing and publishing	3.3	5.6	4.6	5.0	4.8	4.9
28/31	Petrochemicals	2.2	5.1	5.7	11.9	15.5	16.9
32	Construction materials	4.7	4.8	3.0	3.5	3.7	4.1
33/37	Metals & engineering	20.5	25.4	25.2	27.9	34.2	35.1
38/39	Other	2.7	1.9	1.3	3.4	2.9	2.9
Total		100	100	100	100	100	100
Value (x million guilders, current prices)		602	1,452	1,416	5,865	14,241	22,267

* Standard industrial classification of the CBS
† Figures for 1913 are net rather than gross value added

Sources: Year 1913: Smits, Horlings & Van Zanden, *Dutch GNP*, 130–141. Years 1921, 1938: De Jong, Measuring, 216. (Based on figures made kindly available by Gert den Bakker of the CBS.)
Years 1950, 1960 and 1965: CBS, *National Accounts*.

The classification of industries has not always been the same. Before 1945, the classification system used was the same as the classification in the census of population and employment. From 1945 however, the United Nations' International System of Industrial Classification was used. From 1969 onwards, the classification of industrial sectors was again changed, this time under the CBS's own standard classification of industries (SBI). The reconstruction of the distribution of the value added in the inter-war period also employs the SBI classification system. These changes in the system complicate comparisons over time. The problem is largely confined to the classification of the clothing, footwear, leather and rubber industries.[8] To make the data series consistent, I have recalculated them for 1950, 1960 and 1965 using the 'new' SBI system, so that they correspond to the classification of the inter-war years. The recalculation is based on tables given in the CBS's overviews of national accounts that are detailed at the level of industrial sectors and individual industries (*bedrijfsklassen* and *bedrijfstakken* respectively). To relate this data to the situation before the First World War, a column has been added for 1913.

The table gives the percentage distribution of the total value added (the value of production minus the value of raw materials and other items consumed) in manufacturing industries. Total value added in current prices is also presented. At the beginning of the period, about 75 percent of total value added in the industry was produced in the food and beverage industry, metals and engineering and the clothing and textile industry. In the course of the period, the relative position of the food and beverage sector declined, although in 1965 it was still the second largest sector, accounting for 20 percent of production. The share of the textile and clothing sector declined markedly, especially between 1950 and 1965. Its place in the top three was taken by the rapidly growing petrochemical industry. The latter developed strongly during and after the First World War, with products such as rubber and fertiliser. During the inter-war period, a chemicals industry linked to coal mining (coal tar, coke, etc.) was established. After the Second World War this sector expanded with oil refining, bulk chemicals, plastics and pharmaceuticals. Over the period as a whole, the metals and engineering industry is the largest sector. After 1950 its share increased from about 28 percent to 35 percent of total value added. Growth was especially strong in electrical and mechanical engineering and in the vehicle industry. If we look at the sectoral classification used here, it is striking that sectors 20/21 and 33/37, i.e. food and metals, together account for some 50 percent or more of industry during the whole period. At first sight this indicates a considerable specialisation of Dutch manufacturing, which also fits with the picture of an open economy. However there is a wide diversity within the two largest classes. The products of the food and beverage industry in the Netherlands include dairy products, sugar, flour, margarine, cocoa, potato starch, beer, tobacco and preserved food, fruit and fish. The metal industry can be subdivided into metallurgy (iron and steel production, zinc, tin and aluminium), metal products (wire, sheet metal processing), machine construction and steel construction, the manufacture of means of transport (shipbuilding and vehicles, including bicycles, coachwork and cars) and electro-technical products.

The importance of the diverse industries can also be judged from their relative employment levels. However there is a problem, in that the figures in the national

---

8 In the former classification, clothing and footwear were considered together, along with non-footwear leather products and rubber products. In the new classification, clothing is a separate category (sector 23), leather and footwear are combined (sector 24) and rubber is included under the petrochemical industry (sectors 28/31).

surveys for labour volume per industry for the period 1913–1965 do not have the same statistical basis and classification as the figures for value added. We are therefore forced to use other sources such as the census of employment. Table 1.5 shows percentage distributions for the years 1938 and 1960.

Table 1.5. Employment shares (%) and relative labour productivity by sector in manufacturing in 1938 and 1960

SBI classification*		Employment 1938	Employment 1960	Relative Productivity 1938 ratio**	Relative Productivity 1960 ratio
20/21	Food and beverages	23.5	15.0	1.5	1.4
22	Textiles	12.2	9.2	0.6	0.7
23	Clothing	11.1	7.5	0.8	0.5
24	Leather and footwear	2.8	2.5	0.9	0.9
25	Wood and furniture	5.2	5.2	0.6	0.6
26	Paper	2.5	2.6	1.0	1.2
27	Printing and publishing	5.6	5.3	0.8	0.9
28/31	Petrochemicals	4.4	8.3	1.3	1.9
32	Construction materials	4.4	4.5	0.7	0.8
33/37	Metals and engineering	27.1	37.7	0.9	0.9
38/39	Other industry	1.3	2.2	1.0	1.3
Total		100	100	1	1

* Standard industrial classification of the CBS
** The percentage of value added divided by the percentage of employment.[9]

Sources: Employment 1938, measured in total working hours: Den Bakker & De Gijt, Labour force. Employment 1960, measured in number of workers: CBS (1966) results of the 13th national census. Relative productivity: see Table 1.4.

The figures for 1938 are obtained by extrapolation from the results of the census of employment of 1930. They indicate the percentage distribution of wage and salary earners. That is, they do not include the self-employed.[10] The employment figures for 1960 are based on the census of employment of that year. To make the comparison with 1938

9 This is a very crude approach, because the percentage shares of value added are calculated from ratios of nominal values and not from real values, which would be the ideal procedure. However the CBS does not have price indices available for all industrial sectors.

10 See Den Bakker and De Gijt, Labour force. The researchers took the 1930 census of employment as a starting point. They then corrected the wage-earning population for each sector of industry to allow for the unemployment for each sector, giving a figure for employment volume. Then employment levels over the course of the 1930s were extrapolated on the basis of the recorded labour years (of wage and salary earners) for each sector, as given in the accident statistics of the National Insurance Bank. The figure for 1938 therefore shows the number of recorded labour years worked in that year.

as accurate as possible I have deducted the self-employed and unemployed from the recorded working population for each sector of industry, so that both columns refer only to the employment of wage and salary earners. Nevertheless there is still a difference between the two estimates, in that the results of 1938 should be interpreted in terms of labour volume (total hours worked) and those for 1960 in terms of number of workers. Therefore it would not make sense to compare the absolute numbers with one another. The relative numbers can be compared, supposing that the relationship between labour volume and number of workers has not changed very much over time or between industries in this period. Part-time work was almost unknown in these years.

It can also be seen from these figures that Dutch manufacturing was dominated by the food and metals industries. Nevertheless, employment in the textile and clothing industry was still considerable, while the chemicals industry played a much more modest role in this distribution. In 1960 the percentage of realised value added in the chemical industry was larger than its share of employment. The ratio between the two percentages provides an indicator of the relative labour productivity. For the chemicals industry this ratio is greater than one, i.e. that average value added per person working in this sector is higher than for manufacturing as a whole. The relative labour productivity for the textile and clothing industry is less than one. In Table 1.5, the relative labour productivity for 1938 and 1960 is given in the last two columns.

A high relative labour productivity is apparent in the food and beverage, paper and chemicals industries, for both 1938 and 1960. The other industries have values that are lower than one. These industries are characterised by a relatively labour-intensive production process, whereas the first group of industries is more capital-intensive. It is striking that the metals industry also has a below-average relative labour productivity. However the range of values between industries is enormous. On the basis of the underlying data one can calculate values of about 1.5 for the metals processing and electrical engineering industries, while the value for the vehicle industry is less than 0.7.

1.4. The Dutch Statistics of Production

The results presented here flow from a process in which individual industries and companies grow or decline. In studying the process of industrial development and the rise in average labour productivity in industry, it is very important to obtain an understanding of the structure of value added and of the associated employment. The level of aggregation of the national accounts is too high for the purpose. Moreover we have seen that the figures for value added and employment do not have the same statistical basis. Furthermore the portion of production that cannot be directly measured is estimated in the national accounts on the basis of employment figures. This means that quantitative analyses based on the outcomes of the national accounts are unavoidably superficial. This study is based only on the directly measured production, as that can be found in the official Statistics of Production.

The data in the production statistics is central to this study. From 1921 this source provides detailed annual information for some twenty-five industries, covering production, inputs and value added. The data is collected by means of the CBS's direct company surveys. Detailed information is also available about the corresponding annual labour inputs. However one limitation of the statistics of production is that the information covers only part of total manufacturing.[11]

Table 1.6. Production reported in the Statistics of Production, as a percentage of total industrial production in the National Accounts in 1950

SBI classification		1950
20/21	Food and beverages	12
22	Textiles	99
23	Clothing	55
24	Leather and footwear	60
25	Wood and furniture	0
26	Paper industry	57
27	Printing and publishing	0
28/31	Petrochemicals	13
32	Construction materials	68
33/37	Metals and engineering	85
38/39	Other industry	0
Total		49

Sources: Appendix A and CBS, *National Accounts.*

Table 1.6 indicates the relationship between the data from the Statistics of Production and those from the national accounts for 1950. The percentages indicate the proportion of the value added per industrial sector in the national accounts that is covered by the figures given in the Statistics of Production. In 1950 the Statistics of Production covered almost half of industrial value added. However there are considerable differences between the various industrial sectors. The percentages in the food and beverages industry, which is an important industry in the Netherlands, are low. The chemicals industry is also represented only very modestly in the Statistics of Production. In contrast, a large portion of the value added in the textile and metallurgical industries appears in the statistics, along with more than half the value added in the clothing, leather, footwear, paper and construction materials industries. The wood and furniture industry, and printing and publishing are not represented.

At least three reasons can be suggested to explain the difference in the figures of the Statistics of Production and those in the national accounts. In the first place, the Statistics of Production do not give an equally good picture of all sectors of manufactur-

11 However the data available from the two sources is not independent. In both the national accounts after 1945 and the reconstruction of the accounts for the period between 1913 and 1939, the data in the Statistics of Production is the most important element in the estimates of aggregated industrial production.

ing. From 1921 on the CBS chose to gather its data annually, but they did not have the resources to cover all industries: at that time about twenty industrial sectors were included in the statistics. More industrial sectors were added over the course of time. Just before the Second World War the 'sample' consisted or twenty-five industrial sectors. In 1960 the Statistics of Production included fifty industrial sectors.

Second, the Statistics of Production relate only to medium-size and large companies, to facilitate the efficient processing of the data by the CBS. The criterion for including companies within the selected industrial sectors in the statistics was in most cases the number of workers, but sometimes also the volume of production. For instance, the mechanical engineering industry in the statistics for 1950 included only firms with 25 or more workers, and after 1950 it included only those with more than 49 workers. Elsewhere I have indicated the effects of these changes on the total recorded production and productivity in the statistics of the relevant sectors. It will be clear that there may be sudden changes in recorded production and employment that are not due to cyclical effects, but simply to statistical redefinitions.[12]

The third reason why the figures presented here differ from those in the national accounts is that I chose to base my analysis of industrial production on consistent times series for both the individual industrial branches and the total production calculated from the Statistics of Production. If newly added industries were also included in the calculations, this would produce an artificial appearance of growth in the statistics that would make it more difficult to evaluate the effects of the wars and the Depression. For example, to ensure the consistency of the data over time, the industrial sectors added to the Statistics of Production after 1945 are not included in the analyses.

This general outline of the reasons for differences between the data in the Statistics of Production and the national accounts highlights the question of how representative the sample used in the Statistics of Production is of manufacturing as a whole. In the first place, particular industrial sectors and groups of companies are entirely omitted from the Statistics of Production. In the second place there is a bias in favour of larger companies. Moreover it is clear that these industries are not a random sample from the total population of Dutch industries. This limits the role of stochastic theory in making reliable judgements about industry as a whole. On the other hand, the high degree of detail in the data available from the Statistics of Production offers a good insight into the forces lying behind the processes of industrial growth and changes in productivity. On the basis of these insights we can reach conclusions that have validity extending beyond the industries included in the statistics.

The working methods in this study are based on data collection and analysis at the level of aggregation of individual industrial branches rather than industrial sectors, as in the national accounts. This 'industry-of-origin' approach was first used systematically by Rostas in a comparative analysis of the British and American manufacturing industries. Paige and Bombach later refined this approach by basing comparisons of productivity between the industries in two countries on the value of the total production in an in-

---

12 De Jong, *Nederlandse industrie*, 421–423.

dustry rather than on quantities of some of typical goods, as Rostas did.[13] My estimates of production and labour productivity in Dutch industry are based on the approach described here, both in comparing and explaining industrial performance in the Netherlands over the long term and in comparing that performance with manufacturing of the neighbouring countries, Belgium, Germany and the United Kingdom. The new comparisons enable us to form a much better picture of differences in productivity and changes over time than was previously possible.

---

13 When translating the value of production into a common unit (which, incidentally, is always expressed in the currency of the country concerned), the official exchange rate is not used, but rather a value ratio calculated from the data in the Statistics of Production itself, i.e., this method is based on an industry-specific 'exchange rate', and guarantees much more representative value ratios in comparisons between the production figures in two different countries. Van Ark and Maddison's 'International Comparisons of Output and Productivity' project at the Faculty of Economics in Groningen has made many systematic comparisons of the level of labour productivity in diverse countries using this method. See Maddison and Van Ark, International.

Chapter 2: Comparing levels of industrial productivity: the Netherlands, the United Kingdom, Germany and Belgium

This chapter focuses on an international comparison of industrial labour productivity in the Netherlands, as compared to its neighbouring countries Belgium, Germany and the United Kingdom. Few statistics are available regarding production in these countries in the period before the Second World War, which leaves us with little choice in selecting suitable years for the comparison. The years chosen are 1935, 1936 and 1937 for the United Kingdom, Germany and Belgium respectively.

The analysis presented here reveals a pattern of comparatively high Dutch levels of industrial labour productivity. In 1935, labour productivity in Dutch industry was about five percent above that of the United Kingdom; in 1936 it was seven percent higher than that in Germany; and in 1937 five percent above the level in Belgium. This might be regarded as a surprising outcome, given the general opinion that the three neighbouring countries were then important industrial states with strong industrial sectors, while the Netherlands was characterised mainly by a productive agricultural sector and a large national and international services sector. This chapter will present not only the results of the comparative analysis, but also the methods of calculation and the underlying data material.

2.1. International comparisons of industrial productivity

Detailed comparisons of productivity are made at the aggregate level of the various industries, for example for an industrial branch (e.g. the manufacture of vehicles and other means of transport), or an industry such as shipbuilding, or even for a product, such as ship-tons built. Most existing international estimates for the period before 1945 are so-called physical comparisons, i.e., comparisons of the quantities of rubber tyres or tonnes of steel that were produced. Many of these studies have used the methods that Rostas applied in his British-American comparison for 1948.[1] This method of comparing output and productivity is rather approximate, because in some cases only parts of the production process are measured, while information about employment levels often relates to industry as a whole. This can lead to statistical distortions when calculating comparative productivity levels.

---

1 Rostas, *Comparative*; Broadberry & Crafts, Explaining; Broadberry & Fremdling, Comparative; Hjerppe, Productivity.

In productivity analyses covering the period after the Second World War, this problem has been steadily diminished by basing comparisons on the total value of production or, even better, on the value added (i.e., the value of production less the value of inputs such as raw materials and intermediate products). If we take this value as a starting point in international comparisons, it gives a good representation of the whole activity of an industry, but in monetary terms that differ from one country to another. Therefore in comparisons between countries, national production must be shown in terms of a common currency. One could use the official exchange rate for the purpose, but this is not always a good reflection of the actual purchasing power. Exchange rates are determined in part by capital flows and speculation and by the economic and monetary policies of governments and central banks (this applied especially during the economically turbulent 1930s, in which trade barriers and exchange rate manipulation distorted the free exchange of goods). Even if the above factors had little influence, the exchange rate would still not be a good reflection of the comparative values of domestic production in two countries, because it only reflects price differences for goods that are traded internationally. Purchasing power parities offer an alternative to the use of exchange rates. These are calculated relative values of the buying power in two countries, based on weighted comparisons of the domestic prices of identical products. But once again these do not always provide a good representation of the relative values of domestic industrial production in the two countries. International purchasing power parities are generally based on official wholesale or retail prices. Imported goods also determine these prices, which means that foreign price levels, and the exchange rate, still have an undesirable influence on the calculation of the real value of production.[2] The best method is therefore to ascertain the average price level of the goods produced in each industry on the basis of price information from the industry itself. By following the same procedure with a comparable industry in the comparison country, we can calculate relative values for each product or industry, i.e., a 'unit value ratio'. This unit value ratio is then used to express the comparative values of output and the productivity per sector in a common unit of measurement.

A comparative level for the whole sector is then calculated as a weighted aggregate of the ratios for each industry. The weightings are based on the relative size of the various industries in the total industry of the two countries. The advantage of this step-by-step procedure is that relatively small industries are not given any great weight in the final aggregated figure.[3] Moreover this bottom-up approach produces a high degree of detail, which makes it possible to analyse the result further and explain differences between the comparative productivity levels (see chapter 4).

The comparisons of productivity in the 1930s presented here include the maximum possible number of industries, whether the data is available in physical units or in output

---

2 There is an extensive literature on the use of purchasing power parities rather than exchange rates. See, for example, Clark, *Conditions*, 19–35; Paige & Bombach, *Comparison*, 29 et seq.; Kravis, Survey; Kravis, Heston & Summers, *World*, 3 et seq. For a more extensive treatment of the characteristics of purchasing power parities, as compared to unit values, see Van Ark, *International*, 32–34 and Van Ark & Timmer, Industry.

3 Van Ark, *International*, 27–29.

values. The most important criterion for each industry or product is that the data concerning production and employment correspond precisely, i.e., they relate to the same industrial process. However the industry-of-origin approach described here places rather high demands on the source data. In making international comparisons it is difficult to meet these requirements, because the comparability of products and qualities is made even more difficult by country-specific circumstances and specialisation.

The British-Dutch comparison is based on unit values and on the corresponding unit value ratios for seventeen of the thirty industries that were examined. These ratios are used to compare the productivity levels in real terms. The other comparisons of British and Dutch industries are based on physical quantities of production, especially in those industrial classifications in which production is relatively homogeneous. The Belgian-Dutch comparison for 1937 is based entirely on physical quantities of production because of the lack of data on prices and values in Belgium. The comparison between Germany and the Netherlands is based on both physical and real indicators. Because the German statistics of 1936 provide no detailed information at the product level, the comparison of real production is based on price data that derives not from the production data but from other statistics.

Thus in many cases we do not have access to the right material to be able to compare real productivity levels, and we will have to confine ourselves to physical indicators. Where physical indicators are employed as a proxy for the value added (and labour productivity), it is implicitly assumed that the relationship between the use of raw materials and the volume of production in the industries concerned is the same in both countries. For example, to compare production in the shipbuilding industry in two countries on the basis of an estimate of the tonnage produced per worker, we suppose that the same amount of material is used for a given tonnage of shipping built in either country. This supposition may well be defensible for comparisons within a country over time, but in comparisons between countries there is a real risk of large distortions. Production methods can differ fundamentally between countries. A product may be produced as a principal product in one country, and as a by-product in the other. The degree of vertical integration of companies or industries can also differ markedly between countries, so that measurements do not cover the same production phases. For example, there may be differences in the production chain (one country producing only pig iron, for example, and another also processing it). Furthermore there may be differences in the extent to which maintenance and repair are counted as part of production (for example with shipyards), or in the extent to which other extra-industrial activities such as transport or electricity generation are included. Differences in the statistical classifications used in the production data can produce the same effect.[4] The quality issue is closely related to these questions. For example, if goods with differing qualities are compared with one another on the basis of their physical weight or number (cars, footwear, yarns, etc.), this will generally produce a distortion to the 'advantage' of the low-income countries.

---

4 Kravis, Survey, 8; Rostas, *Comparative*, 11–12.

Differences in composition can have a strong influence on comparisons. Specialisation may result in a high level of labour productivity in one production process in a country, while the overall productivity in the sector concerned is low because of the composition of the production. This is the case for example when production has a low value added content, such as components for the footwear and clothing industry.[5] Another possibility is that there may be an extensive industry in one country that does not exist in the other. For example, in the 1930s the Netherlands still had a very large cigar industry, while cigar making in the United Kingdom was almost negligible. The reverse applied in the cigarette industry. Only a proper weighting procedure can prevent strong overvaluation of such a sector.

There are also differences with regard to the labour factor, which can lead to problems when estimating international comparative productivity levels. For example, in most cases the various production figures include only contract labour and employees, and not the owners and members of their families who also work in the firm. It is generally thought that this is only a measurement problem in the agricultural sector, where the family (and not only the head of the family) is the usual production unit. However the problem is also relevant in industry, particularly in small firms engaged in the industrial trades. If the statistics cover only companies of a certain minimum size, it is necessary to form a good estimate of the effect of such a limitation on the calculated average production. Such a lower limit will often have a bigger effect on reported employment than on production. The average production per worker in smaller companies is generally less than in larger companies. This can produce a distortion in the direction of lower average productivity levels where the figures include a greater number of companies.[6]

Allowance must also be made for possible differences in the definition of value added in the diverse statistics. The Dutch Statistics of Production distinguish between the following categories of inputs: raw materials and fuels, manufactured inputs, and subcontracted manufacture. The value of production, less the total of these categories, is the value added according to the definition in the census of production. In addition to labour costs (wages and social security premiums), profit and depreciation there are other costs that contribute to determining the value added, such as the maintenance and repair of machines and buildings, travel costs and (financial) services. However if we use the definition of value added that is applied in the national accounts, all of these latter costs are subtracted from the difference in the values of inputs and outputs, to avoid double-counting on the national level. The concept of value added as applied in the

5 See Mensink, Comparisons, 32.

6 The 1935 census of production in the United Kingdom provides no detailed information on companies of less than 10 employees. In the factory trades this leads to the exclusion of 536,600 people (as compared to 5.2 million people who are counted). The effect of this on the calculated productivity depends on the relative efficiency of the smaller businesses. It is generally assumed that their productivity is lower. This would mean that the exclusion of these small businesses results in an over-estimate of actual productivity. However if the extent of exclusion is the same in all the statistics, this will not lead to any great distortion in comparative terms.

national accounts therefore always yields a lower result than the definition used in the census of production. In this study the broader definition of value added that is applied in the census of production has been followed.

In contrast, the British production statistics do show the costs of maintenance and repair. The resulting difference between the values of output and input is called 'net output' or 'census value added'. The Dutch 'difference in value' and the British 'net output' are thus not entirely identical concepts, since they treat the costs of maintenance and repair differently. In practice this may lead to a systematic overestimation of the Dutch value added in comparison to the British. Unfortunately neither the British nor the Dutch production statistics offer any possibility to correct for this; no separate overviews of maintenance and repair are given.[7]

National systems of taxes and subsidies can also bias international comparisons of the value added per worker. If the aim is to measure the contribution of particular industries to the national product of a country, the value added should preferably be expressed at market prices, i.e., without subtracting the net effect of taxes that raise unit costs and subsidies that lower prices. But if the value added is measured at factor costs, the net effect is included in the value added. For example, if the government provides subsidies, industries that are heavily subsidised will appear in a very favourable light using the factor cost approach. When measured at factor costs, subsidised sectors (such as agriculture) are relatively much bigger than is 'actually' the case. The reverse applies for taxes. If the calculation is based on market prices, the production of the sugar, or the cigarette and tobacco industries is greater than if it is calculated from factor costs, because duties multiply the sales value of the production. However this means that in international comparisons these indirect taxes, in particular, can produce a considerable distortion if only market prices are used. Differences in duties cause artificial differences in the value of production. There is no directly measurable productive performance from the government that can be matched with the duties. The same can be said about value added tax. Because taxation systems differ markedly from one country to another, it is advisable to choose the factor cost approach wherever possible in international comparisons of production and productivity, so that the analysis does not suffer from the effects of national fiscal differences.[8]

Finally there is the question of the dimension in which the factor labour is measured. The labour input should be expressed in comparable units in the various countries,

---

7 Mensink, Comparisons, 43; Van Ark, *International*, 57–61. The same applies to a comparison of productivity in Belgium and the Netherlands in 1960. See De Jong & Soete, Comparative, Appendix 1 and 2.

8 In the production figures, the value of production as recorded includes turnover tax and other indirect taxes. When calculating unit value ratios there is therefore a risk of a distortion if the tax and subsidy structures in the two countries differ. In fact, if one has a good measure of the unit values in the countries, the effect of a tax such as turnover tax on the unit cost should be visible: it will result in higher relative unit values. The total value added can then be corrected for this, so eliminating the effects of higher or lower taxes in the comparison of productivity. Our international comparisons at the higher aggregation level ('industrial sectors') will be based, wherever possible, on the factor costs approach.

whether this is the number of people working, working years or working hours. Naturally the last of these is preferable: absenteeism due to sickness, the length of holidays and the standard working week differ from one country to another (and differ over time) and there should be a correction for this. Unfortunately for the period 1913–1965 there are no comparable times series of the average labour input per industrial worker.[9] According to figures from Maddison, around 1938 the average working year in the four countries was roughly the same, at 2,267 hours for Belgium, 2,316 hours in Germany, 2,244 in the Netherlands and 2,267 in the United Kingdom.[10] In the light of these small differences we will use the number of people working as a proxy for the labour input. Over the whole 1913–1965 period, the standard working weeks in industry in the four countries were broadly comparable.

Moreover the labour volume can be strongly affected by cyclical effects in the year for which comparisons are made. In the short term there may be large fluctuations in the average labour productivity of an industry as a result of changes in capacity utilisation, labour hoarding or changes in the structure of output.[11] The year chosen for the comparison has been determined by the availability of production figures in neighbouring countries. For the comparison between the United Kingdom and the Netherlands the chosen year is 1935, for the German-Dutch comparison it is 1936, and for the Belgian-Dutch comparison it is 1937. Cyclical effects have a strong influence on the average labour productivity in the Netherlands: the levels we have calculated for these three years therefore also vary markedly. Although capacity utilisation rates and unemployment levels in these years differ, we cannot correct for this. In fact such a correction would only make the outcomes less transparent. In Chapter 3 we will analyse the calculated levels in the light of long-term trends, so as to give some perspective on the effects of the economic cycle.

2.2. The structure of industrial employment

To prevent the over-representation of an industry in the comparisons of productivity, the overall productivity of industry is calculated in a two-step aggregation procedure. The first step is to calculate a weighted productivity figure within an industrial sector. This is then weighted by a factor based on the employment volume of that sector in relation to total industrial employment.

Table 2.1 shows the industrial employment structure of the four countries. Although there is data available for every year for the first three countries, this structural overview shows data for the different years on which the comparison is based, because the weights of the productivity comparisons are based on these years. We should remember that the business cycle in the 1930s had uneven effects on the production and employment levels

---

9 Van Ark, *International*, 189 presents figures from 1950, including Germany and the United Kingdom, but not for Belgium and the Netherlands.

10 Maddison, *Dynamic*, 270–271.

11 De Jong & Albers, Industral output, 11–12.

Table 2.1. Structure of industrial employment in the Netherlands (1935), the U.K. (1935), Germany (1936) and Belgium (1937), in percentages

	Netherlands	U.K.	Germany	Belgium
Food and beverages	27.1	11.0	15.4	13.2
Textiles and clothing	23.6	30.1	21.7	28.5
Leather and footwear	2.9	3.0	3.7	5.2
Wood and furniture	5.3	4.8	9.3	9.3
Paper and printing	9.3	7.2	5.4	4.4
Petrochemicals	4.5	3.7	4.2	6.2
Construction materials	4.5	4.3	6.7	6.1
Metals and engineering	21.3	34.8	31.8	23.6
Other	1.5	1.1	1.8	3.5
Total	100	100	100	100

Sources: Netherlands: Den Bakker and De Gijt, Labour force, Table A 3.5. United Kingdom: Feinstein, *Statistical tables*, Table 59, T130. Germany: Hoffmann, *Wachstum*, 191–199.[12] Belgium: De Jong and Soete, Comparative, Appendix 2, 32.

of the various industrial sectors. For example, the figures for the Netherlands show that the employment share of the food and beverage industry in 1938 declined to 23.5 percent (see Table 1.5). At the same time the share of metals and engineering, which had been relatively hard hit by the Depression, had recovered to reach 27.1 percent.[13] We therefore use different weightings for the Netherlands in each of the international comparisons, referring respectively to 1935, 1936 and 1937.

Despite shifts in the employment structure from year to year, it is clear that the Netherlands had a relatively large food and beverage industry, compared to the other countries. The same is true, to a lesser degree, for the paper industry. The metallurgical industry in the Netherlands was smaller than in Germany or the United Kingdom, but the difference is not great when compared to the Belgian metallurgical industry. This is a very heterogeneous industry, including iron and steel production, sheet-metal works, electrical and mechanical engineering, shipbuilding, foundries, and vehicle industry (motor cars, bicycle, rolling stock). Shipbuilding was relatively large in the Netherlands.

---

12 A different distribution can be derived from the 1936 German census of production: Food 10.3%; Textiles and clothing 19.0%; Leather and footwear 3.3%; Wood and furniture 6.1%; Paper 6.4%; Chemicals 6.0%; Construction materials 9.5%; Metallurgical industries 37.8%; Other 1.6%. See *Die deutsche Industrie*, 1936. Rostas (Industrial, 44) used these figures in his comparisons between the United States, the United Kingdom and Germany. However the German census does not cover the whole industry and overestimates the importance of the metallurgical sector. The difference between this and Hoffmann's estimates (which are based on accident statistics and company surveys) is therefore especially great in the food and beverages and metallurgical industries.

13 Den Bakker & De Gijt, Labour force data, Table A 3.5.

Finally it is striking that employment in Dutch industry was more evenly spread over the various industries than in the other countries. In 1935 the three largest industrial sectors were of comparable size. The difference between the largest and third largest sector amounted to 5.8 percentage points. In the United Kingdom, Germany and Belgium the differences were greater: 23.8, 16.4 and 15.3 percentage points, respectively. The following four sections are devoted to the calculation of the comparative productivity levels of these countries compared with the Netherlands.

2.3. Comparison of productivity levels in British and Dutch industry, 1935

The data used for the British-Dutch comparison comes largely from the statistics of production of the two countries. The source for the United Kingdom is the Final Report on the Fifth Census of Production and the Import Duties Act Inquiry of 1935 (henceforth the 'Fifth Census') and for the Netherlands it is the 'Statistics of Production'. However supplementary data has also been used for the Netherlands, to make it possible to compare the maximum numbers of products and/or industries. This comes from the annual figures (*Jaarcijfers*) of the CBS, the accident statistics (*Ongevallenstatistiek*) maintained by the National Insurance Bank, and the OECD's *Industrial Statistics* for 1900–1962. Table 2.2 provides a brief overview.

Table 2.2. Productivity comparison between the U.K. and the Netherlands, 1935 (Netherlands = 100)

Flour	83	Paper	88
Cocoa and chocolate	70	Rubber	121
Sugar	176	Soap	89
Edible oils	126	Rayon	80
Margarine	161	Bricks	96
Beer breweries	127	Cement	59
Cigarettes	124	Blast-furnace	155
Cigars	73	Foundries	94
Cotton spinning	87	Zinc	134
Cotton weaving	114	Wire	84
Wool spinning	87	Mechanical engin.	91
Machine knitting	108	Shipbuilding	56
Clothing	117	Cars and coachwork	134
Leather	108	Bicycles	115
Footwear	80		

Source: De Jong, *Nederlandse industrie*, 472–486.

The total labour volume of these 29 industries and products has been calculated at 2.62 million workers in the United Kingdom and 224,000 workers in the Netherlands. This represents 41 percent and 38 percent, respectively, of the total industrial employment in the two countries.

The highest levels of comparative productivity in the United Kingdom were in the margarine and sugar factories (161 and 176), the car industry (134) and in the metallurgical industries (zinc and pig iron: 134 and 155). British industry had relatively low productivity levels in the cocoa and chocolate industry (70), cigar-making (73), the soap industry (89), the cement industry (59) and in shipbuilding (56).

Rostas has made previous comparisons between the United Kingdom and the Netherlands for the inter-war period. He gives six comparisons based on data for 1937 and 1938. Rostas' comparisons are based on physical indicators of production. However the observations are not sufficiently representative of industry as a whole, for instance because large industries such as the textiles and metallurgical industries are not included.[14]

The productivity in the individual industries within each industrial sector (food and beverages, textiles, etc.) is weighted by the share of that industry in the total employment in the sector. The weighting has been carried out using both the British and the Dutch employment structure for these industries. The results are shown in columns 1 and 2 of Table 2.3.

Table 2.3. Sectoral productivity levels and unit value ratios in the United Kingdom and the Netherlands, 1935 (Netherlands = 100)

Sector	Employm. Weights U.K.	Employm. Weights Netherlands	Unit value ratio guilders per pound
Food	101.4	86.2	10.0
Textiles	105.2	108.0	7.9
Leather & footwear	84.3	85.4	7.4
Paper	87.6	87.6	6.9
Chemicals	94.7	90.4	7.5
Building materials	91.0	93.4	5.3
Metals and engin.	92.0	89.6	7.0
Total	96.8	92.4	7.7

Source: See Table 2.2.

14 Rostas, *Comparative*, 72. Rostas calculated the following British levels (Netherlands = 100): cement 59, rayon and silk 123, beer breweries 111, soap 44, margarine 161, brick 116. In the case of cement and margarine, Rostas used the same data as I have, and it is striking that the productivities he has calculated in these cases are precisely the same. It appears therefore that Rostas has based his comparison on figures for 1935 and not those for 1937/38, as was said in the study. In the case of rayon and silk, Rostas has added the physical quantities together using the system used in the British Fifth Census. I have taken only rayon. In the case of the soap industry, Rostas has clearly over-estimated the Dutch productivity, because he has added the various sorts of soap together, without allowing for the various qualities of soap. In the brick industry the difference has arisen because I have calculated the comparative productivity on the basis of real production value instead of physical indicators.

The figures in Table 2.3 show that the differences in productivity between industrial sectors were much less than those between individual industries, as a result of the averaging of extreme values. With the exception of the food and beverage industry, the structure of the sample in the two countries has little influence on the outcomes, as can be seen from the similarity of the productivity levels shown in columns 1 and 2. A structural effect is most evident within the food and beverage industry.

We can clearly see that the United Kingdom had a productivity advantage in the textile industry. In this case its comparative productivity is even higher if it is weighted with the Dutch employment structure. A study by Broadberry and Fremdling of the comparative productivity of the United Kingdom and Germany, which is also based on 1935, produced the same result. Productivity in the United Kingdom was relatively high in the 'light' industries of textiles and food and beverages, and relatively low in the metallurgical and chemicals industries.[15] Moreover it is striking that the metallurgical sector, which is such a feature of the industrial image of the United Kingdom, did not have high productivity levels compared to the Netherlands. Between the wars industries such as shipbuilding and the mechanical engineering industry dominated the metallurgical sector, which were very large in both countries. However British labour productivity in shipbuilding in particular was low.[16]

This brings us to the second step in the weighting procedure, which is to weight the comparative levels of productivity of each industrial sector according to the overall structures of British industrial employment and of Dutch industrial employment, respectively. It is assumed that in wood products and the other industries for which we have not been able to calculate the comparative productivity levels, the British level was equal to the Dutch. These industries accounted for 8.1 percent and 6.8 percent of industrial employment in the United Kingdom and the Netherlands, respectively.

If we use the British structure, Britain's productivity was 96.8 percent of the Dutch level. If we apply the Dutch employment structure, the comparative productivity is 92.4 percent. Thus the industrial structure does have some influence, but the difference is slight.[17] The geometrical average of the two outcomes gives a British level of 94.5 percent of the Dutch productivity.

In about the half of the comparisons between specific industries or products we have used unit values taken from the British and Dutch production censuses. The third column of Table 2.3 shows the unit value ratios for each industry. The calculated values vary from 5.3 for construction materials to 10.0 for foodstuffs. The weighted average is 7.7 Dutch guilders, which is 6 percent above the official exchange rate of 7.24 guilders.

---

15 Broadberry & Fremdling, Comparative, 405.

16 Broadberry cites various studies showing that British shipyards were characterised by high labour intensity. Given that this industry is very sensitive to the cyclical variations in the economy, companies were very cautious about building up fixed capital, since the high fixed costs that accompany them could lead to financial problems in times of declining demand. Nevertheless the industry was able to maintain a good competitive position by external economies of scale and specialisation. See Broadberry, *Productivity Race*, 176–178; Lorenz, Labour Process. Lomax, Production, 201 points to the underdevelopment of the British mechanical engineering industry.

17 See also Rostas, *Comparative*, Table 10, 41.

Thus in terms of the buying power of industrial production, the guilder was slightly over-valued in comparison to the pound in 1935. This is to be expected, in view of the exceptional monetary circumstances of the 1930s. The United Kingdom had abandoned the gold standard in 1931, leading to a depreciation of the pound. The Netherlands, in contrast, was to remain faithful to the gold standard until 1936. To compensate for the effects of the high guilder, the prices of export products had to fall. However that was not achieved equally well in all sectors. In the food and beverage sector, for example, we find a much lower purchasing power parity as compared to the official exchange rate. Clearly this sector was not able to achieve the necessary price reductions. But there were also big differences within this sector. In the cocoa and chocolate industry, the calculated unit value ratio is 5.6 guilders to the pound, which is far below the exchange rate. The price of cocoa beans, the most important raw material in this industry, had seen an unprecedented fall in these years. The relatively strong guilder resulted in still lower domestic prices for this raw material. Products made chiefly from Dutch raw materials, or from imported materials whose prices were adjusted to match Dutch prices (as in the case of wheat), faced a different situation. In 1935, wheat flour and butter both had a unit value ratio of 14.9, twice the exchange rate, while the figure for margarine, whose price was largely determined by the price of butter, was even higher, at 28.9.[18] However in the case of shipbuilding, the unit value ratio being calculated in shipyard products, the pound was worth less than four guilders. In this case the official guilder exchange rate of 1935 was therefore a clear under-valuation of the 'shipyard-exchange rate'. The unit value ratios of the remaining industries in the table lie around the official exchange rate. From this we can conclude that these industries were reasonably successful in adapting to lower foreign price levels.

Because of the variation in the unit value ratios, the application of an overall purchasing power parity to the various industrial sectors leads to large differences in the estimated comparative productivity levels. The difference between the industry with the highest and the industry with the lowest ratio is a huge 80 percent, and the difference from the average value ratio is no less than 30 percent.[19] In general, if we use an overall ratio (such as the official exchange rate) to convert the values rather than an industry-specific ratio, we over-estimate the amount of currency required to buy a relatively high-productivity article as compared to the currency needed to buy low-productivity goods. Since the nominal value of a productivity level is divided by the purchasing power parity in this method, this implies that the productivity of the high-productivity industries is under-estimated in comparison to low-productivity industries. Another result is that the individual observations are biased towards the average; the spread of the individual comparisons of productivity is then smaller.[20]

---

18 De Jong, *Nederlandse industrie*, 475–477; *Fifth Census*, part III, 121; CBS, *Vijfennegentig*, 183.

19 See Rostas, Industrial, 48, who also notes this reservation in his sectoral comparison of productivity between the United Kingdom, Germany and the United States.

20 See Kravis, Survey, 35 and De Jong & Soete, Comparative, 4, in which this effect is demonstrated for a Dutch-Belgian comparison in 1960.

Comparisons at higher levels of aggregation

An alternative method of comparing productivity levels is simply to calculate the aggregate value added of all those industries that appear in the statistics of production for both countries, divided by the number of workers related to that industries. The exchange rate used to convert the values into a common currency is crucial here. We have used the aggregate unit value ratio derived above. Data for the Netherlands comes from the Statistics of Production, and for the United Kingdom from the Fifth Census of 1935. The figures from the latter were also used by Rostas and by Broadberry and Crafts for their British-American comparison and by Broadberry and Fremdling for their British-German comparison.[21] The Fifth Census does not include manufacturers with a staff of ten or less. These companies employed about 536,600 people.[22] The total net production of the manufacturing industries included in the census is 1,182 million pounds, with a corresponding employment of 5.16 million workers.[23] The calculated average value added per worker for 1935, calculated from this, is 229 pounds per year. According to the British national accounts, the total value added in industry was 1,171 million pounds, with a total employment of 6.39 million.[24] Thus the Fifth Census gives figures that are slightly more than the total production and cover 80 percent of the employment. However the totals in the British national accounts are expressed in factor costs, while the figures in the Fifth Census are in market prices. The national gross domestic product calculated at factor costs is 89 percent of the GDP at market prices. If we correct the figures of the industrial sector by this factor, the census then covers 90 percent of total production.[25]

Table 2.4 compares the totals of the British and Dutch production censuses. As we have seen in Chapter 1, the Dutch census gives a comparatively limited coverage of industrial production. In 1935 the Statistics of Production covered 26.6 percent of the total industrial value added according to the national accounts, and 30.7 percent of the employment. The average production per employee in 1935 was 1,675 guilders. If we

Table 2.4. Value added and employment in the production censuses in the United Kingdom and the Netherlands, 1935

	U.K.	Netherlands
Value added	1,181.7 million pounds	298.6 million guilders
Employment	5,157,587	178,266
Value added/worker	229.1 pounds	1,675 guilders

Sources: See the text.

21 Broadberry and Crafts, Explaining; Broadberry and Fremdling, Comparative.
22 Rostas, *Comparative*, 25.
23 See also Melman, *Dynamic*, 137, who finds exactly the same totals on the basis of his calculations.
24 Feinstein, *Statistical Tables*, Table 9, T 26 en Table 59, T 129.
25 Ibid., T 11, T 27, T 130.

convert the British productivity into guilders, using the purchasing power parity rate of 7.70 guilders, British productivity was 1,764 guilders per worker, or 105 percent of the Dutch level.

A similar calculation at the even higher level of aggregation used in the national accounts results in an average British productivity of 97 percent of the Dutch level.[26] The difference between the results is due to the skewed composition of the Dutch Statistics of Production in comparison to the whole industrial sector. In particular, the important food and beverage industry is under-represented, accounting for just 5 percent of the Statistics of Production. Table 2.1 shows that in 1935 the Dutch food and beverage industry accounted for more than 27 percent of industrial employment. In the British Fifth Census, this industry accounts for 11.3 percent of industrial employment, and the figure in the British national accounts is almost the same, at 11.0 percent. The difference would not in itself produce any great distortion, were it not that the level of productivity of this industry is exceptionally high in comparison to other sectors. The British statistics of production show that the average value added per worker in the food and beverage industry was 387 pounds per year, or 69 percent more than the average value added in industry as a whole (229 pounds). We see the same relationship in the Dutch statistics of production: value added per worker in the food and beverage industry in 1935 was 2,745 guilders, 64 percent above the overall average of 1,675 guilders.

Since this relatively productive industry is under-represented in the Dutch census, it is difficult to compare the census figures directly to the totals from the British census. Therefore the British comparative productivity of 105 percent, which has been calculated from the production censuses, is clearly an upper limit.[27] We must therefore be cautious in making a general comparison on the basis of totals from the statistics of

---

26 Feinstein calculated the value added of British industry using the income method, i.e. by estimating wages and profits. His estimate of 1,171 million pounds, divided by 6,387,000 employees (see text) gives an average production of 183.34 pounds. This is lower than the value calculated from the Fifth Census, which can be explained from the fact that the Fifth Census covers a larger part of the total value added than of total employment.
The Dutch production figures derive from unpublished calculations from den Bakker of the CBS: the value added at factor costs can be estimated on the basis of this material at 76% of the value added at market prices: 76% of 1,124 million guilders = 854 million guilders. Industrial employment is estimated from data in the Accident Statistics (see De Jong, *De Nederlandse industrie*, appendix B) at 586,000 workers and self-employed. This gives an average value added of 1,457 guilders per worker. Using the purchasing power parity rate of 7.70 guilders, British productivity was 1,412 guilders per worker, 97% of the Dutch level. Using the exchange rate to translate the average British industrial production into Dutch prices, we get 1,329 guilders per worker, or 91% of the Dutch level.

27 For example, if we were to exclude the food and beverage industry from both the British and the Dutch census of production, the British average value added per worker is 211 pounds and the Dutch is 1,619 guilders. Translating these at the purchasing power parity of 7.7 guilders per pound, as calculated here, results in a British productivity exactly equal to the Dutch. Because the weighting of the food and beverage industry in the Netherlands is more than twice that of the United Kingdom, if the British comparative productivity is calculated from the national accounts of both countries the result is lower still.

production of the two countries. This is only possible if these are a fair reflection of all industrial sectors.

The fact that the figure calculated from the national accounts is just 2.5 percentage points above the figure calculated at the industry level provides a good degree of confidence about the present productivity-estimates of the United Kingdom and the Netherlands. In 1935 British manufacturing productivity was between 94.5 percent and 97.0 percent of the Dutch level.

2.4. A second British-Dutch comparison of productivity

To estimate the comparative productivity after World War II, we can base ourselves on a calculation for the year 1958, made by the CBS staff member Mensink. This calculation results from an industry-of-origin comparison, so there is a low level of aggregation. Mensink estimates British comparative productivity at 92 percent of the Dutch.[28] This figure is very close to Van Ark's estimate, that British productivity in 1956 was 89 percent of Dutch productivity.[29] The clear divergence between the productivity in the two countries has already been presented in Figure 1.2, Chapter 1. This figure shows that the Netherlands did not equal British productivity levels again until around 1960 and that the comparative British value for 1958 was still 113 percent of the Dutch.

Mensink's calculation of Dutch manufacturing productivity is some 25 percent higher than our own estimate presented here, which is based on an extension of the comparison for 1935 with the aid of long-term productivity data for both countries (see chapter 3). The question is, which estimate is correct? This is important mainly because the different outcomes would justify large differences in the interpretation of the postwar recovery of Dutch industry and the state of British industry in the 1950s. The figures given by Van Ark and Mensink point to a much faster recovery in Dutch productivity after the war, resulting in it quickly catching up with British industry, which at that time was the European leader. My extrapolation from the estimate of 1935 shows a much slower catch-up process, lasting ten more years, mainly because productivity declined after the war.

What did Mensink find at the level of the individual industries? In simple terms, his method is a mixture of physical and value comparisons at the industry level. The comparisons of production that were based on physical indicators were for industries with homogeneous production, such as bricks, whereas 'real' comparisons (based on price indicators) were used in the case of more heterogeneous production processes (such as machine knitting). The industrial sectors and individual industries that were compared, and the productivity level found in the United Kingdom (as compared to the Netherlands = 100) were as follows: in Food and beverages: dairy products (93), tobacco (73) and beer (76); in Textiles: wool (93); in Clothing and footwear: leather (82), footwear

28 Mensink, Comparisons. Mensink has also included agriculture, forestry, fisheries and mining in his comparisons. In the analysis below we will ignore these, and concentrate on industry.

29 Van Ark, *International*, 191.

(112), machine knitting (96), ready-made clothing (93); in Construction materials: brick (111); in the Metallurgical industries: shipbuilding (69). If we weight these comparative productivity levels using the structure shown in Table 2.5, we get the British productivity level cited above, about 92 percent of Dutch productivity.[30]

However this sample is not very representative of manufacturing industry as a whole. The industries listed represent about 19 percent of total industrial employment in the Netherlands and 10 percent for the United Kingdom. By way of comparison, our 1935 estimate is based on 38 percent and 41 percent of industrial employment in the two countries, respectively.

What do we find if we look at industry as a whole? We can begin by comparing the gross industrial value added (at factor costs) and the corresponding labour volumes in the two countries. These are calculated from the national accounts. Table 2.5 provides an overview of the results.

Table 2.5. Gross value added (at factor costs), labour volume and productivity levels in manufacturing in the United Kingdom and the Netherlands, 1958

	United Kingdom			the Netherlands		
	Gross value added million pounds	Labour (man-years) ×1,000	Average productiv. level in pounds	Gross value added million guilders	Labour (man-years) ×1,000	Average productiv. level in guilders
Food & B.	752	833	900	1,761	217	8,100
Textiles	545	932	580	721	113	6,400
Clothing	276	590	470	602	145	4,200
Wood	178	299	600	347	55	6,300
Paper	506	579	880	848	89	9,500
Chemicals	575	514	1,120	1,050	83	12,700
Constr. Mat.	269	328	820	368	48	7,700
Metals	641	581	1,100	430	24	17,900
Machines	2,011	2,474	810	2,079	249	8,300
Vehicles	998	1,170	850	876	127	6,900
Other	232	347	670	487	87	5,600
Total	6,983	8,647	810	9,569	1,237	7,700

Source: Mensink, Comparisons, 20–21.

The total gross value added in British industry in 1958 was 6,983 million pounds and the labour volume was 8.65 million man-years, giving an average production of 810 pounds per man-year. In the Netherlands the gross value added at factor costs was 9,569 million

30 Kravis (Survey, 34) uses the figure 84, but this has apparently been calculated from Dutch weights.

guilders and the labour volume was 1,24 million man-years, giving an average productivity of 7,700 guilders per man-year. If we apply the official exchange rate (1 pound = 10.59 guilders), we find that British productivity in 1958 was 111 percent of Dutch productivity. This is very close to the productivity that we calculated above, of 113, and is considerably higher than the average productivity of 92 percent calculated by Mensink on the basis of comparisons of individual industries. How can this difference between Mensink's estimate and the result of the comparison from the national accounts be explained?

In the first place we have to allow for the possibility that there may be differences between the structures of the British and Dutch industry, at the level of industrial sectors and at the level of the individual industries. On the basis of Mensink's figures, the calculated total industrial value added for the Netherlands would be 8.5 percent higher if the Dutch employment structure at that time was the same as in the United Kingdom. Conversely, British industrial production is 3 percent lower if the average value added is weighted with the Dutch employment structure.

These are indications that the industrial structure in the Netherlands was sub-optimal from the point of view of production efficiency. This is due mainly to the small metallurgical industry in relation to the United Kingdom; in both the United Kingdom and the Netherlands the value added per man-year in the smelting and metallurgical industries was higher than in industry as a whole. The production of vehicles and ships, which is part of this sector, had a much lower relative productivity in the Netherlands (i.e. compared to the average in the Netherlands) than in the United Kingdom. The relatively high British labour productivity is exaggerated when using British employment weights. Such a difference in structure could mean that the Netherlands had a productivity advantage at the level of individual industries, but that the composition of the industrial sector gave the British an advantage in overall productivity.

Secondly, one might well ask whether the currency exchange rate is the correct conversion factor for use in these calculations. A study by Gilbert *et al.* has shown that the British pound was over-valued in the 1950s in comparison to the Dutch guilder. In their comparison of the prosperity levels of Western countries, they converted gross national incomes using purchasing power parities based on the prices of final products ('expenditure purchasing power equivalents'). For both 1950 and 1955, the actual purchasing power ratio was calculated at about nine guilders to the pound. This indicates that the exchange rate overvalued the British pound by almost 20 percent. This would appear to support Mensink's thesis that British productivity was already lower than Dutch productivity at that time, since we would then have to translate the value of British industrial production at a rate lower than the official exchange rate. Leaving aside the question of whether purchasing power parities based on the prices of final products can be used to compare productivity levels,[31] we need to examine whether this over-valuation, which has been demonstrated for the economy as a whole, also applies to industrial production. From the data given by Gilbert, it appears that it does not. They calculated purchasing power parities for forty items (types of products and services), ten of which

---

[31] The price level is then partly determined by other factors such as the price of imports.

are industrial products. The purchasing power parities for agricultural products, at 9.4, and for services such as health, household services and education (7.2, 7.8 and 8.5, respectively) are lower than the official exchange rate. But the calculated purchasing power parities for industrial products were much higher: oil and fats 16.8, non-alcoholic beverages 19.1, footwear 13.0, clothing 11.4, household articles 10.3, vehicles 11.1 and investment goods 11.3.[32] Although the price level of a portion of these goods will be determined by imported items, it is evident that low price levels in the non-industrial sectors cause the lower purchasing power parity for the whole economy. The comparative purchasing power for industrial products during the 1950s was not lower than the exchange rate of 10.59 guilders to the pound. Thus translating the British and Dutch industrial value added figures using the official exchange rate does not in this case overvalue British productivity.[33]

To summarise, we can conclude that Mensink's detailed comparisons of productivity may be correct in themselves, but that they do not give a representative picture of the total manufacturing industry. Dutch productivity in 1958, at the level of industrial sectors, was higher than the British level in a number of cases. However the structure of Dutch industry was less favourable than in the United Kingdom, and around 1958 British industrial productivity was about 10 percent higher than Dutch productivity.

2.5. Comparison of productivity levels in German and Dutch industry, 1936

For the comparison of productivity with Germany we have used the census of German industry in *Die deutsche Industrie: Gesamtergebnisse der amtlichen Produktionsstatistik*, published in 1939. This extensive census of production for the year 1936 is an indication of the priority that the Nazi government gave to planning the domestic production of goods, as part of its preparations for war. However the census is incomplete on two points. In the first place, it does not include the small businesses in manual production (*handwerkliche Kleinbetriebe*), which effectively excludes all companies with a staff of less than five people.[34] This probably has a very slight effect on the total production reported: a similar issue has been dealt with above, in the treatment of the British and Dutch production censuses. In the second place, there is reason to suspect that figures

---

32 Gilbert *et al.*, *Comparative*, 80, Table 27.

33 Even the industry-specific comparisons made by Mensink also do not show that the exchange rate in the 1950s differed strongly from the British-Dutch purchasing power ratio in 1958. The advantage of these value ratios as compared to the purchasing power parities calculated by Gilbert et al. is that they refer to factory prices. His calculated ratio for fertilizer was 12.7; for steel 11.9; ships 9.7; bricks 9.99; footwear 10.5; leather 11.7; and fuels 11.5. Naturally these price ratios cover only a few items, but they do indicate that, although the British pound may have been overvalued in 1958, this was not true of industrial products.

34 Sometimes the lower limit was based on a minimum volume of production; see *Die deutsche Industrie*, 11–12, and 44–54. For a recent analysis of these statistics, see Sleifer, *Falling behind*.

from diverse companies engaged in important war industries, such as mechanical and electrical engineering and the car, optic and chemicals industries, are not included in the publication. These industries employed about 500,000 to 600,000 people. Rostas drew this conclusion on the basis of a comparison between these statistics and the *Gewerbezählung*, the regular company survey of all trades and industrial companies. For example, aircraft construction is not included in the statistics of production, but is represented in the *Gewerbezählung* as having 200,000 employees.[35]

In the census of production, at the level of sectors or *'Industriegruppen'* such as mechanical engineering, and at the next level down of individual industries or *'Industriezweige'* such as boiler-making and appliance manufacturing, we find information about the number of companies, the number of workers, the total wages, input costs, the value of production (*Bruttoproduktionswert*) and the value added (*Nettoproduktionswert*). The total value added of the industries included in the statistics in 1936 was 34.2 billion Reichsmark (RM).[36] (The value of the Reichsmark at that time is discussed below.) For manufacturing industries alone (i.e. excluding mining, utility companies and construction), the figure was 25.7 billion RM, giving an average value added per worker of 4,283 RM.[37]

Table 2.6. Value added and employment in the production censuses of Germany and the Netherlands, 1936

	Germany	Netherlands
Value added	25.7 billion RM	335.4 million guilders
Employment	6,000,741	203,909
Value added/worker	4,283 RM	1,645 guilders

Sources: See the text.

As we have already seen in the British-Dutch comparison, the Dutch Statistics of Production in this period cover about 25 percent of the total value added and about 30 percent of the employment.[38] The total industrial employment in Germany is taken from an estimate by Hoffmann, based on an interpolation of the company and professional

35 See: Rostas, Industrial, 42 and *Statistisches Handbuch*.

36 The net value added, after deducting depreciation, was estimated at 31.4 billion RM: *Die deutsche Industrie*, 37.

37 The German census covers a total employment of 7,950,000 people, of whom 6,842,000 were regarded as workers, 593,000 as sales personnel, 361,000 as technicians and 155,000 as family co-workers. Women accounted for 21.2% of the total employment. The average value added per worker for industry as a whole can be estimated at 4,300 RM. To obtain a figure for manufacturing industries alone, we deduct the value added and employment figures for the utility companies and the construction industry (8.47 billion RM and 1,949,452 workers respectively) and for mining. This results in an average value of 4,283 RM.

38 From Dutch accident statistics we can calculate a total employment for 1936 of 667,604 (manufacturing industry alone, including the self-employed).

surveys between 1925 and 1939.[39] Total employment in manufacturing (including tradesmen and the self-employed) is estimated at 9,767,000. The German census therefore has a coverage rate of about 60 percent of employment. Thus, if we take the total number of workers given in the national accounts as a measure, the German industrial sector in 1936 was fifteen times larger than the Dutch.[40]

We can certainly not use the official exchange rate to convert the average German production into guilders. The year chosen for our comparison is unfortunate in that respect, since the guilder was taken off the gold standard in September 1936, resulting in depreciation. The official exchange rate between the RM and the guilder also changed. From January to August, one RM cost 59.44 Dutch cents, and from September to December it was 73.05 cents. The average exchange rate in 1936 was 63.15 Dutch cents to the RM.[41] The devaluation adjusted the value of the guilder against the Netherlands foreign trading partners in the right direction, making Dutch exports cheaper. However in comparison to the RM, the actual exchange rate for the guilder just before 1936 was higher than the official rate. The under-valuation in the official rate was amplified by the devaluation. While Germany still linked the RM officially to gold, there was no free flow of currency. Trade with the Netherlands was entirely on a bilateral basis.[42] For this reason, the official exchange rate is not a good reflection of the actual purchasing power of the guilder in comparison to the RM. To be able to express the above productivity levels in a common currency, I will now attempt to calculate a better relative value for the two currencies.

The first estimate of the actual exchange rate starts from the official exchange rate in 1913, the last year in which there was free trade between the two countries. Taking this rate as a starting point, I compared the series of domestic wholesale price indexes in the two countries. These indexes were then extrapolated to 1936. On the basis of these extrapolations, I calculate a purchasing power parity for 1936 of 43.3 Dutch cents to the RM.[43] This is significantly below the official exchange rate, indicating that the RM was overvalued.

The second estimate is a purchasing power parity, calculated from a direct comparison of the wholesale prices of about 35 industrial goods. These are then weighted according to the proportion of value added contributed by the relevant industries in the two countries. The result is an average purchasing power parity of 45 cents to the RM[44].

---

39 Hoffmann, *Wachstum*, 190.

40 The total population of Germany in 1936 was 7.9 times greater than the Dutch population. See Svennilson, *Growth*, 236.

41 CBS, *Vijfennegentig*, 150.

42 See Klemann, *Tussen*, 71–100; Hirschfeld, *Actieve*, 78–79 and Hirschfeld, *Jaren*, 38–52 regarding the so-called. '*Sonderkonto*'.

43 In 1913 the exchange rate (based on the gold standard) was 59.25 Dutch cents to the RM. The index for wholesale prices for 1936 can be calculated at 88.6 (index 1913 = 100) for the Netherlands and 121.2 for Germany. (For the Netherlands, see De Jong, *Nederlandse industrie*, 380, 445. The German price levels are taken from Statistisches Reichsamt, *Wirtschaft und Statistik* 1938, nr, 1, 23: Preise und Löhne.)

44 See De Jong, *Nederlandse industrie*, 498.

These two outcomes were checked using an indirect estimate of the purchasing power parity for 1935, via a comparison between the United Kingdom and Germany, on the one hand, and the United Kingdom and the Netherlands on the other hand. The exchange rate for the U.K. and Germany was provided by the German *Institut für Konjunkturforschung*, and is 17.08 RM to one pound sterling.[45] For the U.K. and the Netherlands, we have already calculated a unit value ratio for industry of 7.7 guilders to the pound. Combining these two ratios, we obtain a German-Dutch value ratio of 45 Dutch cents to the RM.

The results of these three independent estimates are very close, and clearly show that the official exchange rate considerably overvalued the RM during the 1930s. If we were to use the official exchange rate to convert German production figures into guilders this would introduce an error of more than 40 percent. In the calculations below I use a parity of 45 cents to the RM.[46]

The average productivity per worker from the German census of production of 1936 is therefore 0.45 times 4,283 RM, or 1,927 guilders. According to this calculation, German productivity in 1936 was 17 percent higher than productivity in the Netherlands (1,645 guilders). However this result is not very representative. The two census totals are not very comparable; as in the comparison between the United Kingdom and the Netherlands, the diverse industrial sectors are not equally represented in the production censuses. The figures are again affected particularly by the relative under-representation of the food and beverage industry in the Dutch census. Because this industry has a relatively high level of value added per worker, this produces an under-estimation of productivity in the Netherlands. We will therefore try first to draw a comparison on the basis of the totals of the national accounts, since these do include all sectors.

For the German data we have to rely on the work of Hoffmann, who estimated the total value added of industry in 1936 (excluding mining, but in this case including the utility companies and the construction industry) at 27,286 million RM (in 1913 prices).[47] Value added in 1913 prices is converted into 1936 prices using the general wholesale price index for manufactured goods that has already been mentioned. The index value for 1936 is 121.2, on the basis of 1913 = 100. This gives a value added for the sector *Industrie und Handwerk* (manufacturing and trades) of 33,071 million RM in 1936, which is very close to the estimate of total German industrial value added that was made in the census of 1936, which is 32,000 million RM (excluding mining).[48] Hoffmann estimates

---

45 Cited in Rostas, Industrial, 43.

46 A fourth independent estimate, but for 1929, has been made by C. Clark (*Conditions*). He calculated purchasing power parities, which he calls 'international units', on the basis of the relative prices of goods and services. For Germany and the Netherlands he calculated a rate of 48.3 Dutch cents to the RM. This indicates that the official exchange rate overvalued the RM, even before the depression had begun.

47 The figure is obtained by linking an index for the volume of industrial production to an estimate of price levels for 1913, made by J. Hirsch (*Wandlungen im Aufbau der deutschen Industrie*, 1929). The latter estimate is made using the income method; see Hoffmann, *Wachstum*, 453–455.

48 This means that the total production reported in the German census of production was almost equal to the total from the national accounts, although the census represents only 60% of total employment (see text and Hoffmann, *Wachstum*, 199). The production associated with 40% of

total industrial employment (in this case including utility companies and the construction industry, in view of the composition of the value added) at 12,048,000 persons.

For German industry as a whole, we now have a value added (at factor costs) of 33,071 million RM and an employment level of 12,048,000. The average labour productivity is therefore 2,745 RM per person employed. The Dutch value added per person in 'industry', broadly defined, comes to 1,411 guilders for 1936.[49] When converted into Dutch guilders at the rate of 45 Dutch cents per RM, this gives a German productivity of 1,235 guilders per worker per year, which is 87.5 percent of the Dutch level. At the average official exchange rate of 63 cents to the RM, average German productivity would be more than 20 percent above Dutch productivity. However this is as much as can be said on the basis of the totals from the national accounts; the data is simply too rough. The totals in the national accounts are built up from reconstructed micro-data and still contain a certain degree of inaccuracy. Therefore, we will try to make comparisons at the level of individual industries and products, as was done in the British-Dutch comparison. Table 2.7 gives an overview of the most important outcomes.

Table 2.7. Productivity comparison between Germany and the Netherlands, 1936 (Netherlands = 100)

Flour	70	Rayon	87
Cocoa and chocolate	74	Brick	82
Sugar	52	Calcium silicate	56
Edible oils	64	Cement	55
Margarine	82	Smelters	216
Beer breweries	79	Foundries	105
Cigarettes	52	Zinc	114
Cotton weaving	88	Tin	96
Wool weaving	85	Rolling mills	110
Machine knitting	105	Wire	101
Clothing	132	Mechanical engin.	140
Leather	80	Metal products	125
Footwear	89	Electrical engin.	107
Paper	66	Shipbuilding	94
Rubber	135	Cars and coachwork	189
Soap	97	Bicycles	78

Source: De Jong, *Nederlandse industrie*, 486–497.

all employment in industry and trades is therefore either very slight or is not correctly reported. Although the text of the 1936 census indicates that the reported employment covers only manufacturing companies and not tradesman's businesses, it also claims that small companies' production is not inconsiderable (*Die deutsche Industrie*, 12–13, 56–58). Hoffmann's study does not address this question. The values of production given in the census have only been used to estimate the relative sizes of industrial sectors; the total is not related to the total employment or Hirsch's estimate.

49 For this purpose I add the estimates for the construction industry and utility companies (a total of 330 million guilders) to the figure for manufacturing industry (915 million guilders at factor costs). Employment in manufacturing was 667,604; to this are added 195,450 workers in con-

Most of the thirty-two comparisons relate to the food and beverage industry and the metallurgical sector (seven and twelve items, respectively). During this period these two industrial sectors combined accounted for almost 50 percent of the total industrial employment in both countries. The only industrial sector in which we were not able to make any comparison was the wood and furniture industry. Fourteen of the thirty-two comparisons were based on physical indicators, and the remainder on nominal values of production, which have been converted into a common currency using industry-specific purchasing power parities.

The German industries that are included in the comparison employed about 3,650,000 people, which is 60 percent of the employment reported in the census of production and 37 percent of Hoffmann's estimate of total industrial employment in Germany. Dutch industries in the comparisons employed about 254,300 workers, which is about 38 percent of the total industrial employment in the Netherlands as reported in the accident statistics.

A closer examination of the comparison of industries shows clearly that German industry had a high comparative productivity in metal products, most remarkably in smelters, automobile production and mechanical engineering. German productivity was also relatively high in the rubber, machine knitting and clothing industries. In the other industries, German productivity was lower than Dutch productivity, particularly in the food and beverage sector in which, leaving aside the margarine industry, German productivity did not exceed 80 percent of the Dutch level. German productivity was also relatively low in the construction materials industry. This pattern very much resembles the results of another comparison that has been made, between Germany and the United Kingdom, which also established that Germany had relatively high productivity in metal products, and low productivity in foodstuffs.[50]

As before, the general comparative productivity has been determined using a two-step weighting procedure. The weighting within the industrial sectors is based on the employment volumes in the individual industries. The geometrical average of the weightings using the German and the Dutch structure, respectively, gives a productivity comparison for each industrial sector. Then the comparative productivity levels per sector are weighted according to the employment structure of the industrial sectors within industry as a whole. This has been based on Hoffmann's estimate of the sectoral distribution (see Table 2.1), and on the distribution of employment in Dutch industry.[51]

In the British-Dutch comparison we saw that the comparative productivity levels in the diverse sectors were quite similar, but in this German-Dutch comparison it is striking that there are large differences between sectors. In the first place we see once again that Germany had very high comparative productivity in metallurgical industries, but very low comparative productivity in the food and beverage sector. In the textiles sector the productivity levels in the two countries were almost the same. The structure within

---

struction and 19,197 in the utility companies. The resulting average value added per worker for 1936 is 1,411 guilders. Production figures come from den Bakker and from CBS (1948), *Nationale*, 24–25, respectively. The employment figures are calculated from the accident statistics.

50 See Broadberry & Fremdling, Comparative, 405.

51 Den Bakker & De Gijt, Labour Force.

Table 2.8. Sectoral productivity levels and unit value ratios in Germany and the Netherlands, 1936 (Netherlands = 100)

Sector	Employm. Weights Germany	Employm. Weights Netherlands	Unit value ratio guilders per RM
Food	62.1	61.0	.48
Textiles	102.2	101.7	.45
Leather and footwear	85.7	86.2	.44
Paper	66.3	66.3	.38
Chemicals	110.3	99.2	.30
Construction materials	76.7	78.5	.28
Metallurgy	133.4	114.2	.53
Total	101.1	86.2	.45

Source: See Table 2.7

the industrial sectors in the sample has some influence in the chemicals and metallurgical sectors. In the first of these, the German advantage in productivity disappears if we use weights based on the Dutch employment structure. This is due to the relatively small rubber industry and large rayon industry in the Netherlands. These have low and high productivity levels, respectively, in comparison to the corresponding German industries. Something similar can be seen in the metallurgical industry: if we use Dutch weights the German advantage in productivity is considerably lower, because the comparatively productive shipbuilding industry is relatively large in the Netherlands. The same effect is found in the electro-technical industry, which in the Netherlands has a higher productivity than the average for metallurgical industries. The comparative productivity levels elegantly confirm the complementarity of the two economies that is so striking in the statistics on imports and exports: the Netherlands exported mainly foodstuffs, and Germany exported mainly metal products.[52]

Finally, the overall comparative productivity is estimated at 101.1 and 86.2, based respectively on the German and Dutch employment structure. The large difference between the results with the two different weightings is striking: in the comparison between the Netherlands and the United Kingdom the difference was much smaller. The geometrical average of the two outcomes is 93.3. This is reasonably close to the estimate that was made on the basis of total figures, using the conversion factor calculated previously (87.5). The fact that the productivity levels calculated above are in close agreement with the productivity based on the industry-of-origin comparison may indicate that the calculated purchasing power parity is indeed a good reflection of the relative purchasing power of the products. Unit value ratios for each industrial sector have also been calculated in the same way as in the British-Dutch comparison. These are shown in the last column of Table 2.8. The ratios in this column have been calculated from the

---

52 Fremdling, niederländischen; Klemann, *Tussen*.

price ratios for each article for the years 1935, 1936 and 1937. These prices have then been averaged so as to compensate, to some extent, for price fluctuations as a result of the depreciation of the guilder. The ratios vary rather widely between sectors, as they did in the comparison between the United Kingdom and the Netherlands. Production in the metallurgical industries, for example, has a purchasing power parity of 53 cents per RM, which is just 10 percent below the official exchange rate prior to September 1936. On the other hand, the unit value ratio in the construction materials industry is low; construction materials that cost one RM in Germany could be bought in the Netherlands for just 28 cents. Once again it is evident that it is necessary, in any sectoral analysis, to use sector-specific purchasing power parities and not a general value ratio, because that has the effect of levelling out the comparative productivity levels in the various sectors.

Finally, if we combine the results of the British-Dutch comparison and the German-Dutch comparison, we can derive from them a German-British ratio for 1935/1936 of 93.3/94.5 = 99. This is close to the German-British ratio of 102 calculated by Broadberry and Fremdling.[53] We have thus established mutually consistent industrial productivity levels for the three countries.

2.6. Comparison of productivity levels in Belgian and Dutch industry, 1937

As was the case with Germany, there is only one year in the inter-war period for which there is sufficient data to make a reliable comparison with Belgium, and that is the year 1937.[54] That was the year of the Belgian *'Economische en Sociale Telling'* (Eco-

Table 2.9. Productivity comparison between Belgium and the Netherlands, 1937 (Netherlands = 100)

Flour	99	Footwear	100
Cocoa and chocolate	93	Paper	69
Sugar	78	Rubber	102
Preserved food	97	Rayon	102
Edible oil	103	Superphosphate	98
Margarine	81	Soap	116
Beer	159	Brick	90
Tobacco	89	Roofing tiles	147
Cotton spinning	61	Cement	60
Cotton weaving	135	Smelters	175
Wool spinning	103	Zinc	147
Wool weaving	86	Shipbuilding	74
Leather	106		

Source: De Jong & Soete, Comparative, 2.

53 Broadberry & Fremdling, Comparative, 404.

54 The data in this section derives from a study performed jointly with Antoon Soete: De Jong & Soete, Comparative.

nomic and Social Census), which collected data on employment and employees' wages, but unfortunately no data on production values. It is therefore not possible to make a productivity comparison based on real value added. The analysis is thus based entirely on physical indicators. Nevertheless comparisons were possible for 25 industries, employing 212,000 people in Belgium, or 20.2 percent of the total industrial employment there, and 178,000 people in the Netherlands, which is 24.6 percent of total employment in Dutch industry.

Belgian productivity appears to have been relatively high in the metallurgical and chemicals sectors, which is not surprising since these are sectors in which Belgium had established a good international reputation. We find relatively low ratios in the paper, shipbuilding and food and beverage industries, with the exception of beer breweries. However the range of productivity levels within the textile and construction materials sectors was very great. Belgium's comparative productivity in cotton spinning was on the low side, which can be explained by differences in quality: the Belgian spinning mills focused very much on spinning higher qualities of cotton threads, as compared to the Dutch mills.[55]

Table 2.10. Sectoral productivity levels in Belgium and the Netherlands, 1937 (Netherlands = 100)

Sector	Employm. Weights Belgium	Employm. Weights Netherlands
Food	109.7	94.2
Textiles	89.1	105.5
Leather and footwear	101.6	101.6
Paper	68.5	68.5
Chemicals	104.0	104.8
Construction materials	85.9	97.3
Metallurgy	116.2	78.4
Total	99.5	89.8

Source: De Jong & Soete, Comparative, 35–42.

If we weight the productivity levels in the same way as was done in the British-Dutch comparison, we obtain a productivity ratio for Belgium of 94.5 percent. Although there are substantial outlying values in the sample, they have little effect on the average, at least if we cut off both the top and bottom of the sample. The weighted productivity without cement, cotton, beer breweries and smelters is exactly 1 percentage point higher: 95.5 percent. At the same time, the coefficient of variation drops from 0.276 to 0.197. The comparative productivity is thus a reasonably robust estimate.

55 Hogg, *Structural*, 38.

A second way to estimate the comparative productivity is by comparing the reconstructed totals of the industrial sectors in the two countries. This has been calculated on the basis of the gross value added at factor costs in manufacturing industries and a calculation of the number of wage earners. This gives a figure of 1,773 guilders per wage earner for the Netherlands and 26,108 Belgian francs (Bfr) for Belgium.[56] If we convert this into Dutch guilders using the official exchange rate of 1 Bfr = 6.14 Dutch cents, this gives a Belgian average productivity of 1,603 guilders. This is 90.4 percent of Dutch productivity and about five percentage points lower than the first estimate. In view of the large uncertainties involved in this calculation, my preference is for the comparative productivity calculated from comparisons between the industries, i.e. Belgian productivity at 95 percent of that in the Netherlands.

A comparison has also been made for the year 1960, this time on the basis of production data for each industry. Table 2.11 presents an overview of the results.[57] In a two-stage weighting procedure, the unit value per industrial sector has been determined, and from this the average value added per worker, which is then expressed in a common currency.

Table 2.11. Sectoral productivity levels and unit value ratios in Belgium and the Netherlands, 1960 (Netherlands = 100)

	Productivity level	Unit value ratio (Bfr. per guilder)
Food	97	12.3
Textiles	93	14.9
Leather and footwear	76	14.0
Wood products	95	14.3
Paper	80	13.9
Chemicals	94	12.4
Construction materials	97	12.7
Metallurgy	99	12.3
Total	93.5	13.0

Source: De Jong and Soete, Comparative, 4

The purchasing power parity for industrial products calculated from the census data is 13.0 Bfr per guilder. For industrial products the guilder was officially somewhat over-valued in comparison to the Belgian franc that year, because the official exchange rate was then 13.2 Bfr. per guilder. This might well come as a surprise, in view of the general opinion that it was the Belgian franc that was over-valued in comparison to the guilder during the 1950s. In fact this was only true for 'traditional' sectors such as textiles,

56 For details see De Jong & Soete, Comparative, 3.

57 Ibid., 4–5, 25–28 en 44.

leather and wood. The productivity levels in the food and beverages, construction materials and metallurgical industries given in the table are practically the same in the two countries. There are some differences in the textiles and chemicals sectors, and big differences in leather and paper industries. The comparative productivity for Belgian industry has been calculated at 93.5. Thus between 1938 and 1960, Belgian-Dutch comparative industrial productivity levels seem to have changed very little. To substantiate this notion, productivity levels will be linked to long-term productivity trends in the next chapter.

2.7. Conclusions

In this chapter we have tried to estimate comparative levels of labour productivity in industry, using various approaches. From the results it appears that Dutch industry in the second half of the 1930s enjoyed a high comparative productivity. The picture for the period after the Second World War is not so clear: little appears to have changed in comparison to Belgium, but we have seen that Dutch productivity in comparison to the United Kingdom was lower in the 1950s. It has been shown that the official exchange rate does not provide a good ratio for translating the productivity levels. Purchasing power parities based on unit value ratios give a more accurate picture of the comparative productivity. There may sometimes be considerable differences in comparative productivity levels between the industrial sectors. The sectoral comparisons have shown that the Netherlands had a relatively productive food and beverage sector and paper industry in the inter-war period. In the textile industry, productivity in this period was somewhat below the average. The metallurgical industry had a low comparative labour productivity, especially in comparison to Germany. Big differences in comparative productivity levels between the industrial sectors were also found especially in the German-Dutch comparison.

The industry-of-origin approach has shown that a simple comparison of average labour productivity levels on the basis of the totals from national statistics of production or national accounts does not give a representative picture of the comparative productivity. This is explained by the fact that the censuses do not all give the same coverage of industry as a whole. Detailed industry comparisons lead to reliable estimates for total manufacturing, provided that a stepwise aggregation procedure with proper weights is applied.

Chapter 3: Productivity performance in the long run

Trends in comparative productivity over the long term can be estimated by extending the calculated productivity levels for the years 1935–1937 backwards and forwards, using time series of the industrial labour productivity in each country. This gives us series that are mutually comparable between the Netherlands and each of the three other countries, showing the comparative productivity from year to year. In some cases it is possible to check the accuracy of these extensions by laying them alongside the results of benchmark comparisons of labour productivity levels between the countries for other years.

The extrapolation of time series from comparisons for a particular year does not give any easy guarantee that the comparisons for the other years will be valid. This depends on the quality of the benchmark comparison and of the time series, as well as the consistency between them. Although these questions will be addressed in the discussion of the data series that are used, they are mentioned briefly here. In the first place, the index number problem plays a role. A long-term output-index becomes steadily less representative, since it is evident that production and price relationships change. Structural changes in manufacturing are not always adequately reflected in time series of output or productivity data. There is often some delay before prices, quantities and weights of new products or industries are included in official series. Another problem is the lack of consistency when applying weighting: the comparisons are made using a weighting based on common weights for both countries, while the separate time series that are compared are based on the weights of one country.[1]

In this chapter, as in the previous chapters, labour input is defined in terms of the number of workers. It would undoubtedly have been preferable to measure labour in working hours, since this would increase the accuracy of the comparisons. However in this comparison we have assumed that the number of working hours per worker changed in parallel in all four countries.[2]

The three time series of productivity in Great Britain, Germany and Belgium are all compared to a single series of productivity data for Dutch industry. This series has been calculated from data in the Dutch Statistics of Production. We do not have data for every year in the period 1913–1921, although there are estimates for 1913, 1916, 1919 and 1921, but the calculated values of real labour productivity between 1913 and 1921

---

1 For an extensive discussion of this question see Krijnse Locker & Faerber, Space and Time Comparisons; Szilagyi, Procedures.

2 Rostas, *Comparative*, 26 and 29; Broadberry, Manufacturing, 776.

are internally consistent, because they are based on the same industries. The same applies to the data concerning the Second World War period and after.[3]

3.1. British/Dutch productivity performance, 1913–1965

The time series of industrial production between 1913 and 1965 in the United Kingdom originates from Feinstein.[4] He based this series on estimates by Lomax, for the period 1913–1938, and by Brown, who compared the census results of the years 1935 and 1948 to provide a coherent picture of levels of industrial production around the Second World War. There is no official production data for the period between 1938 and 1946.[5] The figures for the period after 1948 are based on calculations made by the British Central Statistical Office on the basis of the census, supplemented with estimates of production for the intervening years.[6] The index is consistent and is based on the same source throughout, which in my opinion makes it sufficiently accurate for long-term comparisons.

The data series on employment that Feinstein gives for the period before 1920 is based on census figures adjusted for unemployment. The figures for the period 1920–1938 are calculated from Chapman's analysis of the 1931 Census.[7] Figures for 1939–1947 are based on a modified series from the Ministry of Labour, expressed in units of 'manpower'. The modifications relate to part-time workers and to employees

---

3 For a detailed account of the method of calculation for the Dutch series see De Jong, *Nederlandse industrie*, 339–394, see also appendix c in this book.

4 Feinstein, *Statistical Tables*, Table 51, T112–T113.

5 Lomax, Production, 191–194, Brown, Industrial, v–vii. These estimates are based largely on data from the *Census of Production* and the *Import Duties Act Enquiries* (1924, 1930, 1933, 1934, 1935, 1937 and 1948). For the period 1913–1938, the developments in the intervening years have been interpolated from scores of separate data series relating to the use of raw materials, employment and gross production in many of the individual industries. These separate series were then weighted according to the relative sizes of these industries, based on the industry's value added ('net output') in the census years 1924, 1930 and 1935. Then the geometrical average of the three series was calculated. Although Feinstein expressed his reservations about the possibility that growth was over-estimated as a result of his use of weights from the beginning of the period, it is no longer possible to recalculate Lomax's series using only 1935 weights. See Feinstein, *National Income*, 209 and the commentary by A. Maizels on Lomax' article: Lomax, Production, 214.

6 Feinstein, *National Income*, 208–211. Feinstein expressed some reservations about the value of the index for estimating the level of production: "The reliability of the index has to be considered in the context of measurement of the changes in real output and not of the actual level at any point in time."

7 Chapman has constructed time series for the whole inter-war period for each industry from the estimated level of employment for 1931, itself based on figures for unemployment benefits, the census of production and company estimates. Self-employed persons are included, and there are corrections for unemployment, strikes and part-time work, so that the employment is expressed in full-time equivalents (man-years). Chapman, *Wages*. See also Feinstein, *National Income*, 217–223.

older than 60 and 65 years. Data for the period after 1947 again comes from the Ministry of Labour, providing a figure for total employment, broken down to the level of industrial sectors. Some reclassification work was required to achieve a good match with the series in the inter-war period. No separate employment figures are available for manufacturing industry between 1938 and 1948, so there is a gap, extending for a full decade, in the British estimates of average productivity.[8]

According to these official figures the post-war level of British labour productivity was only a fraction higher (index value = 101) than the level of the base year 1938 (= 100). Other estimates, such as those in the *Economic Survey of Europe since the War* from 1950, point to a somewhat higher level after the war. This report states that British productivity in 1949 was 118, in comparison to the average of the years 1935–1938.[9] If we translate these figures to make 1938 the base year, the productivity for 1948 is 113, which is even higher than Feinstein's estimate. Note, however, that these figures are based on an employment index that includes only employees, and not the self-employed. Nevertheless this source does point to a clear increase in productivity in the war period.

Van Dierendonck provides us with a second estimate of comparative industrial productivity in the United Kingdom. He calculated a level of 104 for 1947, and estimated a level of 108 for 1949. His method was explicitly intended to ensure that the weighting method was in agreement with the way Dutch productivity was calculated.[10] Table 3.1 compares the rates of growth in British and Dutch productivity levels, for the whole period (1913–1965) and for a number of sub-periods.

Table 3.1. Industrial labour productivity growth in the United Kingdom and the Netherlands, 1913–1965 (annual compound growth rates)

	U.K.	Netherlands
1913–1921	–0.9	2.3
1921–1929	4.0	3.3
1929–1938	2.1	2.3
1938–1950	0.8	–0.6
1950–1965	2.5	5.0
1913–1965	1.7	2.5

Sources: United Kingdom: Feinstein, *Statistical Tables*, T114, T125, T129. Netherlands: Appendix C.

8 See Feinstein, *Statistical Tables*, Table 59, T129.

9 This report originates from the Economic Commission for Europe and is cited in the *Central Economic Plan*, 1950, 11 and in Brakel, *Industrialisatie*, 57. By way of comparison, note that the European report estimates Dutch industrial productivity for 1949 at 81 percent (1935–1938 = 100). Thus there is considerable variation in the productivity trends.

10 Van Dierendonck, Niveau, 828–829. Sandee cites an estimate made by the British statistician Seers (*Bulletin of Oxford University Institute of Statistics* Vol. 9 (1947), 228), who calculated the real productivity per man-year for 1945 and 1946 at 119 and 112, respectively (1938 = 100). See Sandee, Meting 863–864.

Labour productivity in the Netherlands between 1913 and 1965 increased faster than in the United Kingdom, with a calculated rate of growth that was about 0.8 percentage points higher than in the U.K. However there are big differences between the sub-periods. Figure 3.1 shows the long-term trends in productivity levels in the two countries. For the sake of standardisation, the Dutch index has 1938 as a base year (1938 = 100). The British series is then linked to the Dutch using the 1935 benchmark comparison, in which British productivity was 94.5 percent of the Dutch level.

Figure 3.1. Comparative levels of British and Dutch manufacturing productivity, 1913–1965 (Netherlands 1938 = 100; British 1935 benchmark: 94.5 % of Dutch level)

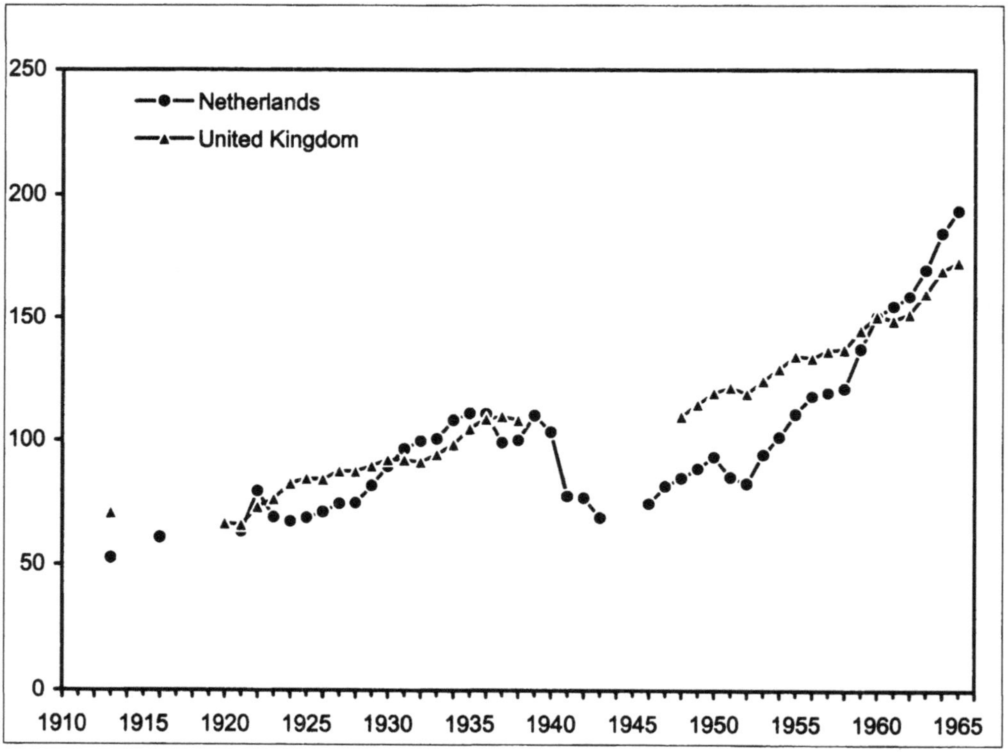

Sources: See Figure 1.2 and Table 2.2.

The figure shows that in 1913, British productivity was about 25 percent higher than the Dutch was. However immediately after the First World War, this difference had been entirely eliminated. Industry in the United Kingdom encountered big problems in adjusting, as a result of the war and its after-effects.[11] During the twenties, British productivity regained some of the relative position it held before the war. About 1930/31, there

[11] See Dowie, 1919–20, 441; Broadberry & Ritschl, Real wages, 327–349; De Jong & Albers, Industrial output, 12.

was a reversal in their relative positions, as Dutch productivity increased considerably while British productivity was stagnant. Dutch labour productivity increased very rapidly between 1925 and 1935.

After the Second World War there was a large productivity gap. According to the figures used here, British productivity in 1950 was 28 percent higher than Dutch productivity. The time series indicates that it took Dutch industry a very long time to catch up to the level of the United Kingdom. According to these figures, it was not until about 1960 that Dutch productivity equalled the British level. Thus the catch-up phase, in comparison to the United Kingdom, lasted some fifteen years.

The further the comparative levels that we have estimated on the basis of the two time series are from the comparison year of 1935, the more likely it is that their accuracy will decline. To check for this, we can compare the comparative levels derived from the time series to other benchmark comparisons. Table 3.2 compares the calculations from other studies with the figures presented here.

Table 3.2. Estimates of the comparative productivity levels between British and Dutch industry, 1913–1965 (Netherlands = 100)

	Present series	Benchmark estimates	Other series
1913	132	135	
1935	95	95	
1937	111	87	
1950	128		104
1955	122		94
1958	113	92	89
1960	100		83
1965	89		79

Sources: Column 1: See Figure 3.1. Column 2: 1913-estimate, Burger, Five-country, 9; 1935-estimate, see Table 2.2; 1937-estimate, Rostas, *Comparative*, 40; 1958-estimate, Mensink, Comparison. Column 3: Van Ark, *International*, 190.

If the comparative productivity series used here is extended back to 1913, we get a British productivity level of 132 (Netherlands = 100). This is close to an independent calculation made by Burger, who gives the figure of 135. Burger's calculation is based on the real values of production, not on physical indicators, with the British and Dutch levels of productivity being expressed in a common currency.[12] The benchmark comparison for 1937 has already been discussed above in relation to the 1935 comparison. The figure given has little significance, because it is based on only six observations that together are not very representative.[13] According to my estimate, British productivity was already higher than the Dutch level, while Rostas' calculation for 1937 points to the Dutch level being higher.

12 Burger, Five-country, 11.

13 Rostas, *Comparative*, 40.

The estimates for the early 1950s, in the third column of Table 3.2, are a different story. These estimates are based on a British-Dutch benchmark comparison for 1984, made by Van Ark. The comparative British-Dutch level of 1950 that is calculated by working back from 1984 suggests that the Netherlands had caught up with the United Kingdom as early as 1953.[14] However this cannot easily be harmonised with what has been discovered thus far about the comparative productivity levels of the two countries just before and after the Second World War. From the sources and the calculations mentioned in the present study it would appear that Dutch industry did not reach the level of productivity it had in 1938 until 1953.[15] According to Van Ark's estimate, Dutch industry caught up with the British in 1953, which, if we suppose that both countries had about the same level of productivity in 1938, implies that British industry also did not achieve the pre-war level of 1938 until 1953. This contradicts what we know about the development of British productivity around the Second World War. On the basis of Feinstein's figures, we can calculate a level of 116.7 for 1953 (1938 = 100).[16] To bring the comparative level derived from Van Ark's figures in line with the pattern of changes as a result of the war, we would have to suppose that British productivity in 1938 was about 80 percent of productivity in the Netherlands. But that would be an unlikely low level for 1938.

Van Ark justifies his relatively high estimates of Dutch productivity levels by referring to Mensink's comparison, which was discussed in the previous chapter. The latter comparison also yields lower British comparative productivity than emerges from my calculations (British levels of 92 and 113, respectively in 1958). However it has been shown that this comparison is not very representative of industry as a whole.

I conclude here that Dutch industry had attained a high level of productivity in international terms before the Second World War, but that its comparative position declined markedly after 1945. It was not until the 1960s that Dutch industrial productivity again exceeded the level in the United Kingdom. The rapid rise in productivity in the Netherlands in the 1950s should therefore be seen in the light of the very low levels of Dutch productivity occurring just after the war.

3.2. German/Dutch productivity performance, 1913–1965

The data series on German industrial productivity is based largely on Hoffmann's historical national accounts statistics. The production figures for 1913–1950 are based on a data series for industry as a whole, which has been recalculated to cover only manufacturing industry.[17] No totals are available for the years 1914–1924, and the period 1939–1949

---

14 Van Ark, *International*, 185 en 191.

15 See Chapter 9, and other sources such as Brakel, *Industrialisatie*, 57.

16 Feinstein, *Statistical Tables*, Table 59, T129.

17 Hoffmann, *Wachstum*, Table 76, 392–395. The totals in column 13 have been recalculated excluding utility companies and the construction sector (columns 11 and 12, respectively). See also Broadberry, Manufacturing, 788–792.

is still a statistical *terra incognita*. The recalculated index of productivity for 1950, derived from Hoffmann's work and confined after the war to production in West Germany, is 57 percent of the 1938 value. The data series is extended after 1950 using data based on the value added in constant prices given in the national accounts of West Germany, as calculated by Van Ark.[18] The employment figures for 1913–1950 also come from Hoffmann. The pre-war figures are based on company surveys and occupational censuses from 1913, 1925, 1933 and 1939, with interpolations using wage statistics and industrial accidents statistics.[19] Employment after 1950 (for West Germany only) has been estimated from the annual counts of wage earners, to which we have added the self-employed. From 1960 the labour volume is based on the number of people in work, taken from the official publications of the *Statistisches Bundesamt*, as cited by Van Ark.[20]

By dividing the production index by the employment index, we obtain a long-term series for labour productivity. The rate of growth in productivity, over several sub-periods, has been compared to the trend in Dutch industrial productivity. The results are given in Table 3.3.

Table 3.3. Industrial labour productivity growth in Germany and the Netherlands, 1913–1965 (annual compound growth rates)

	Germany	Netherlands
1913–1925	−0.4	2.2
1925–1929	3.9	4.4
1929–1938	2.4	2.3
1938–1950	0	−0.6
1950–1965	4.9	5.0
1913–1965	2.0	2.5

Sources: See the text.

Just as for the British-Dutch comparison of growth rates, it is striking that there are large differences in the period of the First World War and the following years. The German productivity level, even as late as 1925, was lower than in 1913. The average annual rate of growth is therefore negative in contrast to the Netherlands, for which the calculated rate of growth is 2.2 percent per year between 1913 and 1925. The countries' growth rates in the other periods are fairly similar, although it is striking that the period of the Second World War saw a smaller decline in productivity for Germany than for the Netherlands. In broad terms, the rate of growth in the Netherlands is half a percentage point higher than in Germany.

18 Van Ark, *International*, 202.

19 Hoffmann, *Wachstum*, Table 15, 196–200.

20 Van Ark, *International*, 202.

Figure 3.2 shows the changes in comparative productivity levels from year to year, working from the calculated comparative productivity for 1936 (Germany/the Netherlands = 93.3/100). The figures for 1913 point to Germany having a considerable advantage in productivity: some 50 percent. In the 1920s the difference became smaller, due to the effects of the war, which saw German levels falling while Dutch levels continued to rise. The very fast rise of the Dutch level, especially from 1929, is also striking. At the end of the 1930s both levels were approximately equal. After the Second World War, German productivity was again higher than Dutch productivity. With the exception of 1951 and 1952, the two series run very much in parallel. Even the fluctuations due to the trade cycle appear in the same way in the two series. According to our measurements, German industrial productivity in this period was about 15 percent above the Dutch level.

However doubts have been expressed about the quality of Hoffmann's indices of industrial production. Ritschl has shown that Hoffmann's figures for industrial production for the inter-war period probably strongly overestimate actual production. This would imply that production in 1925 was probably even lower than the level in 1913. Supposing that the employment volume is not affected, the effect would be lower pro-

Figure 3.2. Comparative levels of German and Dutch manufacturing productivity, 1913–1965 (Netherlands 1938 = 100; German 1936 benchmark: 93.3% of Dutch level)

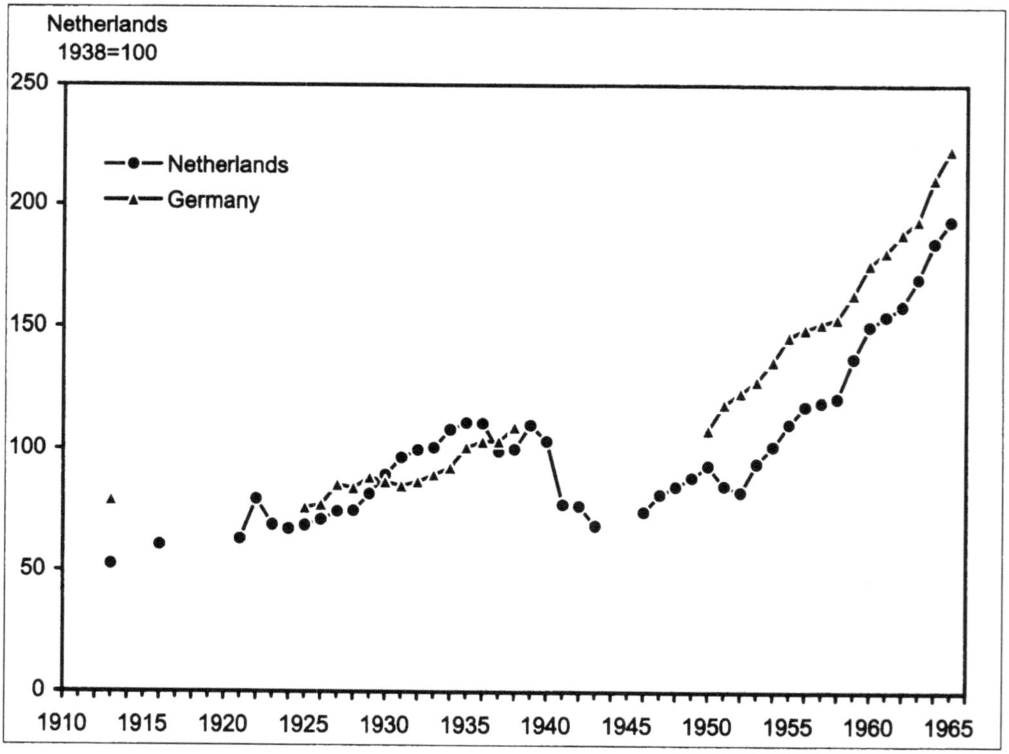

Sources: See Figure 1.2 and Table 2.7.

ductivity levels in the inter-war period. In other words, in the comparative figure, the 1913 comparative level would be even higher than it now is.[21]

The second weak point in the data series on German productivity used here is the extent to which an allowance has been made for the effects of the Second World War and the division of Germany. From 1950 onwards, that data on production and employment refer only to West Germany. While this will have had less effect on the average productivity than on the production figures (since both the numerator and the denominator have been corrected for the new territorial limits), it is not possible to say what portion of the decline in both series is due to the circumstances of the war and its after-effects, and what can be attributed to statistical effects due to the division.[22]

The aggregated series of German labour productivity from 1938 to 1950 do not reveal the same decline we have found in the Netherlands. From a more detailed examination of Hoffmann's figures we can calculate the gain in productivity in each industrial sector between 1938 (all Germany) and 1950 (West Germany). The results are shown in Table 3.4.

Table 3.4. Change in sectoral productivity levels between 1938 (Germany) and 1950 (West Germany)

	% change as compared to 1938
Food	1.5
Textiles	8.4
Clothing	10.3
Leather	–24.6
Wood	14.7
Paper	17.3
Chemicals	– 2.7
Construction materials	9.8
Metallurgical industries	–20.8
Total	– 0.9

Source: Hoffmann, *Wachstum*, Table 15, 196–200 and Table 76, 392–395.

Note that the figures in Table 3.4 are not annual growth rates, but changes in levels of labour productivity in comparison to 1938. We can see that in 1950 West Germany's productivity in the metallurgical and leather industries had fallen in comparison to pre-war Germany. Since metallurgical industries were a major part of manufacturing industry as

21 Ritschl, Origins, 15.

22 The complication is even greater if we consider that several million refugees were also being hosted in the 'new' territory of West Germany. Because this was not directly linked to increased production capacity, this implied a strong increase in unemployment in the post-war years. For a comparison of the initial positions of East and West Germany, see Ritschl, East German, 504–513; see also Sleifer, *Falling behind*.

a whole, this pulled the average industrial productivity sharply down, to the extent that the average productivity for industry as a whole in 1950 was a fraction lower than in 1938. Leaving aside the effects of the division of Germany, which are difficult to estimate, it is striking that the war conditions did not have a greater impact on production and average productivity. In the Netherlands the average productivity fell much more sharply in comparison to 1938.

Table 3.5 relates German-Dutch comparative productivity levels based on these figures to other available estimates.

Table 3.5. Estimates of comparative productivity levels between German and Dutch industry, 1913–1965 (Netherlands = 100)

	Present series	Benchmark estimates	Other series
1913	150	113	157
1929	109		
1936	93	93	
1938	109		
1950	116		103
1960	117		116
1965	115		115

Sources: Column 1: See figure 3.2.
Column 2: 1913: Burger, Five-country, 11; 1936: Table 2.3.
Column 3: 1913, Broadberry, Manufacturing, 774; 1950, 1960 and 1965: Unpublished ICOP-estimates by Van Ark, based on a comparison between the Netherlands, the U.S. and Germany for 1992.

According to two estimates, German comparative productivity in 1913 was some 50 percent higher than the Netherlands. However the two estimates are not independent of one another. The figure in the third column has been derived by extending backward from a comparison of productivity levels in the United Kingdom and Germany in 1937. For 1913, this estimate gives a German productivity of 119 in comparison to the British level. Using our British-Dutch comparison for 1913, in which British productivity was calculated at 132, the German-Dutch comparative level can be calculated at 157.[23] A German-Dutch comparison by Burger for 1913 (see column 2) gives a lower figure for German comparative productivity. However it is not clear how he compiled the employment figures in this benchmark estimate, so we must treat his estimate with great caution.[24]

At the same, the high German productivity levels presented here do seem to reinforce Fremdling's earlier doubts about the low German productivity levels for the early 20th century that he found in a comparison with British productivity. He based his work in

---

[23] For the German-British comparison see Broadberry & Fremdling, Comparative, 405 and Broadberry, *Productivity*, 49.

[24] Burger, Five, 7.

part on figures given by Hoffmann, whom he therefore criticised. However the problem here is that if we adopt corrections in accordance with this criticism – and with Ritschl's opinion about the over-estimation of German industrial production in the 1920s in comparison to 1913 – which was discussed above, this would imply very high levels of comparative production and productivity for 1913, even higher than the figures presented here.[25]

We can compare our productivity levels after the Second World War with an estimate by Van Ark, which is based on a comparison of productivity in 1992 and extended back using series on production and employment. If we start with the 1936 comparison and extend it forward we come to the same levels for 1960 and 1965 as are obtained by starting with the 1992 comparison and extrapolating back. We can conclude that in the early 1960s industrial productivity in Germany was about fifteen percent higher than in the Netherlands.[26] The changes in comparative productivity in the Netherlands are again striking, with a catch-up phase after the First World War, an exceptional acceleration between 1925 and 1935, and considerable ground to catch up after 1945, because of a low post-war level.

3.3. Belgian/Dutch productivity performance, 1921–1965

Productivity figures for Belgium are available from 1920. The data series comes from Soete. For the period before 1953 it consists of weighted sub-series of production data

Table 3.6. Industrial labour productivity growth in Belgium and the Netherlands, 1913–1965 (annual compound growth rates)

	Belgium	Netherlands
1913–1921	–	2.1
1921–1929	2.6	3.3
1929–1938	0.8	2.3
1938–1950	0.8	–0.6
1950–1965	3.3	5.0
1913–1965*	2.1	2.5

* The Belgian rate of growth for the whole period is based on the growth between 1920 and 1965.

Source: De Jong and Soete, Comparative, 48.

25 Fremdling, Productivity, 39–42. This critique was made more pointed in later publications: see Fremdling, German, 25–55, which also cites Ritschl's opinion.

26 In Van Ark, *International*, 191 we find comparative levels for the Netherlands for this period that are higher than the German level. The difference is due to the third country with which the comparisons are made. The 1992 figures come from a comparison via the United States, whereas Van Ark has used the United Kingdom. This can produce considerable differences, especially in combination with extrapolation.

on the basis of physical and real indicators. The series after 1953 is based mainly on national accounts. The indices for production and employment are based on all companies in manufacturing industry, and not only on the larger companies.[27]

Once again, there are fairly large differences between the sub-periods. During the inter-war period, growth in Belgian productivity was quite modest. However it is not yet possible to determine what the Belgian level before the First World War was. During the 1940s there was a slight net increase in productivity, comparable with growth in the United Kingdom and significantly higher than the Dutch rate of growth. The rate of growth during the 1950s was again much lower than the Dutch rate, and in this respect is again comparable to the British experience.

Taken over the whole period, the rate of growth is slightly more than two percent per year, but this does not include the period 1913–1921. If we compare the change in productivity period by period, it is striking that Belgium enjoyed somewhat faster growth than the Netherlands during the period 1925–1929. However, productivity growth declined markedly in the 1930s, leading to a big productivity gap compared to the Netherlands. This situation continued until the Second World War. In 1937, the year for which the benchmark comparison is made, the difference is still very slight (the Belgian level being 95.5 percent of the Dutch). If we take 1938 as a starting point (index = 100), Belgian productivity regained its pre-war level in 1948. In 1949 Belgian productivity reached a level of about 96 percent of the top pre-war year of 1937. This figure is very close to the value for 1949 that was calculated in the previously mentioned report of the *Economic Commission for Europe*, which is 93 percent.[28]

Figure 3.3 shows that the comparative productivity between the two countries was much the same during the period 1946–1953, but from that point onwards their paths of growth were very different. For the entire 1950–1965 period, the calculated average difference in the growth rates of the two countries is 1.5 percentage points per year. The result in 1960 was that productivity in Belgium was 87 percent of Dutch productivity. The comparative productivy levels estimated here are based on an extension from the comparative productivity in 1937. The direct comparison for 1960 gave 93.5 percent (see section 2.6). Given the variations that were found earlier, this estimate stays within acceptable limits; it confirms that the estimates and the time series are reasonably accurate.[29]

---

27 Soete, Evolution.

28 Economic Commission, *Economic Survey*.

29 Further extrapolation of the time series for productivity shown here, to 1987, points to a comparative Belgian productivity of 97 percent. This is only three percentage points different to a direct Belgian-Dutch comparison for that year. See de Jong and Soete, Comparative, 45, 48.

Figure 3.3. Comparative levels of Belgian and Dutch manufacturing productivity, 1913–1965 (Netherlands 1938 = 100; Belgian 1937 benchmark: 95.5 % of Dutch level)

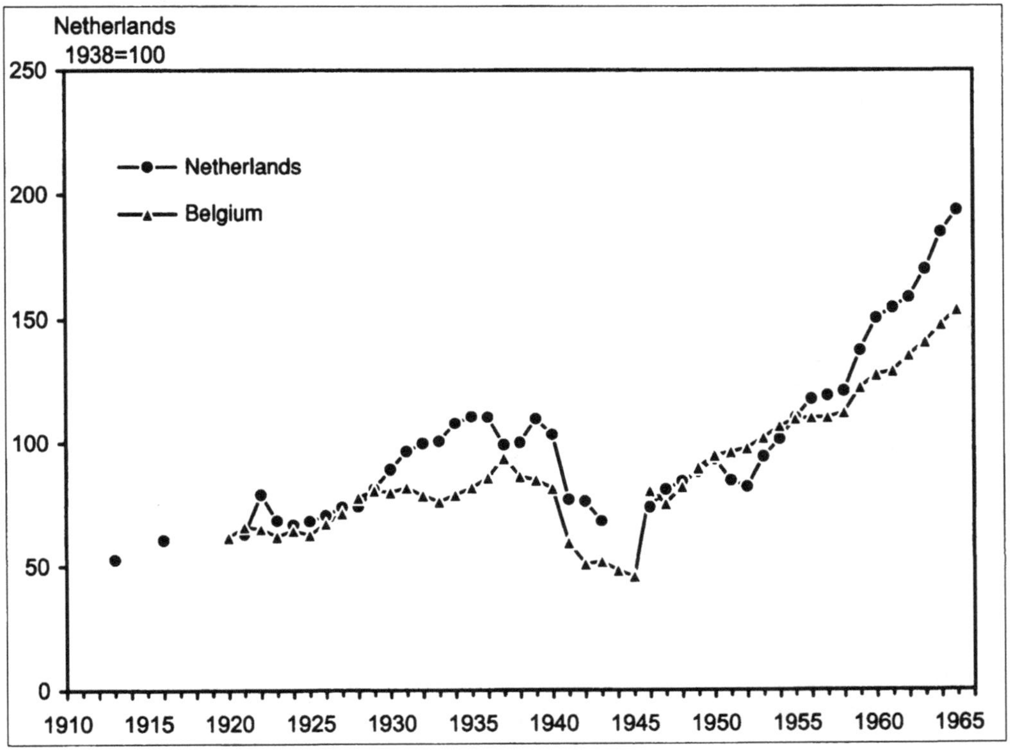

Sources: See Table 1.2 and Table 2.9.

3.4. Productivity levels in manufacturing and in the total economy, 1913–1992

Changes in industrial productivity do not necessarily show the same movements as productivity changes in the economy as a whole. Chapter 1 has shown that in the period 1913–1965, the output of manufacturing industry in the Netherlands grew faster than total gross domestic product. Labour productivity in industry also increased faster than total economy productivity. This implies that combined growth in the other sectors of the economy, i.e. the service sector and agriculture, was slower. Thus if structural shifts take place at different times in different countries, trends in the comparative industrial productivity will not parallel trends in the comparative growth of gross domestic product per worker. This brings us to the question of structural shifts in the economy. For a given employment level in the national economy, a shift of employment and output from less productive sectors to more productive sectors can increase productivity. It is generally assumed that the shift of the economic centre of gravity from the agricultural sector to the industrial and service sector was the main cause of the spectacular increase in productivity in many countries during the 19th and 20th centuries. This massive transfer of employment has led some researchers to assume that each country has its own path of economic growth. Economic crises, wars and other disasters can temporarily obstruct these deeper economic forces in a country, but an acceleration in the productivity growth returns the country to its own path of growth.[30]

This section will examine the relationships between developments in industrial labour productivity and the productivity in the whole economy in the four countries. From Maddison's data we can deduce that productivity levels among the rich countries converged strongly in the period following the Second World War.[31] Countries in which labour productivity was initially relatively low grew faster than those with a higher initial productivity. It was not just a question of convergence towards a mean, but of catching-up with the lead country. During this period the gap between the United States, being the productivity leader, and the other rich countries became smaller. The convergence and catching-up processes can be explained using the Solow-type neo-classical theory of growth. In the long term, population changes and increases in technological knowledge, which leads to labour-saving production processes, determine the growth of a country. In many neo-classical growth models, technological development is assumed to be exogenous.[32] This implies that the international diffusion of technological knowledge (for example through imitation and adaptation) will lead to a convergence in the levels of productivity in different countries. Similarly, in the more historically orientated theories of economic development, such as Gerschenkron's theory, it is assumed that countries that lag behind in economic development can catch up by imitating technical knowledge from the leading countries. A prerequisite is, however, that national institu-

---

30 Clark, International, 272. There is a discussion and evaluation of the catching-up hypothesis in relation to the German *'Wirtschaftswunder'* in Dumke, Reassessing, 451–494. See also Lindlar, *Wirtschaftswunder*.

31 Maddison, *Dynamic*; Maddison, *Monitoring*.

32 This theory assumes that an ongoing accumulation of a factor of production leads to diminishing marginal returns, and that knowledge is a public good. Each country tends towards its own steady state: However there may be conditional convergence, i.e. paths of growth may differ, depending on the savings rate, population growth and factors such as educational levels. For example, a high savings rate leads to a steady state with a greater capital intensity. Mankiw, Romer & Weil, Contribution, 407–437, have demonstrated conditional convergence between many countries for the period 1960–1985.
Declining economic growth after 1973 and the absence of convergence between rich and poor countries gave way to the 'new growth theory', which assumes technological development to be endogenous, i.e. it is explained by the economic factors themselves. Endogenous growth theory assigns a bigger role to the effects of a higher quality of human capital through accumulation. In this case, diminishing marginal returns are outweighed by favourable spillover effects from an increase in knowledge, extending to other economic sectors. This means that the cumulative production of knowledge ('learning processes') and research and development within countries does not necessarily lead to convergence processes between countries.

tions create appropriate conditions to promote the diffusion of technology and production methods.

On the basis of these diffusion mechanisms, one would expect to find catching-up processes and a convergence between productivity levels in the manufacturing sector. Especially in the 20th century, industry was a growth sector that experienced rapid increases in productivity. Moreover it is the sector in which international technology transfer can take place most easily, so production methods that are technically and economically superior can be copied or imported along with capital accumulation.[33] Do we also find convergence processes between the four countries that are compared with one another in the present study?

From comparative studies by Broadberry and Van Ark, among others, it appears that productivity changes in the manufacturing sector are not parallelled in the economy as a whole. Broadberry, for example, has shown that labour productivity in American industry was far above that of the United Kingdom even in the 19th century. His figures show, moreover, that German industry was approaching the productivity of British industry by the beginning of the 20th century, although the productivity of the German economy as a whole did not surpass that of United Kingdom until long after the Second World War. From Van Ark's data follows that from 1950 until the mid 1970s there were roughly parallel processes of convergence in ten industrialised countries between the manufacturing sector and in the economy as a whole, but that in the 1980s diverging trends emerged in the manufacturing industry.

How can we harmonise these findings with the theoretical notions outlined above? In various publications Broadberry has defended the thesis that there has been a long-lasting gap between the levels of industrial productivity in the United States and those of Germany and the United Kingdom since the 19th and 20th centuries. In other words, the convergence between the gross domestic product per worker in the United States, on the one hand, and the United Kingdom and Germany, on the other hand, has not been reflected in industrial productivity. According to him there have been long-lasting differences in industrial productivity across the Atlantic as a result of different technological choices in the industrial production process. These choices were said to be linked to divergent relative factor costs and to country-specific factors in connection with demand.[34] The implication of this hypothesis is that the process of convergence is determined mainly by productivity trends in the agricultural and service sectors and by structural shifts in the total economy, but not in industry. The differences in the productivity trends at the sectoral level of the economy are just part of the process of overall convergence.[35] However there does appear to have been a convergence between the European countries on a common path of growth in industrial productivity.

33 Fremdling, *Voorsprong*, provides a certain relativisation of the logic of convergence.

34 See for example Broadberry, Technological.

35 'Employment shift' is an important structural force. It also has effects within the sectors. Maddison, among others, has indicated that the productivity growth within a sector is not independent of the shifts between sectors: the two kinds of change influence one another. Maddison, *Phases*, 115–121.

Using Maddison's comparisons of gross domestic product per worker, we will now examine to what extent the changes in industrial productivity that we have found have also been reflected in the comparative productivity levels of the national economies. Because the comparative time series of industrial productivity are reasonably compatible with the estimates for the period after 1965 (at any rate for Germany and Belgium), the long-term perspective for this analysis has been extended to the 1990s. Table 3.7 compares the comparative national productivity levels to industrial productivity levels.

Table 3.7. Comparative productivity levels for manufacturing and for the total economy in the U.K., Belgium and Germany, 1913–1992 (Netherlands = 100)

	U.K.		Belgium		Germany	
	Ind.	Total	Ind.	Total	Ind.	Total
1913	132	110	–	90	150	87
1929	110	88	99	76	109	69
1938	108	96	87	84	109	77
1950	128	121	102	93	116	67
1960	100	97	87	88	117	85
1973	61	84	75	86	91	88
1992	75	83	102	99	86	96

Sources: Industry: See Tables 3.2, 3.5 and 3.6. U.K. and Germany 1973 and 1992 unpublished ICOP data from Van Ark. Belgium 1973 and 1992: De Jong & Soete, Comparative 2, 48.
Total economy: Maddison, *Monitoring*, 47; 1960: Maddison, *Dynamic*, figures from Appendix C2 divided by employment.

It is clear that the comparative levels of the foreign industrial sectors in comparison to the Netherlands were higher than the comparative levels of total economic productivity, at least until about 1960. This indicates that in the Netherlands the agricultural and service sectors combined has always had a higher comparative productivity than the industrial sector. This is not surprising, since the Dutch economy has had well-developed primary and tertiary sectors for many centuries. Moreover, both sectors were strongly internationally oriented.[36] The differences between industrial and total productivity are quite considerable, especially in 1913 and 1929, for which there are differences of twenty percentage points or more.[37] Moreover in 1929 the comparative productivity of the whole economy was very high.

The comparison of productivity levels in the Netherlands and the United Kingdom reveals that the Dutch economy was catching up with the British economy in both the industrial sector and the economy as a whole. In the last quarter of the 20th century the British economy was overtaken. At the beginning of the century, British productivity

36 See for example Brakel, *Comparison*, 123.

37 See also Van Ark & de Jong, Accounting, 32. Table 10 shows that the difference in comparative productivity levels between Dutch industry and Dutch agriculture declined after the Second World War, but around 1992 it was still some thirty percentage points. The service sector is not included in these figures.

was higher than the Dutch level. However the very favourable development between 1913 and 1929 meant that the productivity of the whole Dutch economy remained higher than British overall productivity during the inter-war period. The Second World War then led to a decline in the Netherlands. Around 1950, Dutch productivity had returned to the low comparative level of 1913, but this abnormal situation lasted only a decade. Around 1960, Dutch labour productivity in industry and in the whole economy had again achieved equality with the U.K. One might describe this as a process of 'local' convergence, interrupted only by the wars. During the 1960s, however, productivity in the Netherlands rapidly attained a higher level than in the U.K. This is attributable not only to the fact that Dutch industry was much more capital intensive during this period, but also to the poor performance of British industry.[38]

In our comparative study of Belgium and the Netherlands, Soete and I have shown that the employment structures in the two countries showed increasing similarities after the Second World War. This was coupled with a convergence between their overall productivity levels. In manufacturing industries, in contrast, there were strongly divergent trends in productivity between 1955 and 1973, attributable in part to differences in the timing of changes in the industrial structure. For example, in Belgium many labour-intensive industries such as the textile mills continued to operate much longer than in the Netherlands. But after 1973, Belgian manufacturing productivity caught up rapidly.[39]

Looking at the German-Dutch comparative productivity levels, we can see a striking difference between the comparisons for industry and for the whole economy in 1913. At that time industrial productivity in Germany was a full 50 percent higher than in the Netherlands, yet if we consider the whole economy, the Netherlands had a productivity advantage over Germany of 13 percent.[40] This shows that the German agricultural and service sectors were much less productive than those in the Netherlands. If we look at the rest of the comparisons between Germany and the Netherlands, then the catch-up process in overall German productivity in comparison to the Netherlands is striking, but this was much affected by the two wars. In 1913 and 1960, German overall productivity was about 85 percent of the Dutch level. In the intervening period it was even lower. Comparative productivity in the manufacturing industries alone does not show such a clear pattern. Figure 3.2 shows both convergence and divergence patterns in the industrial productivities of the two countries. Between 1950 and 1965 there was a constant productivity gap in manufacturing of about fifteen percent in Germany's favour. After the 1960s, this was reversed, and Dutch industry had an advantage.

If we consider the four countries together, it is clear that there was convergence in their manufacturing industries up to 1929, but no clear underlying pattern after that. As for the productivity of their total economies, we can only observe convergence in the

---

38 See this chapter and Van Ark, *International*, 126 and 191.

39 De Jong & Soete, Comparative, 18–20. This paper develops the idea that international competition meant that less productive industries in the Netherlands, such as shipbuilding and the cotton and textiles industry, were forced to restructure earlier than the less productive sectors in Belgium, partly because of the higher wage levels in these sectors as compared to Belgium.

40 There was a similar, but somewhat less extreme, relationship between the United Kingdom and Germany. See Broadberry, Manufacturing, 777 and 784.

German-Dutch comparison. Differences in industrial productivity between countries have remained, although some have changed places. In 1913 British productivity was still high, but this has since been considerably reduced, especially during the 1960s. In the Netherlands there is a clear trend in the opposite direction that points to increasing comparative industrial productivity. The productivity handicap of Dutch manufacturing industry at the beginning of the century was progressively eliminated after 1913, and the Netherlands must have gained the lead during the 1960s. Thus there was no overall convergence in industrial productivity after 1929. Rather we can observe lasting differences, and we must consider the differences in impact of the two wars in these countries. In the 20th century, the two World Wars make it difficult to form a clear picture of long-term convergence processes between these countries. In the second half of the 20th century, the various changes in the Netherlands' comparative industrial productivity in relation to Belgium had little net effect, while Britain's position in comparison to the Netherlands clearly worsened. After 1950 the German position in comparison to the Netherlands also worsened in the industrial sector, but grew much stronger with regard to the productivity of labour in the whole economy.

3.5. Conclusions

The international patterns outlined here show that Dutch industrial productivity has gone through three distinct periods. The first was the period around the First World War, during which productivity in manufacturing was clearly catching up in comparison to British and German industry. The second was the 1925–1935 period, when productivity increased very rapidly to reach levels clearly above those in the neighbouring countries. This increase in comparative productivity coincided with the Great Depression, which had drastic effects on the Dutch economy after 1929. The third was the phase following the Second World War, when the productivity of Dutch industry was low by international standards. The explanations of these distinct phases will be considered in those chapters that focus more on chronological developments. In the following chapter we will first try to throw more light on the question of how to explain the differences in productivity levels between these countries.

Chapter 4: Explaining international variations in productivity

In Chapters 2 and 3 we have seen that the labour productivity comparisons between the Netherlands and the three neighbouring countries have shown alternating periods of convergence and divergence. The identification and analysis of the determinants of differences in the productivity levels and growth between countries is the domain of growth accounting, the quantitative analysis of economic growth on the basis of a production function. In growth analysis often a distinction is made between 'ultimate' causality based on underlying factors influencing the economy and 'proximate' causality based on primary causes.[1] The underlying factors are difficult to quantify. To cite Angus Maddison: "The investigation of ultimate causality involves consideration of institutions, ideologies, pressures of socio-economic interest groups, historical accidents, and economic policy at the national level ... These 'ultimate' features are all part of the traditional domain of the historian."[2] Differences in geographical, historical and institutional factors (the latter including taxation systems, income distribution and trade policies), may mean that the combination of given quantities of labour and capital in one country may yield a higher productivity than in another country.[3]

The primary causes, however, are among the quantifiable variables in the explanatory model. Beginning with the standard neo-classical production function, we can differentiate three categories of factors that determine the volume and growth of output: the quantity of labour, the quantity of capital goods, and a residual factor.[4] This is the factor that indicates the growth in productivity; productivity being that part of growth that is not explained by a quantitative change in the labour and capital inputs to production. Growth analysis focuses chiefly on measuring the size of the residual factor and analysing its components. The residual factor often includes not only the level of technical progress, but also, for example, the standardisation of production, methods of production control, the quality of the inputs (investments in education and research and development) and the size of the market.[5] By including these factors in our quantitative analysis, we can increase our knowledge on the components of the 'unexplained' residual.

This chapter is devoted to a more detailed explanation of the differences in the productivity of labour that we have found in the comparisons for the second half of the

---

1 See Van der Klundert, *Groei en instituties*, 1.

2 Maddison, *Dynamic*, 11. See also Abramowitz, Search, 237–238.

3 Melman, *Dynamic*, 3.

4 Solow, Technical, 312–320. See also Paige & Bombach, *Comparison*, 68.

5 The market size is a demand factor rather than a supply side factor. For a discussion of its significance see Frankel, *British*, 64–80.

1930s. The method that I will use here differs from traditional growth accounting, which measures and explains changes over time, rather than differences between economies at a particular moment.[6] Moreover I will consider only manufacturing, which has been subdivided into about thirty industrial sectors. For each of the three international comparisons, I will use a cross-section in a particular year to try to explain the differences between the productivity of labour in Dutch industries and in the corresponding industries in neighbouring countries.

What indicators can we use for this purpose? Comparative studies of the period around the Second World War generally examine the following primary factors: degree of mechanisation, human capital, market size and factory plant size.[7] Comparative studies for the period after 1960 also include factors such as the stock of capital (the value of the capital stock in real prices) and research and development investments. This data is available for several countries at the level of industrial sectors or individual industries. However this approach is not possible for the period considered here. The availability of data has therefore had a large influence on the analysis that follows.

Table 4.1 summarises a number of coefficients of correlation that can be calculated on the basis of the data that will be presented in this chapter. These are simple statistical correlations between the comparative levels of labour productivity per industry in the three countries in comparison to the Netherlands (see Chapter 2) and the comparative levels of the four defined indicators. The index values of comparative productivity for each industry have been associated with the comparative index values for that industry for four explanatory variables: the installed horsepower of the power sources that drive the machines (hp. per worker, as an indicator of the capital intensity), the average wage per worker, the size of the market and the average plant size (measured by labour volume).

Table 4.1. Coefficients of correlation between comparative labour productivity and explanatory variables U.K./Neth, Germany/Neth, and Belgium/Neth, (1930–1937)

Variable	U.K./Netherlands (1930/1935)	Germany/Netherlands (1933/1936)	Belgium/Netherlands (1937)
Installed power	0.34	0.48	0.09
Wages	– 0.39	0.54	0.55
Market size	0	0.64	0.91
Plant size	0.60	0.55	0.06

Sources: See Tables 2.2, 2.7, 2.9, 4.2, 4.5, 4.8, and 4.9.

6 Van Ark has applied the growth accounting framework for a productivity-level comparison across industrial sectors in Western economies in the 1980s. Van Ark, *International*, 115–147.

7 Rostas, *Comparative*; Frankel, *British*; Broadberry & Crafts, Britain's; Broadberry & Fremdling, Comparative.

The table contains several high coefficients of correlation. There is a positive correlation in Dutch and British industries between the productivity of labour and average plant size. Those industries in which labour productivity is high in comparison to the corresponding industry in the other country also have a comparatively large plant size. If we look at Dutch industry, on the one hand, and German and Belgian industries on the other hand, we find a positive correlation between comparative labour productivity and the level of comparative wages, as well as the size of the market. The industries that offer higher average wages and serve large markets have relatively high levels of comparative productivity. It would appear that the cost of labour inputs and the extent to which industries can benefit from economies of scale have a strong positive association with productivity levels. This chapter will elaborate on these statistical relationships and analyse the underlying phenomena in more detail. It is evident that the four differentiated variables can also influence one another. The average plant size might, for example, have an effect on the capital intensity in an industry. Therefore in the final section of this chapter I will use multiple regression analysis to estimate the separate contributions that the explanatory variables make simultaneously to labour productivity.

4.1. Machinery and horsepower

The first variable to consider here relates to capital as a factor of production. There has been a general tendency in industrial development since the late eighteenth century to use ever-greater amounts of capital in comparison to labour in the production process. This has led to an increase in the productivity of labour. The combination of factors of production that will be used, for a given state of technical knowledge, is determined by the relationship between the costs of the input factors: as labour becomes more expensive in comparison to machinery (capital), machinery will be substituted for labour. The extent to which this happens is determined by the elasticity of substitution between labour and capital. If we compare countries we would expect, on this basis, that where the relative costs of labour are high there will be a higher degree of mechanisation and probably also of labour productivity. This does not automatically mean that there is also a technological advantage; while this substitution does involve changes in mechanisation and capital intensity, it does not necessarily change the level of technological advancement.[8]

Many studies have shown that labour productivity in American industry has always been considerably higher than in Western European countries. This is thought to result from higher capital intensity, attributable to differences in the relative factor costs on the

8 Witteveen, Vraagstuk, 116. A reservation should be noted here, in the light of the vintage approach on capital measurement. It is assumed that capital stocks are built up from a series of capital goods built in successive years. The most recently installed machines generally embody the more modern technology. Therefore in countries with high relative costs of labour, there may be relatively many capital goods that are more recent and modern. Within a given branch of industry, this results in higher average labour productivity compared to the same branch in other countries, because more plants will use best-practice production methods. See for example Salter, *Productivity*, 69–70 and Maddison, *Phases*, 22–24.

two sides of the Atlantic. Raw materials were relatively plentiful in the United States while labour was relatively scarce, and this favoured a system of production employing machinery that used relatively large amounts of raw materials but were economical on labour.[9]

A good example of this is the difference in the design of steam turbines before the Second World War between the United States and Germany. Although the same knowledge was available in both countries for the construction of steam turbines, the turbines designed and built in Germany worked at higher temperatures and under higher pressure than in the United States. This difference can be attributed to differences in relative prices. In Germany, where the wages were lower than in the United States, while fuel costs were relatively higher, many hours of design work were devoted to achieving greater energy efficiency. In the United States, turbine builders economised on expensive development costs and accepted lower energy efficiency, because fuel was relatively cheap.[10]

Can we see similar patterns within Western Europe, in this case between the Netherlands and the surrounding countries? In other words, is there a demonstrable relationship between comparative level of labour productivity and degree of mechanisation in the industries of the various countries? For this we need to know the value of industrial capital stocks. However, given the lack of reliable and comparable data on investments, as well as the real value of industrial capital, we have to seek another indicator. Following earlier studies of Rostas (1948), Broadberry and Crafts (1990) and Broadberry and Fremdling (1990) the installed horsepower per unit of labour is used as a proxy for the capital/labour ratio. It refers in fact to that part of the stock of capital that is used to drive machines and production vehicles. Data for the British-Dutch comparison comes from the British *Census of Production* of 1930 (the capacity of powered machinery is not reported in the census of 1935) and from the Dutch company survey of 1930, as well as the Statistics of Production of the same year.[11] From these sources we calculated

---

[9] See, for example, Habakkuk, *American*; David, *Technical Choice*, and more recently Broadberry, Technological. The latter also points to demand factors such as the existence of a large homogeneous home market. The same argument is given in Frankel, *British*, 69 and Melman, *Dynamic*, 110–113: a higher relative price of labour causes increasing mechanisation and therefore an increase in productivity. Rosenberg, (*Exploring*, 117–118), also points to these mechanisms, but implicitly applies a model of embodied technical progress. The specific factor endowments gave rise to a technological dynamic that did in fact result in a technological advantage that was even capital saving.

[10] Melman, *Dynamic*, 103.

[11] In making international comparative analyses using this indicator, it is important to base the comparison on years in which the countries were, as far as possible, in the same phase of the business cycle, because this variable is sensitive to the capacity utilisation. Industries generally adjust the quantity of capital to match the level of business activity more slowly than they adjust the factor labour. One implication is that at the low point of the trade cycle, when the production per unit of capital is lower, the calculated productivity of capital may be much reduced, while the capital intensity has been increased by lower capacity utilisation. If the countries being compared are at different points of the business cycle, this will distort the comparison of comparative capital intensities.

the average installed horsepower per worker (the 'capital intensity') for each industry. Table 4.2 compares the capital intensity in British, German and Belgian industries to that in the Netherlands.

Most of the 23 British industries that could be compared had a lower intensity than their Dutch counterparts. The table shows that in six British industries the average installed horsepower per worker was higher than in the Netherlands: margarine, sugar,

Table 4.2. Capital intensity in the United Kingdom, Germany and Belgium (Netherlands = 100)

	U.K. (1930)	Germany (1933)	Belgium (1937)
Flour	53	72	92
Cocoa and choc.		68	64
Sugar	117	79	114
Preserved food			110
Edible oils	83	92	
Margarine	107	30	
Beer	42	96	67
Tobacco	125	21	176
Cotton spinning	93		
Cotton weaving	75	49	58
Wool spinning	78		
Wool weaving		61	55
Machine knitting	53	70	
Ready-made clothing		65	
Leather	81	71	42
Footwear	74	86	168
Paper	69	57	38
Rubber	98	110	40
Soap	124	115	155
Rayon	86	158	
Brick	145	105	51
Calcium silicate		82	
Roofing tiles			76
Cement	61	91	
Smelters	88	112	
Foundries	70	142	
Zinc	140	135	
Tin		125	
Sheet metal works		162	
Wire		53	
Mechanical engin.	88	86	
Metal products		67	
Electrical engin.		125	
Shipbuilding		50	45
Cars and coachwork	88	160	
Bicycles		75	

Source: See the text.

tobacco (cigarettes), zinc, soap and brick. In the first four of these, Dutch comparative labour productivity was higher than the British. On the other hand, capital intensity in Dutch breweries was extremely high, while the average labour productivity there was about 25 percent lower than in the United Kingdom.

For the sample as a whole, there is a positive coefficient of correlation between comparative capital intensity and comparative labour productivity (see Table 4.1), but the coefficient of regression of the equation is statistically not significant.[12]

For the German-Dutch comparison we have used the *Gewerbezählung* of 1933[13] and the Dutch Statistics of Production of 1933, supplemented with a number of figures from the company survey of 1930. Since capacity utilisation in both countries was low in 1933, there will be scarcely any distortion due to trade cycle effects in the comparison for that year.[14]

From column 2 in Table 4.2 we can see that the measured capital intensity of German industry was higher in ten out of 32 cases. These are industries in the chemicals and metallurgical sectors, especially the primary metallurgical industries. It is striking that the companies that performed continuous-process technologies and construction work (shipbuilding, metal products and the wire industry) had a lower intensity than their Dutch counterparts, the much larger automobile industry being an exception. Once again there is some relationship between comparative capital intensity and comparative labour productivity, with a coefficient of correlation of 0.48, which is somewhat higher than in the comparison with British industry.

Fourteen industries could be selected for the comparison with Belgium. The Belgian figures derive from the *Economische en Sociale Telling* (Economic and Social Census) of 1937, while the Dutch figures are from the Statistics of Production for the same year. Five Belgian industries had a higher capital intensity than their Dutch counterparts: soap, footwear, tobacco, preserved food and sugar. This higher intensity is only coupled with higher comparative labour productivity in the case of the soap industry. The Belgian and Dutch indicators do not point to a statistical relationship.

In general we can say that the data on comparative capital intensity presented here points to a relatively high horsepower per worker in Dutch industry. The German

---

12 This weak relationship between comparative labour productivity and capital intensity is also found in comparisons between the United Kingdom and the United States and the United Kingdom and Germany. Moreover these are negative correlations; $r = -0.25$ and $r = -0.077$, respectively. See Broadberry & Crafts, Explaining, 392 and Broadberry & Fremdling, Comparative, 392 and 412.

13 The results are, for example, quoted in *Statistisches Jahrbuch 1937*, 136–140.

14 From the tables and graphs of employment in the *Vierteljahrsheft* of 1937 (pt. 3, p. 77ff.) it appears that industrial employment in Germany reached a low point at the beginning of 1933. It is possible that some Dutch figures from the *Bedrijfstelling* (company survey) of 1930 may contain an under-estimation of the Dutch level of capital intensity, because employment levels then were somewhat higher than in 1933. Moreover it is not always clear to what extent the German statistics may include electrical horsepower using internally generated electricity. If that were the case, this would produce an over-estimation in the German capital intensity. Thus the possible distortions are all in the direction of a relative over-estimation of the German capital intensity.

chemical and metallurgical industry is the only area where we find systematically higher capital intensities than in the Netherlands. However the statistical connection with comparative labour productivity is not significant.

Does this mean that there is no relationship between comparative levels of productivity, labour and machinery? To test this we have also calculated the comparative productivity levels of machinery (the capital productivity, i.e., output divided by capital, measured in hp.). This is shown in Table 4.3.

Table 4.3. Capital productivity in the United Kingdom, Germany and Belgium (Netherlands = 100)

	U.K. (1935)	Germany (1936)	Belgium (1937)
Flour	158	97	108
Cocoa and choc.		109	145
Sugar	151	66	68
Preserved food			88
Edible oils	152	70	
Margarine	151	273	
Beer	302	82	237
Cigarettes	99	247	51
Cotton spinning	93		
Cotton weaving	151	180	143
Wool spinning	111		
Wool weaving	139		171
Machine knitting	204	150	
Ready-made clothing		203	
Leather	133	113	251
Footwear	108	103	59
Paper	127	116	179
Rubber	124	123	255
Soap	72	84	75
Rayon	93	55	
Brick	66	78	177
Calcium silicate		67	
Roofing tiles			194
Cement	96	62	
Smelters	175	193	
Foundries	134	74	
Zinc	96	84	
Tin		77	
Sheet metal works		70	
Wire		191	
Mechanical engin.	103	163	
Metal products		187	
Electrical engin.		86	
Shipbuilding	188	162	
Cars and coachwork	153	118	
Bicycles		104	

Sources: See the text.

If we compare these figures with the figures for comparative labour productivity in Tables 2.2, 2.7 and 2.9, we can see that industries with high levels of labour productivity in comparison to their Dutch counterparts also have higher levels of capital productivity. In particular, the comparisons with the United Kingdom and Germany are clearly positively correlated.[15] In short, high comparative levels of capital productivity are accompanied by high comparative labour productivity. Apparently in these European countries, at any rate in bilateral comparisons with the Netherlands, differences in levels of labour productivity cannot be explained by a greater quantity of machinery per worker. Thus the figures do not point to substitution effects.[16]

Broadberry and Crafts have also observed this in their analysis of productivity differences between American and British industries in the 1930s.[17] Not only labour productivity but also capital productivity was usually higher in the American industries. This suggests that there was not only a shortage of labour in the United States (and thus a tendency to substitute capital for labour), but also a shortage of capital in relation to the production potential in general.[18] Melman also suggests that, in addition to the substitution of factors of production (deriving from the change in the relative costs of machinery and labour), there have also been changes in the organisation of production and in technology. These changes would have led to capital savings.[19]

However installed horsepower is of only limited use as an indicator of the total quantity of fixed assets, including buildings, vehicles, and tools and installed systems. Although this proxy comes closest to reflecting the capacity of the machinery installed in an industry, it is only a limited indicator of the quality and age of the capital, and tells us nothing about the state of technology that it embodies. An innovation is generally a qualitative change in the applied technology. For example if newer machinery can be used more efficiently with less power consumption and less horsepower needed, this indicator would point to a relatively lower use of capital per worker and per unit produced. In that case the criterion of shaft horsepower may even be misleading. In the light of this, the very low coefficients of regression and the low (in some studies nega-

---

15 The calculated regression lines also resemble one another closely (Y = labour productivity, X = capital productivity: For U.K./Netherlands $Y = 57 + 0.42X$ (St. error = 0.17, r = 0.48; without the breweries $n = 22$), for Germany/Netherlands. $Y = 53 + 0.41X$ (St. error = 0.13, $r = 0.51$; without margarine and tobacco $n = 33$). For Belgium/Netherlands: $Y = 81.6 + 0.12X$ (St. error = 0.09, $r = 0.34$, $n = 16$).

16 Section 4.6 describes a multiple regression analysis that takes into account the simultaneous influence of the other variables.

17 Broadberry & Crafts, Explaining, 377.

18 See Frankel, *British*, 38 and Temin, Labor, 251–264.

19 Melman, *Dynamic*, 114–115. Salter has also emphasised this point. During the first phases of industrialisation manpower was replaced by mechanical power, but there is still a question as to whether the factor substitution was permanent. In his eyes, labour-saving techniques are not a direct consequence of labour becoming relatively more expensive. Much depends on the elasticities of substitution. Entrepreneurs consider it important to reduce total costs. If costs rise as a result of the higher cost of labour, any innovation that yields a saving is welcome, whether it is realised via savings on capital or on labour (Salter, *Productivity*, 43).

tive) correlation coefficients between labour productivity and horsepower per worker are hardly surprising.

For industries in Germany and the Netherlands, the installed horsepower can be differentiated into electrical and non-electrical horsepower. This allows some refinement of the analysis, since the electrification of the production process can be regarded as a crucial industrial innovation of the first half of the twentieth century. Some industries were quick to introduce the generator and the electric motor, others moved more slowly. Electrification led to changes in the production processes of all industries, without exception. Thus we can regard the degree of electrification as an approximation of the modernity of the stock of capital goods of the industries differentiated here. This topic is considered further in Chapter 7, but at this point we can describe a comparison between Dutch and German industry that relates the degree of electrification to comparative labour productivity. By the electrification ratio we mean the total horsepower of installed electric motors as a proportion of the total shaft horsepower in an industry. The latter includes the horsepower of steam engines and internal combustion engines. Table 4.4 shows the absolute and comparative electrification ratios for both countries for 1933.

Table 4.4. Electrification ratios in manufacturing in Germany and the Netherlands, 1933

	Germany	Netherlands	Germany/Netherlands
Flour	29.5	51.1	57.7
Cocoa and choc.	90.1	98.4	91.6
Margarine	90.9	90.8	100.1
Cotton	61.8	63.5	97.3
Wool	70.4	77.3	91.1
Machine knitting	84.7	73.5	115.2
Ready-made clothing	89.1	86.4	103.1
Footwear	92.2	78.8	117.0
Paper	73.0	78.6	92.9
Rubber	97.7	80.5	121.4
Soap	88.6	91.1	97.4
Brick	45.2	58.6	77.1
Calcium silicate	34.3	52.3	65.6
Foundries	95.5	91.5	104.4
Wire	84.9	82.4	103.0
Mechanical engin.	93.6	93.0	100.6
Metal products	91.3	87.4	104.5
Electrical engin.	97.9	98.1	99.8
Shipbuilding	90.4	96.5	93.7
Bicycles	93.0	89.9	103.4

Sources: See Table 4.2.

There are large differences between Germany and the Netherlands in the building materials, flour and rubber industries. In the latter, Germany had a higher electrification ratio. It is remarkable that there are only very slight differences in the metallurgical industries, where Germany clearly led in productivity. Nevertheless there is a demonstrable positive correlation between the comparative electrification ratio and the comparative labour productivity. The coefficient of correlation is $r = 0.64$.[20] This is higher than the correlation between the comparative installed horsepower per worker and the comparative productivity: $r = 0.48$.

The electrification ratio, as a proxy for the modernity of the capital stock, has the advantage of avoiding the problem of a misleading statistical effect as a result of capital savings (where better technology also entails less machine power per worker). I conclude here that the electrification ratio provides the closest approach to showing the inherently plausible connection between capital intensity and labour productivity in the inter-war period. For this period it may well be the only available indicator that represents the modernity and quality of the tangible capital at the aggregation level of industries.

4.2. Average wages and human capital

The second factor to be associated here with the productivity of labour is human capital, or the quality of the labour input. Can we reveal this connection in a comparison of the productivity of labour in the two countries? We will apply an approach that has been used previously, for example by Broadberry and Fremdling who, in their comparison of German and British productivity levels, employed the average level of wages per worker per industry as an indicator of the level of human capital.[21] The assumption behind this is that the remuneration of labour is related to its marginal productivity. High comparative wages in particular industries can thus be an indicator of higher labour performance as a result of higher comparative levels of human capital.[22]

Dutch wages for the years 1935, 1936 and 1937 are calculated from the accident statistics compiled by the National Insurance Bank (*Rijksverzekeringsbank*). The data on British wages comes from the *Census of Production* of 1935, the German data from the Statistics of Production of 1936 (*Die deutsche Industrie*) and the Belgian from the Eco-

---

20 The regression equation is: Y (comp.lab.prod.) = 18.2 + 0.96X (St.error = 0.27, $r = 0.64$). The idea is that by looking at the electrification ratio we can gauge technological advance. For a somewhat similar approach see Goldin & Katz, Origins, 10, who relate this to a higher demand for skilled workers. In the present case technological advance is related to higher productivity levels.

21 Broadberry & Fremdling, Comparative, 412.

22 In the growth accounting literature, the average number of years of education of the workforce is generally used as a proxy for human capital, rather than the average wage. This is seen as a better indicator for the macro level than the average wage, because the latter is very closely related to changes in the average production per hour worked. Denison used the number of years of regular education per head of the working population (Denison, *Why*, 78–108, also Maddison, *Phases*, 110–112. A comparable method has been used for the Netherlands, in Van Ark & de Jong, Accounting, 15, 27–28). However it is not possible to derive such an indicator for the aggregation level of the present industries.

nomic and Social Census (*Economische en Sociale Telling*) of 1937. The average wages have been converted into Dutch guilders using official exchange rates and expressed as a percentage of the Dutch level.

Table 4.5. Wage levels in the U.K., Germany and Belgium (Netherlands = 100)

	U.K. (1935)	Germany (1936)	Belgium (1937)
Flour	94	116 (75)*	58
Cocoa and choc.	84	128 (91)	73
Sugar	96	52 (37)	53
Preserved food			71
Edible oils	80	111 (79)	
Margarine	71	129 (92)	
Beer	76	116 (83)	47
Tobacco	91	73 (52)	73
Cotton spinning	78		
Cotton weaving	72	100 (71)	57
Wool spinning	69		
Wool weaving		91 (65)	60
Machine knitting		110 (78)	
Ready-made clothing	78	112 (80)	
Leather	100	108 (77)	50
Footwear	99	121 (86)	65
Paper		101 (72)	54
Rubber	91	149 (106)	71
Soap	77	134 (95)	76
Rayon	67	105 (75)	
Brick	107	90 (64)	72
Calcium silicate		90 (64)	
Roofing tiles			72
Cement	92	105 (75)	
Smelters	79	106 (75)	
Foundries	90	121 (86)	
Zinc	102	163 (116)	
Tin		110 (79)	
Sheet metal works		115 (82)	
Wire	81	118 (84)	
Mechanical engin.	82	111 (79)	
Metal products		110 (78)	
Electrical engin.		138 (98)	
Shipbuilding	82	125 (89)	65
Cars and coachwork	71	100 (72)	
Bicycles		141 (100)	

* For Germany the wages in parentheses were converted using an estimated industry purchasing power parity as against the official exchange rate.

Sources: See the text.

Table 4.5 shows that British wages in 1935 were considerably below the Dutch level except in the brick and zinc industries.[23] Measured over all industries, the British average wage was about 85 percent of the Dutch level.[24] The variations within the two sets of wage data are nearly identical; the coefficients of variation of the British and Dutch series are 0.208 and 0.216, respectively, which indicates that the wage structures were similar. The German-Dutch comparative wage level varies strongly with the exchange rate that is chosen. Using the official exchange rate, the German comparative wage level is higher than in the Netherlands. However this exchange rate is not very representative for the domestic cost structure and the purchasing power of the German currency. In the previous chapter it was shown that the German-Dutch purchasing power parity in this period was very different to the official exchange rate. Therefore the column for the German comparative wages also shows, in parentheses, the comparative wage converted using the previously calculated parity of 1 Reichsmark to 0.45 Dutch guilders. The wages are then generally significantly lower than in the Netherlands, about 80 percent of the Dutch level on average. Only in the zinc and rubber industries the German comparative wages are higher than the Dutch wages. Extreme low values are shown for the tobacco, sugar and brick industries. The reason for this, at any rate in the latter two industries, may be that these are seasonal industries in which the recorded wages have been spread over a full year, which would produce an under-reporting. If we exclude these three industries, the inter-industry variation in wages is little greater than in the Netherlands. The coefficients of variation for the German and Dutch data are 0.220 and 0.215, respectively.

The Belgian average wages for all the compared industries were lower than corresponding Dutch wages, especially in the textile, clothing and leather industries. In 1937 the average level was a little over 60 percent of the Dutch average. However it should be noted that the composition of the 'sample', which includes only those industries included in the comparison of productivity, has led to a slight distortion. For example, the metallurgical industries, in which the highest average wages were being earned at this time, are under-represented. Moreover there is no separate wage data for two of the three metallurgical industries in our sample (smelters and the zinc industry). The comparative level for the whole industrial sector is estimated at about 64 percent of Dutch average wages for all industries.[25] The cross-industry variation of the Belgian wages is fairly small, with a coefficient of variation of 0.140, the Dutch coefficient being 0.213.

---

23 If the British wages in each industry are translated using a purchasing power parity based on prices in the industry, of 1 Pound to 7.7 Dutch guilders (rather than the official exchange rate of 7.24 Dutch guilders), the wages in the sugar, leather and footwear industries are also higher than the Dutch.

24 This was also noted in studies at that time. It appears that during the depression it was well known that Dutch industrial wages were high. While wages in the Netherlands had increased less than in other European countries, the 'gold wages' (wages converted at the official exchange rate) in the Netherlands were substantially higher than in the surrounding countries. See, for example, Oortwijn Botjes, Peil, 185.

25 See De Jong & Soete, Comparative, 17.

The association between comparative average wages and comparative labour productivity per industry can now be quantified. This can be done by relating the distribution of the comparative wage levels to the distribution of comparative productivity levels, as shown in the tables of comparative productivity in Chapter 2 (Tables 2.2, 2.7 and 2.9). For the comparison between the United Kingdom and the Netherlands this results in a slight negative correlation. This means that in many British industries, low comparative wages, in comparison to the Netherlands, are associated with high comparative productivity. If we exclude some extreme values, including those of the zinc industry, the strength of the relationship is as high as $r = -0.39$.

In the German-Dutch comparison there is a positive relationship, with a coefficient of correlation of $r = 0.54$, between the two variables.[26] Finally, there is a strong positive correlation in the Belgian-Dutch comparison between the comparative wage levels per industry and the comparative labour productivity: the coefficient of correlation is $r = 0.55$. High average wages are coupled with high labour productivity. Thus we find relatively high wages in Dutch industry, and in a number of cases a strong relationship between the wage levels and labour productivity. However the correlation coefficients found in the comparison with the United Kingdom are strongly negative.[27] These contradictory outcomes make it difficult to offer any unambiguous interpretation of the relationship between comparative wages and labour productivity.

The first question to be addressed is how we should interpret the causal relationship between average wages and average productivity at the level of the various industries. If we assume that labour is rewarded according to its marginal productivity, the wage level can be regarded as an indication of the quality of the labour. The direction of the causality and the sign of the relationship are then clear: higher levels of human capital should lead to higher productivity levels, both over time and between countries.

However this causality could also be reversed. If we assume a labour market in which there is differentiation in the wages paid for the same labour, it is possible that higher nominal wages in particular industries are the result of a premium for higher productivity or higher profits. The sign of the relationship would again be positive. Nevertheless the latter effect is unlikely. Research by Salter into British manufacturing industries between 1924 and 1950 has shown that nominal wages in industries with high productivity growth did not rise faster than in industries with low productivity growth. Salter attributed this to the existence of a unified national (homogeneous) labour market. This is not to deny that there may be segmentation of well-qualified and unqualified labour,

---

26 Because there are twelve observations from the metallurgical industries alone, we can also examine this sector separately. Wages in these industries were between 71% and 116% of the Dutch level, while productivity was between 78% and 216%. It is striking that there is a strong negative coefficient of correlation, $r = -0.70$, between comparative wages and labour productivity in this sector, whereas in the other sectors we find a positive correlation. A very strong correlation, of $r = 0.91$, was found in the food and beverages sector, which in Germany was characterized by relatively low wages and low productivity levels.

27 A similar correlation analysis for the 1930s between Germany and the United Kingdom also has a negative correlation, although this is not significant. Broadberry & Fremdling, Comparative, 412.

and high and low wages, in the labour market.[28] According to this approach, differences in average wages between industries are a reflection of the composition of types of employment offered in different industries, and thus reflect differences in human capital between the industries in the countries.[29]

This would lead us to the conclusion that wage differences between industries within a country do not primarily reflect differences in average labour productivity, but rather the variation in the composition of employment per industry. There are differences in the ratios of male to female labour, in the extent to which young people are employed in the production process, and in the proportion of labour provided by workers or employees. This variation determines the variation in the average wage per worker, not only between the industries within a country, but also between comparable industries in different countries.

The first factor to be considered is the extent to which the wage structures (here defined as the cross-industry variation in wage levels) within these countries resemble one another. In the four countries examined, the highest wages were earned in industries such as the automobile industry, beer breweries, smelters and the shipbuilding industry, while the lowest average wages were found in the cotton and wool industries, ready-made clothing, footwear, and in the tobacco and cocoa industries. If we compare the structure of the average wage levels in each industry in the Netherlands with the structure in each of the three neighbouring countries, we find coefficients of correlation of $r = 0.80$ 0.81 and 0.66 between the Netherlands and United Kingdom, Germany and Belgium, respectively. It would appear that there is an identical underlying pattern in the structure of employment in the four countries. The factors underlying average wage levels include the extent to which women and youth workers (who earn lower wages) participated in paid labour, the size of non-production workers such as sales and administration, and the percentage of managers and specialists (the bosses and engineers).

Table 4.6 shows the proportions of male workers in the diverse industries, for the Netherlands, the United Kingdom, Germany and Belgium. The bottom line of the table shows totals for manufacturing as a whole. The overall percentage for the Netherlands is 82 percent. This average has been calculated from the census of employment of 1930, while the percentages for each industry come from the Statistics of Production of 1938. The British percentages are calculated from the *Census of Production* of 1935. The overall level there is 63 percent. The proportion of German industrial employment held by males is calculated from the overviews of the *Erwerbspersonen nach Branche* from the *Statistisches Jahrbuch* of 1933. Because there was a substantial decline in economic

---

28 Compare this to the theories on segmented labour markets, see f.i. Schippers and Siegers, Labour market, 403.

29 Salter, *Productivity,* 115, 156; see also Melman, *Dynamic,* 58–60. For a different opinion see Rostas, *Productivity,* 36, who in a cross-sectional analysis between British industries (on the basis of the Census of 1935) found a close relationship between higher productivity and higher average wages and explained the latter as due mainly to the differences in productivity levels. Within a particular industry, companies with a higher productivity paid higher average wages because there was more budget flexibility for this, because the workers were well organised or (reversing the causal relationship) because they used more skilled labour.

Table 4.6. Male labour shares in the Netherlands, the U.K., Germany and Belgium (% of total employment)

	Netherlands 1938	U.K. 1935	Germany 1933/1939	Belgium 1937
Flour	97	91	87	95
Cocoa and choc.	51	31	36	
Preserved food	61	37	47	48
Margarine	69	68	83	
Cotton	68	37	50	46
Wool	68	43	50	52
Machine knitting	24	20	31	
Ready-made clothing	19	18	36	26
Leather	95	88	83	73
Footwear	67	56	77	58
Paper	90	76	81	78
Rubber	73		64	62
Soap	64	54		83
Pottery	77	45	68	
Brick	99	95	92	
Foundries		92	93	82
Wire	92	67		79
Mechanical engin.	97	92	91	93
Metal products	92	76	71	85
Electrical engin.	88		75	
Shipbuilding	99	98	98	
Cars and coachwork	99	82	92	
Bicycles	99		89	
Total industry	82*	63	72	76

* The overall figure relates to the year 1930

Sources: See the text.

activity in that year, which might affect the gender structure of labour, a figure for 1939 from the *Statistisches Handbuch 1928–1944* is also given. The male labour shares from these two sources are 73 percent and 71 percent, respectively. The figures for each German industry are averages of the two counts.[30] In the case of Belgium, the *Economische en Sociale Telling* of 1937 gives an overall percentage of male labour of 76 percent. The complements of these proportions represent the labour share of women in industry. Big differences can be seen between the countries. Rostas saw the high participation rate in the United Kingdom as a structural characteristic of the British economy and explained

[30] From the 1936 census of production we can calculate a male participation rate of 73%. Somewhat higher percentages are given in the *Vierteljahrshefte zur Statistik des deutschen Reichs* 1937, Drittes Heft, page 94: about 75%.

it in relation to the low real wages for men, in comparison to the United States, where there was less economic need for women to have paid work.[31] It has also been said that the relatively high wages of adult male workers in the Netherlands led to lower female participation rates.

At the level of industries, the low participation rates of men in the machine knitting and ready-made clothing industries are notable. The rates in the cotton and wool industries are higher, especially in the Netherlands. In these branches the figures for the United Kingdom reveal clearly higher percentages of female labour than in the Netherlands, with Germany and Belgium lying between these two. The food and beverages sector, with the exception of the flourmills, had a reasonably high employment share for women, particularly in the United Kingdom. Finally, in the metallurgical industries employment shares of women were exceptionally low, especially in the Netherlands.

Women were paid much lower wages than adult male workers were. This was caused either by the sort of labour that women did, or by lower wages paid for the same labour. In the United Kingdom the average women's wage was about 50 percent of the male wage.[32] In the Netherlands the average women's wage between the wars was about 60 percent of the wage of adult male workers.[33] There were similar differences in wage levels in Belgium.[34]

What influence did these differences in female participation between countries have on their average wage levels? From Table 4.6 we can see that the male shares of overall manufacturing employment in the Netherlands, the United Kingdom, Germany and Belgium were 82, 63, 72 and 76 percent, respectively. Supposing that the wage of women in all four countries during the 1930s was 60 percent of the average male wage, if the Dutch average wage is taken as 100 percent then the British average wage was 92 percent, the German was 96 percent and the Belgian wage was 97.5 percent. In other words; the downwards effect on the average wage as a result of sex differences in the structure of employment, in comparison to the Netherlands, was 8, 4, and 2.5 percent, respectively. For the United Kingdom, this accounts for half of the difference between British and Dutch average wages that was given above.[35] In the German-Dutch comparison it explains about a quarter of the difference, in the comparison with Belgium only a few percent.

A similar analysis is possible at the industry level. Naturally the correction to average wage levels is different for each industry, depending on the employment share of

---

31 In 1937, men accounted for 74% of all industrial employment in the United States. Rostas, *Comparative*, 23.

32 Rostas, *Comparative*, 32. See also Maddison, *Dynamic*.

33 Bölger, Beteekenis, 60, gives the following percentages for the various categories (in comparison to adult educated workers): experienced 88%, uneducated 75%, women 60%, boys 50% and girls 40%). See also CBS (1960), *Statistiek der lonen*, 5.

34 In Belgium in 1936 the average wages for women, boys and girls were 60%, 50% and 40%, respectively, of the average male wage. See Pott, Lonen, 13.

35 If we adopt Rostas' assumption that the average female wage was 50% of the average male wage, the difference in female employment shares would actually explain the entire difference between average wages in the United Kingdom and the Netherlands. See Rostas, *Comparative*, 32.

women.[36] However when the coefficients of correlation are recalculated, the results show no important changes.

This raises the question of the influence of the employment structure on comparative wage levels. The correction for the lower wages paid to women shows that part of the absolute differences in the wage levels between the countries is explained by differences in the gender structure of labour. Thus far we have considered how the structure of employment may directly influence labour productivity. It is clear that firms had a preference for male or female employees for specific parts of the production process.[37] However it is not clear to what extent this may have influenced the comparative productivity levels in particular industries. During the inter-war years, expensive, skilled labour in highly mechanised industries such as the cotton industry was replaced with new, faster machines creating a new mix of skilled and unskilled labour. Thus in particular production processes there was a need for cheap labour. However, besides substitution there was also complementarity between labour and capital. The continual mechanisation of the production process steadily decreased the importance of low-skilled labour.[38] The census data is not sufficiently detailed for us to trace the net effect of this qualitative change in the labour input, or to trace changes in the age structure of the workforce in each industry.

The proportion of salaried staff in the workforce offers another indicator of the quality of human capital. The proportion of industrial workers and operatives who work on the shop floor has fallen considerably in the course of the twentieth century, while the number of employees has grown. Once again we can consider what connection there may be between the proportion of staff positions in the workforce and the average labour productivity in each industry.

Table 4.7 shows the proportion of the total workforce of each industry, in each country, who hold staff positions. The Dutch Statistics of Production distinguish between

---

36 In the comparison between the United Kingdom and the Netherlands, the recalculation to allow for differing rates of female employment results in every case in a higher relative figure, by a few percentage points. The effect is especially large (larger than the average 8 percentage points) in the cotton mills, wool spinning and the wire industry. However it is striking that the new outcomes increase the negative coefficient of correlation between comparative wages and comparative productivity (see the first part of this section) rather than weaken it. That is, after making allowance for this factor, the comparative wages in the industrial sectors with a lower comparative productivity still increase the most.
In the comparison between Germany and the Netherlands, the correction for female participation does not produce a higher German comparative wage in every case, because in particular industries such as the machine knitting and ready-made clothing industries, the Netherlands had a higher proportion of female employment than Germany. The biggest effects (bigger than the average of 4 percentage points) are in the cotton industry and metal products. A similar picture emerges in the comparison with Belgium: after making the correction, the Belgian comparative wages are higher in almost all industries (with the strongest effect in the cotton, wool and leather industries), but the relationship between wages and comparative productivity is scarcely affected.

37 See for example Schrover, *Het vette*, 93–101, 191–203. The lower valued work (packing, etc.) was done mainly by girls, whose wages were in the lowest category.

38 Von Tunzelmann, *Technology*, 402; Goldin & Katz, Origins, 2–5.

'workers' and 'administrative, technical and service personnel'. In 1938 the latter category accounted for almost 12 percent of the employment in the companies included in the census. The British Census distinguishes between operatives, on the one hand, and administrative, technical and clerical staff on the other hand, with the latter having a total share of 13 percent in 1935. The German statistics of Production of 1936 distinguish between *Kaufmännische Angestellte*, *Technische Angestellte* and *Arbeiter*.[39] The first two categories together account for 12.6 percent of the total employment. According to the Belgian *Economische en Sociale Telling* of 1937, 'auxiliary personnel' accounted for almost 11 percent of industrial employment. Thus the total percentages do not differ widely, although it must again be said that the Dutch statistics have a more limited coverage of the total manufacturing industry than the other statistics.

Table 4.7. Industrial non-production workers in the Netherlands, the U.K., Germany and Belgium (% of total employment)

	Netherlands (1938)	U.K. (1935)	Germany (1936)	Belgium (1937)
Flour	23.1	24.2	23.5	18.2
Cocoa and choc.	14.5	16.5	17.8	
Preserved food	21.2	19.9	9.3	16.4
Margarine	33.8	23.6	32.5	
Cotton	6.3	3.5	9.0	7.3
Wool	6.5	6.0	9.1	8.1
Machine knitting	7.9	9.0		
Ready-made clothing	11.7	10.7	14.1	9.5
Leather	8.9	10.1	9.2	9.0
Footwear	9.0	6.8	9.2	7.5
Paper	7.5	8.8	9.7	10.4
Soap	35.8	29.8	28.8	21.9
Pottery	10.2	6.7	8.8	8.9
Brick	3.1	6.1	4.0	
Foundries	8.6	9.5	7.9	9.4
Tin	8.2	3.7	10.0	
Sheet-metal works	12.9	12.2	13.8	
Wire	10.4	10.5	10.5	8.3
Mechanical engin.	17.1	18.2	17.4	15.7
Electrical engin.	20.1	22.2		
Shipbuilding	8.1	8.5	11.2	
Cars and coachwork	8.8	14.1		
Bicycles	21.0	12.8		
Total industry	11.7	13.0	12.6	10.8

Sources: See the text.

39 *Die deutsche Industrie*, 70ff.

The 'staff' category is particularly large in the flour, margarine, soap and electrical engineering industries. In all countries it is generally smallest in the textile and leather industries.

Expressing these percentages as comparative values, in comparison to the Netherlands, gives us ratios that can be associated with comparative productivity. The comparisons between the Netherlands and Germany and Belgium, respectively, yield a positive coefficient of correlation that is similar in size to the correlation between average wages and comparative productivity (r = 0.47 and r = 0.61). Thus there is some relationship between high comparative labour productivity and higher proportions of non-production workers. However the comparison between the Netherlands and the United Kingdom again yields a negative correlation, as we have already seen in the comparison between wages and productivity.[40]

4.3. Market size and scale economies

Relative market size is the third factor that could explain differences in labour productivity. Of the various explanatory indicators presented here, this is the only demand factor. A large market may influence the level of productivity of industries because it enables them to benefit from economies of scale and allows companies or plants within a particular industry to specialise. If large capital investments are required in particular industries, a large market may be necessary to achieve cost-efficient production. Various studies have demonstrated a positive relationship between comparative labour productivity and output volume.[41]

In his study of industrial productivity in the United States and the United Kingdom, Frankel estimated the comparative market size from the total gross value of production of the industries he compared.[42] The same criterion will be used here. In principle this should be adjusted to allow for the net effect of imports and exports, since the market size consists not only of domestic production but also of imports. This is a more important consideration in more open economies. However no correction for net imports has been made. Many trade barriers existed in the 1930s, when the Netherlands, Belgium and the United Kingdom developed an extensive system of quotas and import duties, while Germany even pursued an economic policy aiming at self-

40 On the other hand, the association between 'staff' functions and wages in the Dutch-British comparison does have a relatively high positive correlation coefficient of r = 0.64. From this we can conclude that in the United Kingdom, in contrast to the other countries, the highest relative wages as compared to the Netherlands are in industries where the share of staff functions is also relatively high. The situation is reversed in the comparisons between the Netherlands and Germany and Belgium: wages in industries with relatively large numbers of salaried staff are relatively low.

41 Rostas, Comparative, 36, 71; Kravis, Survey, 38; Frankel, *British*, 65–66; Paige & Bombach, *Comparison*, 70.

42 Frankel, *British*, 67.

sufficiency. Furthermore there is the possibility of quality differences between imports and domestic production.[43]

Table 4.8. Market size in the U.K., Germany and Belgium (Netherlands = 100)

	U.K. (1935)	Germany (1936)	Belgium (1937)
Flour	1,282	1,138	133
Cocoa and choc.	763	790	93
Sugar	1,493	837	154
Preserved food			63
Edible oils	437	1,115	60
Margarine	297	655	81
Beer	2,632	2,511	1,111
Tobacco	1,538	412	88
Cotton spinning	1,370		
Cotton weaving	532	755	120
Wool spinning	3,333		
Wool weaving	775	940	196
Machine knitting	1,370	1,533	
Ready-made clothing	1,298	983	
Leather	1,010	1,176	159
Footwear	1,053	1,079	123
Paper	735	1,184	79
Rubber	2,083	916	270
Soap	833	508	83
Rayon	521	478	119
Super phosphate			55
Brick	467	864	139
Calcium silicate		520	
Roofing tiles			119
Cement	1,667	2,917	
Smelters	2,632	5,277	1,250
Foundries	1,667	3,552	
Zinc	448	446	909
Tin		2,291	
Sheet metal works		5,173	
Wire	2,041	2,519	
Mechanical engin.	2,857	4,538	
Metal products		5,787	
Electrical engin.		1,789	
Shipbuilding	787	400	30
Cars and coachw.	16,667	17,521	
Bicycles	990	832	

Sources: See the text.

[43] Frankel claims that the scale and method of production are determined mainly by the market that is actually served and not the 'potential' market; Frankel, *British*, 64.

Table 4.8 shows the comparative market size of industries in the United Kingdom, Germany and Belgium in comparison to the Netherlands (= 100). The underlying data here is the same as was used in Chapter 2 to calculate productivity levels. All the industrial branches in the United Kingdom are larger than their Dutch counterparts. This is not surprising in view of the fact that the British population in 1935 was 5.6 times larger than the Dutch population.[44] Even if we adjust for this by dividing the market size by the size of the population, the market in the United Kingdom is in many cases larger than the Dutch market. Cotton weaving and the margarine, zinc, seedcrushing, brick and rayon industries are then smaller than the Dutch markets. However the variation of comparative labour productivity levels in these six industries is rather large (from 80 for rayon to 161 for the margarine industry) and does not point to any statistical relationship with market size. We also found no relationship between comparative productivity and comparative market size between other British industries and their Dutch counterparts.

A comparison of the German and Dutch markets shows that the market available to German companies in the 1930s was also much bigger than the Dutch market, especially in the metallurgical industries. If we adjust the market size to allow for population differences (the German population in 1936 was 7.9 times larger than the Dutch population), the comparative market size for German companies was smaller in the cocoa, tobacco, margarine, cotton, soap, rayon, calcium silicate, zinc and shipbuilding industries. The significantly larger German industries such as smelters, machine building, metal products and the automobile industry also have a higher labour productivity. Thus, in contrast to the British-Dutch comparison, there is a reasonably strong relationship between higher comparative productivity and greater comparative market size. The calculated coefficient of correlation is $r = 0.64$ (excluding the automobile industry: $r = 0.58$).

The comparison between the Netherlands and Belgium also reveals a statistically significant relationship between the comparative market size and productivity, chiefly because of three industries that were very large in comparison to the Netherlands: the zinc industry, smelters and beer breweries. These are also industries with high levels of productivity (147, 175 and 159 percent of the Dutch productivity, respectively). If we include all industries the coefficient of correlation is $r = 0.91$. Without these three industries, the correlation is lower. With the exception of the textile, leather, rubber, and metallurgical sectors, in which Belgium's production was clearly larger, neither country has a systematically higher or lower market size in any industrial sector. This is due in part to the fact that the populations of the two countries in 1937 were nearly the same.[45]

An analysis of the comparative levels of labour productivity between industries in the United States and the United Kingdom during the inter-war period has also demonstrated a significant positive correlation between market size and productivity.[46] Nevertheless

---

44 Maddison, *Dynamic*, Table B.2: both populations are calculated without considering colonies.

45 Maddison, *Dynamic*, Table B.2, 233–234: in 1937 the Dutch population was 3% larger than the Belgian population.

46 See Broadberry & Crafts, Explaining, 384 and 392. The same authors to some extent refute this in a later article (Britain's, 544). The difference is due to the indicators for market size that they used in the two studies: volume of production in the first study and employment in the second. In both cases the correlation is positive, but in the second case no statistically significant relation-

the comparison between Germany and the United Kingdom in the inter-war years, which has been mentioned several times, revealed no strong relationship between the two variables. The authors attribute this to the lack of standardisation of production processes in both the United Kingdom and Germany, which meant that the effective market size for individual companies was slight.[47]

However the direction of causality between market size and productivity is not entirely self-evident. An initially large comparative market could have a positive effect on labour productivity because of scale effects. But the reverse is also possible: high productivity may mean relatively lower prices for the products and higher sales as a result. A third possibility is that underlying forces may simultaneously influence the market size and productivity. For instance the standardisation of products and production processes (including standardisation between companies within an industry, resulting in Marshallian 'external economies', and higher quality due to mass production (cars and textiles), could influence both market size and productivity. The extent of competition and the prevalence of cartels could also play a role. For example, if inefficient producers can remain in the market through price-fixing or by similar agreements in relation to the volume of production or market share, this will influence the average level of productivity and in the long term also the market size. Well-known examples are the British cotton and steel industries in the 1910s. Manufacturers opted for extensive product differentiation, but were at the same time making agreements among themselves about prices and market shares. The British government had not established the strong anti-cartel legislation that was introduced, for example, in the United States. The result was that inefficient companies were also able to survive. The aversion to technological innovation displayed by both management and the unions is a recurring theme already in the early literature on British manufacturing.[48] Moreover the taste of the British public was focused on differentiated products rather than the traditional staples. The depression of the 1930s only strengthened these tendencies.[49]

Do the comparisons presented here reflect a similar picture? The four countries in this analysis all took a different line to that of the United States, especially after 1930, with restrictive measures and legislation that allowed or even supported trade restrictions. From the 1920s, Dutch industries had participated in domestic and international cartels (the soap syndicate, Phoebus light bulb cartel, etc.) and the quota policy, and legislation in response to the agricultural crisis of the 1930s resulted in even more extensive cartels.[50] The result was that domestic markets were protected, but also that export possibilities were limited. This may have had an overall negative effect on labour productivity, because inefficient producers were also able to remain in the market. At the same time, in such a restrictive world the volume of sales was largely determined by the size of a country's population.

---

ship could be demonstrated. In addition, Frankel has found a reasonably strong correlation between the two variables for these countries for 1948/1949, with $r = 0.70$ (Frankel, British, 66).

47 Broadberry & Fremdling, Comparative, 414.

48 See Frankel, *British*, 78, 94 and 116 and Rostas, *Comparative*, 63.

49 Broadberry & Crafts, Britain's, 546.

50 See van Schaik, *Crisis*; De Hen, *Actieve*.

4.4. Average plant size

The last of the factors to be associated with labour productivity here is average plant size. In the literature, this variable is generally regarded as a derivative of market size and of the state of the production technology. Plant size in this context is not the size of the companies or organisations concerned, but the size of a production unit or factory plant. In the neo-classical model of industrial organisation, market size and technology determine the optimal plant size.

A graph of the average total costs of a production unit is U-shaped: the lowest point indicates the production volume at which average costs are lowest. We assume that a company that operates in a competitive environment moves to the efficient point at the bottom of this curve. If we divide the employment in a particular industrial branch by the total number of production units, the resulting average company size can be regarded as an indicator of the optimal size of a typical company in that industry.[51] It is obviously a very rough indicator, because it does not explain the actual discernible differences in plant sizes.[52]

In general plants became larger during the age of mass production in the nineteenth and twentieth centuries. This resulted not only in internal efficiencies and subsequently productivity gains, but also in external efficiencies. The concentration of many large companies in a region may lead to benefits from general agglomeration effects such as better transport facilities and specialised suppliers of components and industrial services.

The effects of the size of plants and companies have always had an important position in the economic history literature, precisely as an explanation of differences in productivity and economic growth between countries. According to Chandler, the emergence of large companies in the United States and Germany at the end of the nineteenth century was the engine behind the rapid economic growth of these two countries.[53] The period between 1875 and 1914 was characterised by many technological and organisational innovations.[54]

Among the effects of this 'second industrial revolution' was a shift from steam power to internal combustion motors and electrically powered machines, to mass production and to new products (chemicals, steel, consumer goods), and to increasing scale and the more effective management of production processes by company managers (Taylorism and 'scientific management'). This process was accompanied by an increase in factory size. The other side of the coin is that the comparative industrial stagnation of France and especially of the United Kingdom (compared to the United States, but also in comparison to Germany) can be attributed to the persistence of small scale companies there

---

51 Broadberry and Fremdling have described this variable as a '*challenge and response*' indicator that indicates how industries have responded to the new challenges of changes in demand and in production technology. See Broadberry & Fremdling, Comparative, 414–418.

52 Van Ark used the median company size as an as indicator, to minimise the effects of very large and very small companies. Van Ark, *International*, 137.

53 Chandler, *Scale*.

54 Svennilson, *Growth*, 20.

and an apparent resistance to adapting to the new developments. According to this interpretation, the British and French response to the new challenges of the second industrial revolution should have been to increase average plant size, as an expression of economies of scale and product and process innovation. But relatively small-scale production remained the central characteristics in both countries until well into the twentieth century.[55] Van Zanden has applied this vision in his analysis of the rise and significance of large companies in the Netherlands (Shell, Philips, Unilever, AKZO, and DSM). His conclusion is that the development of these companies is a good fit with this theoretical framework.[56]

Chandler's general approach has been attacked by, among others, Broadberry and Crafts. They pointed out that in the 1930s there is no observable statistical connection between differences in the size of production units in manufacturing and comparative productivity between the United States and the United Kingdom.[57] Moreover research by Kinghorn and Nye has shown that the average company size in France was in reality much bigger than has always been assumed, because of systematically incorrect interpretations of the source material (the relevant company surveys). For example, the average company size in France has always been under-estimated because the French company surveys include all companies, including one-person firms or *isolés*, in contrast to the statistics for the United States and Germany. They claim that in reality the average company size in France around the First World War was actually larger than in Germany.[58]

To what extent does the comparative analysis between the countries considered here support a Chandlerian interpretation? The comparative factory size, using employment figures as criteria, can be determined from company surveys and/or the Census of Production. It is important that the data sources that are compared are drawn up in approximately equivalent ways, so as to avoid problems such as those mentioned above. The average factory size in British industry has been determined from the *Census of Production* of 1935 as the number of workers in an industry divided by the number of plants. The figures for the Netherlands are based on the Statistics of Production and the Accident Statistics for 1935.

Table 4.9 shows the calculated comparative factory sizes per industry. It is striking that the average British factory size is larger in almost all cases, with the exceptions being flour and cotton factories. In the metallurgical industries, the average company in 1935 was up to twice as big as in the Netherlands and in the food and beverages sector it was – with a few exceptions – two to three times as big.

There may be a slight bias here, because the smallest companies are not included in the census. In the British census the threshold size is a labour volume of ten workers. However the smallest companies are also excluded from the Dutch Statistics of Production. Moreover small firms account for only a very small part of most of these indus-

55 Caron, *Economic*, 167; Elbaum & Lazonick, *Decline*, 5.

56 Van Zanden, *Klein land*, 48–76. See also Sluyterman & Winkelman, Dutch Family Firm.

57 Broadberry & Crafts, Explaining, 375–402 and idem., Britain's, 533–535.

58 Kinghorn & Nye, Scale, 99. See also Herrigel, *Industrial constructions*.

Table 4.9. Plant size in the U.K., Germany and Belgium (Netherlands = 100)

	U.K. (1935)	Germany (1936)	Belgium (1937)
Flour	63	11	64
Cocoa and choc.	136	96	88
Sugar	256	47	69
Preserved food			68
Edible oils	393	93	
Margarine	215	75	125
Beer	288	87	76
Tobacco	273	70	61
Cotton spinning	81		
Cotton weaving	91	91	31
Wool spinning	142		
Wool weaving	169	231	36
Machine knitting	246	111	
Ready-made clothing	240	110	
Leather	220	111	102
Footwear	165	81	24
Paper	104	52	47
Rubber	233	134	66
Soap	215	38	68
Rayon	126	91	
Brick	141	61	97
Calcium silicate		60	
Roofing tiles			45
Cement	117	116	
Smelters		123	
Foundries	122	119	
Zinc		108	
Tin		592	
Sheet metal works		329	
Wire	192	98	
Mechanical engin.	101	139	
Metal products		79	
Electrical engin.		129	
Shipbuilding	126	57	58
Cars and coachw.	159	756	
Bicycles	318	302	

Sources: See the text.

tries, in both countries. Therefore there is no reason to question the degree of representation and comparability of the comparative figures.

The largest British comparative factory size was in the food and beverages sector, which had relatively high productivity levels. A reasonably strong statistical relationship can be observed in the whole sample. The simple coefficient of correlation is $r = 0.60$.

The German-Dutch comparison reveals a weaker connection between comparative productivity and comparative factory size. The figures for the German average company come from *Die deutsche Industrie*. Because only companies with five or more people are included the calculated value overestimates the actual average company size. However, as we have seen with the British figures, this will have little effect on the degree of representation of the comparative figures since the figures for the Netherlands also exclude small companies. The comparative size of the companies is smallest in the food and beverages sector and in the paper and building materials industries, and is largest in the metallurgical sector. If we exclude the extreme values of the automobile and tin industries, the coefficient of correlation is $r = 0.55$. Thus there is again a positive correlation between factory size and average labour productivity per industry.

The Belgian figures are based on the *Economische en Sociale Telling* of 1937, which includes the whole workforce and all companies, including employment in the smallest companies. This means that the Belgian comparative values may have a downward bias in comparison with the Dutch Statistics of Production. Therefore in this case the Dutch average figure has been calculated from the Accident Statistics of 1937, which include all working people (expressed as the equivalent number of standard workers) and all companies. However it is striking that even then the number of registered companies in Belgium is in many cases considerably larger. The Dutch Accident Statistics for 1937 record 64,304 manufacturing companies, while the Belgian census found 181,194 companies and a total industrial employment that was somewhat more than 40 percent higher than the Dutch level.[59] The differences are especially large in the textile, clothing and wood industries, where the number of Belgian industrial plants was 8, 6 and 7 times, respectively, as large as in the Netherlands. In view of these figures it is not surprising that the average plant size in Belgium in the industries compared was smaller, with the exception of the leather industry. The comparative factory size was largest in the food and beverage and chemical industries, at about 70 percent of the Dutch size. Despite the small scale of Belgian companies, no strong connection can be established between comparative factory size and comparative productivity.

In their comparison of productivity between the United Kingdom and Germany, Broadberry and Fremdling calculated a coefficient of correlation between productivity and company size of $r = 0.51$.[60] This comparison shows clearly that in Germany the average factory size and productivity in heavy industry (mining and the metallurgical industry) were generally higher. In the light industry, such as food production and textiles, the position is reversed. This shows that in the United Kingdom, industries with relatively larger production units had a higher relative labour productivity.[61] We can conclude that the average Dutch plant size was much smaller than in the United King-

---

59 In Belgium, industrial employment in 1937 was more than 1 million workers, as compared to more than 700,000 in the Netherlands. De Jong & Soete, Comparative, Appendix 2, 32.

60 Broadberry & Fremdling, Comparative, 415.

61 Moreover it is striking that diverse comparisons between the United States and the United Kingdom have shown that production units in the latter were not significantly smaller than in the United States. This contrasts sharply with accounts in the literature of the weaknesses of British industry (see, for example, Elbaum & Lazonick, *Decline*).

dom: it is only in the flour and cotton industries that British production units were smaller.

The comparison between Germany and the Netherlands confirms that factories in Germany were not on the whole larger than in the Netherlands. Therefore differences in factory size can tell us little about the supposed irrationality, mismanagement or lack of adaptation to new circumstances. The cartels that were permitted in Germany could create an environment in which external economies were realised, while retaining relatively small-scale production.[62] We might add that the electrification of production processes, especially the introduction of the electric motor, also had a positive effect for relatively small-scale production processes because this source of energy offers greater flexibility.

A separate study could be devoted to the trends in average plant size in the Netherlands. My impression is that on average plants became smaller in many industries, in part due to the effects of measures taken during the 1930s in response to the Depression. A statistical analysis of data from the Accident Statistics might throw more light on this. However the question remains to what extent a smaller scale of production, if it exists, can influence the average labour productivity. The smaller scale of companies in Belgium offers a good example. Although the average company size in most industrial sectors was 60 percent to 75 percent of the corresponding Dutch average, the average productivity of Belgian industry was about 95 percent of the Dutch level. However it must be said that the comparative Belgian productivity in earlier and later years was lower.

In the light of these outcomes, it appears that the optimal plant size is not determined by the market size. It should be recalled that plant size could be seen as a variable that indicates the extent to which an industry is responding to the state of technology and the organisational possibilities and limitations of the production process. Nevertheless a strong relationship between comparative productivity and factory size has been found only in the comparison between the United Kingdom and the Netherlands (and to a lesser extent between Germany and the Netherlands). How can we explain the relationship that was found in the British-Dutch comparison? We find for most British industries in which the average plant size was up to twice the Dutch average, a lower comparative productivity. Industries in which the companies were more than twice as big as in the Netherlands had a higher productivity than their Dutch counterparts. It would appear that there is a 'critical' average plant size in the comparison, above which scale effects are more likely to play a role. It is striking that there is only one assembly industry – bicycle manufacturing – among the industries in which average plant size in Britain was more than twice that in the Netherlands. Many of the others are continuous-process industries: sugar, margarine, beer, rubber, seedcrushing, leather and tobacco. From this list it is again evident that the comparative advantage of British industry, in comparison to Dutch industry in the 1930s, was mainly in the food and beverages industry.

---

62 Kinghorn & Nye, Scale, 110.

4.5. Productivity and competitiveness

The calculated coefficients of correlation that have been given above could be misleading, because of the indirect effects of the variables on one another. For example, the average plant size may effect capital intensity. To precisely determine the statistical affect of one of the independent variables on the dependent variable (comparative labour productivity), the other variables must be held constant. This is done through a multiple regression analysis.

In the first equation (1), a multiple regression equation was calculated with the variables of installed horsepower, wages and market size. Then in a second equation (2) the plant size is added, as an indicator of how industries have responded to market developments and developments in technology. In the third equation (3), all the variables that

Table 4.10. Results of multiple regressions between comparative productivity levels and explanatory variables: U.K., Germany, Belgium and the Netherlands.

United Kingdom/Netherlands (1935)

Variable	Equation 1 Slope (SE)	Equation 2 Slope (SE)	Equation 3 Slope (SE)
Installed power	0.40 (0.28)	0.27 (0.23)	
Wages	– 0.29 (0.62)	– 0.25 (0.51)	
Market size	0.01 (0.01)	0.01 (0.01)	
Plant size		0.20 (0.07)	0.21 (0.06)*
R^2	0.15	0.46	0.35
St.error Y	29.8	24.6	23.4
N	19	19	26
Intercept	93.0	65.0	65.0

* t-value = 3.5; p-value smaller than 0.1 %

Germany/Netherlands (1936)

Variable	Equation 1 Slope (SE)	Equation 2 Slope (SE)	Equation 3 Slope (SE)
Installed power	0.05 (0.15)	0.08 (0.16)	
Wages	0.76 (0.33)	0.78 (0.33)	0.80 (0.31)*
Market size	0.06 (0.01)	0.07 (0.01)	0.06 (0.01)**
Plant size		– 0.04 (0.04)	
R^2	0.53	0.55	0.53
St.error Y	26.2	26.2	25.8
N	32	32	32
Intercept	16.5	16.2	16.1

* t-value = 2.6; p-value smaller than 1 %
** t-value = 6; p-value smaller than 0.05 %

Belgium/Netherlands (1937)

Variable	Equation 1 Slope (SE)	Equation 2 Slope (SE)	Equation 3 Slope (SE)
Installed power	0.07 (0.07)	0.09 (0.07)	
Wages	0.56 (0.40)	0.46 (0.43)	0.70 (0.38)*
Market size	0.08 (0.01)	0.08 (0.01)	0.08 (0.01)**
Plant size		0.11 (0.15)	
R^2	0.78	0.79	0.76
St.error Y	11.1	11.4	11.1
N	15	15	15
Intercept	40.8	39.2	37.9

* t-value = 1.8; p-value smaller than 5%
** t-value = 8; p-value smaller than 0.05%

Notes: SE = Standard error of the slope-coefficient of regression, N = number of observations.
Sources: See the text.

have only a limited explanatory value in the multiple regression are omitted. What remains is a regression formula for each pair of countries that can be regarded as the optimal statistical relationship on the basis of the available data.

In the comparisons with Germany and Belgium, the regression variable for comparative wages has a significant positive value in both cases. The variable for comparative market size is also significant in Belgium and Germany. Although the coefficient is very small, it has been included in the definitive regression equations for these countries. The comparative factory size is only statistically important in the comparison with the United Kingdom, and is the only variable that remains in the British-Dutch comparison.

If we now specify the regression equations that have been derived, using the actual comparative values for factory size (U.K.-Netherlands 1935, from Table 4.9) and for comparative wages and market size (Germany-Netherlands 1936 and Belgium-Netherlands 1937, Tables 4.5 and 4.8), we can calculate an estimated comparative productivity according to the least squares method. If this produces a result that is significantly above the actual comparative labour productivity that we have found, this implies that the relevant Dutch industry had a lower than expected comparative productivity (on the basis of the defined regression variables). If the result is lower than the comparative productivity found above, the reverse is true: the Dutch productivity is higher than expected. Table 4.11 shows the residuals concerned.[63]

If we consider only those residuals that are about one standard deviation or higher, we note the following points of interest. In the British-Dutch comparison, we find a higher than expected Dutch performance in the following industries: cocoa and chocolate, edible oils, wool spinning, soap, cement, wire and shipbuilding. A lower than expected performance in comparison to British industry is found in the sugar and margarine industries, cotton weaving, and in cars and coachwork. The German-Dutch

63 This method has been derived from a similar analysis in Broadberry & Crafts, Britain's, 543–545.

regression equation produces relatively well Dutch performances for the food and beverage industries except for the sugar and tobacco industries, as well as for the soap, paper, cement and bicycle industries. Lower comparative performances are found in ready-made clothing, smelters and machine building. In comparison to Belgium, Dutch comparative productivity is higher than expected (according to the equation) in the paper, brick and shipbuilding industries, and lower in the flour, leather and soap industries.

Table 4.11. Residuals of the productivity regressions between the Netherlands and the U.K., Germany and Belgium

Standard Error Y	U.K. (1935) SE = 23.4	Germany (1936) SE = 25.8	Belgium (1937) SE = 11.1
Flour	5	-21	9
Cocoa and choc.	-23	-21	-4
Sugar	58	0	-10
Preserved food			4
Edible oils	-20	-24	
Margarine	52	-13	
Beer	3	-23	-4
Tobacco	3	-9	-8
Cotton spinning	5		
Cotton weaving	30	9	7
Wool spinning	-48		
Wool weaving		10	2
Machine knitting	-8	15	
Ready-made clothing	3	44	
Leather	-2	-7	16
Footwear	-19	-4	6
Paper	2	-17	-13
Rubber	8	5	-8
Soap	-20	-19	18
Rayon	-11	7	
Brick	2	8	-10
Calcium silicate		-15	
Cement	-30	-44	
Smelters		99	
Foundries	4	-8	
Zinc		2	
Tin		-1	
Sheet metal works		-12	
Wire	-21	-2	
Mechanical engin.	5	25	
Metal products		1	
Electrical engin.		-1	
Shipbuilding	-35	4	-12
Cars and coachwork	36	-20	
Bicycles	-16	-25	

Sources: See the text.

Higher than expected productivity levels may indicate relatively strong competitive positions, and lower than expected outcomes may indicate weak competitive positions. However this analysis is based on a comparative approach: if a particular industry has a strong competitive position in one country this may say as much about a weak position of the corresponding industry in the other country. The Dutch shipbuilding industry, which appears to have a strong competitive position in the British-Dutch comparison, would appear to be flattered by the comparison because the British shipbuilding industry in the 1930s had strong cartels. The protection of this industry during the Depression was coupled with relatively high employment levels. The same could be said for the British cement and wire industries.[64] There are also examples of cartels and production constraints in the Dutch sugar and margarine industries, which is confirmed by the figures in Table 4.11.[65]

---

64 Broadberry & Crafts, Britain's, 547.

65 De Jong & Oude Vrielink, Voedingsmiddelenindustrie, 302 and 310.

Chapter 5: Productivity growth and structural change

Following the comparative statistical analysis of industry in the Netherlands and surrounding countries in the three previous chapters, this chapter and the next two chapters (Chapters 5, 6, and 7) will concentrate on analysing changes in output and productivity across industrial branches in Dutch manufacturing. In the discussion concerning the first (and second) industrial revolution, and in the analysis of industrial development during the inter-war period, a distinction is generally made between 'old' and 'new' sectors or industries. The rubber, rayon and electro-technical industries are generally seen as new industries that emerged in the inter-war period as being distinct from the 'old', existing industries such as textiles and shipbuilding. The terms 'old' and 'new' are strongly linked with the economic historical analysis of structural change. The distinction is used not only in Rostow's *leading sector* analysis but also in Schumpeter's analysis of economic development and the role of innovations and the abandonment of old production methods (in Schumpeter's terminology *creative destruction*).[1] Rostow's work in particular assumes that economic renewal is mainly embodied in new, emerging sectors and industries with a higher than average level of labour productivity. The relative expansion of these industries in the total economy and the diffusion of innovations through favourable demand and supply effects on other industries accelerates the growth of output and productivity. However the time series of Dutch industrial production and labour productivity I have used thus far do not reveal any cross-industry variations in growth, because output and productivity have been shown only in terms of aggregates.[2] This chapter will examine whether increases in output and productivity in the Netherlands took place over the full range of industry, or were limited to a small number of industries.

---

1 Rostow, *Stages*; Schumpeter, *Theory*; Schumpeter, *Capitalism*, 83.

2 O'Brien refers in this connection to *misplaced aggregation*: "When we plot the growth of all the individual industries for which data is available, marked deviations around the average rate or growth for industry as a whole appear on the graph. This challenges the notion of an industrial sector with components growing at comparable rates along a similar cyclical path." O'Brien, Introduction, 14, see also Fabricant, *Output*, 9 and Harberger, Vision, 4–10. Harberger in his analysis of the growth process makes a distinction between yeast- and mushroom-like expansions. In fact, these analogies can be related respectively to macro- and industry-level types of explanation.

5.1. Defining old and new in manufacturing

In his analysis of the European economy during the inter-war period, Svennilson has explicitly employed a conceptual framework in which economic success of a country depends ultimately on the outcome of the competitive struggle between old and new industries. Industry and society in the inter-war period benefited from many technological advances: electrification, the use of internal combustion motors in road transport and shipping, new chemical products such as rubber and rayon, and new, mass-produced products such as automobiles and electrical appliances. Nevertheless the total effect of these innovations was modest, according to Svennilson, because the transformation from 'old' to 'new' in Western Europe proceeded only with difficulty and stagnating industries with old-fashioned capital structures had a tight hold over the economy.[3] These generalisations require some clarification. The relationship between growth and the structure of the economy in the Netherlands has received little systematic study to date. This is in sharp contrast with British industry, for example. By way of introduction we can mention here a few points that have emerged in the British discussion.

In contrast to the Netherlands, the economic performance of the United Kingdom in the first years after the 'Great War' was – frankly – bad. A true industrial recovery followed during the 1930s, but unemployment remained high. Aldcroft, following Richardson, ascribed this recovery to shifts in resource allocation from stagnating towards expanding sectors. This is said to have led to higher productivity for the 'new' invested capital in sectors like electricity generation, electro-technical products, automobiles, aircraft and chemical and related products such as artificial silk. The rubber, oil refining, metallurgy and machine building industries, which were closely linked to the leading industries, also grew rapidly.[4] The *export staple industries* performed badly: steel and shipbuilding, cotton and wool, and mining had dominated British industry from the nineteenth century but were declining, some already before the First World War. However Broadberry and Crafts have strongly relativised the effect of the structural change suggested here, by pointing out that the structural change in industry in the preceding and following periods (i.e. 1913–1924 and 1937–1951) was actually greater than in the period around 1930. Moreover they have shown that the effect of structural change on the growth in industrial productivity must have been negligible.[5] The growth in productivity was mainly an *intra*-sectoral phenomenon, taking place within industries. It was not the result of a shift in employment to more productive industries. Moreover the level of investment in the new industries was modest, compared to investments in other sectors.

---

3 Svennilson, *Growth*, 10, 20 and 47: "... the physical stagnation of industries was often accompanied by a deterioration in their financial position. Stagnation of demand usually went hand-in-hand with falling prices and profits. As a general rule, therefore, stagnating industries were also depressed industries and their depression was often intensified by the struggle between old and new forms of capital and enterprise." See also Rostow, *Stages*, 175–176.

4 See Aldcroft, Economic, 49 and Richardson, *Economic*, 95. For a similar analysis of Swedish industry during the inter-war period see Dahmén, *Entrepreneurial.*

5 Broadberry & Crafts, Impact, 600. See also Arnold, Profitability, 45–68.

Dowie has also sharply criticised the concept of *new industries*, on both empirical and analytic grounds. During the 1930s the average growth in labour productivity in British industry was 2.4 percent, but the differences between industries were enormous. Industries that enjoyed rapid productivity growth included old *staples* such as the cotton, wool and metallurgical industries, while many 'new' industries (vehicles, chemistry, electricity and paper) had a very modest growth in productivity. Moreover he found it difficult to defend the excessive disaggregation of the data that would be required to form a picture of the new industries: "... If all new products are removed from the equivalent old staple area, then it becomes impossible for the latter to transform themselves in the way called for by, above all, the economic historian." Thus there are not only empirical but also analytic arguments against an excessively simplistic dichotomy. The shift from old to new as a source of growth may easily become a tautology.[6]

5.2. Levels and growth of productivity across Dutch industries

Analyses on the structural development of Dutch industry generally give only qualitative views of the process of growth. In his overview of the inter-war period, De Graaff demonstrates that the economy underwent a "renewal, enrichment and deepening" of its industrial structure within a single generation. He points to the increasing importance of coalmines, smelters, the salt industry and the chemicals industry. However his quantitative details focus mainly on general modernising trends, such as mechanisation, and they tell us less about structural effects.[7] In Brugmans' overview of the economic history of the Netherlands, the section concerning industry in the twentieth century is limited to a summary of new industries, under the chapter title 'the second industrial revolution', without giving a quantitative picture of its significance.[8] Only Klein has attempted to examine developments in Dutch industry in the light of structural changes, and to relate this to the British discussions that were just mentioned. He claims that the inter-war period in the Netherlands did not witness a transformation like that in the United Kingdom, and that modernisation occurred only in a few multinationals such as Unilever, Philips and AKU. Klein says that in fact the Netherlands had an ageing production structure, dominated by 'old' industries (coal, iron industry, textiles and food), producing articles that no longer matched what increasingly affluent customers wanted. Nevertheless the equipment in these industries was more modern than in the United Kingdom.[9] However Klein's conclusions regarding the economic effects of this situation

6 'New' should not be defined as identical to 'expanding'. Not only can expansion not be a criterion, industries that are called 'new' must also be shown to have actually expanded. Even then, the fact that all expanding industries were new does not explain why that was so. The data in the British statistics of production does not enable us to make a fundamental distinction between what is old and what is new. See Dowie, Growth.

7 De Graaff, Industrie, 3, 139.

8 Brugmans, *Paardenkracht*, 471–498. Joh. de Vries, Economisch leven, especially 104–131.

9 Klein, Depressie, 325–327.

for Dutch industry are not very clear.[10] More recent overviews of the Dutch economy in the twentieth century also fail to provide a systematic treatment of the phenomenon of industrial change and renewal and its effects.[11] In his survey of the Dutch economy, Van Zanden does address the emergence of large multinational enterprises in the Netherlands and their effects on the economy, but does not give output figures.[12] In the remainder of this chapter I will make an attempt to identify structural changes in Dutch industry, and the factors that have influenced these movements.

The data in the Statistics of Production enables us to calculate the value added per worker for 24 industries for the period 1938–1965. In addition, the value added per worker for the period 1921–1938 can be calculated for 15 industries. Unfortunately it is not possible to calculate labour productivity levels for the period 1913–1921, so this period is not included in the analyses in this chapter. The figures are shown in Table 5.1, in which industries are ranked in ascending order according to their value added per worker in 1965. The value added per worker is high in the flour, soap, calcium silicate and paper industries. These are manufacturing industries that are characterised by high levels of power consumption and relatively high levels of installed horsepower, particularly in the form of motors driving machinery for processing raw materials (see further Chapter 7). Labour productivity in most of the metallurgical industries is average, with automobile and electrical engineering industries forming exceptions. Relatively low levels of productivity can be found in the textiles and clothing industries. However the relationships between productivity levels in the various industries have changed over time. The table shows fairly high levels of labour productivity in the wool and cotton industries for 1921 and 1950, whereas in 1921 the productivity of labour in electrical engineering was still very low. The relative spread of productivity levels in the four chosen years remains reasonably constant, except that in 1938 there is a relatively wide spread with a coefficient of variation (the quotient of the standard deviation and the average of the 24 observations) of 0.479. However this is due to one exceptionally high value of an observation in the flour industry. In the 1930s the market mechanism had been completely suspended in this industry, as part of the policies for dealing with the agricultural crisis. This led to a strongly monopolistic situation and thus to unusually high profit margins. If this industry is excluded, the coefficient of variation is 0.312, which is very close to the values for other years.

However the variations in comparative levels of labour productivity between industries, and over time, are to be ascribed not only to the exceptional market situation but also to specific movements in the prices of the raw materials and final products for each industry. For example, the remarkably high value added for the paper industry in 1950 is attributable to high prices for paper products as a result of the Korean War. And last but not least, real growth in labour productivity also plays a role. If we are to identify

---

10 See the review by Drukker, *Waarom*, 69–75.

11 Several publications from the Centraal Planbureau (Central Planning Bureau) must be excepted from this criticism, but these publications all relate to the period after 1950. See CPB, *De Nederlandse economie in 1973* and CPB, *De Nederlandse economie in 1980*.

12 Van Zanden, *Klein land*, Chapter 3.

Table 5.1. Value added per worker in current prices for 24 industries, 1921, 1938, 1950, and 1965 (in guilders)

	1921	1938	1950	1965
Ready-made clothing		1,143	4,527	9,677
Machine knitting	1,807	1,268	5,024	11,939
Cotton	2,335	1,490	8,037	12,174
Footwear	2,537	1,371	4,433	12,839
Wool	2,456	1,370	9,546	13,486
Pottery		1,517	5,247	14,218
Shipbuilding	2,848	2,031	6,451	16,250
Rubber	2,222	1,744	7,458	16,487
Bicycles	2,391	2,244	5,744	16,727
Mechanical engin.	3,130	2,333	5,980	17,773
Steel furniture		1,541	5,299	17,776
Wire	1,318	1,812	7,018	17,825
Leather		2,146	9,439	18,067
Roofing tiles		1,358	5,965	18,765
Sheet-metal work	1,928	1,643	6,200	18,793
Cocoa	2,223	1,935	9,860	19,290
Bricks		1,122	5,442	19,821
Preserved food		1,485	6,774	21,728
Cars and coachwork		1,589	7,344	21,954
Electrical engin.	2,202	2,501	7,718	22,724
Paper	2,600	2,891	13,494	25,218
Calcium silicate		1,972	8,773	27,308
Flour	3,585	5,683	9,426	32,351
Soap	4,539	3,524	10,172	33,200
Weighted average	2,498	1,798	6,862	17,756
Coefficient of variation	0.293	0.479	0.294	0.307

Source: Appendix A.

the effects of labour productivity, the value added must be adjusted for price changes relevant to each industry. This will give us a picture of the real value added.

The first two columns of Table 5.2 show the real value added for 1921 and 1965 in index numbers (1938 = 100), broken down by industry. The figures in the last two columns show the annual rate of growth in real labour productivity for the periods 1921–1938 and 1938–1965, respectively.

The table reveals large differences in growth performance of the present industries. Between 1938 and 1965, the increase in real value added was greatest in the electrical engineering, sheet metal working, rubber and automobile industries. In the case of the first three of these, we can also show that this growth had been considerable as from 1921 onwards. The real value added in the electrical engineering industry in 1965 was 130 times its level in 1921. The metallurgical industries as a group enjoyed the greatest increase, with only the shipbuilding industry as an exception. On the other hand, in half of the industries the volume of production increased at the most only three-fold

Table 5.2. Levels of real value added (index numbers, 1938 = 100) and real labour productivity growth (annual compound growth rates), 1921–1965

	Value Added		Labour productivity	
	1921	**1965**	**1921–1938**	**1938–1965**
Cars and coachwork		1340		4.1
Electrical engin.	11	1340	8.8	3.7
Sheet-metal work	53	1046	3.2	2.5
Rubber	15	862	7.1	3.1
Preserved food		775		4.9
Steel furniture		738		3.5
Wire	47	605	4.0	2.7
Mechanical engin.	43	525	3.8	2.0
Bicycles	31	374	6.9	2.8
Paper	22	347	7.1	2.3
Machine knitting	18	322	4.3	2.9
Ready-made clothing		316		1.9
Soap	41	264	3.7	0.9
Calcium silicate		258		2.6
Wool	77	243	0	3.2
Pottery		233		1.9
Cocoa an choc.	71	203	3.6	2.2
Footwear	36	195	4.3	2.2
Leather		184		2.7
Flour	39	164	6.6	2.2
Shipbuilding	88	162	1.2	0.9
Cotton	59	159	2.3	1.1
Roofing tiles		150		2.7
Brick		130		3.2

Source: Appendix A.

between 1938 and 1965. These include the construction materials, clothing and textile industries.

To what extent does the growth in real value added in each industry relate to productivity increases? From column 3 of the table we can see high growth rates for average labour productivity in the electrical engineering, rubber, bicycle and paper industries. The first three of these could be characterised as 'new' industries. They emerged during and soon after the First World War and enjoyed considerable growth in the 1920s and 1930s. The growth in labour productivity in the shipbuilding, wool and cotton industries between 1921 and 1938 was much more limited. In the period 1938–1965, the rates of growth in labour productivity are not so high, but once again the higher rates are in industries that also enjoyed rapid growth in real value added, such as the automobile, electrical engineering, steel furniture and rubber industries. The first of these grew out of coach-making and wagon building, and provides a nice example of the analytic objection presented in section 5.1 to the use of the categories 'old' and 'new', that excessive disaggregation in effect deprives existing industries of the fruits of their innovation.

The greatest growth in productivity over the whole period was in the electrical engineering industry, with an annual rate of growth of 5.8 percent. This means that production per worker increased by a factor of 12 between 1921 and 1965.

Figure 5.1 compares for the fifteen industries the annual rate of growth in real value added to the annual rate of growth in labour productivity in each industry.

Figure 5.1. Real value added and real labour productivity in 15 industries, 1921–1965 (annual compound growth rates)

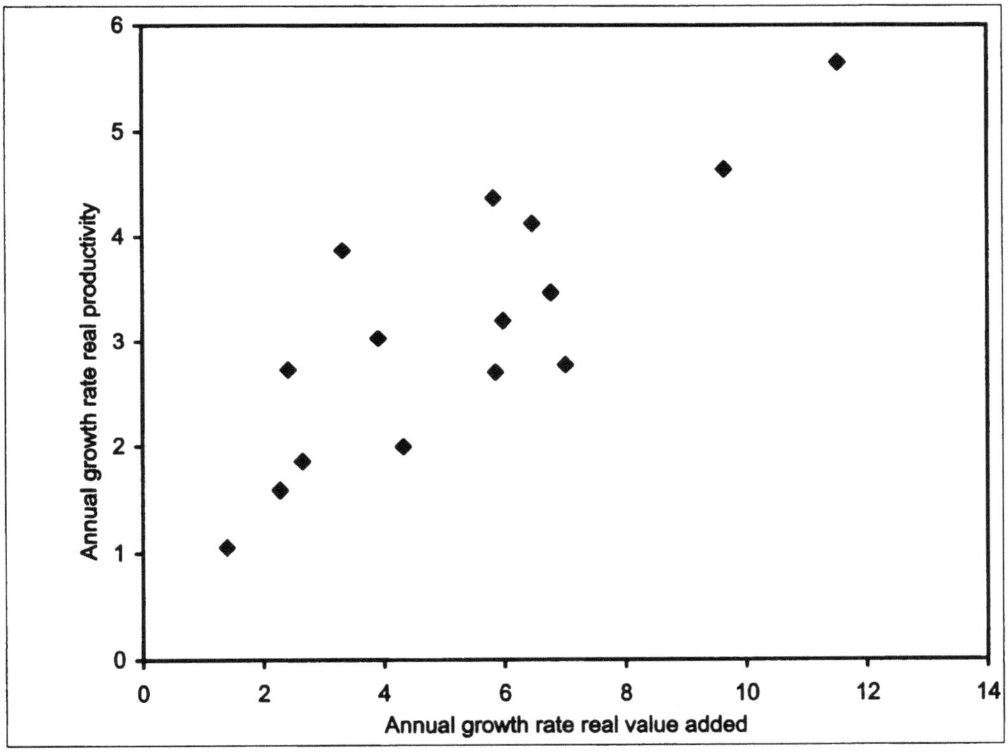

Source: Table 5.2.

There is a strong connection between the annual growth rates of the two variables. The greatest increases in productivity took place in industries in which production increased the most. The correlation is fairly strong, with a coefficient of correlation of 0.83. If we make the same calculation for shorter periods and for the larger sample of 24 industries, the coefficient of correlation is still between 0.70 and 0.80.

The British economist Salter arrived at similar results for a comparable sample of 28 British industries between 1924 and 1950. He found a coefficient of correlation of 0.81. In the long term, an increasing volume of production and increasing labour productivity go together.[13] In the following sections we will examine the effect of structural

13 See Salter, *Productivity*, 123–126 and 206–208. Kendrick found coefficients of correlation of between 0.55 and 0.6 for the United States. Kendrick, *Productivity trends*, 111–112.

changes resulting from the uneven growth of the sample-industries on productivity growth in manufacturing.

5.3. The role of dynamic industries in total industrial expansion

All industries in the sample faced real growth of value added between 1921 and 1965 and between 1938 and 1965, but Table 5.2 shows considerable differences between industries. The relative importance of large industries such as the cotton industry and shipbuilding declined sharply while the importance of the electrical engineering and car industries increased rapidly. Employment volumes changed accordingly. This process of structural change also affected aggregate productivity in manufacturing, not only because there was relatively high productivity growth in these quickly growing industries, but also because an increasing portion of the labour volume was employed in these industries. We will analyse this by comparing the productivity effects of the shift of employment between industries to changes in productivity within industries.

Figure 5.2 shows the effect of the rapidly growing industries on the increase in aggregate labour productivity. Aggregate labour productivity (the real productivity of labour for each industry, with weights according to the share in total employment in the sample) is shown in this figure both with and without the four fastest growing industries, i.e. the electrical engineering, sheet-metal work, automobile and rubber industries.

It is striking how modest this effect on total labour productivity was at first. Until the mid-1950s there is little difference between the two lines in the graph. However from the second half of the 1950s on the lines diverge. The small size of the initial structural effect occurs because the level of labour productivity in the industries in which productivity grew rapidly was not very high at the beginning of the period. Table 5.1 indicates that productivity levels (the value added per worker in current prices) in large industries such as the cotton and wool industries, and mechanical engineering and shipbuilding, were significantly above those of the rapidly growing industries. The amplifying effect of the shift of employment from low growth sectors to sectors with high productivity growth is counterbalanced by the dampening effect of the low levels of labour productivity in the rapidly-growing industries in comparison to the low growth industries. After 1950 these relationships changed, in the sense that the productivity increase in the four rapidly growing industries had a greater effect on total productivity in the sample.

We can now also determine the relative importance of the rapidly growing industries in the total value added of the sample. The index of real value added without the four fastest growing industries reached a value of 260 in 1965 (1938 = 100) compared to the figure of about 400 if the growth industries are included. Thus growth since 1938 without these four industries is about 65 percent of the total growth. The four rapidly growing industries accounted for 16.1 percent of the total value added of the sample in 1938 and for 55.3 percent in 1965. Their share of employment also rose, but not as rapidly. In 1938 the four industries accounted for 13.5 percent of total employment, and in 1965 for 34.1 percent. These shares are lower than we saw for the value added, point-

Figure 5.2. Real labour productivity growth and the most dynamic industries, 1921–1965 (1938 = 100)

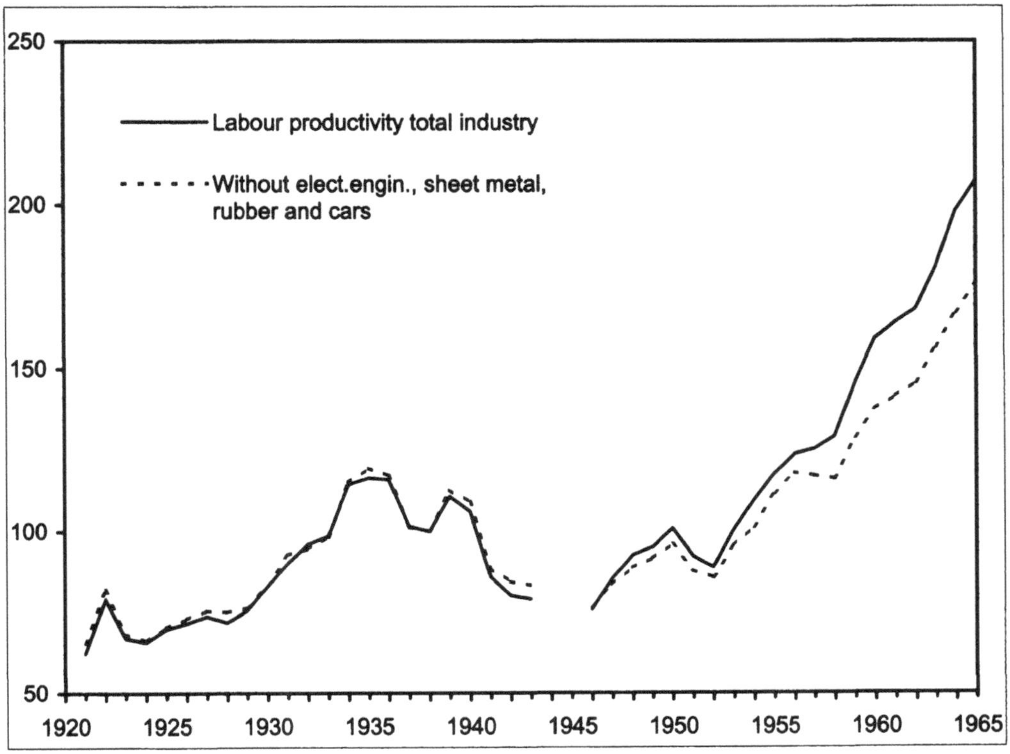

Source: Appendix A.

ing to a higher than average productivity, as well as a faster than average increase in productivity between 1938 and 1965.

5.4. The components of labour productivity growth: internal and structural effects

The contributions of the different industries to the increase in total labour productivity can be split into two components. In the first place, labour productivity within every industry increased, but not at the same rate in all industries. In addition there were structural changes because the rapidly growing industries accounted for an increasing share of all industry. This led to shifts in the structure of employment. Surplus labour in industries that were not growing rapidly was as it were reallocated to the more expansive sectors. These two effects will be referred to as the 'internal' effect and the 'structural' effect, respectively. In determining the structural effect, allowance can be made not only for the growth in productivity, but also for the level of labour productivity within every industry in a particular year.

To measure the effects of these shifts, we will use a composite index of production in which production, employment and levels of labour productivity are differentiated. We will compare this index with the results of similar calculations by Salter and Von Tunzelmann for British industry.[14] The technique used here is based on a breakdown of the overall change in the aggregate productivity in manufacturing over a period into two components. The first component measures the increase in aggregate productivity, under the restriction that the productivity of labour in each industry remains constant and the total employment does not change (the so-called structural effect: the increase in total productivity as a result of shifts in employment between industries). The second component measures the change in productivity under the restriction that the employment per industry does not change (the internal effect). If the following variables are defined:

O_i is the annual real value added in an industry
E_i is the employment level
P_i is the real labour productivity per worker

Then

$$\frac{\sum_i O_{it}}{\sum_i O_{i0}}$$

represents the change in production from year 0 to year t. Because O is equal to $(O/E) \times E$ we can rewrite this as follows:

$$\frac{\sum_i (O_{it}/E_{it}) \cdot E_{it}}{\sum_i (O_{i0}/E_{i0}) \cdot E_{i0}}$$

We can write O/E as P (i.e. production per unit of labour) so:

$$\frac{\sum_i P_{it}E_{it}}{\sum_i P_{i0}E_{i0}}$$

The aggregate change in productivity is then:

$$\frac{P_{it}}{P_{i0}} = \frac{\sum_i P_{it}E_{it}}{\sum_i P_{i0}E_{i0}} \cdot \frac{\sum_i E_{i0}}{\sum_i E_{it}}$$

This can be rewritten as:

$$\frac{P_{it}}{P_{i0}} = \frac{\sum_i P_{it}E_{it}}{\sum_i P_{it}E_{i0}} \cdot \frac{\sum_i E_{i0}}{\sum_i E_{it}} \cdot \frac{\sum_i P_{it}E_{i0}}{\sum_i P_{i0}E_{i0}}$$

[14] Salter, *Productivity*, 184–185; Von Tunzelmann, Structural, 2–5.

In this equation the two first components measure the change in production if the labour productivity within each industry is held constant and total employment also remains constant. The two components together measure the structural effect, i.e. the increase in production as a result of employment shifts between industries. The last component is an index of aggregate labour productivity, with the various industries being weighted according to their employment volume in the base year.[15]

Naturally it is also possible to define this decomposition using productivity rather than employment for the base weighting. In this case the first two components are a base-weighted structural effect, and the internal component is based on the current year.

$$\frac{P_{it}}{P_{i0}} = \frac{\sum P_{i0}E_{it}}{\sum P_{i0}E_{i0}} \cdot \frac{\sum E_{i0}}{\sum E_{it}} \cdot \frac{\sum P_{it}E_{it}}{\sum P_{i0}E_{it}}$$

Both formulas produce different results. The outcomes that Salter obtained for his sample of 28 industries for 1924–1948 differed quite widely depending on the weighting method. Using the first method, Salter broke down the total productivity increase of 181 (1924 = 100) into an internal effect of 136 and a structural effect of 133. The second method produced an internal effect of 152 and a structural effect of 119.[16] Leaving aside the fact that the structural effects in his calculations are relatively strong (see my figures and those of Von Tunzelmann, below), it is important to ask which weighting method is best suited to our empirical data. In theoretical terms the two methods are equally good.

In the light of the discussion concerning British *new industries* that has already been described above, it is evident that the choice of weighting method depends on the question that is to be answered and the theoretical approach that has been chosen. If the aim is to evaluate the extent to which entrepreneurs were successful in developing innovative activities, their behaviour should be seen as a rational response to existing market conditions and the available technology. In this neo-classical approach, the behaviour of entrepreneurs is evaluated in comparison to the alternatives available at the time (in this case, the relative productivity levels during the first year of the time series). For this, one must use the second formula, since this incorporates weighting according to productivity levels in the base year. However the discussion about industrial renewal – especially in the United Kingdom – has also examined the extent to which entrepreneurs had, or should have had, foresight about future relative productivity levels. This neo-Schumpeter-

---

15 A typesetting error slipped into Salter's equation for a multiplicative index. The weighted internal component for the final year is incorrectly given as P_0E_t/P_0E_t. Naturally this should be P_tE_t/P_0E_t. See Salter, *Productivity*, 185.
There is a multiplicative relationship between the components. Fabricant has translated this index into a formula in which there is an additive relationship between the components. However one has to ask whether such a breakdown is logical in view of the weighting problem. Employment shifts change the aggregated productivity due to the structural effect, but they also change the component of the internal effect, if employment in the final year is used to determine weightings. See Fabricant, *Employment*, Appendix G, 336–337. Fabricant's method has also been applied in international comparisons. See for example Van Ark, Sectoral. The same objection applies in this case. The problem is dealt with by introducing an 'interaction effect', which proved to be quite small in practice.

16 Salter, *Productivity*, 151.

ian approach focuses on innovation, represented in the nineteenth century by the *entrepreneur*, in the twentieth century by large companies. Qualitative changes of technology may imply that a production process that initially appears to be inefficient will in the long term prove to be efficient (dynamic efficiency rather than static efficiency). Using this approach, the first equation is appropriate, since this includes a weighting scheme according to employment volumes in the base year and relative labour productivity levels in the final year.[17] Both weighting methods will be used with the Dutch data.

The first analysis is based on the fifteen industries for which data is available for the 'long' period, 1921–1965. Table 5.3 shows the size of the two effects, including a breakdown into shorter periods. The change in labour productivity for industry as a whole (second to last column) is split into structural and internal components. These components are weighted according to employment in the base year (first and second columns) and then according to labour productivity levels in the base year (third and fourth columns). The first two columns can be considered in terms of entrepreneurs' ability to predict future relative labour productivity in the diverse industries (the neo-Schumpeterian approach). Columns three and four should be considered in the light of the relative labour productivity of the alternatives that were available in the base year (the neo-classical approach).

The most notable feature is that for all but one period, the internal effect is many times greater than the structural effect. The largest part of the increase in labour productivity in industry as a whole can thus be explained by improvements in labour productivity within the different industries.

If we look at the effects for various sub-periods, it is striking that for the variant in which weighting is based on productivity levels in the base year, the structural effects are negative for the periods that have 1921 as the base year. That is, if we start with the relative productivity levels in the base year, the movement of employment to other industries had a negative effect on productivity. We can also see that using this variant the structural component in the two other periods was very small.

The variant in which employment in the base year is used as weight (columns one and two) yields larger structural effects. Entrepreneurs were apparently well able to identify activities that would later yield higher relative labour productivity levels.

The 1938–1950 period is exceptional in many respects. The internal effects in this period are negative, and in contrast to other periods are of the same order of size as the structural effects. In the first variant the positive structural effect actually outweighs the negative internal effect. This is related to strong differences in productivity changes between industries: in large industries such as cotton, shipbuilding and mechanical engineering productivity actually fell between 1938 and 1950.

For the 1938–1965 period we can use a larger sample of 24 industries. The structural and internal effects have again been differentiated. Moreover the bottom half of Table 5.4 also shows a calculation based on productivity levels. My reasoning is that the effect of an employment shift to sectors with a higher rate of productivity *growth* could in some cases be negated if these sectors had a relatively low labour productivity *level*. For

17 Von Tunzelmann, Structural, 5.

Table 5.3. Labour productivity growth in 15 industries, internal and structural components, 1921–1965

Period	(1)	(2)	(3)	(4)	(5)	(6)
21–38	0.7	58.9	– 5.6	69.6	60.1	101.0
38–50	3.1	– 4.9	0.0	– 2.0	– 2.0	61.2
50–65	6.5	96.5	3.7	101.8	109.3	166.1
21–65	19.7	174.2	–19.8	309.5	228.2	762.0

Notes:
Column (1): the size of the structural component, with employment in the base year as weight factor in the internal component.
Column (2): the size of the internal component, with employment in the base year as weight factor in the internal component.
Column (3): the size of the structural component, with productivity in the base year as weight factor in the structural component.
Column (4): the size of the internal component, with productivity in the base year as weight factor in the structural component.
Column (5): percentage changes in labour productivity.
Column (6): percentage changes in real value added.
All values are expressed as percentage points change from the reference value of 100. Multiplying column 1 by column 2 gives the value in column 5, and likewise column 3 and 4 are factors of column 5.

Source: Appendix A.

example, the relatively rapid increase in employment and in labour productivity in an industry such as the preserved foods industry had only a slight effect on overall productivity. The value added per worker in this industry was below the nominal value added per worker of the total sample throughout this period. We can highlight this effect by comparing the outcomes when allowance is made for productivity levels against the outcomes if this factor is not included.

If we compare the top half of this table with the corresponding periods in the table based on fifteen industries, we can see that production grew a little more slowly in the sample of 24 industries. However the differences are slight. The same may be said for the increase in productivity. The developments in the nine extra industries have scarcely any influence on the picture that emerges if we consider only fifteen industries. This is partly because these are relatively small industries (in terms of employment), which make little impression on the overall outcome. The nine extra industries also had little effect on growth rates for the structural and internal effects. In general, the structural effects for the whole period shown in this table are a little stronger than in the previous table.

If we base the calculations on the levels of labour productivity levels in each of the 24 industries (for 1938 prices), this leads to higher outcomes in the final year, 1965, using both production and labour productivity. A comparison between the two methods of calculation shows that if we make allowance for the labour productivity levels, the structural effect is a few percentage points higher than with the first method. This indicates that there has been a small shift in employment in favour of industries with a higher real value added per employee. However this 'level effect' is also fairly slight, chiefly because the rapidly growing industries (the electrical engineering, sheet metal work, automobile and rubber industries) were not among those with the highest productivity in 1938.

Table 5.4. Labour productivity growth in 24 industries, internal and structural components, 1938–1965[18]

Period	(1)	(2)	(3)	(4)	(5)	(6)
Index numbers						
38–50	1.6	− 0.8	− 0.1	0.9	0.9	60.6
50–65	5.5	94.5	2.3	100.6	105.3	156.3
38–65	10.6	87.3	0.0	107.1	107.0	311.6
Levels (1938 price level)						
38–50	3.0	− 2.1	0.8	0.0	0.8	60.5
50–65	9.6	95.9	6.6	101.3	114.6	167.9
38–65	16.5	85.7	4.0	108.0	116.3	330.0

Notes: See the explanations to Table 5.3. All values are expressed as percentage points change from the reference number 100.

Source: Appendix A.

The overall conclusion therefore is that in these two samples (for 15 industries between 1921–1965 and 24 industries between 1938–1965) the structural effect is completely overshadowed by the internal effect. In other words, the aggregate change in productivity in the samples is chiefly determined by productivity changes within industries and not by employment shifts to more productive industries.

These results contrast sharply to Salter's findings for British industry for 1924–1948. He found much higher structural effects. However Von Tunzelmann, using a more disaggregated sample of about hundred industries, has replicated Salter's analysis and found much lower structural effects. He explained this by pointing to the consequences of the processes of change that were taking place at the same time as the structural effects, such as declining marginal returns and the reduction in the advantage that relatively productive sectors have over less productive sectors, as more employment is created in those industries. These processes would be more clearly seen in an analysis in which the industries are differentiated at a lower level of aggregation.[19] However our sample of Dutch industries has a similar level of aggregation to that used by Salter, so this cannot account for the difference between the structural and internal effects in

[18] The rise in labour productivity reported here differs from growth figures given earlier, in which there was actually a decline from 1938 to 1950. This discrepancy arises because the underlying calculations are based either on index figures for productivity alone, or on productivity on the basis of 1938 prices. In both cases this gives a faster rise in productivity, compared to the figures that were presented earlier. This index number problem is discussed in more detail later in this chapter.

[19] Von Tunzelmann, Structural, 13. Moreover, it is significant that Von Tunzelmann, in contrast to Salter, used a general price index to estimate the real productivity. In other words, the nominal production of the diverse industries is translated into real production using one time series of prices. This method is rather inexact.

British and Dutch industry. On the contrary, the small size of the Dutch sample would explain low structural effects: since there are only fifteen industries in the sample, it is logical that there is little chance of detecting structural effects.

The greater rigidity in the Netherlands could also be caused by a less dynamic industrial structure, as a whole. Almost all of the industries we have considered had rising employment levels. Obviously this will tend to cancel out effects relating to changes in the employment structure. Another related measurement problem is the fairly high level of aggregation of the sample. There may have been important changes in productivity as a result of structural changes within the industries, which would not be directly visible as structural effects. One clear example is the automobile and coach-making industry. The rapid growth of the Dutch automobile industry in the second half of the 1950s in fact entailed a structural change within this industry. What have appeared as internal productivity effects might well turn out to be structural effects if we used smaller and more precise categories, in spite of Von Tunzelmann's conclusions. The introduction of new processes and products in industries had essentially the same effect. In the end this problem cannot be solved unless the level of aggregation is reduced to individual products.[20]

The role of structural effects in explaining changes in industrial productivity in the period 1921–1965 must therefore be quite small. This is not to say that there were no structural effects in manufacturing. For example, the emergence of the chemicals and petroleum refining sectors, which were still largely outside the sample in the 1950s, led to large structural changes from the second half of this period on. However the slight differences between the long-term movement in the total productivity of the sample industries, as calculated here, and the productivity movement of all manufacturing industries shown in the Dutch national accounts (see Appendix A) gives us no reason to suppose that employment shifts between sectors played a big role. In so far as there were fundamental structural effects in manufacturing, these only became important in the 1960s.

5.5. Production and price levels

The influence of new industries on changes in industrial labour productivity in this period is not seen in any exceptionally high productivity levels or exceptional increases in productivity, but rather in the opening up of new sources of activity on a significant scale. Demand effects, and the resulting broadening of manufacturing, is just as impor-

---

20 Another explanation is that the structural component has been under-estimated because employment shifts themselves have effects on the individual industries. If, for example, more employment is created in highly productive industries, the production per worker in those industries is reduced, presuming diminishing marginal returns. This not only reduces the potential effect of employment shifts, it also strengthens the internal effect in the formula. In principle the formula should therefore contain a term that ensures that an industry's contribution to the structural effect is added if an industry with above-average productivity generates more employment, or if a below-average industry loses employment, and *vice versa*.

tant in this process as Schumpeterian 'creative destruction' or Rostowian 'unbalanced growth'. However that does not mean that the latter processes played no role. The differences between the productivity growth rates for industries indicate different, industry-specific, developments. There was a considerable employment shift in our sample. This is a growth phenomenon that relates to changing patterns of consumption and to technological developments.

We can form a better idea of the dynamics of inter-industry developments using the cross-sectional analysis applied by f.i. Fabricant, Kendrick and Salter.[21] In *Productivity and Technical Change* Salter systematically compiled key industrial statistics that include production and inputs, prices, wages and labour volumes, for 28 different industries. The data derives from the British *Census of Production*.[22] He used correlation analysis to produce a complete picture of the dynamics of industrial growth in the United Kingdom between 1924 and 1950. Below, and in the following chapters, we will see whether it is possible to do the same for the Netherlands, although we must again note that the sample is of limited size.

If we start with 1938 and end with 1965, we can obtain data for 24 industries. Both years were in the rising phase of the business cycle, thus minimising the possibility that productivity changes may be distorted by differences in capacity utilisation. The variables to be used are:

1. Real value of production
2. Real value added
3. Employment
4. Real labour productivity
5. Average money wage
6. Wage costs per unit of production
7. Output prices

Real value of production (1) is the value of the gross production in constant prices. Real value added (2) is the real gross value added, obtained by subtracting non-labour input costs (costs for raw materials and intermediate products) from the value of production, and then adjusting for price changes using an industry-specific production price index. Employment (3) is the total number of reported workers and non-production workers per industry. Real labour productivity (real value added per worker) (4) can be calculated from variables 2 and 3. The average money wage per worker (5) is the only quantity that cannot be derived entirely from the Statistics of Production. This is partially based on a retrospective extrapolation of wage levels as reported in the Statistics of Production for 1950 (using wage indexes from the Accident Statistics) with due regard for changes in social security costs. Nominal wage costs per unit of production (6) for each industry are obtained by dividing the index of wages by the index of production. Product prices

---

21 Fabricant, *Employment*; Kendrick; *Productivity trends*; Kendrick, *Postwar*.

22 Salter, *Productivity*. As mentioned above, the British *Statistics of Production* is not available for all years; the period Salter covered was very much determined by the availability of census data. In the second edition of the work (1966), W. B. Reddaway has extended the analysis to cover the period 1954–1963.

(7) are calculated for each industry. The price series for each industry consists of linked sub-series that are re-weighted every five years. Table 5.5 shows the values of the begin-year and end-year of these variables for each industry for the period 1938–1965, indexed to 1938.

Table 5.5. Levels of key variables per industry in 1965 (1938 = 100)

	1 Output Volume	2 Value Added	3 Empl	4 Real Labour Product.	5 Money Wage	6 Unit Wage	7 Output Price
Cars and coachw.	1684	1340	486	276	794	288	474
Electrical engin.	1604	1340	498	269	757	288	338
Rubber	858	862	378	228	919	403	413
Sheet metal	820	1046	533	196	856	436	583
Steel furniture	654	738	292	253	875	346	583
Preserved food	608	775	215	360	868	241	407
Mechanical engin.	523	525	307	171	753	440	446
Wire	512	605	297	204	832	408	477
Bicycles	489	374	178	210	1016	484	373
Machine knitting	385	322	147	219	872	398	432
Paper	357	347	189	184	795	433	533
Ready-made cloth.	292	316	188	168	702	418	504
Wool	244	243	105	231	773	334	425
Pottery	224	233	142	164	952	580	572
Soap	221	264	205	129	858	666	732
Calcium silicate	218	258	128	202	970	481	703
Footwear	212	195	107	182	853	468	514
Cocoa & choc.	209	203	113	180	788	439	555
Cotton	159	159	117	136	902	664	601
Leather	150	184	89	207	743	359	411
Roofing tiles	150	150	74	203	1029	508	688
Shipbuilding	143	162	126	129	894	695	623
Brick	132	130	56	232	1092	470	766
Flour	124	164	91	108	754	418	327

Sources: Appendix A and Table 6.1.

From Kendrick and Salter's studies of the different long term growth rates of industries in the United States and the United Kingdom, respectively, it appears that the fastest growing industries generally also face the largest falls in the prices of their products.[23] In a growing economy there is a trend towards producing goods that can be produced at relatively low costs. Can we demonstrate this for the Dutch industries in our sample?

23 See Kendrick, *Postwar,* 119 and Salter, *Productivity*, 122.

Figure 5.3. Levels of output prices and output volumes in 24 industries, 1965 (1938 = 100).

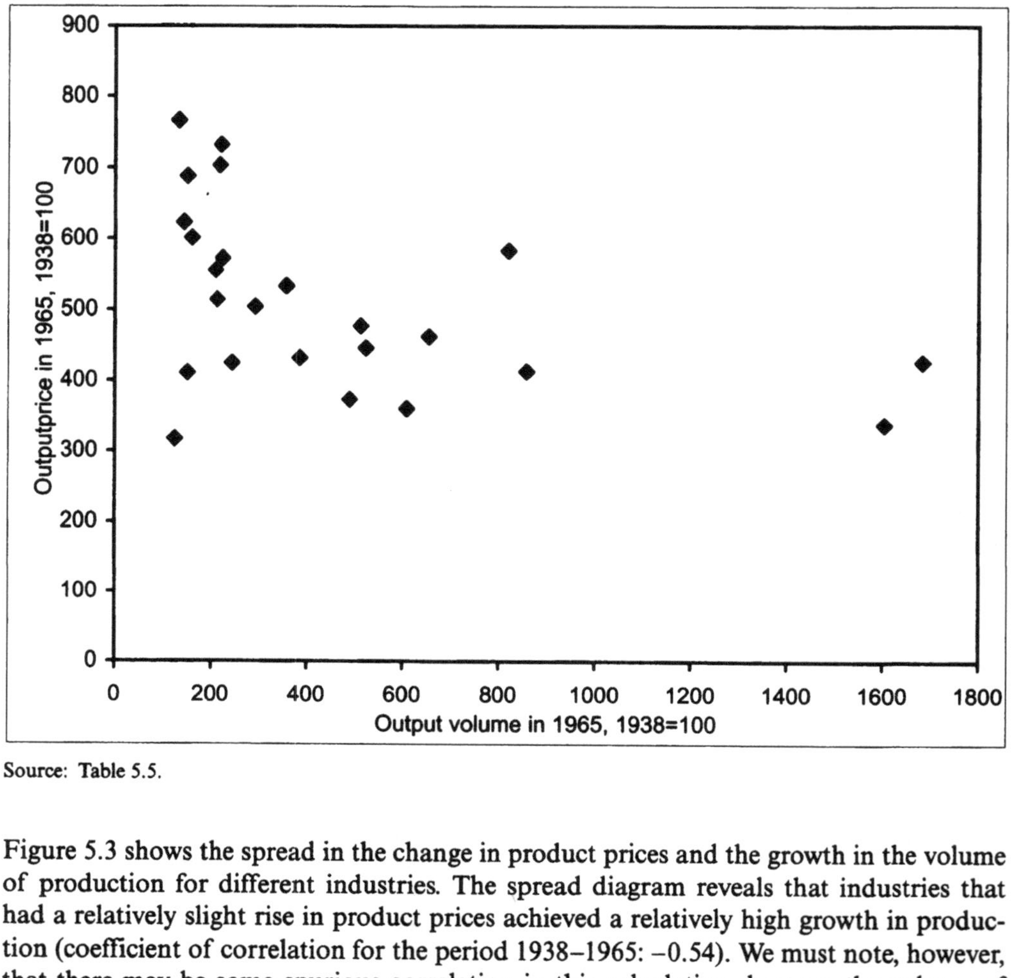

Source: Table 5.5.

Figure 5.3 shows the spread in the change in product prices and the growth in the volume of production for different industries. The spread diagram reveals that industries that had a relatively slight rise in product prices achieved a relatively high growth in production (coefficient of correlation for the period 1938–1965: –0.54). We must note, however, that there may be some spurious correlation in this calculation, because the volume of production for each industry is obtained by dividing the nominal production values by a product price that is also calculated from the production data for industries given in the Statistics of Production. If the product price is reported too high, the calculated production volume will be too low. Thus measurement errors could have amplified the correlation. However if we look at the outcomes over the other periods and compare our results with the outcomes for the United Kingdom, it would appear that the results are not very sensitive to measurement errors. The coefficients of correlation for 1924–1963 and 1924–1950 are –0.57 and –0.64, respectively. The latter figure is lower than the coefficient for the comparable period in the United Kingdom, yet the regression equations are in reasonably close agreement.

In general one may assume that an economy will in the long term produce more and more of those goods whose relative prices rise most slowly. These goods are produced in greater physical quantities precisely because improved technology and productivity increases make it possible to produce them at a lower cost. This can also be related to the observation in Section 5.3, that the industries in which productivity grew fastest were also those in which the volume of production increased the most. This positive relationship between production and productivity within industries can be regarded as reciprocal. Faster growth as a result of expanding demand leads to economies of scale, to the optimal utilisation of productive capacity or to new investments, which in turn has a favourable effect on productivity improvements. The increase in labour productivity results in lower costs and lower prices, which increases demand and stimulates production.[24]

5.6. The index number problem

The relation between sectoral price levels and total value added is crucial in the quantification of the process of economic growth. If real production figures are calculated on the basis of price weights referring to the first stage of a developing industry, these calculations will over-estimate real growth. For example, prices for electro-technical products in the early 1920s were relatively high. In the course of the twentieth century the prices of these products rose much less rapidly than those of other industries. In a composite industrial production index, the electrical engineering industry will be given more weight and the value of output will increase faster if prices at the beginning of the period are used as weights, then if one used the prices found in the final year of the period. So the relative prices of 'new' products tend to decline, which is characteristic of any developing economy. This *Gerschenkron-effect* is the result of contrary movements in relative production and relative prices.[25] Some studies have focussed on relative prices as a means of tracing broad long-term transformation processes in an economy.[26] The same effects must also be taken into account when comparing countries' income levels,

---

24 The positive relationship between increased production volume and higher labour productivity across industries is known as *Fabricant's Law*. P. J. Verdoorn has demonstrated this phenomenon for the economy as a whole. Verdoorn's Law states that production growth results from increased demand, which stimulates increases in the productivity of labour. Verdoorn's claim is that there is a fairly unambiguous causality between production increases and productivity increases, in the sense that production growth exerts an independent, structural influence on labour productivity. In fact the production growth variable includes a whole range of factors, such as economies of scale, changes in the capital/labour ratio, improved management and organisation, and higher investments. All of these have a positive effect on labour productivity. The growth in production is something like a composite proxy variable that explains changes in the productivity of labour. Salter claims that it is mainly cost reductions, and thus supply factors, that stimulate productivity and thus also production. See Verdoorn, Empirical, 209; Salter, *Productivity*, Chapter 10; for a discussion of the diverse approaches see Von Tunzelmann, *Technology*, 220–221.

25 This effect was first extensively studied by Alexander Gerschenkron. He applied it to his concept of the *Great Spurt*, the transformation from manual labour to industrial production. Gerschenkron, *Economic*, 202–204.

26 See for example Ljungberg, Prices, 49–63. For a sceptical response to the use of Gerschenkron effects to explain long-term transformations, see Larssen & Nilsson, Some remarks.

Figure 5.4. Real labour productivity growth in the sample industries, 1921–1965 (1938-price weights and 1960-price weights)

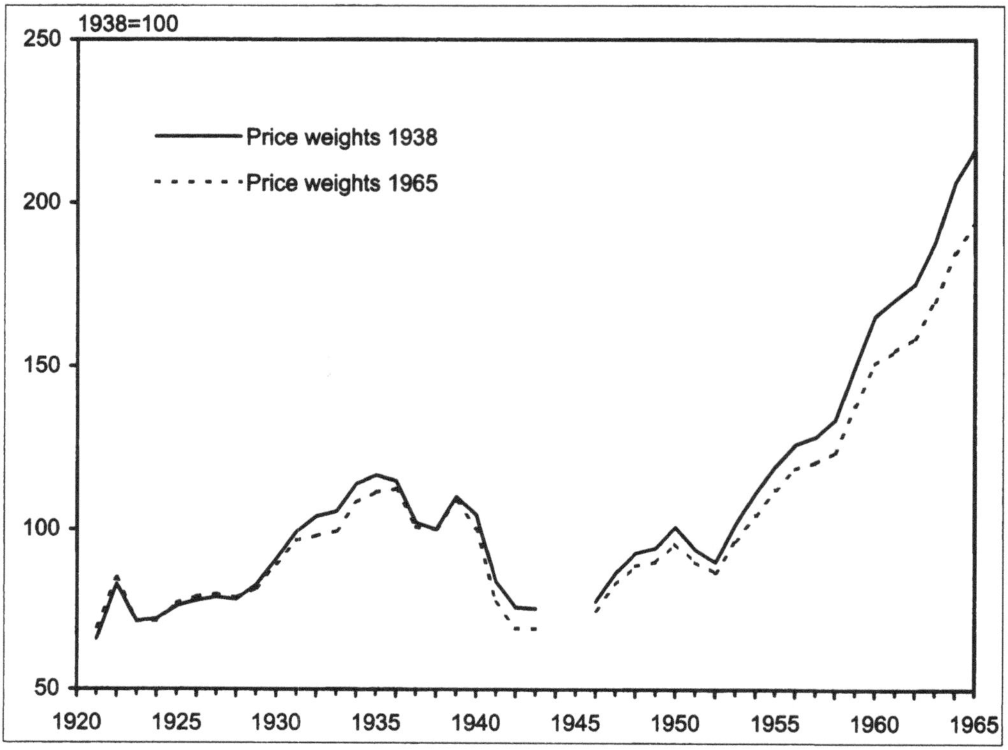

Source: Appendix A.

especially if the comparison is between highly industrialised countries and developing countries.[27]

The effects we have seen in relation to the real production volume also come into play when calculating the real productivity of labour. Long term changes in industrial productivity in the Netherlands are also affected by simultaneous changes in the price and quantity of products. What effect does this have on the levels of productivity in the diverse periods? Figure 5.4 shows the effects of shifts in the price and quantity structure on real labour productivity in the total sample. The figure shows the changes in productivity if real values are expressed in 1938 and 1965 prices, respectively. The differences between the two methods are fairly slight in the period before 1945, but the gap increases after that. In 1965 the index of real labour productivity in comparison to 1938 (1938 = 100), weighted using 1938 prices, is 216.4. If the weighting is based on 1965 prices the index is 193.7, a difference of almost 12 percent, despite the equally good theoretical foundations of the two outcomes.

---

27 Kravis, Survey.

However the weighting system used in this study is not based on a particular beginning- or end-year. Instead, the weightings are adjusted every five years in accordance with the changing output and price structure. The successive weightings are then linked to one another. Similarly the sub-series that I have compiled is a compromise between the Laspeyres and Paasche indexes. As a compromise, I used the Fisher *ideal* index, the geometrical average of the two outcomes. This leaves us finally with three estimates of real labour productivity. The first is measured in prices of 1938, the second in prices of 1965 and the third according to a 5-year-adjusted weighting scheme. By way of comparison, Table 5.6 shows the levels and growth rates of the three series of real labour productivity.

Table 5.6. Real labour productivity in manufacturing 1921–1965. Levels (1938 = 100) and compound growth rates (% change)

Weighting scheme	1921	1938	1965	rate of growth 1921–1965
1938 prices	65.7	100	216.4	2.75
1965 prices	69.3	100	193.7	2.37
5-year-adjusted weights	62.9	100	193.5	2.58

Sources: Appendices A and B.

The last column shows that the productivity growth estimate is highest using 1938 prices. This is in agreement with what has been said above. The quantity of goods produced per worker increased, but this was accompanied by structural changes; the largest production increases being found in sectors where prices declined most. If this structural change is measured in the relative prices of the begin year, real productivity is being overestimated. If we use the 5-year adjusted weighting scheme, the calculated rate of growth falls between the estimates using constant weights.

5.7. Conclusions

The productivity of labour in all the industries in the sample increased at a rate of 2.6 percent per year between 1921 and 1965. This increase was mainly due to changes in productivity within the different industries and not to structural changes as a result of shifts in employment between industries.

There is a positive relationship at the industry level between growth in value added and growth in labour productivity. In this situation, demand and supply factors reinforce one another. The near absence of *leading sectors* in the present sample is related to the fact that the relative level of labour productivity in rapidly growing industries was below the average for industry as a whole. The topics that will be considered in the following chapters relate especially to explanations of the levels and growth of labour productivity within the industries.

Chapter 6: Labour input and productivity in Dutch manufacturing

In most of the industries considered in this book, wages are the largest constituent of the value added. In the international comparisons in Chapter 4, the average wage per worker was treated as an indicator of the quality of the labour input. If an industry has a high average wage level compared to other industries, this is indicative of high quality labour and may explain the level of labour productivity and, thus, international differences in productivity. We have already seen that this variable has its limitations as an indicator of human capital, in that this factor of production is not rewarded in accordance with its marginal product. Institutions play such an important role in the labour market that average wages do not always have a direct relationship to the actual work performance or labour productivity of workers and employees. Moreover, the labour market is segmented because of differences in skills and qualifications. For these reasons, some studies have used other indicators of labour quality, such as the number of workers who have vocational education relevant to the industry or the number of people working in R&D. However this data is not available in the Dutch Statistics of Production, so we must in the first place examine what relationship there may be between the average wage level in an industry, the quality of the labour input and the actual level of labour productivity and the movement of these variables over time.

6.1. The industrial wage structure

The industries in the sample are characterised by a certain pattern and variation of levels of average money wages across the manufacturing branches. Table 6.1 provides an overview of this wage structure.

During the period 1921–1965, low average wages were earned in machine knitting factories, footwear, ready-made clothing, pottery and bicycle manufacturing industries. The highest average wages were in shipbuilding and in the margarine, flour, electrical engineering, mechanical engineering and calcium silicate industries.

Van Zanden and Griffiths have pointed out that the gradual institutionalisation of wage-setting in the twentieth century in the Netherlands led to smaller wage differentials between regions and between qualities of work. This is also said to have played a role between the various industrial sectors. They illustrate this with a number of observations that point to a decrease over the course of the twentieth century in the coefficient of variation (the quotient of the standard deviation and the average) of wages in the diverse industries. For the seventeen industrial sectors that are differentiated in the Accident

Table 6.1. Average wage per worker in current prices in 25 industries, 1921, 1938, 1950 and 1965 (index numbers, sample average in each year in guilders and index = 100)

	1921	1938	1950	1965
Machine knitting	63	70	70	73
Footwear	80	80	83	82
Ready-made clothing	80	77	71	64
Bicycles	80	79	87	99
Pottery	87	92	88	96
Cocoa and choc.	90	82	92	90
Soap	90	103	101	104
Cotton	94	89	95	89
Wool	98	99	102	92
Brick	99	89	93	98
Roofing tiles	99	89	98	96
Preserved food	99	90	88	92
Wire	104	101	104	98
Cars and coachwork	104	101	111	106
Flour	104	122	113	123
Leather	106	111	112	100
Paper	106	125	113	116
Sheet-metal work	108	93	101	111
Rubber	112	95	106	105
Calcium silicate	113	111	108	113
Electrical engineering	115	110	115	109
Mechanical engineering	118	133	114	109
Steel furniture	104	101	101	99
Margarine	120	127	119	121
Shipbuilding	122	129	116	113
Average (In guilders)	1,306	1,037	2,498	8,245
Coefficient of Var.	0.140	0.172	0.132	0.136

(Coefficient of variation in 1924 = 0.136 and in 1960 = 0.135.)

Sources: 1921 and 1938 Ongevallenstatistiek Rijksverzekeringsbank (Accident Statistics National Insurance Bank); 1950 and 1965 CBS, *Statistics of Production.*

Statistics, this indicator fell from 0.31 in 1906 to 0.25 in 1939, and further to 0.16 in 1950.[1] They conclude that there was a trend towards smaller differences in average wages in these industries.

1 On the Dutch developments see Van Zanden and Griffiths, *Economische*, 25; Van Zanden, *Klein Land*, 41. Cramer, Loonverschillen, 31–33, shows that the difference between low and high wages between the diverse sectors declined over the Second World War period. Other authors have also related the levelling trend to managed wage policies during and after the war. See, for example, Weststrate, *Economic*, 167–172 and Levenbach, Nederlandse 21. In addition to the wages policy,

The question then is whether the data in Table 6.1 also reveal a trend of declining differences between the various manufacturing industries in our sample. The coefficients of variation below the table range from a maximum of 0.172 in 1938 to a minimum of 0.132 in 1950. However, if we put the values for all the years between 1921 and 1965 in chronological order, we have to conclude that for these industries there was no long-term decrease in the variation in average wages over time. During the 1920s the coefficient of variation averaged 0.147, and in the 1930s the average was 0.165. During the war the coefficient was low, at 0.120, but it rose thereafter to 0.150 in 1952. At the end of the period the coefficient reached 0.136, which is also the average value for the whole post-war period. This average differs only slightly from the average for the 1920s.

On the basis of our figures, the most remarkable period is not the 1950s but the 1930s when, despite a labour surplus, wage differences increased, after a relatively stable situation during the 1920s.[2] In contrast, the strict wage regulation during the German occupation (at first by the Board of Mediators, and from late 1942 onwards by a separate Commissioner of Labour, who drew up prescriptions for the various industries) had a strong levelling effect.

How did the relationship between average money wages and levels of the value added per worker across industries change over time? Table 6.2 shows the coefficients of determination (the square of the correlation coefficient) between the wage structure and the labour productivity structure.

Table 6.2. Coefficients of determination between the structure wages and of value added per worker in the sample industries

1921	0.01
1938	0.49
1950	0.32
1960	0.55
1965	0.59

Sources: See Tables 5.1 and 6.1.

The table illustrates that the relationship between the average wage and the value added has become stronger in the course of time. After the First World War there was scarcely any connection between the two spreads. However, in 1938 and 1950 there was a link. In 1960, and especially in 1965, the link became even stronger: in the industries in which productivity (measured as the value added per worker in current prices) was above average, the average money wage was also high in comparison to other industries.

Weststrate who also points to the effects of the greater mobility of labour, which increased the homogenisation of wages in diverse industries. Moreover, Weststrate shows that the standard wages of unskilled labour rose much more quickly from 1939 to 1947 than the wages for skilled labour. He attributes this to government measures to combat poverty.

2 See also Goldin & Katz, Origins, who see the widening wage structure in the U.S. during the first half of the 20th century as an indicator of technology-skill complementarity.

Here, as in section 4.3, we are faced with the question of the causality between wage and productivity levels: do high wages as an indicator for human capital provide the basis for high productivity. Or the other way around, is there a wage premium for workers to bargain over in high productivity industries? To consider this we must first examine which variables determine the wage structure, that is, the pattern of wage differentials between industries.

6.2. The relation between the composition of the workforce and average wages

The Statistics of Production distinguish between categories of labour, such as workers and administrative, technical and service personnel, as well as differentiate these by gender and by age. As was shown in section 4.2 the latter two categories are important in explaining the wage level in an industry. The CBS statistics on wages reveal that around 1960 women earned about 60% of the wage of adult men. Boys aged 18 earned an average of 50%, and girls of the same age earned 40% of the male adult wage.[3] Bölger's estimate for 1930 points to the same percentages for the three categories.[4] These general wage differentials changed little between 1930 and 1960. Part of the difference in wages between the diverse categories can be attributed to the degree of training and education: boys and girls were certainly not regarded as skilled. The post-war wage surveys also showed that few women workers were categorised as skilled labour.[5] In 1960 only a few industries employed women who are treated in the statistics as skilled. The highest proportion was in the printing industry, where 1.3 % of all skilled workers were women. In the pottery, ready-made clothing, wool and cotton industries about 0.2 to 0.4% of skilled workers were women.[6]

---

3 CBS, *Statistiek der lonen 1960* (5, 35). In 1965 the percentages were 70, 50 and 45%, respectively (*St. der Lonen 1966,* 43).

4 Bölger, Beteekenis, 124.

5 Compound effects also played a role in the wage differentials between men and women, as we can see by comparing the wages for skilled adult men and skilled adult women for 1960. The weekly earnings of women were 75% of those for men, for industry as a whole. The hourly rates of women were 80 % of those for men. The difference between this hourly 20% gap and the weekly 40% gap reported on the basis of the CBS statistics is due to the lower average qualification of women workers (fifteen percentage points) and their shorter working week (five percentage points). The hourly 20% gap is thus sex-specific and cannot be explained by the economic statistics.
In their study of labour market inequalities between men and women, using data from 1984/1985, Schippers and Siegers found that 40% of the difference in wages between the sexes in the Netherlands was determined by differences in training, experience and age; 28% was determined by the allocation of men and women to levels and categories of jobs, and 32% by the fact that men are paid more than women with the same characteristics. See Schippers & Siegers, Labour market.

6 CBS, *Statistiek der Lonen 1960*, 21.

Given the large wage differences between the diverse categories of labour, the composition of categories of workers has a big influence on the average wage. Table 6.3 shows the percentages of women, young workers and skilled labourers (expressed in number of workers) in the total workforce for 1938 and 1960, for all the industries included in the Statistics of Production. There is a considerable overlap, especially between the first two categories, since many female workers were younger than 18 or 21 years.

Table 6.3. Share of women, young workers and skilled workers in industrial employment, for 1938 and 1960 (percentages)

	Women 1938	Women 1960	Young workers 1938	Young workers 1960	Skilled 1960
			<18yr	<21yr	
Bicycles	0	0	20	14	14
Roofing tiles	0	2	24	12	4
Calcium silicate	1	2	4	4	4
Brick	1	1	13	10	6
Shipbuilding	1	2	12	10	61
Cars and coachwork	1	5	20	14	53
Mechanical engin.	3	1	14	17	50
Flour	3	8	4	9	13
Steel furniture	3	7	23	13	28
Leather	5	5	11	10	5
Sheet-metal work	8	5	16	16	29
Wire	8	8	22	15	28
Paper	13	7	10	14	25
Electrical engin.	14	18	20	15	24
Pottery	23	16	25	19	11
Rubber	27	10	22	15	7
Margarine	31	15	18	9	12
Cotton	32	17	20	18	30
Wool	32	20	21	28	24
Footwear	34	25	31	29	1
Soap	36	34	22	22	9
Preserved food	39	25	25	16	7
Cocoa and choc.	49	44	32	23	14
Machine knitting	76	68	25	44	4
Ready-made clothing	81	77	28	42	1

Sources: CBS, *Statistics of Production*; CBS, *Statistiek der Lonen* 1960 (*Statistics of Wages*, 1960)

The table shows that women accounted for a relatively large proportion of the labour in the food and beverage, textile and chemicals industries and for a small proportion in the metallurgical industries. Between 1938 and 1960 there was a trend in industries that employed many women for the female share of employment to decline. However the structural distribution of female labour across industries changed very little.

The young worker share of employment varied less between industries, falling below 10 percent only in the calcium silicate and flour industries. The highest shares were in the footwear, wool, machine knitting and ready-made clothing industries. In the 1940s the definition of young workers in the Statistics of Production changed from those under 18 to those less than 21 years old, which would introduce a systematic distortion to any comparison between 1938 and 1960. As was the case with women's share of industrial employment, there is a general trend for the share of young workers to decline. Machine knitting and ready-made clothing were the only industries in which the proportions of young workers increased.

Industries' use of skilled labour can only be studied systematically for the post-war period. The figures in the last column of Table 6.3 show that in 1960 skilled labour played an important role in industries such as shipbuilding, mechanical engineering and the car industry, in which 50 percent or more of the workers were skilled. The production processes in these industries require a good deal of expertise and craftsmanship, more than in the routine operation of machines in other industries. However not all machine operators were unskilled: in the cotton industry the weavers were skilled workers. In the other metallurgical industries and in the cotton, wool and paper industries, skilled workers accounted for about 25 percent of employment.

How strong is the relationship between the various categories of labour and the average wages in the sample industries? We can estimate some statistical relationships using the figures of Table 6.3. The first is the coefficient of determination between the wage structure (the average money wage in Dutch guilders) and women's share of the employment across industries. For 1938 this coefficient of determination is 0.28, and for 1960 it is 0.50, implying that 28 and 50 percent, respectively, of the differences in wage levels between industries can be statistically explained by differences in women's shares of employment in each industry. The higher the proportion of female labour, the lower the average wages in an industry. An even stronger negative association was found between the share of young workers and wage levels, with coefficients of determination of 0.51 and 0.62 for 1938 and 1960, respectively.

The average level of skilled workers in the workforce is linked much less strongly to the industrial wage structure. The coefficient of determination for 1960 is only 0.16. The influence is so slight because there were only small wage differences between skilled and medium-skilled workers (the largest group in industry) working within the industries. These differences were outweighed by the greater wage differentials between men and women and between men and young workers. The average weekly wages for skilled and unskilled workers in 1960 were 109 and 100 guilders, respectively.[7] Among the medium-skilled workers, wages ranged between a low of 92 guilders in the footwear industry and a high of 106 guilders in the machine knitting industry. With a coefficient of variation of

---

7 See also *Economisch-Statistische Berichten 1924* no. 432, 325–327, in which the differences in hourly wage rates for the categories of skilled, medium skilled, and unskilled workers are given in proportional terms: 100, 90 and 85, respectively. In no. 435 of the same publication, pp. 391–393, the proportions for the metallurgical industries in 1923 alone are given as 100, 87 and 76, respectively. In 1915 the proportions for the metallurgical industries were 100, 94 and 82, respectively. Thus there were increasing wage differences after the First World War.

only 0.03, the spread in the standard wages is very slight and much lower than the previously calculated spread in average wages. Thus the standard wages of a category of workers (unskilled, medium-skilled or skilled) are a poor indicator of differences in average wages between industries. The dominant influences come from the employment shares of women and young workers.

There might also have been a link between standard (contract) wage levels for skilled workers and levels of labour productivity per industry. Unfortunately no industry-by-industry data on contract wages is available for the inter-war period, but it is available for 1960. If we compare this with the cross industry labour productivity levels, we find however a very slight correlation between the variance in weekly earnings for skilled workers on weekly wage contracts and the variance in average value added: the coefficient of determination is 0.09.

If we measure the direct correlation between the share of women workers and the labour productivity per industry for 1938 and 1960, the coefficients of determination are 0.15 and 0.26, respectively. The correlation between the employment share of young workers and labour productivity yields values of 0.30 and 0.43. These are negative correlation coefficients, meaning that industries with an above-average value added per worker have lower than average proportions of women and young workers in their workforce.

We can conclude that it is mainly the composition of the workforce, and especially the number of young workers per industry, which is related to the cross-industry variation in labour productivity levels. This relationship became stronger after the Second World War. The increased correlation between average wage levels and labour productivity per industry (see Table 6.2) can therefore be attributed to this relationship. If we are to regard average wages as an indicator of human capital, we must do so in the sense that average wages are related to the shares of women and young workers in the workforce of each industry. These categories of workers had relatively low educational levels, were assigned low-status jobs, and were therefore paid less. Industries with a high percentage of low-status jobs did not have a high intensity of human capital. Their average money wages were relatively low, as was their labour productivity.

6.3. The share of non-production workers in the workforce

We can also make a breakdown of the workforce by distinguishing between manual workers, on the one hand, and administrative, technical and service personnel, on the other hand. For simplicity's sake the latter will be called non-production workers here. It is often said that the processes of mechanisation and the substitution of manual labour by machines were accompanied by a decline in the first category of labour in comparison to the second.[8] Unfortunately changes in definitions make it impossible to trace this process accurately in the Statistics of Production, since the descriptive distinction just mentioned was abolished in the Statistics of Production as from 1950. A distinction between workers with weekly wages and those with monthly salaries replaced it. Table 6.4

[8] Melman, *Dynamic*, 69–94.

shows the percentage shares, first of 'non-production workers' (those not directly involved in the production process) and then of those on monthly salaries, for several industries, over several years.

There are high percentages of non-production workers in the margarine and soap industries. This is mainly attributable to the large number of sales staff in these industries. Even after the Second World War, the proportion of non-production workers in these industries remained high. We also find relatively high percentages in the flourmills and in electrical engineering. The first is very capital intensive, and the second is knowledge-intensive (e.g. a company such as Philips had a research and development department at an early date). There were low percentages of non-production workers in the textile, leather and construction materials industries.

Table 6.4. Share of non-production workers (1921, 1938 and 1948) and monthly salaried staff (1950 and 1960) as percentage of the total employment

	1921	1938	1948	1950	1960
	Non-production workers			Monthly salaried personnel	
Brick		3	5	3	5
Roofing Tiles		6	8	6	9
Cotton	4	6	8	8	12
Wool	5	7	8	8	12
Calcium silicate		8	8	5	8
Machine knitting	6	8	10	6	10
Paper	5	8	10	12	17
Shipbuilding	7	8	12	11	17
Footwear	7	9	12	8	11
Leather		9	12	10	14
Cars and coachwork		9	17	12	21
Pottery		10	8	9	14
Wire	9	10	12	10	17
Ready-made clothing		12	13	9	12
Rubber	20	12	18	16	18
Sheet-metal working	7	13	12	12	18
Cocoa and choc.	12	15	24	17	21
Steel furniture		16	16	14	22
Mechanical engin.	14	17	20	19	24
Bicycles	20	21	17	7	14
Preserved food		21	19	14	18
Electrical engin.	24	20	28	27	30
Flour	18	23	28	23	27
Soap	24	36	36	30	40
Margarine		49	44	31	39
Average					
15 industries	13	16	19	15	20
25 industries		14	17	13	18

Source: CBS, *Statistics of Production*.

The cross-industry variation in shares of non-production workers remained very constant over time, just as we have seen with the shares of women and young workers. The coefficients of determination of the percentages of workers in the sample industries from year to year are about 0.90. This points to a constant composition of the workforce across all industries, a composition that was also influenced only slightly by the gradual growth in the number of non-production workers. Although this is not shown in the table, the increase in the proportion of non-production workers during the inter-war period occurred mainly in the 1930s; between 1921 and 1929 the proportion of workers remained constant in most industries.

The years 1921, 1938 and 1948 cannot be compared directly to the years 1950 and 1960. Therefore, we have calculated regression equations for the whole sample for each period, by defining the figure for each industry for the final year as the dependent variable and the value of the first year as the independent variable. The coefficient of regression then shows the average annual increase in the percentage of workers for the period concerned.

From 1921 to 1938, the proportion of non-production workers in the total workforce increased by 20 percent (not by 20 percentage points). From 1938 to 1948 the proportion grew by about 15 percent. Between 1950 and 1960 the category of non-workers increased by 30 percent. Over the whole period, 1921–1960, the proportion of non-production workers increased by approximately 80 percent, i.e. it almost doubled.[9]

For 1921, 1938, 1950 and 1960 we have sufficient observations to measure the correlation between the percentage share of the non-production workers and a number of other variables.

Table 6.5. Coefficients of determination between the share of non-production workers and the level of productivity (in current prices), the average money wage per worker, and the wage share per industry

	1921	1938	1960
Productivity	0.20	0.45	0.42
Average wage	0	0.10	0.26
Wage share	0	0.46	0.27

Sources: Tables 5.1, 6.1, 6.4 and Appendix A.

For 1938 and 1960 there is a reasonably strong connection between the proportion of non-production workers and the labour productivity per industry. In these years, industries with a relatively high proportion of non-production labourers also had higher levels of productivity.

9 Melman has calculated the following percentages of workers for British industry: 1907, 0.08; 1924, 0.12; 1930, 0.12; 1935, 0.13; 1948, 0.17 (Melman, *Dynamic*, 73). There are two periods of acceleration in the increase in workers, one around the time of the First World War and the other around the Second World War.

The relationship between the relative proportion of non-production workers and the average money wage per industry is much weaker, but does increase slightly over time. The increasing proportion of people on monthly salaries probably causes the gradual increase during this period, which meant that the influence of their wages on average wages was somewhat greater. However this assumes that the average wage for non-production workers was higher than for manual labourers.

The correlation between non-production workers and the wage share in value added (the total wage bill divided by the total value added) is negative. Industries with a high percentage of people on monthly salaries had a lower than average wage share. This indicates that the capital-intensive industries have relatively more non-production workers. This negative connection is strongest for 1938 and this suggests a movement toward capital-skill complementarity.[10]

This statistical analysis answers part of the question about the relationship between differences in average wages and labour productivity. The production processes specific to the industry determine both productivity of labour and average wages in an industry. This structure shapes the composition (and quality) of the employment offered, and thus the productivity of labour. Thus there is a segmented labour market, one in which the characteristics of a job (and the associated wage) determine the unequal labour market positions of workers in it.

6.4. Changes in wages and productivity per industry in the long term

Figure 6.1 compares the variation in the growth of real wages per industry to the growth in real labour productivity, based on the values given in Table 5.5. Each point represents a combination of these two variables for one of the industries in the sample. The figures for the increase in real labour productivity are taken directly from the table. Real wages have been calculated by dividing the numbers given in the column for average wages by the corresponding figures in the column for product prices. The resulting real product wage is related to particular price movements in that industry. It represents the real cost of the wage of a worker, i.e. in terms of the prices that industry can earn for its products.

The distribution shows a wide variation in the development of average labour productivity in the sample industries. In the car industry and in electrical engineering, labour productivity grew by a factor of 2.5 between 1938 and 1965. This contrasts with the negligible increase in productivity in the shipbuilding, cotton and soap industries. Real wages increased the most in industries with the fastest growth in real labour productivity. The calculated coefficient of correlation is $r = 0.60$ (without the two outlying values, $r = 0.80$). In a cross-sectional analysis of the Dutch economy at industry

10 See Hiscox, Factor mobility, 406. Studies on the U.S. economy suggest that in the first half of the 20th century the historic shift of industrial capital substituting labour came to an end with the move from assembly-line to continuous-process technology. The result being that there was need of more professional and skilled workers, for the management and operation of complex tasks.

Figure 6.1. Changes in real labour productivity and the average real product wage in 24 industries, levels of 1965 in comparison to 1938 (index numbers 1938 = 100)

Source: Table 5.5.

level, Kuipers and Kuper also found such a connection for the period 1951–1960.[11] The correlation is in part due to relative price movements between the industries in the sample. Because both money wages and labour productivity in current prices for each industry are divided by the same production price index, they tend to correlate to some extent. Nevertheless the calculated correlation is quite strong. The slope coefficient in the regression equation is about 0.45. This implies that in an industry in which the increase in labour productivity is ten percentage points above the average increase, the increase in real wages will be four to five percentage points above the average.

How can we explain the positive relationship between growth in real wages and in real labour productivity? Let's look first at the elasticity of substitution between labour and capital. If the elasticity of substitution is equal to 1, the increase in real wages will be equal to the percentage increase in labour productivity. If it is less than 1, an increase in real wages will be accompanied by a smaller rise in labour productivity. However what we see is that productivity increases are larger than the rise in real wages. My explanation is that although the factors of production can be substituted for one another, wage

11 Kuipers & Kuper, Wage formation, 492–493.

costs are just one cost category for companies, alongside the cost of capital and of raw materials and intermediate products. Management knows the prices of the various alternative inputs, and therefore selects a mix of inputs in accordance with the company strategy (for example cost minimisation or maximisation of sales). An increase in labour productivity or increasing mechanisation can be seen as the result of a wider process involving both economic and financial considerations.[12] However this does not necessarily mean that rising labour costs always leads management to economise on labour, resulting in higher labour productivity. Various studies have shown that the elasticity of substitution between labour and capital is not the same for all sorts of labour: unskilled labour competes more directly with capital than highly skilled labour, which can be even complementary to capital.[13]

We should also consider the effects of an increase in real wages on the composition of all the industries that make up an industrial sector. The international comparison in Chapter 4 suggested that high wages in an industrial sector force the under-performing industries within that sector to retrench or renew, both of which increase the average productivity of the sector. The causality in this case works in one direction only: higher wages lead to higher productivity.

Does this also work in reverse: can higher labour productivity in an industry lead to higher average wages for the employees? In other words, is there a wage premium to bargain over? To examine the relationship between changes in productivity and in wages, we have first to look at the comparative prices for labour on the labour market, using the changes in money wages over time for each industry given in Table 5.5. It can be seen that there is no statistical relationship between changes in nominal wages and real labour productivity. Both the regression coefficient and the coefficient of correlation in the equation relating the two variables have very low values ($b = 0.04$ and $r = 0.02$, respectively). Moreover, the spread of wage increases across industries is much smaller than the spread of labour productivity levels. Thus the change in money wages in an industry is not closely related to productivity growth. Similar results have been found for the United Kingdom and the United States over similar periods.[14] Apparently there is considerable homogeneity within the diverse segments of the labour market, due to the high mobility of labour or to agreements between agents or to government prescriptions (such as the principle of equal pay for equal work). If nominal wage increases in the industries had reflected the increase in labour productivity, the industrial wage structure as a whole would have changed radically within a few years, which did not happen.

Because the change in average money wages per industry has scarcely any correlation to changes in real labour productivity, there must by definition be a connection between the nominal wage costs per unit of product and the real output per unit of labour.

---

12 See, for example, Melman, *Dynamic*, 58.

13 Goldin & Katz, Origins; Broer & Jansen, Employment, 442; Hebbink, Employment by level, 397.

14 The outcomes for the period 1924–1963 are also similar. Salter also calculated a much lower coefficient of correlation (0.09) for British industry for 1924–1950 (Salter, *Productivity*, 115). The figure for the Netherlands for 1924–1950 is $r = -0.05$. Naturally this analysis can also be performed using growth rates rather than index figures. We have used index figures so that the results can be compared to Salter's findings. For the United States see Kendrick, *Postwar*, 114–119.

Figure 6.2. Changes in real labour productivity and unit wage costs in current prices in 24 industries, levels of 1965 in comparison to 1938 (index numbers 1938 = 100)

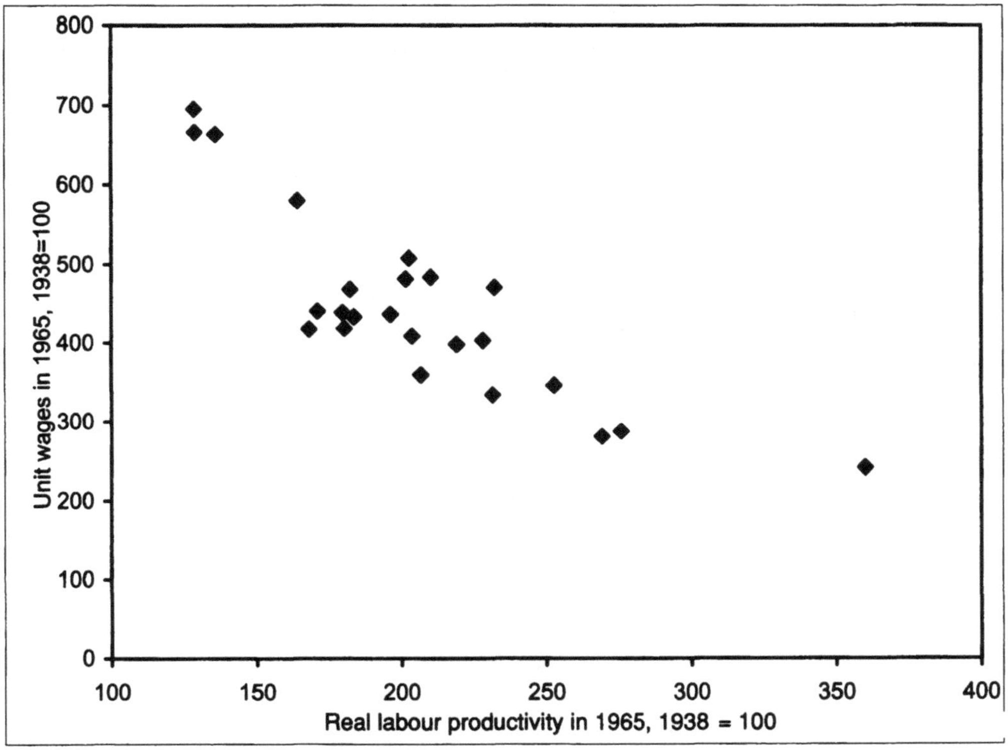

Source: Table 5.5.

Figure 6.2 shows the combinations of changes in nominal wage costs per unit of product and changes in the variance in labour productivity by industry.

There is a clear association between variances in the wage component of unit costs and changes in labour productivity. The spread of wage costs per unit of product is greater than the spread of wage costs. Manufacturing industries that achieved high increases in labour productivity were better able to reduce the wage costs per unit of product. Here productivity increases went hand in hand with a reduction in nominal wage costs per unit of product. The estimated relationship is strong in statistical terms: a coefficient of correlation of $r = -0.85$.[15] I conclude that the reduction in wage costs per unit of output made it possible to reduce relative product prices in industries that had high productivity increases.

---

15 Salter's analyses for 1924–1950 yield a regression equation of $Y = 272.4 - 0.67X$, $r = -0.89$ (Salter, *Productivity*, 116). The relationship for the corresponding period in the Netherlands is almost identical: $Y = 252.9 - 0.67X$ (Standard error = 0.07), $r = -0.93$.

6.5. Labour costs per industry

Not only do average wage costs differ from one industry to another, the total wage sum as a proportion of the value of production also varies across industries. When comparing industries at a given time, the size of this share can be regarded as an indicator of the labour intensity of an industry. In a dynamic analysis (between industries, or for industry as a whole), this ratio is an indicator of shifts in the relative importance of different categories of income (labour and capital). Both approaches are presented in this section.

The total wage sum can be calculated from wages and salaries and social security premiums as recorded in the Statistics of Production. For 1921–1950, this component is calculated by reverse extrapolating of the wages of 1950 using the indices of wages for each industry as shown in the Accident Statistics. Social security premiums are then added to this. In 1921 the rate was 3.6 percent of the wages paid, while in 1938 it was 5.1 percent.[16]

In an earlier publication the total sales value of production per industry for 1921, 1938, 1950 and 1965 is broken down into the percentage shares of inputs (raw materials and intermediate products), wage costs and the gross surplus, consisting of capital costs and profits.[17] The share of input costs in the total value of production gives an indication of the industry's place in the chain of production. This share can sometimes vary sharply over time within one industry – because of price fluctuations of raw materials. Because of such fluctuations the wage ratio also varies strongly. A sudden increase in the prices of raw materials will reduce the percentage share of wages and salaries, even if money wages have not changed. Therefore in the following overviews I will define the wage share as a percentage of gross value added, this is gross output minus the share of inputs. To provide an idea of the size of the cost categories, Table 6.6 provides an overview of all industries in the sample for 1938.

The wage sum in the total value of production varies markedly across the diverse industries. As a rule, this share is high in those industries where the value of the raw materials and intermediate inputs is low in relation to the quantity of labour employed. One would expect that the wage sum in the total value of production would be relatively slight in industries that are higher in the production chain, because all the previous stages of manufacture are included in the value of production as input costs.

The table shows that the input costs were high in the food and beverage and textile industries. Input costs were low in the construction materials industry. Continuous-process industries such as the rubber, soap and paper industries lie between these extremes. The position in the metallurgical industries varies strongly, with low input costs in electrical engineering and high input costs in the sheet-metal working and wire industries.

One would also expect that the share of wages in the total value added would be relatively low in industries that are relatively capital-intensive or machine-intensive, since more of the value added will be used for depreciation and the return on capital. The

[16] Van der Does, *Economische*, 231.

[17] De Jong, *Nederlandse industrie*, Appendix F.3.

Table 6.6. Components of the total value of production in 1938

	Input costs (1)	Wage costs (2)	Surplus (3)	Wage Share (2/(2+3))
Brick	16.2	63.4	20.4	75.7
Roofing tiles	20.5	52.2	27.3	65.7
Pottery	25.5	46.2	28.3	62.0
Electrical engineering	33.1	35.4	31.5	52.9
Calcium silicate	43.4	26.8	29.8	47.3
Footwear	44.5	36.3	19.2	65.4
Mechanical engineering	45.5	32.2	22.3	59.1
Steel furniture	47.8	35.9	16.3	68.8
Rubber	48.0	32.0	20.0	61.5
Machine knitting	48.4	31.4	20.2	60.9
Cars and coachwork	51.4	32.2	16.4	66.3
Paper	51.9	21.2	26.9	44.1
Bicycles	52.0	19.2	28.8	40.0
Shipbuilding	55.5	25.8	18.7	58.0
Soap	57.2	13.5	29.3	31.5
Sheet-metal working	59.2	26.7	14.1	65.4
Cotton	60.3	24.7	15.0	62.2
Wire	61.7	23.2	15.1	60.6
Wool	62.2	30.4	7.4	80.4
Ready-made clothing	64.4	25.8	9.8	72.3
Cocoa	66.7	18.1	15.2	54.4
Leather	70.2	17.6	12.2	59.1
Preserved food	70.4	17.4	12.2	58.8
Flour	89.2	2.8	8.0	25.9
Weighted average	56.5	26.4	17.1	60.6

Source: CBS, *Statistics of Production* for 1938.

wage share in the fourth column gives an impression of these relationships. There are wage shares of 60 percent or more for the construction materials, textiles and clothing industries, and in half of the metallurgical industries. There are relatively low wage shares in the food and beverage, soap, paper and electrical engineering industries.

To consider changes over time in the wage share for industry as a whole, the wage sum in the total value added (both in current prices) of the industries in the sample is calculated by compiling a weighted average wage per worker for the industry based on the nominal wages per worker across all the sample industries. By dividing this by the annual gross value added per worker for industry, we can calculate the annual wage share for industry as a whole. Figure 6.3 presents the long-term trend in the overall wage share.

During the inter-war period, the wage sum averaged around 60 percent of value added. One striking feature in this figure is the rapid rise in labour costs as a proportion of gross value added in 1931 and 1932. The early years of the depression saw a strong relative rise in labour costs. After the war, wages and premiums averaged about 10 percentage points less as a proportion of value added. Even before the German occupation

Figure 6.3. The share of the wage sum in industrial value added 1921–1965 (percentage)

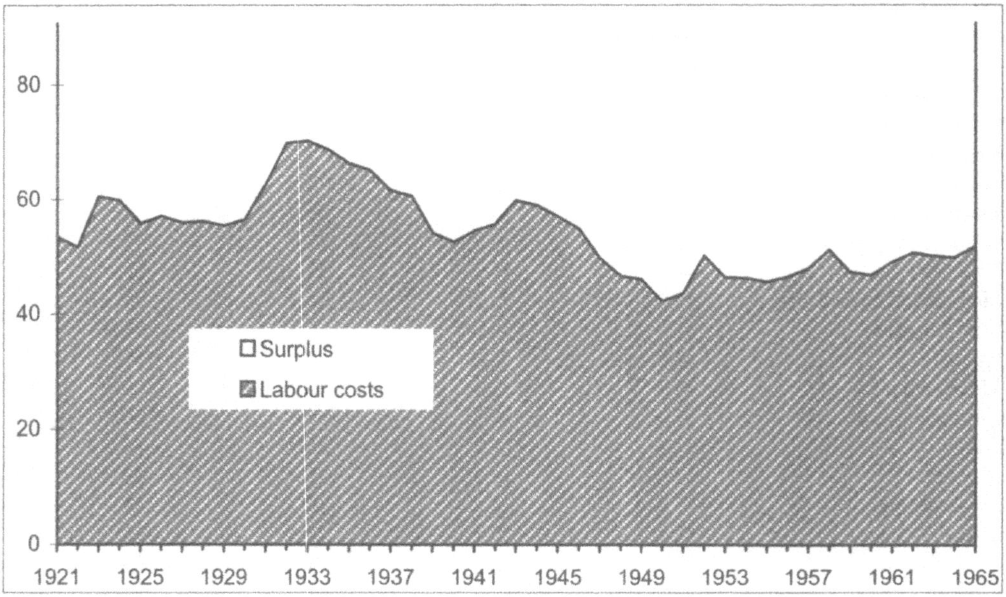

Sources: Appendices A and B.[18]

in 1940, the share of wages in industrial value added had begun to decline.[19] The following section will consider where these changes originated: in the numerator (labour costs), the denominator (gross value added) or in both.

6.6. Real product wages and real labour productivity between 1913 and 1965

Figure 6.4 shows the long-term changes in real product wages and real labour productivity. The real wage costs are calculated using the same production price index of indus-

18 The figures for 1944 and 1945 have been interpolated, but have no real significance since we do not have production figures for these years. In reality the wage share were probably higher than is indicated here.

19 But there were few people in the Netherlands at that time who perceived this. The Central Economic Plan for 1949, for example, said that Dutch wages were still high in comparison to other countries. However at the same time a report of the Economic Commission for Europe revealed that Dutch labour costs per unit of product in 1949, in comparison to the 1935–1938 period, had increased less than all other European countries except the United Kingdom (this was before the 1949 devaluation). See, for example, Roemers, Loonpeil, 908–910 and also the papers by Holtrop and Tinbergen that were published in the *Economisch-Statistische Berichten 1949*, no. 1699, 956–957, from which it appears that they considered low wages should be given top priority, so as to reduce costs and improve the balance of trade.

Figure 6.4. Real product wage per worker and real labour productivity in manufacturing, 1913–1965 (1938 = 100)

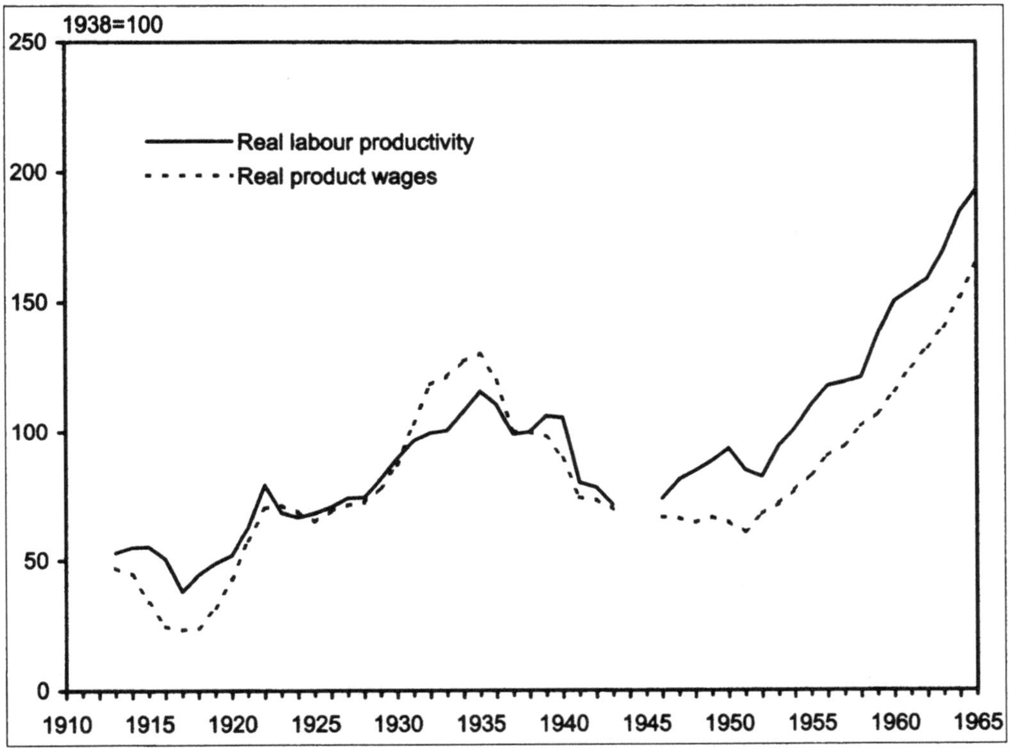

Sources: Appendices B and C.

trial products that was applied when calculating the real value added and productivity of the industries in the sample. This price index was compiled using prices that are relevant to the industry concerned, giving us a picture of long-term trends in the costs of labour inputs from 1913 to 1965, expressed in constant prices.

Over the long term there is a strong correlation between changes in real wages for industry as a whole and changes in real labour productivity. However if we look at the positions of the two curves, there is a clear difference between the period of the First World War, when labour productivity was higher, the 1930s, when it was lower, and the period after the Second World War, when it was higher.[20] These periods were also remarked on in the international comparisons of labour productivity, because of the exceptional developments in Dutch industry.

20 The productivity figures for 1913–1921 are estimated on the basis of recalculated data from Van der Schalk, *Wiskundig-statistische*. This is explained in De Jong, *Nederlandse Industrie*, Appendix E.2. Although these figures may well slightly underestimate actual changes in real productivity, they are preferred in this context because this series contains annual observations, whereas the Statistics of Production only allow us to make estimates for 1913, 1916 and 1919.

Clearly real wages fell very much behind productivity in the period between 1913 and 1920. Between 1920 and 1922 the relationship between wages and productivity returned to the relative proportions of 1913, although the real values of both had increased strongly. During the 1920s the two series follow parallel paths, with labour costs and productivity increasing at the same rate.

In the first half of the 1930s, real product wages rose more quickly than the labour productivity in the industries studied: wage costs in real terms were double the level in 1913 and 1921.[21] From 1935 onwards, both wage costs and labour productivity declined. After 1945, the index of real labour productivity increased rapidly, yet the decline in real wage costs that had emerged before and during the occupation continued until 1951. The figure clearly shows that real wage costs fell continuously between 1941 and 1951. Between 1946 and 1951 the indicator of real wage costs fell by an average of 0.7 percent per year, while productivity increased by an average of 5.9 percent per year. In 1951, labour costs in real terms were comparable to the level of 1921. Only after 1951 was there a turnaround – after sixteen years of decline – the index of real wage costs rose. From 1951 the two lines follow similar paths, which shows in the figure as a widening gap between real labour costs and real labour productivity in comparison to the index year (1938). This difference was locked in place in the 1950s and the first half of the 1960s, and provides a statistical explanation for the difference between the wage shares in the inter-war period and in the post-war period that were noted in the previous section.

The task remains to find an economic-political explanation for this phenomenon. It is obvious to suppose that the difference between wages and productivity was related to the policy of wage restraint that was in place after the Second World War. These policies are discussed briefly in Chapter 9. Most economic analyses of these guided wages policies have focused on their possible effects on the Dutch economy during the 1950s, but this figure shows that wage restraint in industry occurred mainly during the 1940s. During this decade economic and labour policies were very much controlled by the government, first during the German occupation and later under the first post-war administrations. During the 1950s, real wages did not grow more slowly than in the surrounding countries, but in parallel with them.[22] In this light, the most important achievement of the policies of the wage restraint during the 1950s can be seen to be the maintenance of the wage-productivity gap that had emerged during the period of strong government control before 1950.

---

21 This is confirmed by the high relative wages in the Netherlands, as we have seen in the international comparisons in section 4.3. Drukker has also estimated changes in real labour costs during the 1930s, in his analysis of the persistence of the Great Depression in the Netherlands. He showed that real wages in industry in the 1930s remained above those of the late 1920s, despite the decline that began in 1933. However he adjusted for inflation using the price index of the net national product, rather than an index of the prices of industrial products. The result is that the increase in real wage rates that he calculates is quite moderate. See Drukker, *Waarom*, 303–304. See also Schrage, Nijhoff & Wielsma, Inkomensontwikkeling.

22 Van Ark & De Jong, Accounting, 219.

6.7. Conclusions

Over the long term, and for industry as a whole, there is a fairly strong connection between trends in real wages and real labour productivity. Nominal wages increased in all industrial sectors at more or less the same rate. The rate of growth was determined by the overall productivity growth in all industries. The effect of an overall wage rise for a particular industry depends on productivity growth within that industry. If productivity increases faster than nominal wages, wage costs per unit of output will decline, bringing down total costs. This will lead to falling prices in comparison to the average price level.

In the case of the Netherlands the homogeneity in the labour market may have been strengthened by the wage setting policies that were in place in the 1940s and 1950s, and by specific agreements between employers and employees to maintain a stable wage structure. In addition to moderating wage increases, the managed wage policies had a second objective of reducing wage differentials.[23] However it is not clear to what extent the decline in wage differentials can be attributed these policies. In the first place, wage differentials between industries were not exceptionally high before the Second World War. We have seen that differences in average wages in the 1950s were not essentially different to those in the 1920s, but did differ from those in the 1930s. In the second place, similar analyses of industry in the United States and the United Kingdom have found scarcely any demonstrable connection between growth in average nominal wages and real labour productivity between industries. This does show that the fairly constant wage structure in the Netherlands was not an exceptionally Dutch phenomenon.

Within the industries considered here, the highest average wage levels were found in industries characterised by relatively low proportions of women and young workers in the workforce. Because the average wages for women and young workers were much lower than adult male wages, this emerges as the most important factor in explaining the industrial wage structure.

---

23 Weststrate, *Economic*, 165–174.

Chapter 7: Capital indicators and productivity measurement

This chapter focuses on the development of the stock of capital goods in Dutch industry and on the relationship that can be identified between capital and the productivity of labour. The quality of the indicators introduced here as a proxy measure for the volume of capital installed will be extensively discussed. Finally the effects of mechanisation and technological advance on changes in labour productivity in the sample industries will be considered.

The starting point is the relationship between capital intensity and labour productivity in neo-classical theory. Levels and growth rates of labour productivity depend on the capital intensity (the quantity of capital per unit of labour), and the state of technology and direction of technical progress. The mechanisation of production processes leads to a reduction in the quantity of labour per unit of product. The extent to which this occurs is determined by changes in the relative costs of labour and machines, by the elasticity of substitution between labour and capital and by technological developments. Let's ignore the latter for the moment. In the case capital is substituted for labour in the production process (f.i. because the relative costs of labour increase in comparison to capital) capital intensity will increase, implying that the productivity of labour also will increase. Theoretically one can identify all the different combinations of capital and labour producing the same volume of output. This can be shown in a graph as a shift along the isoquant representing all the different combinations of labour and capital producing the same volume of output. However, in the case of technological progress, it becomes possible to produce more with the same intensity of capital per unit of labour. In that case the curve of the production function, showing the relationship between labour productivity and capital intensity shifts outwards.

Moreover, technological progress will generally alter the capital intensity even where the relative costs of capital and labour have not changed. For example, existing manufacturing systems may be replaced with more advanced technology that requires more capital per unit of labour. Such innovations in the installed machinery and processes used in production can be regarded as labour saving. But there may also be technical progress that is capital-saving: in that case the capital intensity will decline, even if the relative prices of the factors of production are constant. In the following sections I will try to show that the electrification of production processes in the sample industries in the first half of the twentieth century provides an example of capital-saving technological progress.

7.1. The productivity paradox

During much of the twentieth century, industrial production processes evolved through labour-saving mechanisation and, later, automation. Machines replaced manual labour, became faster and grew in capacity. A central characteristic of all these processes is that the manual work required from workers, as well as part of the intellectual work, has, in relative terms, declined.[1]

What is the empirical connection between new investments in capital, technological progress and the increase in labour productivity? For example, do the statistics reveal the effects of innovations in production processes? We assume here that techniques used in production can change for two main reasons. In the first place, because of improved technical knowledge and technological progress, and, in the second place, because of changes in the relative prices of machines and labour, and also relative prices of other inputs such as raw materials. When the relative prices of labour and capital change, companies should in theory regard their previous investments in already out-of-date production processes as 'sunk costs' and invest in new combinations of labour and capital. In practice, however, innovations are introduced step-by-step, with the old and new techniques being used next to one another. Thus not all companies in a particular industry will always use 'best-practice' production techniques. It follows that average labour productivity in all companies within an industry, or between industries, is not the same: there will be certain spread in labour productivity levels even within an industry.[2]

According to this line of thought, one would not expect to observe a direct relationship between technical innovations and their effects on productivity levels. Either in terms of the phasing of significant technical breakthroughs, or in terms of productivity effects from sudden increases in capital intensity. The process takes place gradually. Paul David has called attention to the 'productivity paradox' in economic history: the delay between the introduction of large innovations and the resulting improvements in productivity. It is a historical fact that technological innovations such as the steam engine, the dynamo and the computer took a long time before their effects were visible in the productivity statistics. Because new and old technical systems exist side by side, or one above the other in the production chain, the capital coefficient (the installed capital per unit of output) may even be temporarily higher. This implies that the possible effect of new techniques and of capital savings on productivity levels will only become visible after some delay.[3]

Moreover there are many ways to economise on labour that do not necessarily entail large changes in the mechanisation of the production process or in the capital coeffi-

---

1 For a general discussion on mechanisation during the inter-war period see Jerome, *Mechanisation*, 43.

2 Salter, *Productivity*, 5.

3 David, Dynamo, 357. In this article David used electrification during the first decades of the twentieth century and the steam revolution of the eighteenth and nineteenth centuries as examples to illustrate the question of the 'productivity paradox', which Solow had raised. Solow asked to what extent the introduction of the computer had improved productivity. "We see the computers everywhere but in the productivity statistics".

cient. Better organisation of work, improvements in training and in workers' conditions, the standardisation of production and using better raw materials and intermediate products, as well as shorter working hours, can all increase productivity.[4] Moreover these improvements have a cyclic character in some respects, since each new system of production is gradually made more efficient by a process of 'learning by doing'.[5] Such developments can only be quantified with great difficulty. One exception to this is external shocks, such as the widely implemented shortening of the working day in Western Europe around 1920, which forced companies to respond rapidly to a new situation.[6]

Rosenberg has claimed that factor substitution and technical development, which are clearly differentiated in the traditional neo-classical analysis, cannot be separated in principle. In his opinion, much of the *research and development*-effort, particularly in smaller companies, does not focus on fundamental research, but on obtaining information about factor substitution. The reason for this is that individual companies are not so much interested in knowing all available technological options, since these are not all used in the actual production processes anyway. It would be much too expensive to obtain complete information about all options. Rather, changes in the relative prices of factors of production lead to a process of *engineering* and *experimentation* aimed at obtaining precise technical information about new combinations of inputs in the production process.[7] If we accept this reasoning, many *R&D* activities focus on reducing total costs and improving and/or modifying the production process. Thus there is more stress on development than on research. This is a process of small steps and therefore of moderate improvements in productivity. Since these processes also move at different rates in the various industries, the long-term increase in aggregate productivity will be gradual.

7.2. Mechanisation, substitution and capital savings

Statistics of the stock of capital goods in the Netherlands were established only very recently. To compile such statistics, one has to rely on investment data over many years. Although the CBS has data series on investment from 1921 onwards, the estimates based on this data are at such a high level of aggregation that they are not directly applicable to industrial sectors, and certainly not to the industries in our sample.[8]

---

4 See also Fabricant, *Employment*, 25: "... revisions of plant layout; improvements in equipment, notably increases in the size of machines; accelerated speed of operation; more precise control devices; and less susceptibility to breakdown ... air conditioning, lighting, elimination of disturbing pillars and other refinements in factory building and design ... have contributed as much to reducing unit labor requirements as has the growth in the physical stock of productive instruments."

5 Maddison, *Phases*, 102–109.

6 Heerma van Voss, *Achturendag*.

7 Rosenberg, *Exploring*, 14. See also Salter, *Productivity*, 24.

8 Den Hartog & Tjan, Investeringen. As part of the Reconstruction of the National Accounts project, estimates have now been made for capital formation in infrastructure and in the companies

Tinbergen made the first estimate of the relationship between the quantity of capital and changes in productivity in Dutch industry. In an article published in 1932, he tried to establish a statistical connection between capital formation and the increase in capital intensity.[9] The indicators that Tinbergen used to estimate capital formation in industry were variables such as issues of new industrial shares, calls for tenders to build factories, and the physical volume of machines produced and imported. His indicator for the increase in capital intensity was the annual rate of growth in the primary power of the installed machinery per worker, which he calculated from the Statistics of Production. He concluded that, on the basis of his figures, the rate of rationalisation had accelerated since the First World War.[10] Parallel to this, Tinbergen demonstrated that other indicators also point to increasing capital intensity in the 1920s. For example, the amount of labour used per unit of raw material fell steadily.

In Chapter 4 we have seen that in many studies the primary horsepower of engines and motors installed to drive machinery is used as the main direct indicator of the stock of capital goods.[11] Engines and motors provide sources of heat, drive other machines and transport systems, and thus provide a direct indication of the elementary production processes in an industry. The primary horsepower per worker is therefore a very useful indicator for the capital intensity. From the data available to me, I calculated an increase of the installed primary horsepower per worker of 26 percent between 1921 to 1930 (between 1922 and 1930 it was a mere 13 percent). In the same period labour productivity for industry as a whole increased by 36 percent. On the basis of these figures, I can only conclude that just part of the increased labour productivity in this period can be explained by the increased intensity of capital. On the basis of similar calculations, Van Zanden and Griffiths concluded that the growth of capital only partially explains the improvement in labour productivity in these years, and that industrial investments were mainly capital broadening than capital deepening.[12] This implies that labour productivity growth can be located mainly in the residual factors in the production function: improvements in the quality of machines, economies of scale and the shift of employment to more productive sectors.[13] Thus the 1920s saw a moderate rise in the capital intensity of industry, combined with a much larger rise in labour productivity.

---

sector for the period 1800–1913. See Groote, *Kapitaalvorming* and Albers, *Machinery*. On the basis of the estimate of the stock of capital goods in 1913, Groote, Albers and de Jong (1996) made a new estimate for the twentieth century.

9 Tinbergen, Kapitaalvorming, 12ff.

10 Tinbergen defined rationalisation here simply as an improvement in methods of production, through which more profit can be achieved per unit of raw material input, and less labour is used per unit of raw material input. See Tinbergen, Kapitaalvorming, 14.

11 Broadberry, *Productivity*, 108–109; Broadberry & Fremdling, Comparative, 412 and Van Zanden & Griffiths, *Economische*, 118.

12 Van Zanden and Griffiths have also tried to use the Statistics of Production to get a picture of changes in capital intensity and labour productivity during the 1920s. For the somewhat shorter period of 1924–1929, they calculated a productivity growth of 16.5% and growth in the primary horsepower per worker of 7.4%. See Van Zanden & Griffiths, *Econom*ic, 118.

13 In our own sample (see Chapter 5), we found that these had scarcely any influence.

Does this mean that capital, as a factor of production, did not play any important role in the rapid growth in labour productivity during the inter-war period? I have already noted that the technological changes in industry in these years led to the more efficient use of capital goods, so that primary horsepower reveals only part of the contribution made by capital.[14] Thus there may have been capital deepening in the 1920s, despite Van Zanden and Griffiths' findings, but this is not reflected in the figures for primary horsepower or the number of machines, because horsepower and machines could be employed more efficiently.[15]

Another indication of the capital deepening nature of mechanisation is the pattern of energy consumption. Between 1921 and 1929, the energy consumption per unit of labour in industry increased by 3.8 percent per year. However the energy consumption per unit of product and per horsepower of machinery fell gradually.[16] This points to a process of substitution of capital for labour accompanied by greater efficiency in generating and transmitting power. It has been suggested that there was a radical leap in energy efficiency in the Netherlands in the second decade of the 20th century.[17] Perhaps the rapid progress of electrification contributed substantially to the exceptional growth in productivity of the 1920s and early 1930s. And it may be that we can see an example here of what is known in the literature as the 'productivity paradox'.[18]

---

14 Thorp (Horsepower, 380) claims that the statistics for primary horsepower under-estimate the growth in the actual installed capacity. A.J. Field has pointed out that researchers often use the terms capital and machines indiscriminately, which implicitly makes them synonyms. But that is incorrect: machines are only part of the total quantity of capital, is not representative, and may vary strongly over time (Field, Unimportance, 378–379).

15 De Jong and Albers, Industriële, 475–476.

16 CBS, *Maandschrift 1936*, 1335.

17 Gales, Mijnbouw, 13–35. Schot et al, *Techniek*, Vol. 2.

18 Compare this to the situation between the wars in the United Kingdom. There was a considerable increase in production and productivity during the inter-war period in the British economy: "... Britain's economic performance was by no means as black as often painted ..." (Aldcroft, Economic, 35.) In the 1920s, and especially in the 1930s, the growth trend was higher than in the thirty previous years. Aldcroft says that this higher rate of growth could hardly be due to more investments, since the investment rates in the United Kingdom were not exceptional high when compared either to previous periods or to those in other countries. He suggests that the causes for the declining capital coefficient in this period were, first, a shift of investments to higher growth sectors; second, technical improvements which entailed little extra capital such as the rationalisation of production methods; and third, that replacement investments increasingly embodied new technologies. The existing stock of capital goods was better utilised, through the more efficient use of raw materials and other inputs, the rapid introduction of the electric motor, and by external rationalisation by means of the standardisation of components and products. Once again we see a low marginal capital coefficient in such cases: a combination of low investments and a high level of output (for a treatment of this paradox, see Matthews, Feinstein & Odling-Smee, *British*, 382–385).

7.3. Electrification as the embodiment of a new system of production

In the literature on American industrialisation, the significance of mechanisation for the improved labour productivity during the first half of the twentieth century has been related to electrification. New production processes that relied heavily on the use of electricity accompanied technological progress in industry. From the turn of the nineteenth to the twentieth century, the United States saw a rapid transformation from steam to electricity as the primary source of energy in industry.[19] The substitution not only reduced the quantity of energy used per machine; it was accompanied by more efficient ways of organising factories. As a result, output growth was higher than the growth of inputs, such as labour and raw materials, including energy.[20] The shift was also clearly different in character to the shift from waterpower to steam, which had occurred in the United States in the mid-nineteenth century. The steam revolution was not accompanied by fundamentally different methods of energy transmission or by more efficient factory organisation. In the United States the 1910–1920 period seems to have been crucial in this process: from this period onwards, the power consumption per unit of gross national product declined steadily.[21]

The most important effect of the electrification of production processes, occurred through a change in the way machinery was powered. When using steam power, the machines in a factory would generally be powered by one, or sometimes several, steam engines, which drove all the machines and tools in the factory through a system of axles, belts and gears. Electrification made it possible to switch to small electric motors driving one machine (the 'unit drive' system). This change had major effects on the production process. Citing Sonenblum: "Unit drive made fundamental contributions to a more efficient organisation of manufacturing production by allowing a more effective use of space in the factory, by speeding up the movement of materials and parts, by reducing the time required between successive production steps, and enhancing the ability of workers and machines to specialise in particular tasks."[22] Because the system of power transmission was no longer the critical factor in determining factory layout, there was more flexibility in designing and organising factories. In the long term this led to capital savings, for instance because factories did not need to be so sturdily constructed.[23] Maintenance was also simpler and cheaper, because it no longer entailed stopping the whole drive system.[24] Rosenberg describes this characteristic as 'fractionalised power':

---

19 See Du Boff, Electrification; Sonenblum, Electrification.

20 Devine, Electrified, 21.

21 See Schurr & Netschert, *Energy*, 157–167, 170–171. Before 1920, the primary horsepower per worker grew faster than labour productivity, and from 1920 on the two grew in parallel. The authors describe this as a 'transition to a new basic relationship between energy and national product' (p. 164). However, as has already been noted, the influence of such innovations only appears in productivity figures after a long delay (David, Dynamo, 355–361).

22 Sonenblum, Electricity, 292.

23 Byatt, *British*, 85.

24 David, Dynamo, 358.

power was produced in small units, and no excess capacity in generation was required. This flexibility led to an integrated system of production consisting of interlinked machines. "Once the basic technology of generating electric power through the burning of fossil fuels had been introduced at the beginning of the twentieth century, it set the stage for several decades of minor plant improvements."[25] This 'mechanisation of transfer' resulted in better ways of organising labour, which directly and indirectly boosted the long-term growth in productivity.[26]

The transition from steam power to electricity was gradual, and proceeded at different rates in different countries. In relation to these developments, Devine has shown that companies in the United States were interested mainly in cutting the so-called indirect costs, i.e. in savings that did not result from lower energy costs (in many companies the fuel bills were only a fraction of total costs), but rather from better organisation and management of the production process. Electricity was seen primarily as a factor that could improve the overall efficiency of the production process.[27]

In the case of the United Kingdom, Byatt has also pointed to the potential indirect benefits of electrification for British companies, particularly in relation to modernisation: "There is some justice in the comment that it was the state of buildings and layout rather than the age of the machine tools that contributed to the allegedly high costs of British industry".[28] Thus the advantages of electrification in the United Kingdom were again not to be measured only in lower energy costs. Yet British entrepreneurs, in contrast to the Americans, focused mainly on the possible direct cost savings. They saw only small differences between electricity and the existing steam technologies, with the result that this innovation was implemented only slowly in several industries.[29]

Sonenblum calculated that in American manufacturing during the 1920s, productivity growth of 5 percent per year was accompanied by a 2 percent per annum decline in the quantity of energy used to drive machinery. The combined usage of labour and capital declined, while energy use rose faster than capital use, which rose only moderately. "The magnitude of the increase in the ratio of electricity to capital growth rates reflects the fact that the organisational-technological changes that so strongly boosted productivity

---

25 Rosenberg, *Exploring*, 15.

26 Von Tunzelmann, *Technology*, 232; Rosenberg, *Inside*, 177.

27 Devine, Electrified, 30 and 36–38.

28 Byatt, *British*, 86.

29 According to Byatt there was little profit to be made from the lower costs: higher production offered greater opportunities for boosting profits. In the 1910s, demand in the United Kingdom grew only slowly, so there was little incentive for technological changes: "Hence the return to electrification was relatively slower than in countries with faster economic growth". The author seems reluctant to criticise the behaviour of British entrepreneurs. He says that practical electric motors were invented too late to make a difference in the textile industry, because the 'cotton boom' had already happened, in 1905–1908. Electrification was a long time coming in this industry. However he does not mention that British spinners during and after the First World War had very high costs of production, and lost markets as a result (the Netherlands, for example) and missed out on further economies of scale. Byatt, *British*, 91, 213–216.

required relatively small growth in capital but a very rapid increase in electrified production techniques".[30]

From this picture it appears that we can regard the rate of electrification in industries as an indicator of the degree of technical and technological change in their production infrastructure, and can relate this to changes in productivity. The following sections will examine whether a statistical relationship between the two variables can be found for Dutch industry.

7.4. Mechanisation in Dutch industry, 1921–1960

The Statistics of Production report the total primary horsepower of powered machinery for every year to 1960 for all of the industries considered here. The figures are subdivided into steam engines and steam turbines, electric motors, and gas, diesel and petrol motors. The electric motors are again subdivided according to the source of energy: those using only purchased power, using only power from the factory's own generators, and alternately powered by both sources. Steam engines and electric motors are the most important sources of energy in all industries. Gas diesel and petrol motors account for only a fraction of the total installed horsepower. The CBS has avoided double-counting in the figure for total installed horsepower by not counting electric motors powered by the factory's own power (which they call 'secondary' electric motors). This is power that has already been counted, along with the steam engines that drive the generators used for internal power production.

Table 7.1 shows the installed primary horsepower per worker for each industry for 1921, 1938 and 1960. The average capacity per worker is especially high in the paper, flour and calcium silicate industries. Shipbuilding, and the leather, rubber, cotton, and wire industries, are also well above the average. There are low values in the ready-made clothing, machine knitting, footwear, bicycle and car industries. The manufacture and assembly of these products requires relatively little use of mechanical energy. In general terms, the intensity is high in industries that use raw materials that are in their original state and that can be processed easily in large quantities. There is a middle group of industries, those lying between rubber and roofing tiles in the table, which includes those that make less easily worked products in bulk and the 'heavy' assembly industries. There are low intensities in the industries further up the production chain. These industries, producing goods such as bicycles, footwear, machine knitting and ready-made clothing, buy a higher portion of their inputs as intermediate products.[31]

---

30 Sonenblum, Electricity, 298.

31 For another extensive overview of horsepower intensities in Dutch industry, see the ***Bedrijfstelling*** (Company Survey) of 1930. This identifies several other capital-intensive industries, such as the blast furnaces (27.7 horsepower per worker in1930), the cement industry (27.7), and edible oil factories (7.4). In these statistics the cotton industry is divided into cotton spinning and cotton weaving, with the former being relatively capital intensive (6.5 horsepower per worker). Although the classification of industries in the Statistics of Production does not entirely match that in the

Table 7.1. Installed capacity of powered machinery per worker in 25 industries, 1921, 1938 and 1960 (hp per worker and growth rates)

	1921	1938	1960	1921–38	1938–60
	Horsepower per worker			Rate of growth	
Paper	13.2	21.8	24.3	3.0	0.5
Flour	7.5	11.8	16.6	2.7	1.6
Calcium silicate		6.7	11.0		2.3
Margarine	3.4	6.5	5.7	8.2	- 0.6
Leather		4.7	8.9		2.9
Rubber	3.5	4.7	5.2	1.7	0.5
Cotton	2.8	4.6	4.6	3.0	0.0
Wire	3.6	4.1	5.9	0.8	1.7
Shipbuilding	2.2	3.8	6.3	3.2	2.3
Cocoa and choc.	1.5	3.5	5.6	5.1	2.2
Brick		3.0	6.0		3.2
Mechanical engin.	1.6	2.8	3.8	3.3	1.4
Wool	2.6	2.8	3.8	0.4	1.4
Roofing tiles		2.3	5.2		3.8
Soap	0.9	2.0	3.0	4.8	1.9
Pottery		1.7	3.4		3.3
Sheet metal work	1.2	1.7	2.6	2.1	2.0
Electrical engin.	1.2	1.7	2.4	2.1	1.6
Bicycles	0.7	1.7	1.8	5.4	0.3
Steel furniture		1.4	2.3		2.3
Preserved food		1.1	2.5		3.8
Cars and coachwork		0.8	2.1		4.5
Footwear	0.6	0.6	0.9	0	1.9
Machine knitting	0.3	0.5	1.0	3.1	3.2
Ready-made clothing		0.2	0.4		3.2
Weighted average	1.6	2.7	3.7	3.1	1.7

Source: Appendix A

The last two columns of Table 7.1 show the annual rates of growth in installed horsepower per worker over the periods 1921–1938 and 1938–1960. The average growth in machine intensity in the industries shown between 1921 and 1938 was 3.1 percent, with above-average growth in the margarine, cocoa, soap, and bicycle industries. There are very low growth rates in the wire, wool and footwear industries. In the period 1938–60, there is high growth in the construction materials, machine knitting, ready-made clothing, and preserved food and car industries. However most of these industries were only included in the statistics during the 1930s. Although the machine intensity in these industries grew by between three and four percent between 1938 and 1960, the average growth in machine intensity in the sample industries was just 1.7 percent per year. In most of the industries, the growth in the second period was lower than in the first.

Company Survey 1930, a comparison of the two shows that the figures differ little. The figures in the one-off survey of 1930 lie between those given in the industrial statistics for 1921 and 1938.

7.5. Measuring electrification in the Netherlands

The electrification ratio, which is electrical power as a proportion of installed power, will serve as an indicator to measure the increase in the rate of electrification. More accurately defined, the electrification ratio is the electrical power in comparison to the total productive power in the companies. The total productive power is defined as all power minus the power of electric motors driven by internally generated electricity (for example by steam engines), thus eliminating double counting.

Electrical power is counted as the sum of the electric motors driven by purchased electricity and by a factory's own generators. In a 1929 article, Thorp indicated that the statistics on installed power might have been distorted by the shift from steam power to purchased electricity. In the first place, a production plant that initially generated electricity would internally record the capacity of the 'prime-movers' (the steam engines and/or turbines) and not the installed power of the electric motors they drive. If electric motors were sometimes driven using purchased electricity, the installed power of these electric motors would also be recorded. However there is a big difference between the electrical capacity of steam engines and of electric motors. The power of steam engines is often the maximum they can supply, whereas electric motors can, temporarily, provide more power than the stated maximum capacity.[32] In the second place, where a factory shifts from central sources of energy with mechanical transmission to electricity, the improved transmission means that less power is required to do the same amount of work. In the third place, if electric motors are driven by internally generated electricity, the combined capacity of the electric motors will very probably be greater than that of the steam engines, because not all motors will be running at the same time. Calculations indicate that on average, for every 100 horsepower of electric motors driven by internally generated electricity, the available steam capacity was 70 to 75 horsepower.[33] If a factory switches from internally generated electricity to purchased electricity, the capacity recorded will rise, without any actual change in the power of the electric motors that are used, simply because the capacity of the electric motors is now being recorded, rather than the capacity of the steam engines.

As electrification proceeded, the first two of these effects would reduce the recorded amount of installed power, provided the effective power remained the same. Both processes would involve capital savings. The third effect is more statistical in nature: a shift to external sources of electricity means that different *prime movers* are counted, with different energy efficiency.

To express the power of the electric motors in a common indicator, the motors that are driven by internally generated electricity are multiplied by a factor of 0.72. The assumption is that about 72 horsepower of steam power back each 100 horsepower of internally supplied electric motors. This corrects for the statistical distortions that arise during a gradual transition from steam engines to purchased electricity. The capacity of

---

32 Thorp, Horsepower, 380. This means, that the statistics for primary horsepower under-estimate the real rise in installed capacity.

33 Jerome, *Mechanization*, 152.

Table 7.2. Electrification ratios, 1919–1960 (electrical power as a percentage of total power)

	1919/21	1930	1940	1950	1960
Paper	48	59	63	52	81
Flour		55	68	90	
Calcium silicate			53	52	64
Margarine	57	80	82		
Leather	54	58	77	93	
Rubber	65		88	99	99
Cotton	37	54	62	74	
Wire	58	72	92	99	100
Shipbuilding	86	94	94	90	96
Cocoa and choc.	83	93	94	98	98
Brick			61	73	82
Mechanical engin.	81	96	95	98	98
Wool	48	67	85	92	
Roofing tiles			73	84	92
Soap	65	84	94	97	
Pottery			75	84	90
Sheet metal work	86	88	90	94	98
Electrical engin.	95	100	93	91	
Bicycles	69	88	89	100	100
Steel furniture			98	99	100
Preserved food			81	96	99
Cars and coachwork				99	99
Footwear	30	63	87	96	
Machine knitting	48	68	88	96	
Ready-made clothing		89	91	95	
Total	59	72	78	84	92

Sources: CBS, *Statistics of Production* and Appendix A.

the electric motors that are partially powered by purchased electricity and partially by internally generated electricity has been divided equally over the two categories of electric motors. Table 7.2 shows the resulting electrification ratios for the sample industries for the years 1921, 1930, 1940, 1950 and 1960.

The totals at the bottom row point to a very rapid rise in the electrification ratio: thirteen percentage points between 1919/21 and 1930. In the three following decades the electrification ratio rose by twenty percentage points. The greatest increase took place during the 1920s. There was also a considerable increase in the 1950s, even though the variable was approaching a natural ceiling. By 1960 many industries were fully electrified: only the paper, calcium silicate and brick industries still had electrification ratios of less than ninety percent. Metalworking industries such as the electrical engineering, shipbuilding, mechanical engineering and sheet-metal work were among the first industries to electrify, and they all retained their lead over the course of the years.

Figure 7.1. Electrification ratios in manufacturing in the United States, the United Kingdom and the Netherlands, 1900–1960

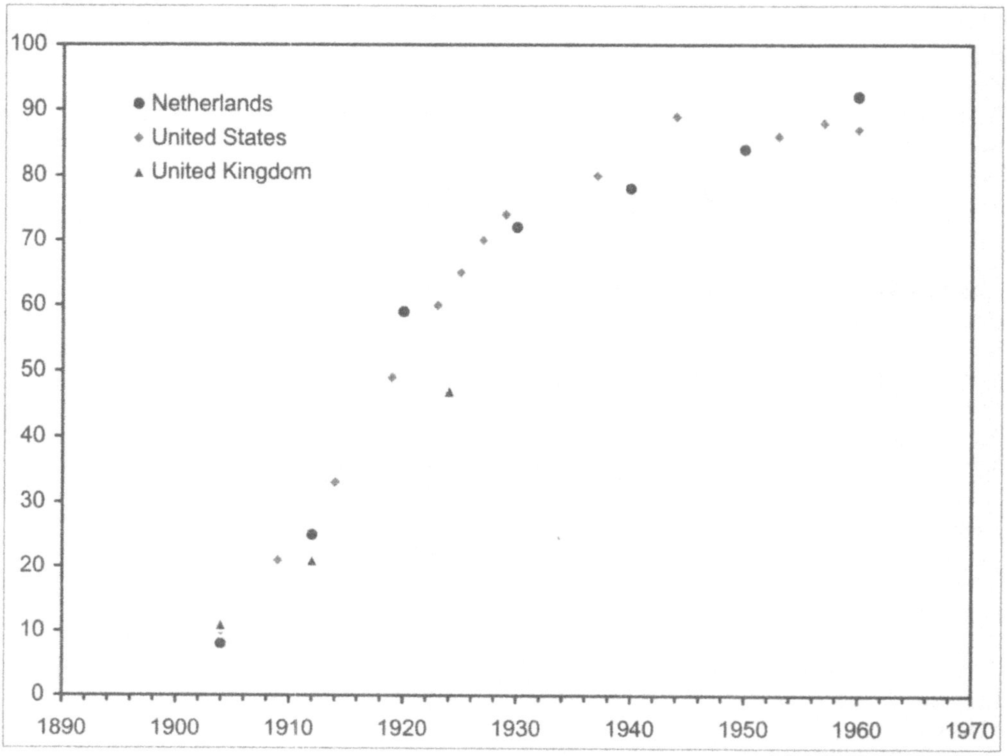

Sources: Netherlands: Table 7.2. U.S.: Jerome, *Mechanization*, 251 and Schurr, *Electricity*, 394.
U.K.: Byatt, *British*, 77.

Figure 7.1 compares the trend in the electrification ratio in Dutch industry to those in the United States and the United Kingdom (until 1924). The figures for these two countries have been corrected for statistical distortions in the same way as the Dutch figures. The development Figure 7.1 shows has the typical form of a diffusion curve. The s-shape of the curve indicates a phase in which the process of diffusion was clearly accelerating (until 1920); a phase in which the acceleration rate became less but the growth remained rapid (to 1930); and then a phase in which the electrification ratio increased more slowly, taking over three decades to grow from 70 percent to more than 90 percent.

One striking feature is that the introduction and speed of diffusion in the Dutch industries we have examined are in line with the progress of electrification in the United States. However the three observations from the United Kingdom shows that this process was not universal. As has already been noted in the literature, electrification in the UK lagged behind the other two countries. Byatt has calculated the electrification ratio in British industry for 1924 at 47 percent. In the United States and the Netherlands the ratio was at least ten percentage points higher.

Even greater international differences emerge if the electrification ratio is broken down by industrial branche. In 1924 the highest British electrification ratios were in mechanical engineering and shipbuilding (more than 80 percent), and in the food and chemicals sectors (about 60 percent). These values are comparable to those in the Netherlands (see Table 7.2). Electrification ratios in the British textile and iron and steel industries in 1924 were low, at 20 and 40 percent respectively. In the Netherlands at that time, the electrification ratio in the textile sector was already more than 40 percent, while in foundries and the sheet-metal work and wire industries it was more than 60 percent. Thus the British were lagging behind in these sectors.[34] The differences between the electrification ratios across the different sectors were much less extreme in the Netherlands than in the United Kingdom.

The picture that emerges is that electrification in the Netherlands took off between 1910 and 1930 over the whole range of industries and at a speed that equalled that in American manufacturing.

7.6. Capital indicators in Dutch industry between 1913 and 1938

The following sections will compare the available indicators of the capital employed in Dutch industry to one another, and to the indicators used above: the total installed power and the electrical power. Unfortunately there is no indicator in real terms (i.e. expressed in constant prices) for the stock of capital goods in industry in our period (1913–1965). However there is a data series available for the whole economy. This non-residential capital stock (the total stock, less houses) is based on a reconstruction of the annual investment data and will be used here as an indicator. From this we can separate out a series for annual investments in machines, which we also will use as an indicator.[35] In fact, machines account for only a modest proportion of the total stock of capital goods. In the years 1913, 1921, 1929 and 1938 machinery accounted for 31, 36, 37 and 35 percent, respectively, of the non-residential capital stock. Industrial machines are a sub-group of this machinery.

Figure 7.2 shows the trends in the diverse capital indicators that can be compiled for the period 1913 and 1938 (1938 = 100). First the total recorded primary horsepower of powered machines as reported in the Statistics of Production (from 1921); then the standardised gross value of the stock of machines in the Dutch economy; and thirdly, the standardised value of the stock of capital goods excluding houses and inventories. Table

---

34 Byatt, *British*, 76–82.

35 Groote, Albers & De Jong, Standardised. The technique used here is the 'perpetual inventory method'. Starting with a value of capital in a base year the value of new investments are added to the stock of capital goods, while subtracting old capital goods from the stock, in accordance with particular assumptions about the life expectancy of the diverse sorts of capital goods. For example, in this study the average life expectancy for machines and other equipment is supposed to be 14 years, and for buildings 39 years.

Figure 7.2. Capital stock growth in manufacturing and in the total economy, 1913–1938 (1938 = 100)

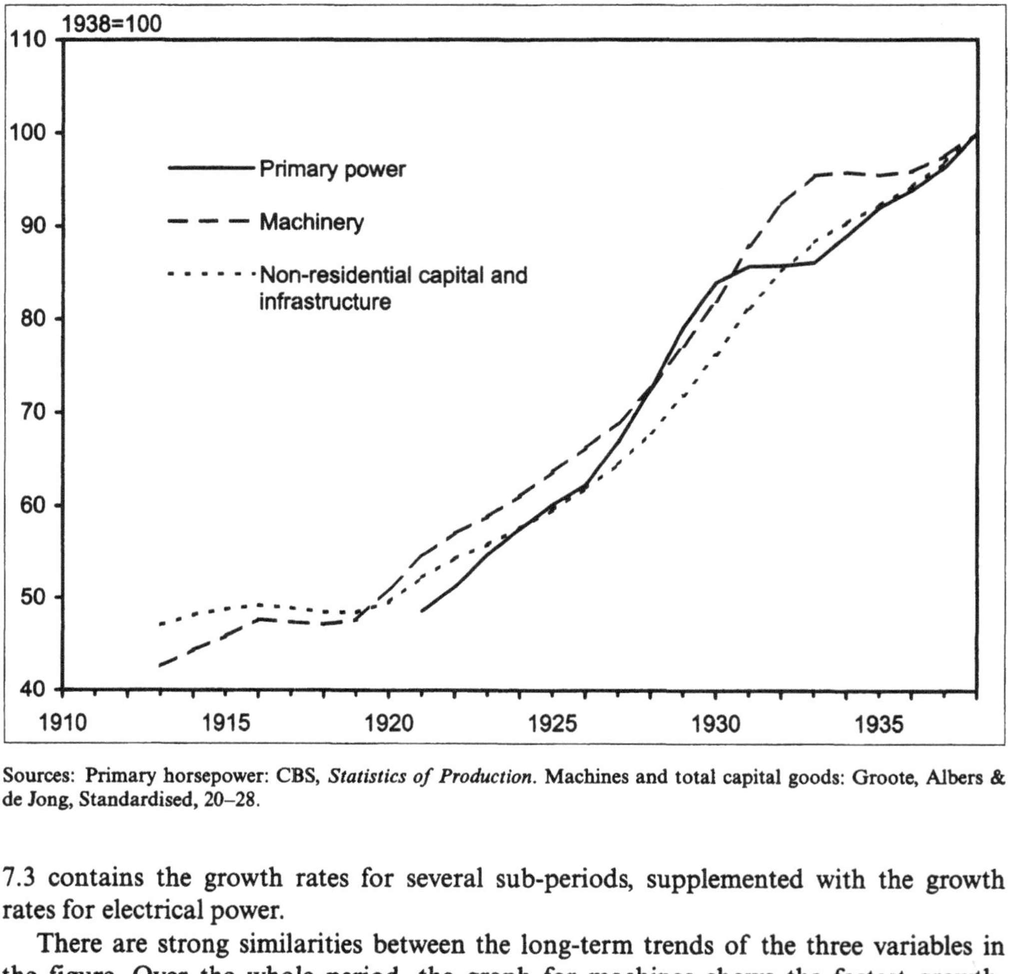

Sources: Primary horsepower: CBS, *Statistics of Production*. Machines and total capital goods: Groote, Albers & de Jong, Standardised, 20–28.

7.3 contains the growth rates for several sub-periods, supplemented with the growth rates for electrical power.

There are strong similarities between the long-term trends of the three variables in the figure. Over the whole period, the graph for machines shows the fastest growth, although if we begin only in 1921, installed primary horsepower grew fastest. The growth during the 1930s is lower than in the 1920s, but there is a striking acceleration visible in all three lines after 1926. This continued into the early 1930s. The indicator from the Statistics of Production represents the actual installed horsepower and appears to respond most immediately to the business cycle. The total stock of capital goods continued to grow in the 1930s, but at a somewhat slower pace than in the 1920s.[36]

It is difficult to say which series represents industry best. In any case, it is clear that the stock of capital goods in the Netherlands increased rapidly during the 1920s. After the First World War the level of investment in the Dutch economy was very high. In fact

36 Compare this to Drukker, who based his analysis of unemployment in the 1930s on the wrong observation that the stock of capital goods declined. Drukker, *Waarom*, 204.

this capital indicator reflects the rapid industrialisation of those years, which also involved numerous outlays of infrastructure, including the further expansion of utility companies and the power transmission grid.[37] These processes are represented in the high growth rates for machines in general, and of machines for primary power production and electrically powered machines in particular.

Table 7.3 shows the calculated growth rates for the diverse indicators for three shorter periods, both for capital and capital intensity (the quantity of capital per unit of labour). The capital intensity can be regarded as an indicator of capital deepening. For 'machines' and 'total capital stock' capital intensity is calculated using an index of the economy-wide volume of total working hours. For primary power and electrical power, capital intensity is calculated by using an index of the volume of employment in the sample industries. Employment is adjusted for changes in the length of the standard working week.

Table 7.3. Capital stock and capital intensity, 1913–1938 (annual compound growth rates)

Capital	1913–1921	1921–1929	1929–1938
Machines	3.1	4.4	2.9
Total capital stock	1.3	3.9	3.6
Primary horsepower		6.3	2.6
Of which electrical		8.9	3.6

Capital intensity	1913–1921	1921–1929	1929–1938
Machines	3.8	2.9	2.9
Total capital stock	1.9	2.5	3.6
Primary horsepower		2.1	3.5
Of which electrical		4.6	4.5

Sources: Primary and electrical power: CBS, *Statistics of Production*. Machines and total capital goods: Groote, Albers & de Jong, Standardised, 20–28. Industrial employment from the Statistics of Production. Total economy employment: See Van Ark & de Jong, Accounting.

For the period 1913–1921, the rate of growth in capital intensity (machines and capital goods) is about half a percentage point higher than the growth in the capital stock. This is because weekly working hours declined quite rapidly after the First World War, so that the total labour volume also declined.[38] During the 1920s the capital intensity grew less rapidly than the capital stock, pointing to a relative increase in labour volume. During the 1930s capital intensity grew just as rapidly as the total capital stock (the cal-

37 Groote, Albers and De Jong, Standardised, 11.

38 Van Ark & De Jong, Accounting, 206.

culated labour volume in the Dutch economy for 1938 is the same as the volume for 1929). Machine intensity grew by 2.9 percent in both periods. The growth in the intensity of primary horsepower is much the same as the growth of the total capital intensity. The rate of growth in electrical power per worker is higher than all the other rates. Capital intensity in the Dutch economy in the 1930s was some 50 percent above the level of the 1920s, which is a clear indication of ongoing capital deepening during the whole inter-war period.

7.7. Capital indicators in Dutch industry between 1938 and 1965

The popular view is that the effects of the war and the occupation hit the Dutch economy very hard between 1940 and 1945. When tracing what happened to the stock of capital goods between 1938 and 1965, it is very important to correctly estimate the effects of the Second World War and the German occupation. In the late 1980s, Van Zanden and Griffiths showed, using the primary horsepower of powered machinery as an indicator, that industrial capacity increased between 1939 and 1946. They based this calculation on data from the Statistics of Production.[39] I have used this source to estimate the combined primary horsepower in all industries. This shows that the level in 1946 was about 25% above that of 1938, and 13% above that of 1943 (see Appendix D). Thus we have an indicator of industrial capacity, which reveals an unexpected increase during the war years. To put this in perspective, this will be compared to capital goods estimates for the whole economy, using the same methods that were applied above for the period 1913–1938.

In the standardised time series of the stock of capital goods prepared by Groote *et al.* – also mentioned above – they make allowance for the effects of the war by estimating new investments, depreciations and war damages. These are combined with one CBS estimate of the national wealth in 1938 and another for the years 1946–1952. Whatever statistics on investments may have been kept during the war years, they have never been published officially. However we do have extensive information about some industries in which capacity increased, such as iron and steel, shipbuilding, various metallurgical industries and some other types of industry (see Section 9.3 for a fuller treatment of these), and about industries that were closed down by the authorities. Despite the closures, there were additional investments, as can be seen from the rise in the installed primary horsepower in the sample industries. Groote *et al.* estimated the changes in investment by equating them to changes in the general index of industrial production.

---

[39] See Van Zanden and Griffiths, *Economische*, 185–186, and Passenier, *Planning*, 49. The latter suggests that investments were made even during the war. The same is mentioned in Klemann, *Nederland 1938–1948*, Chapters 7 and 12.

A continuous series was constructed by making allowance for the net effect of investments after 1938 and for depreciation in the intervening period.[40] The result is an estimate that the total stock of capital goods (without housing) in 1946 was 93 percent of the 1938 level. This is close to a rough computation made by Maddison, who estimated the overall loss at 10 percent of all accumulated investments from before 1946.[41]

According to the estimates made by Groote *et al.*, the war had very different effects on the different sorts of capital goods. Machines and other equipment suffered particularly from obsolescence, because there were insufficient replacement investments. This effect was much more limited in the case of the infrastructure and buildings, because these have a much longer life expectancy and thus do not need to be replaced so quickly. The calculated stock of machines in 1946 is 30 percent lower than in 1938, whereas the infrastructure stock in 1946 was about 20 percent higher, and the stock of non-residential buildings was 7 percent lower.[42]

Figure 7.3 shows that in 1948 the total stock of capital goods returned to 1938 levels, whereas the total standardised volume of machines did not reach 1938 levels until 1952. This contrasts with the level of primary horsepower (calculated from the Statistics of Production), which by 1946 was higher than ever. There are very large differences between the diverse indicators, which makes it difficult to determine the 'true' level of post-war capital in industry from such estimates. However it is very likely that the standardised estimate for machines under-estimates the actual number of machines installed in industry. The stock of capital goods is calculated using a depreciation model in which investments have predetermined service lives, and it may well be that the depreciation of machines during this period was lower than the model supposes. Given the shortage of funds shortly after the war, replacement investments were initially low, and machines were probably kept in service longer than usual.[43] The fact that real wages were low also made it possible to keep them in service longer, effectively extending the economic life of the machines. We can see that the capital formation of machines increased rapidly after 1954.

Table 7.4 shows the growth rates of the various capital indicators I am using. Between 1950 and 1965 machine capital grew by a remarkable 8% per year, as compared to a negative rate of growth of –0.7% between 1938 and 1950. The big difference between the two growth rates indicates that there was some 'catching up' in the second period,

---

[40] A detailed comparison of the two CBS estimates shows that the total stock of capital goods, excluding houses, land and production inventories, was in 1946 seven percent lower than in 1938. This reduction can thus be regarded as the net effect from new investments (which declined during the war years) and the depreciation of capital goods and direct war damages, whether by destruction or plundering. The direct losses due to the war can be derived using standard assumptions concerning capital formation and depreciation. The war losses come to about 7.2% of the stock in 1945, or 7% of the 1938 stock. This does depend on the assumption that the destruction hit all vintages of capital goods equally. See Groote, Albers & de Jong, Standardised, 8.

[41] Maddison, Standardised.

[42] If we exclude infrastructure, the level of 1946 was 18% lower than that of 1938. This standardised estimate is very close to van Zanden & Griffiths' estimate: see *Economische*, 186.

[43] See Brakel, *Industrialisatie*, 58 and also Klemann. Nederland, 290.

Figure 7.3. Capital stock growth in manufacturing and in the total economy, 1938–1965 (1938 = 100)

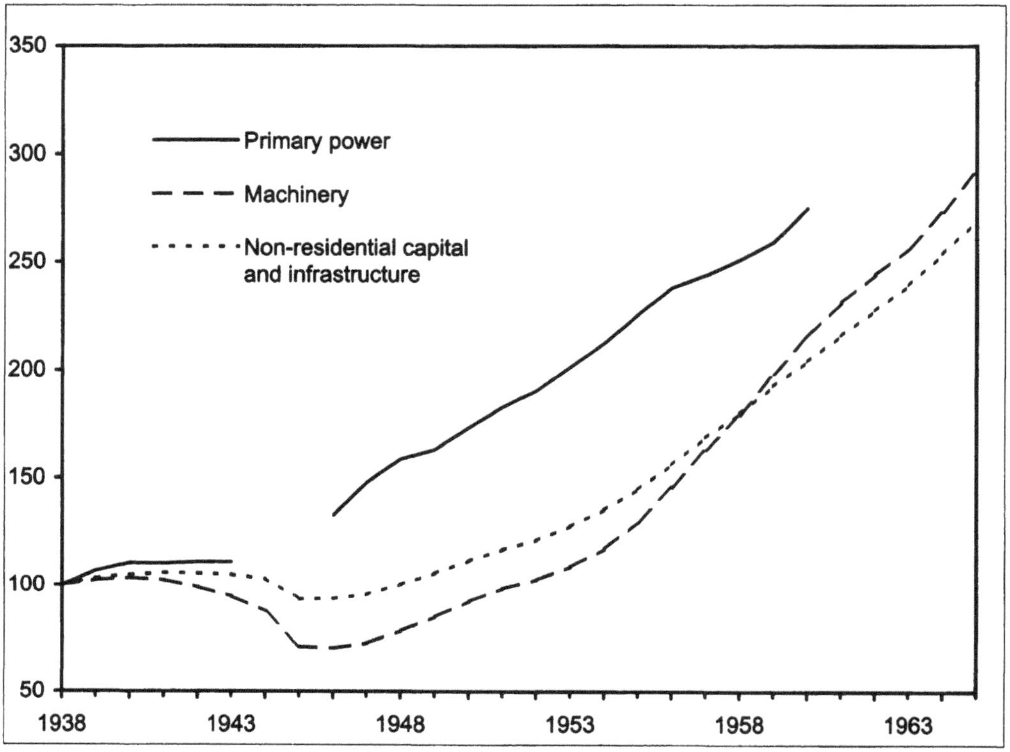

Sources: Primary horsepower: CBS, *Statistics of Production*. Machines and total capital: Groote, Albers & de Jong, Standardised 20–28.

but statistical effects may also play a role here. The same applies to some extent for the total quantity of capital goods. In contrast, the primary horsepower did not grow much more quickly in the second period than in the first.

Rates of growth in capital intensity for the period 1938–1950 were low. If we compare them with rates for 1950–1960/1965, it is clear that the latter includes a catching-up effect. Although the 1950s are generally thought to be characterised by capital broadening investments, in contrast to the capital deepening of the 1960s, we can see here a different picture for the economy as a whole. In the period 1950–1960, the capital intensity increased rapidly. However if we consider only the primary horsepower per worker, the increase during the 1950s appears low in comparison to the 1930s.

When growth rates for industrial labour productivity are compared to the rates for capital intensity shown in Table 7.4, productivity appears to rise in close parallel with the annual increase in capital intensity based on the total stock of capital goods. Between 1938 and 1950, productivity fell by 0.6 percent per year, while from 1950 to 1965 it rose by 5.0 percent per year. During the same periods, capital intensities fell by 1.0 percent and then rose by 5.3 percent. We have already calculated an annual rate of growth in labour productivity for the whole period from 1921 to 1965 of 2.5 percent. This per-

Table 7.4. Capital stock and capital intensity, 1938–1965 (annual compound growth rates)

	1938–1950	1950–1960/65	
Machines (up to 1965)	- 0.7	8.0	
Capital stock (up to 1965)	0.9	6.0	
Primary horsepower	4.2	4.7	
Of which electrical	4.8	5.6	
Capital intensity			
	1938–1950	1950–1960/65	21–60
Machines	- 2.6	7.3	2.5
Capital stock	- 1.0	5.3	2.5
Primary horsepower	0.3	2.8	2.0
Of which electrical	0.9	3.7	3.2

Sources: Primary and electric power: CBS, *Statistics of Production*. Machines and total capital goods: Groote, Albers & de Jong, Standardised, 20–28. Industrial employment from the Statistics of Production. Total economy employment Van Ark & de Jong, Accounting.

centage is exactly the same as the rise in capital intensity in this period. Between 1921 and 1960, the intensity of installed electrical power was the fastest growing indicator, averaging 3.2 percent per year.[44]

The following section will measure the contributions of labour and capital to the growth in production, and then calculate what part of the growth can be explained by the growth of the two factors of production, and what part still remains to be explained.

7.8. Total factor productivity in manufacturing, 1913–1960

We can use the rates of growth of the capital indicators, calculated above, to estimate the contributions of labour and capital to the growth of industrial production in a simple Cobb-Douglas production function. The weights for labour and capital vary per period between 0.40 and 0.60, depending on their shares in value added. Taking the quotient of output change and the change of labour and capital we get the total factor productivity. This is the part of the growth in production that remains to be explained, for instance by broad efficiency effects, such as economies of scale, organisational improvements and technological developments.

---

[44] Melman has also demonstrated a clear parallel, in the United States, between the long-term rise in productivity and the increasing primary horsepower of the powered machinery (per worker) during the first half of the twentieth century. "The result is consistent with the proposition that the productivity in manufacturing as a whole is directly related to the powered equipment available per worker" (Melman, *Dynamic*, 112–113).

In Table 7.5 I made a subdivision into the following three periods: 1913–1921, 1921–1938, and 1938–1960. The figures for 1913–1921 shown here are somewhat speculative because, as we will see in Chapter 8, it is very difficult to find a good indicator for changes in production and employment in manufacturing for 1913–1921. While the growth rates for machine capital and for the total stock of capital goods are based on the total economy, in the following analysis these are assumed to provide a representative picture of industry. Four capital indicators are presented here: primary horsepower (prim.), electrical power (elec.), machines (mach.) and the total non-residential capital stock (cap.).

Table 7.5. Growth of real value added, labour- and capital inputs, and total factor productivity (TFP) in the sample industries, 1913–1960 (annual compound growth rates, relative weights of labour in parentheses, weights of capital as the complement)

	Value added	Labour	Capital	TFP
1913–1921	4.00	–0.37 (0.40)	3.10 (Mach.)	2.0
			1.30 (Cap.)	3.1
1921–1938	4.14	1.34 (0.60)	4.34 (Prim.)	1.6
			6.10 (Elec.)	0.9
			3.62 (Mach.)	1.9
			3.74 (Cap.)	1.8
1938–1960	5.06	3.00 (0.50)	4.67 (Prim.)	1.2
			5.46 (Elec.)	0.8
			3.55 (Mach.)	1.8
			3.24 (Cap.)	1.9

Note: Labour in 1913–1921 from Van der Bie, *Economische*. Employment adjusted for the reduction of the working week from 60 to 48 hours. The number of employed increased by 2.45 percent per year between 1913–1921, but because of the shorter working week the total number of hours worked fell by an average of 0.37 percent per year.

Sources: Appendices B, C and D and Table 8.1.

The calculations for the period 1913–1921 result in growth rates for total factor productivity between two and three percent per year. This corresponds to the estimate made by Van Ark and De Jong for the whole economy in this period (2.5 percent).[45] TFP growth rates between 1921–1938 and 1938–1960 are very much the same, but lower than for the period 1913–1921. The difference between the rates of growth in value added during the two periods (somewhat less than one percentage point per year) can largely be explained by the difference in employment growth.

[45] Van Ark and De Jong, Accounting, 201.

As a result of these similarities, the TFP over the whole period 1921–1960 is constant, for three of the four capital indicators. Nevertheless if we take primary horsepower as the indicator, the difference between the two periods is still 0.4 percentage points. For the whole period 1921–1960, we can conclude that the TFP measured on the basis of machines and capital grew by about 1.8 percent per year. If we take primary horsepower as the capital indicator, a greater proportion of the growth in value added is explained by capital, and the rise in the TFP averages 1.4 percent per year.

If we now consider only the growth in primary and electrical power, we find an increasing capital coefficient in three of the four observations. During the periods 1921–1938 and 1938–1960, electrical power grew faster than the value added. Nevertheless, the higher labour productivity does not result only from the more intensive use of capital. Part of the growth in production cannot be explained by the combined increases in the measured quantities of capital and labour. From 1921 to 1960, electrical power grew fastest. If electrical power is used as the indicator of industrial capital, there are only 0.8 percentage points of productivity growth left to be explained by residual factors. With total annual growth in production in this period running at of 4.66 percent, this means that more than 80 percent of the industrial growth is explained using this indicator.

It has already been established that electrical power accounts for only a limited proportion of the total capital goods. Nevertheless, for the period considered here this indicator represents the improved quality of capital. In other words, for that period it embodies technological progress. It represents a new technological system, in which a factory's machines and 'fractionalised power' are integrated in a manufacturing system. The existing production systems were gradually modified for the new technology, and on that basis innovations in the production processes themselves could progressively be introduced. The emergence of this new approach to production is comparable to the introduction of other fundamentally innovative breakthroughs, such as the introduction of the steam engine in the eighteenth and nineteenth centuries and automation and computerisation in the second half of the twentieth century.[46] The use of this new technology made it possible to economise on all factors of production: not just on labour, but also on capital.

7.9. The process of substitution in the long term

The growth accounting exercise above has been based on the measured quantities of labour and capital. It demonstrates that both the productivity of labour and the capital intensity increased. However it is still not clear how closely these two phenomena are related. In this section I will first try to establish a connection between the relative costs of labour and capital and the capital intensity. The 'primary power' in horsepower per worker, calculated in Section 7.3 will be used as an approximation for the capital intensity. Labour costs are defined as the annual money wage costs (wages and social security

---

[46] See, for example, Von Tunzelmann, *Technology*, 231–232.

levies, per worker), which were calculated in Chapter 6. The capital costs are calculated as the input costs for capital ('*user cost of capital*'). These can be represented in the formula:[47]

$$r_k(t) = \left[r(t) + \delta - \frac{\dot{P}_k(t)}{P_k(t)} \right] P_k(t)$$

The costs are made up of three components. The first is foregone interest r(t), which is approximated by the yield on perpetual government bonds. The second is depreciation costs (δ), which are estimated here at ten percent per year. The third term of the equation is an allowance for changes in the price of capital goods. If the price of a unit of capital falls, input costs rise, since the capital goods already purchased were priced at a higher level. The data series for the prices of capital goods (third and fourth terms) is estimated from a series of price indexes for electric motors, the machine-manufacturing industry and for the construction costs of factory buildings. A series of relative costs is then compiled by taking the quotient of the labour cost index and the capital cost index. This series is shown in Figure 7.4, together with an estimate of the machine intensity.

Figure 7.4. Relative factor costs and machine intensity, 1921–1965 (1938 = 100)

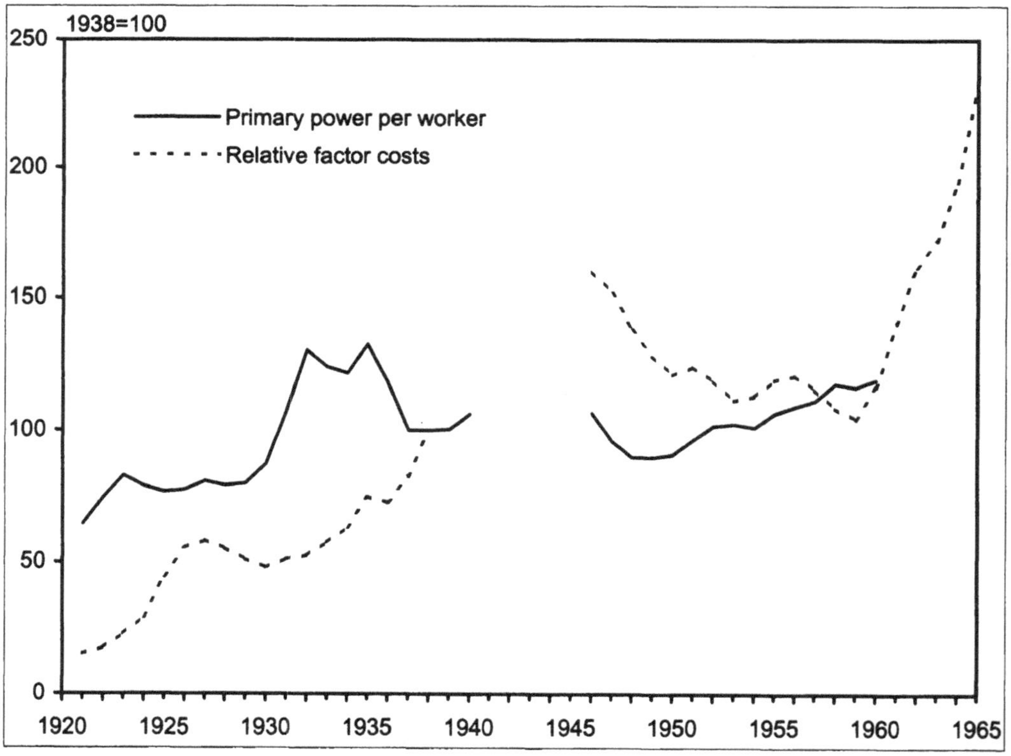

Sources: Machine intensity: primary horsepower per worker. Appendices C and D. Relative factor costs: Appendices A and B and CBS, *Vijfennegentig Jaren*, 90, 150.

47 See Romer, *Macroeconomics*, 346–347, and Collins & Williamson, Capital-goods prices, 59–60.

The curve of relative factor costs indicates that there was a rising trend before the Second World War. Although money wages declined in the 1930s, the prices of capital and the capital cost fell even faster, which means that the relative price of labour rose. At the same time, the machine-intensity increased markedly. The movement in relative factor costs can explain this: labour became more expensive in comparison to capital. After 1946 there was a long period of rising capital costs. In combination with the much less rapid rise in labour costs, this led to a very long-term decline in the relative costs of labour, lasting until 1959. From that year, capital costs began to fall, while labour costs increased rapidly. The result was that relative labour costs more than doubled within five years. The changes in capital intensity must also be considered against the background of the capital losses due to the Second World War. In 1945 capital intensity was low, and we can regard the period after that as a period of catching-up. However in the figure we have taken the primary horsepower of powered machinery as a proxy for machine intensity. This does not reveal any decrease between 1940 and 1945. In contrast, after 1946 we can see an initial decline (as a result of a rapid increase in employment) followed by a moderate increase. This is not unexpected in the light of the declining trend in relative labour costs: at that time labour in the Netherlands was cheap, which did not encourage the substitution of capital for labour. However between 1953 and 1956 the relative cost of labour did rise. After 1960, relative labour costs increased very rapidly; even well before the big wage rises that began in 1963. However this is partly due to the numerator in this quotient: the costs of capital were declining, having reached a post-war high in 1959 (see Appendix D).

The relation between labour productivity and the relative costs of labour and capital for the whole 1921–1965 period can now be shown in a scatter diagram, with the relative cost index on the *x*-axis and the index of labour productivity on the *y*-axis.

The long-term association between both variables is positive: rising relative costs for labour, in comparison to capital, are accompanied by higher labour productivity in the periods 1921–1936 and 1959–1965. From 1937 to 1959 the association is predominantly negative. It appears that during the war years a development began that was contrary to the long-term trend; relative labour costs lagged behind the rise in capital costs. The trend that emerged in the interwar period was taken up again in 1959.

Melman has also sought to relate the long-term changes in labour productivity to the degree of mechanisation.[48] Instead of the real user costs of capital that were used above as the indicator of machine costs, he used the price of electricity, in this case the standard price of a kilowatt-hour (kWh). His indicator of relative costs was the index of hourly money wages divided by the price per kilowatt-hour, giving an index of the number of kilowatt-hours per hourly wage.[49] A similar exercise using the price of electricity

---

48 Melman, *Dynamic*, 3–4.

49 See Melman Appendix A and B. This points to many arguments for using the kilowatt-hour as the indicator: it is a broadly applied industrial input and is strongly homogeneous. During our period there were major investments in electrification. It is a very good example of the continual development of efficiency and cost cutting in the field of inputs, design and production technologies. Melman has shown that changes in the kWh price are a good proxy for direct machine costs in both the United States and the United Kingdom.

Figure 7.5. Levels of labour productivity and relative factor costs, 1921–1965 (1938 = 100)

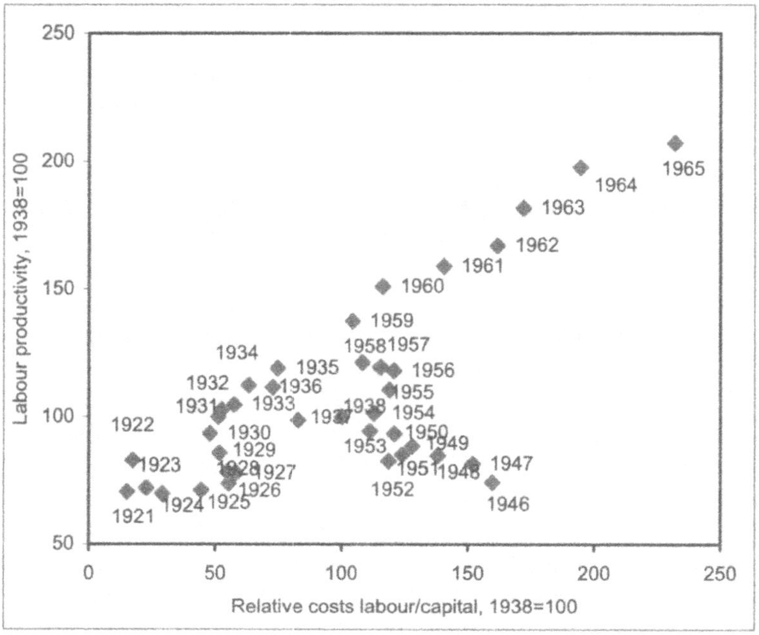

Sources: See Figure 7.4.

and labour costs in the Netherlands yields practically the same picture as that shown in Figure 7.5: the relationship between wages and kWh costs is apparently a good reflection of the relative factor cost for Dutch industry during this period. Melman, too, found a positive long-term correlation between labour productivity and relative factor costs for the United Kingdom and for the United States.[50]

In my opinion the causality between these two variables is that labour productivity in total manufacturing is in the long term determined by changes in the relative factor costs. That is, rising labour productivity at industry-level is an effect of increasing mechanisation, which is caused by the increasing relative price of labour. The rising labour productivity is the result of measures taken to compensate for the increased costs of labour in comparison to capital. While labour costs and capital costs are important considerations when making the decisions that shape the production process, one would seldom chose increased labour productivity or mechanisation as an explicit criterion, let alone as a goal. They can be regarded as by-products or results of a decision-making process.[51]

---

50 He terms relative factors as 'alternative costs', saying that "Alternative costs is the most general statement representing not only costs as such but also factors like labor scarcity, inventory size and floor space problems. For such problems have been solved in ways determined by alternative costs levels" (Melman, *Dynamic*, 126).

51 See Melman, *Dynamic*, 58 and 165; Brown, *Theory*, 97; Fabricant speaks of a *secular rise of wages* (Fabricant, *Employment*, 80).

7.10. Conclusions

The increase in labour productivity in the period studied has resulted in part from an increase in capital intensity: the quantity of capital per worker rose rapidly. The influence of the fixed capital employed is somewhat under-represented in the statistics, because an allowance is not always made for qualitative changes in capital. Technological developments led to capital savings, as demonstrated in the electrification process. The electrification ratio in industry rose especially rapidly between 1910 and 1930, but was still rising around the beginning of the Second World War. If we use installed electrical power as a capital indicator in relation to industrial growth, the increase in labour and capital as factors of production (which includes the technological progress embodied in capital) explains 80 percent of industrial growth in the period 1921–1960.

The substitution of capital for labour has been made visible in a long-term comparison of the machine-intensity and changes in the relative costs of labour and capital. The relationship was particularly strong in the inter-war period, or at least in that period both curves increased. There is also a positive long-term correlation between labour productivity and the relative factor costs. If we look at shorter periods, the relationship is less strong, and may even be negative, as in the period between 1935 and 1958.

In the light of the findings in Chapter 5, we may suppose that economies of scale were mainly responsible for simultaneous savings on both labour and capital. Specialisation and external economies create potential economies of scale. Whether this potential is in fact utilised depends in part on demand factors, which may differ markedly from industry to industry. A growing market can lead to the better utilisation of production capacity in a specific company, and in an entire industry. New investments can help in achieving the most efficient manufacturing production processes. Thus demand factors provide an explanation for differences in productivity growth in different industries. Salter has already demonstrated that technical progress and economies of scale should be regarded as complementary: achieving economies of scale can accelerate expansion as a result of technological improvements.[52] Such growth may develop its own dynamic where production capacity is increased with machinery that embodies new technologies. Industries that do not receive such a technological stimulus also have little chance of achieving the potential economies of scale. The broad lines of Salter's argument are confirmed in the development of Dutch industry.

---

52 Salter, *Productivity*, 141–142.

Chapter 8: Industrial growth and crisis between 1913 and 1938

8.1. Introduction

Figure 1.1 in the first chapter shows that industrial production in the Netherlands increased rapidly in the period after 1913. This industrial expansion took place against a military and political background of the Great War, an uneasy peace settlement in Versailles and rearmament in Europe. In economic terms, the period 1913–1938 was one of international economic disintegration, trade restrictions and economic nationalism. The Netherlands had for centuries focused on free trade and depended on its position as a transit centre. However the country did not become militarily involved in the First World War, and neutrality had very favourable effects on the economic position of the country. Although the war entailed extensive government interference in trade, the bureaucratic government agencies built up during the war to deal with the crisis were quickly dismantled after 1918. The 1920s were years of 'old-fashioned' economic liberalism, in which the government refrained from interfering in the economy. Nevertheless social legislation during and after the war was very extensive. This culminated in the *Arbeidswet* (Labour Act, 1919), in which the legal working hours was shortened to 45 hours per week (and raised again to 48 hours in 1922). The effects of the shortening of the working week on industrial labour productivity will be considered here. More dramatic, however, were the effects of the depression of the 1930s on manufacturing. The stock market-crisis and the severe problems in the banking-sector between 1929 and 1931 were followed by a worldwide decline in demand and economic contraction. Central banks in many countries suspended gold-convertibility with depreciation as a result. However, the Netherlands maintained the gold value of the guilder during the larger part of the 1930s, together with the gold-bloc countries. This had a negative impact on the Netherlands' competitive position. Step by step, the government's liberal economic policy of the 1920s was abandoned under the pressure of circumstances. In practice the changes in the direction of policy – on the question of whether to intervene or not – resulted in a range of official measures in which internal consistency was not a strong feature. Some parts of the economy were supported directly, while others were left to their fate. The debate among economic historians and economists concerning this period is still dominated by the question of whether the Netherlands was correct to remain true to the gold standard.[1] In this chapter I will present data on industrial development before and during the economic turmoil of the 1930s, to identify and explain the effects of the Depression on Dutch industry.

---

[1] See Van Zanden, Economic history.

8.2. Manufacturing industry between 1913 and 1921

On the eve of the First World War, the Dutch economy was booming. Since the last cyclical downturn in 1907 GDP per capita had increased by an average of 3 percent per year.[2] The Netherlands remained neutral during the First World War. The most important effects of the war for the Dutch economy were an increase in both domestic and foreign demand and the elimination of foreign competition. This in itself opened up exceptional opportunities for industry, but within a few years there were large shortages of raw materials and fuels.[3]

Exports were quickly regulated, in compliance with the rules imposed by the principal belligerents (the United Kingdom and Germany). During the early years of the war, the United Kingdom was in a position to dictate terms. The Netherlands Overseas Trust provided guarantees to the British that imported goods would not end up in Germany. From 1917 onwards, unrestricted submarine warfare made overseas trade, including the supply of raw materials, increasingly difficult and Germany was able to exert an increasing influence on the Netherlands, which was especially dependent on German coal.[4]

Nevertheless, industrial production continued to grow strongly until 1916. The prices of raw materials rose rapidly, due in part to high transport costs. However, manufacturers could simply pass this on in their prices, because of the increasing shortage of goods. Other costs did not rise as rapidly as output prices. Until 1918 there was only a moderate growth in nominal wages. What was new was the extensive government intervention in the economy. Price controls and distribution systems were established and enforced, by temporary government agencies.[5] As early as 1914, the government had set maximum prices and implemented export restrictions for basic foodstuffs such as potatoes, wheat, meat, milk, rice, sugar and butter. These measures made it possible to moderate the rise in the cost of living.[6]

During the first half of the war, many companies made large profits. The urge to expand was therefore considerable. Long-term interest rates remained quite stable prior to 1918, despite increasing government lending. There was big interest in industrial funds among investors, not only for long established industries such as the margarine, metal and shipbuilding industries, but also for new industries that were driven by import substitution, such as the rubber industry. At the same time, plans were being made for a basic metals industry, which was later to become the Hoogovens blast furnace.

The extraordinary monopoly profits of the early war years quickly evaporated. In the second half of the war, trade restrictions forced large parts of the industrial sector to reduce production. Industries that depended on other countries for either their raw

---

2 Smits, Horlings & Van Zanden, *Dutch GNP*, 230.

3 For general overviews see, for example, Frey, *Erste Weltkrieg*, Van Dorp, Handel; Zaalberg, Manufacturing industry, De Jong & Albers, Industrial output; Van Zanden, *Economic history*.

4 Moore, *Economic aspects*, 14–17.

5 Smidt, Regulering, 102–133.

6 The resulting reduction in food prices, in relative terms, has been estimated at approximately 20%. See CBS (1939), *Nederlandsche*, 9.

materials or intermediate inputs, or for the sale of their final products, were especially hard hit. In 1918 industries such as the cotton, paper, and food and beverage industries lay almost completely idle. Wage subsidies and suspension of employment on reduced pay (the latter partly financed by the government) were introduced to avoid large-scale redundancies.

After the First World War the special government agencies were rapidly dismantled, and price controls ended. Because international trade was slow to restart in 1919, prices for industrial products, which had reached record heights during the war, rose even more.[7] Thus 1919 and 1920 were years of great optimism and renewed expansion of industrial capital.[8]

The prospects for industry shortly after the war were not good in every respect, however. Two issues were causing great concern in Dutch manufacturing. First, there was increasing competition from countries such as Belgium, Germany and France, which had a much lower exchange rate vis-à-vis the Dutch guilder compared to the pre-war situation. Second, the introduction of the 45-hour working week in 1920 had pushed up wage rates. The first was seen as an annoying but temporary nuisance. The second was, however, considered a more serious problem by industrialists.[9] When corrected for inflation, wage rates during the first half of the war fell at first, but from 1918 on real wages began to rise. The shortening of the working week increased wage costs for employers even further. As the weekly wages remained the same this measure implicitly raised hourly rates and piecework rates.

The tide turned in the middle of 1920, with a downturn in trade, a sharp decline in prices, and in some industrial sectors a decline in real production. The decline in demand continued into 1921 and brought with it a bear market that lasted until the middle of 1923, followed by a strong economic recovery. Prices-levels remained low. This was not just a consequence of a worldwide trend towards declining price levels; it was also due to deflationary government policies to prepare for the return to gold and to restructure government finances.[10]

---

7 Keesing identifies monetary expansion due to a lack of fiscal discipline on the part of the Dutch Central Bank as the most important source of inflation in this period. Keesing, *Conjuncturele*, 16.

8 Keesing, *Conjuncturele*, 17 and 81. See also Saalfeld, *Metallindustrie*, 81–83. Both demonstrate that during this period there was an abundant supply of capital in the Netherlands, and investors were looking for investment funds in the industrial sector. Government propaganda had been advocating industrial investment even during the war. Dutch industry also benefited from considerable German investment.

9 For the introduction of the 8-hour day and the debate, which preceded the legislation, see Heerma van Voss, *Achturendag*, Karsten, *Achturendag* and Kuyper, *Schaduw*.

10 Keesing, *Conjuncturele*, 313. Van de Woestijne has remarked that the steady reduction in prices between 1925 and 1929 should in fact be regarded as a *structural* decline in prices upon which price increases, due to trade-cycle effects, were superimposed (Van de Woestijne, Goede jaren, 379).

8.3. The volume of industrial production, 1913–1921

In quantifying industrial development, we will consider the 1913–1921 period separately, because the statistical basis for this period is not the same as for the period following. Figures from the Statistics of Production will be used for both periods, but the CBS changed the design of their statistics in 1921. Prior to that, the statistics recorded a large number of industries, but only for the years 1913, 1916 and 1919. From 1921 on, the statistical basis was much narrower, covering only about twenty industries, but giving data on an annual basis. Moreover the Statistics of Production for the period between 1913 and 1921 do not give any direct information on employment, so that an additional source had to be used to estimate productivity levels.

The statistics reveal that the development of industry before 1921 was considerably stronger than had previously been thought. Table 8.1 shows growth in real value added for eleven industries.[11] The table contains those industries for which statistics of production continue beyond 1921. They have been selected to make it possible to draw a consistent comparison with the period after 1921. The estimates presented here are based only on the Statistics of Production. The nominal value added of these eleven industries in 1913 was about 90 million Dutch guilders, and in 1921 about 290 million. The value added in manufacturing as a whole (i.e. all industry less mining, utilities and construction) for 1913 and 1921 was 513 and 1458 million guilders, respectively.[12] Thus our sample constitutes about 20% of all industry, in both years.

The real value added is obtained by adjusting the nominal value added using a price index for industrial products. Price indices were computed from the Statistics of Production. The production value in each industry was divided by the corresponding volume of production. The resulting average value of products was then weighted according to that industry's share of the total value added of all the industries in our sample. These calculations show that between 1913 and 1921 the index of output prices rose from 100 to 186.[13] Expressed in 1913 prices, the value added in 1921 was 155 million Dutch guilders, which was 72% above that of 1913. This is equivalent to an annual increase of almost 6.5%. The average rate of growth for all manufacturing industries between 1913 and 1921 is estimated to be about 4.5%.[14] We can conclude that the sample industries witnessed a growth that was two percent points higher than total manufacturing during these years.

Table 8.1 provides an overview of the level of real value added in the sample industries in 1921 in comparison to 1913. The big variations between the levels of value added are reflected in differences between the growth rates, in the second column.

The figures in Table 8.1 show that growth in real value added in these industries varied greatly. In shipbuilding, for example, output levels in 1921 were twice as high as in

11 Only 1913 and 1921 are considered here. Of the other years for which some data is available (1916, 1919, 1920), only the data for 1916 is usable.

12 Based on Van der Bie, *Economische ontwikkeling*, 206 as revised by J. P. Smits.

13 De Jong, *Nederlandse industrie*, 381.

14 De Jong, *Nederlandse industrie*, 447.

Table 8.1. Real value added in 11 sample industries, 1913–1921 (levels, index 1913 = 100; growth in annual compound growth rates)

	Level in 1921 (1913 = 100)	Growth rate 1913–1921
Paper	86	-1.9
Machine knitting	108	1.0
Margarine	121	2.4
Cotton	129	3.2
Wool	150	5.2
Flour	160	6.1
Footwear	203	9.2
Shipbuilding	218	10.2
Cocoa	226	10.7
Soap	240	11.6
Rubber	339	16.5

Source: De Jong and Albers, Industrial output, 4–5.

1913. The demand for shipping capacity increased rapidly during the war, in part due to foreign demand.[15] In those years production capacity expanded rapidly and high demand levels continued in the early post-war years. Production peaked during the period 1921 and 1922. The rapid growth of the rubber industry can be attributed to import substitution as a result of the war. Traditionally the Netherlands had imported many rubber products from the United Kingdom, but these were now produced domestically. The small industry that existed in 1913 had a value added of 476,000 guilders: six years later this had increased to 8 million, only to fall to just over 3 million (in current prices) in 1921.

The paper industry, by contrast, was already well developed before the First World War, and contracted between 1913 and 1921. During the war many companies switched to producing cheaper types of paper, which reduced the value added per unit of product. But this industry did not experience a post-war recovery, and in 1920 and 1921 it had to face competition from Germany, which, with its undervalued currency, could easily sell its products in the Netherlands. Moreover output prices for paper products fell faster than the costs of inputs, resulting in a disappointing financial outcome for this industry.[16]

---

15 To meet this demand, Dutch shipping companies sold their own ships at considerable profit to foreign companies. They then ordered new ships, to be built in the Netherlands.

16 However if one adjusts for both the changes in the prices of inputs and changes in output prices (using a double deflation technique), the real result achieved in 1921 is better than that in 1913, which does indicate that real production had risen. I have chosen to allow only for single deflation here, to preserve comparability with the other industries, for which no input prices are available. See De Jong & Albers, Industrial output, 10–11.

8.4. Trends in labour productivity

The Statistics of Production for the years before 1921 do not include the corresponding data on the volume of employment. Therefore employment levels have been calculated from the Accident Statistics of the National Insurance Bank. To obtain an accurate estimate of the labour volume, an allowance has also been made for changes in the length of the working week. The standard working week was reduced from 60 hours in 1913 to 48 hours in 1922, and in a few industries there was for a short period (1920–1921) a working week of even 45 hours. This is equivalent to a 25 percent reduction in standard labour input. This calculation shows that in the industries considered here, the total labour volume expressed in working hours actually declined during the 1913–1921 period. The workforce increased by 21 %, but this did not entirely compensate for the shorter working week.

Figure 8.1 shows indexes for the average production per worker and per worked hour, for every year for which data is available, i.e. 1913, 1916, 1919 (for a limited number of industries) and from 1921 onwards annually. The topmost series shows the changes in labour productivity calculated per hour worked, while the bottom series is calculated on a worker-basis.

Figure 8.1. Real labour productivity per worker and per working hour, 1913–1929 (index numbers, 1913 = 100)

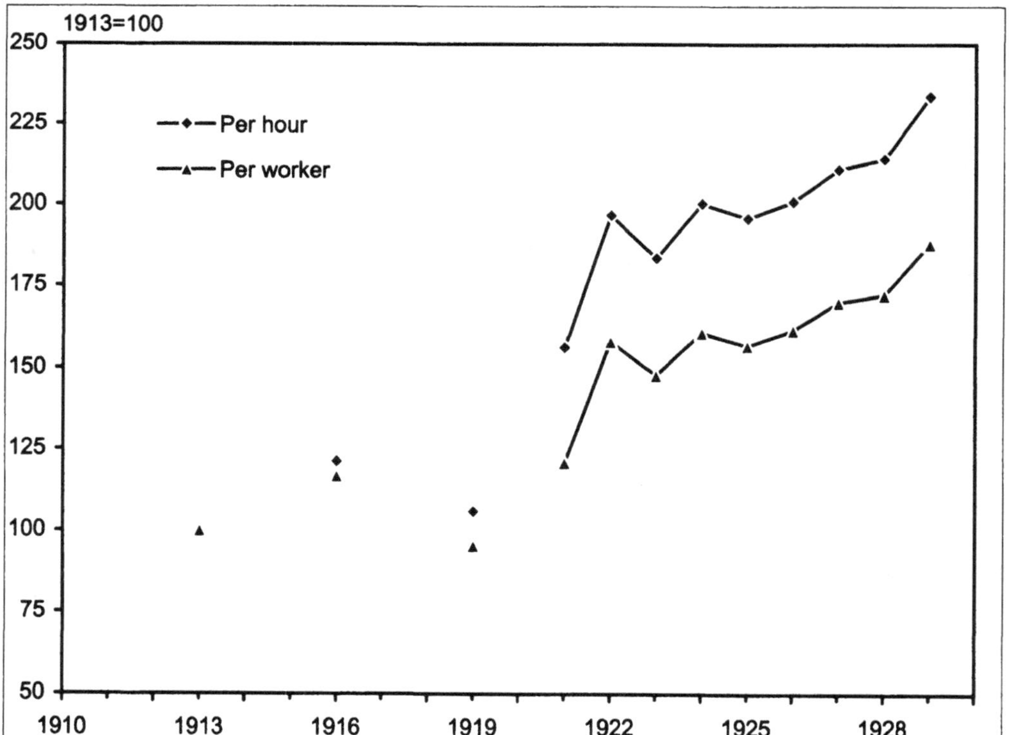

Source: De Jong and Albers, Industrial output, 8.

Although a difference between the two series emerges as early as 1916 and 1919, the effect of the shorter working week becomes clearly visible from 1921. During the 1920s, however, the gap between both series is constant, as the length of the working week remained practically unchanged.

Productivity-levels in 1919 were almost the same as in 1913. There is a striking shift between the years 1919 and 1921, especially in the index for output per working hour, which increased by 50 percent. In terms of output per worker, the increase was more than 20 percent, which is also considerable. From our comparisons with Germany and the United Kingdom, it appears that this was the period in which the productivity of Dutch industry rapidly caught up with international levels. The closing of the gap was due not only to bad economic performances in these two countries, but also to the exceptionally rapid improvement of productivity in the Netherlands.

How can we explain this 'great leap' for productivity in the Netherlands? In the first place, we can examine whether there was also a sudden rise in productivity in other countries after the war. In the case of the United States, real production per working hour increased by 20 percent between 1919 and 1921, but real production per worker increased less, by 14 percent. Once again, taking the shorter working week into account makes a considerable difference, but the difference is much less than for the Dutch figures.[17]

In the case of Sweden, which like the Netherlands remained neutral during the war, we have figures based on the real value of industrial production (rather than value added), and data on working hours.[18] The standard working day fell by almost 30% between 1913 and 1921, i.e. from 10.5 hours to 7.5 hours, rising to 8 hours in 1922). On an index of production per hour of work, with 1913 as the base year, production per hour in 1919 was 84, and in 1921 it was 115. The difference in both levels resembles an increase of 31 percentage points between 1919 and 1921, which is not so far from the calculated rise in the Netherlands.[19]

The rapid rise in productivity in the Netherlands can be attributed to three factors. First, there are the effects of the business cycle on capacity utilisation. In 1919, output volumes in the industries considered here were very low in comparison to 1921. There were shortages of raw materials and other physical inputs, so that the production capacity could not be fully utilised.[20] Verdoorn has attributed the low level of labour productivity during the war to labour hoarding, in the expectation of better economic times to come. Despite the decline in economic activity there was scarcely any incentive for com-

---

17 Fabricant, *Employment*, 331. The figures for the United States presented by Broadberry also show a rise of 14%, but these are not adjusted for the length of the working day. Broadberry, Manufacturing, 789.

18 De Lange, Productiviteit, 10–16.

19 In contrast to the Netherlands, there is a big difference between the levels in 1919 and 1913; my figures for Dutch industry suggest that average production rose significantly until 1916, whereas production per hour in Sweden had already fallen sharply. Thus, while the rise in Swedish productivity following the war was considerable, it did not surpass the level of 1913 until 1920.

20 Keesing, *Conjuncturele*, 14.

panies to restructure, because profits in this period were high and real wages were low.[21] The comparison between real wages and labour productivity in Figure 6.4 highlights the big difference between 1919 and 1913. After 1919, profit expectations among employers were less optimistic and labour costs rose. Because labour capacity had been maintained, companies could increase productivity simply by making labour redundant. Moreover the capacity utilisation in 1921 was higher, yielding greater efficiency.

Second, there were radical changes in the composition of output for some industries immediately after the war, and the effects of this were already noticeable in 1920 and 1921. In some cases the shift was in favour of products with a higher value added. One well-known example is paper, which had lost many of its markets during the First World War. In retaking these markets, paper manufacturers chose mainly to produce and export high quality sorts of paper. Production patterns in, for example, the cocoa and cotton industries also tended to shift progressively towards greater value added per unit of input.[22]

In the third place, there are positive productivity effects associated with the introduction of the shorter working week: workers' average rate of work rose when the working day was shortened. Not only did the shorter working day mean more free time and less fatigue for the workers; it also forced managers to develop more efficient methods of production and to look critically at the organisation of the work. On the basis of 260 observations from the international literature, Heerma van Voss has calculated an average productivity effect of more than 40 percent, on the basis of a working week of 54 hours (measured against the 48-hour week).[23] This means that a 10 percent reduction in the working day led on average to a reduction in the volume of output of just 6 percent.[24]

We can conclude that a significant part of the rapid rise in labour productivity in the statistics after 1919 can be attributed to higher hourly wages. Producers were able to absorb these costs by improving the efficiency of their production processes. Labour productivity growth measured in average output per worker is estimated at 2.3 percent per year. However, if average labour productivity is adjusted for the change in the standard working week, the annual increase in labour productivity between 1913 and 1921 can be estimated to an average of about 5 percent (Figure 8.1).

---

21 Verdoorn, *Arbeidsduur*, 243, 247.

22 De Jong & Albers, Industrial output, 18–22.

23 Heerma van Voss, *Achturendag*. In his industry-level analysis he uses a lower value for the productivity effect, i.e. 25%.

24 See also Van der Schalk, *Wiskundig-statistische*, Chapter VI; Verdoorn, *Arbeidsduur*, Chapter IV. Van der Schalk states that productivity effects were especially strong in sectors that were relatively labour-intensive. He found a weaker effect in the more capital-intensive sectors, where primarily the machines used determined the pace of production.

8.5. Output, employment and productivity between 1921 and 1938

From 1921 onwards, the value added generated in the industries included in the Statistics of Production can be calculated for every year. Figure 8.2 shows the changing volume of value added and employment between 1921 and 1938.

Figure 8.2. Real value added and employment in the sample industries, 1921–1938 (1921 = 100)

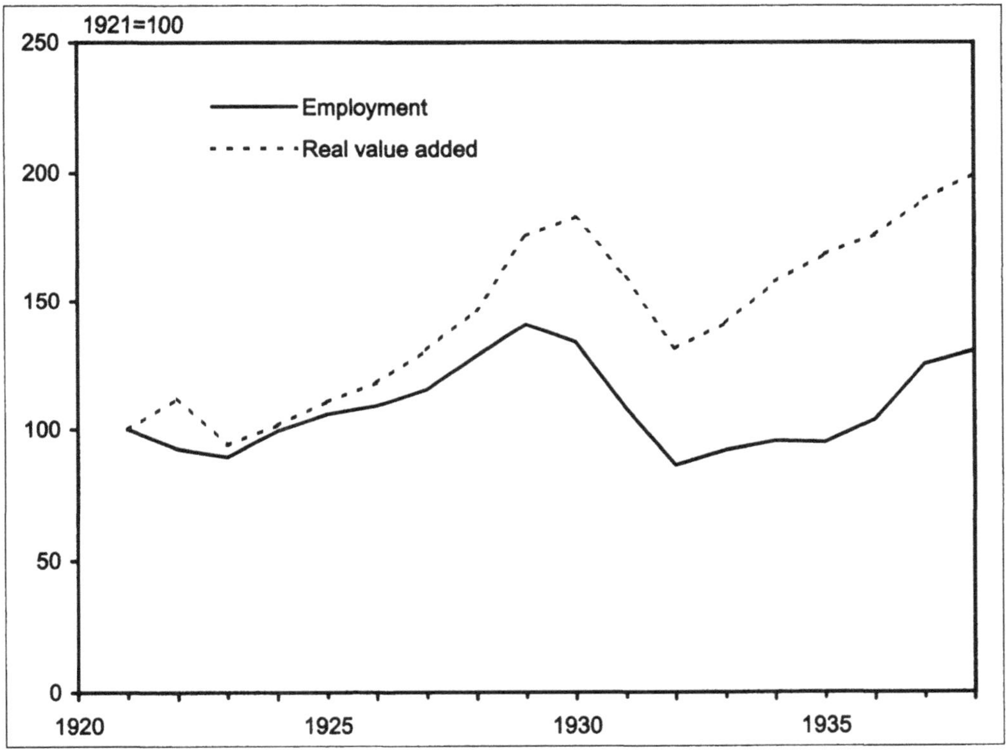

Source: Appendix C.

Despite the downward trend in prices, the volume of production in the second half of the 1920s increased. This period is widely recognised as very favourable. All the main indicators of economic performance (domestic output, employment, investments and exports) are positive year after year.[25]

[25] See Van Zanden & Griffiths, *Economische*, 115. Keesing reports low profit margins. Under pressure from a continuous decline in prices, entrepreneurs tried to lower their costs of production (Keesing, *Conjuncturele*, 80). Van de Woestijne saw this deflationary trend as a persistent (and with hindsight, ominous) warning of the approaching crisis. Even in 1929, when unemployment was very low and nominal wages rose, this did not lead to price increases. In his view the defla-

At the end of the decade manufacturing output growth accelerated. The fast growth in production in 1928 and 1929 is striking. In the course of these two years, industrial production rose by some 35% in comparison to 1927. This highlights the exceptional economic performance of 1929, with a capacity utilisation of more than 100 percent. The peak in the business cycle that was reached in that year can scarcely be compared to any other boom in the twentieth century.

The international financial crisis that followed the crash on the New York stock exchange in 1929 took hold in Europe in 1930, with a decline in production.[26] In the Netherlands, the 1929–1930 period marked the end of the trend of industrial growth of the 1920s. Figure 8.2 shows that production volumes reached a low in 1932, but that the rising trend from that point continued almost without interruption until 1938. By 1938, the index had reached a level that was clearly above that of 1929.

It is also striking that the growth of industrial employment lagged far behind growth in production. In 1929 the index of employment, at 141 (1921 = 100), reached its highest point during the inter-war period, but by that time the index for production was already at 175. This difference continued to grow after 1929. The employment index only begins to rise appreciably after 1935. In 1938 the index of total employment in the industries included in the Statistics of Production had regained the level of 1928, while the index of industrial production was already 36% above that of 1928.

Figure 8.3 shows average labour productivity in real terms for the period 1921–1938. The data has been obtained by dividing the index numbers for value added by the corresponding employment index.

These estimates of the real value added per worker point to an annual increase of 3.3 percent per year between 1921 and 1929. In terms of value added per working hour, the increase is 2.8 percent per year, the difference being due to the extension of the average working week, after 1921, from 45 to 48 hours.

Real labour productivity continued to rise, even after 1929, and at a higher rate than in the 1920s. It reached its highest point in 1935, in the middle of the Depression. In particular, the ten years between 1925 and 1935 saw persistent productivity growth to an extent almost unequalled in the twentieth century. The average growth in productivity in this period was 5.4 percent per year. There is a clear difference between the 1920s and the 1930s in terms of the relationships between the two components of productivity. In the first part of this period, productivity increased in line with an increase in the volume of production. From 1929, productivity continued to rise but in line with falling employment. Improved economic conditions after 1935 brought an end to this 'jobless growth'. In the second half of the 1930s employment levels increased most rapidly in electrical engineering, in the cotton and mechanical engineering industries and in shipbuilding, with rates of increase of 47, 38, 51 and 117 percent, respectively. These sectors had shed high proportions of their employment at the beginning of the Depression. The recovery

---

tionary trend after the inflationary wave during and after the First World War had not been strong enough (Van de Woestijne, Goede jaren, 379).

26 In the United States the tide had turned as early as the summer of 1929. See Kindleberger, *Depression*.

Figure 8.3. Real labour productivity in the sample industries, 1921–1938 (1921 = 100)

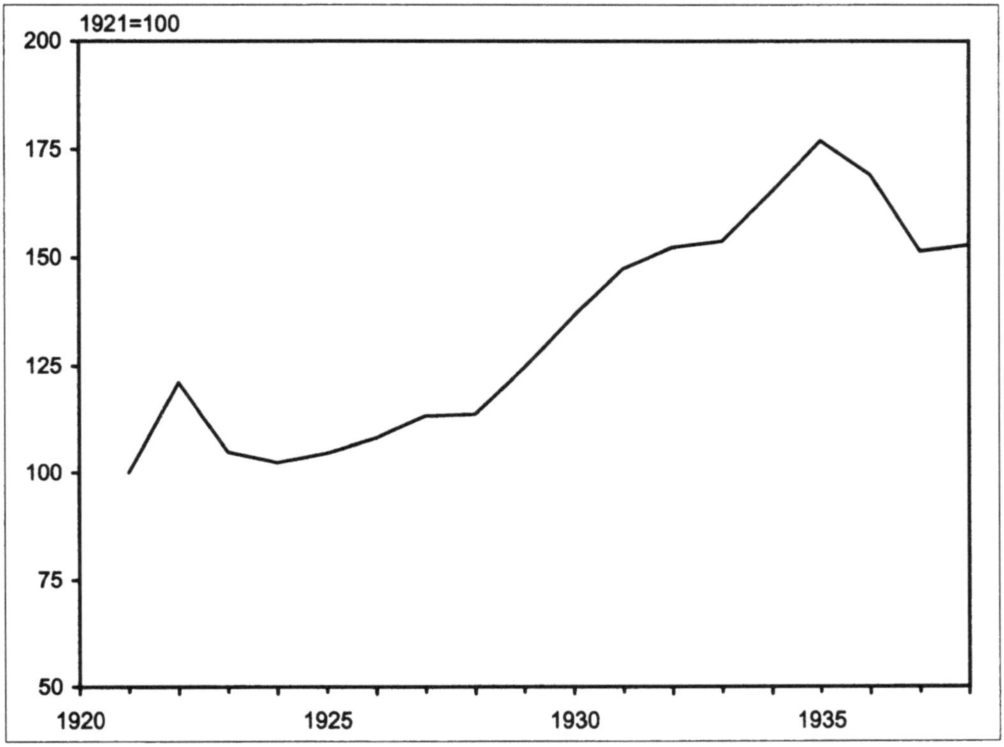

Source: Appendix C.

cannot be attributed to business cycle effects only. Some industries had also gone through structural changes. The recovery of employment in light-bulb manufacturing (part of the electrical engineering industry) was modest. During the 1930s, international protectionism had led to the relocation of much of the light-bulb manufacturing capacity to other countries. Something similar had occurred in the margarine industry. Thus the effect of the upturn in world trade in this period was accompanied by structural shifts in employment.

Table 8.4 provides an overview of productivity growth per industry for the periods 1921–1929 and 1929–1938. The 1925–1935 period, a decade of continuously increasing labour productivity for all industries, is also considered separately in the third column.

There was rapid growth in the flour, paper, rubber and bicycle industries. The first two of these had low productivity in the base year, 1921, which partly explains the high rate of growth in the following years. The latter two, and other industries such as the electrical engineering and the wire and sheet-metal working industries can be counted as emerging industries in which rapid growth in the volume of production was associated with a substantial increase in productivity.

In the period 1929–1938 the average annual increase in productivity was lower than in the 1920s (2.3 percent per annum). However there was much less variation between

Table 8.2. Real labour productivity in 16 industries, 1921–1938 (annual compound growth rates)

	1921–1929	1929–1938	1925–1935
Wire	9.1	- 0.9	0.5
Sheet-metal work	6.2	0.1	1.4
Margarine	8.5	3.1	3.8
Wool	- 1.3	0.7	4.4
Paper	12.9	2.1	4.4
Cotton	1.1	3.2	4.6
Mechanical engineering	3.5	3.7	4.9
Flour	12.2	0.9	5.4
Shipbuilding	- 0.2	3.2	5.5
Footwear	4.1	4.5	5.6
Machine knitting	6.3	0.5	5.7
Electrical engineering	9.4	3.7	6.0
Soap	3.1	3.5	6.6
Rubber	10.1	3.7	7.0
Cocoa	2.0	4.2	8.0
Bicycles	10.9	2.7	8.1
Total (Weighted)	3.3	2.3	5.4

Source: Appendix A.

industries, with no industries achieving growth rates of more than 4.5 percent, in contrast to the earlier period. However the third column of Table 8.4 shows that between 1925 and 1935 annual productivity growth was four percent or higher in almost all industries (exceptions being wire manufacturing and sheet metal working). In fact the rates of growth in the cocoa, bicycle, and rubber industries in this period were as high as seven and even eight percent. In these three industries the volume of production was increasing exceptionally rapidly. Productivity growth in industries like shipbuilding and mechanical engineering was not caused by output growth but resulted from decreasing employment levels, especially after 1929.

Industrial employment fell faster than the volume of production. During the 1920's the manufacturing sector had supplied a sufficient number of jobs for the fast increasing Dutch population. De Graaff was on solid ground when he said that in the Netherlands the depression of the 1930s was mainly an employment crisis. Of course this period was characterised by a significant decline in demand, mainly caused by falling exports. The decline in real value added between 1930 and 1932 that resulted from the downturn in trade set in with unprecedented rapidity. However, domestic demand did not collapse across the board: many industries suffered stagnant sales after 1929 or 1930, but in most cases this was only temporary. There was no long-term decline in output in industry as a whole. Surprisingly, the figures in the Statistics of Production show that the volume of production began to increase again after 1932. Many industries were actually backed by government protectionism or by collusive agreements. During the 1930s the principal characteristics of the crisis, especially high unemployment, were in part due to supply factors. Employment levels declined even in those industries in which production volumes hardly fell. Obviously, in a broad range of industries management was cutting back on labour, prompted by declining output prices.

8.6. The Great Depression and the rise in productivity

How can we explain the exceptional rise in manufacturing productivity around 1930? Figure 8.3 indicates that the increase in average labour productivity continued until well into the Depression. It even accelerated between 1929 and 1931 and between 1933 and 1935. During the first acceleration productivity growth was mainly due to lower production volumes, combined with the extensive shedding of workers. During the second phase increasing production was combined with stagnating employment. This might indicate that capital was being substituted for labour. In the previous chapter it has already been suggested that this could be related to the high relative wages of that time (see especially Figure 7.4). Van Zanden and Griffiths have also suggested, on the basis of their own calculations of industrial productivity during this period, that there must have been substitution of capital for labour. According to them, about a quarter of the rise in unemployment between 1929 and 1936 can be explained by capital substitution.[27]

I support their argument, but their estimate of the negative effects on employment is probably too low. A simple arithmetic example gives an idea of the size of the productivity effect in relation to the decline in industrial employment. Suppose that labour productivity had not increased at the calculated rate of 5.4 percent per year in the period 1925–1935 (see Table 8.4), but at 2.5 percent per year, which is the long-term average between 1913 and 1965. With the measured production volume from the Statistics of Production, employment in 1935 would have had to be more than 30 percent higher than it actually was. If we also assume that this increase in average labour productivity was a general phenomenon that was also felt in the industries that are not in the Statistics of Production, we can use estimates of total industrial employment to calculate the effect on total industrial employment. According to the most recent estimates, there were a total of 528,000 wage earners in manufacturing in 1935. If we suppose employment levels in that year would have been 30 percent higher if productivity had risen at only the 'normal' rate, we can see that there would have been about 160,000 extra jobs. This is more than 20 percent of the manufacturing workforce (773,000). The rate of unemployment in manufacturing for 1935 has been calculated at 31.7 percent of the workforce.[28]

---

27 Unfortunately, the authors do not provide a quantitative basis for the figure. See Van Zanden & Griffiths, *Economische*, 155. They regard the most important causes of the persistent unemployment as declining demand and a general stagnation of economic growth, which meant that there were not enough jobs for the growing workforce.

28 The highest unemployment rates in the 1930s were in the construction (42.9%) and transport (34.1%) sectors. The overall unemployment rate in 1935 was 22.6%, its highest point during this period. See Den Bakker & De Gijt, Labour Force Data, Table A3.7.

Should we follow this calculation for the sake of the argument we may conclude that two-thirds of the unemployment in manufacturing is attributable to the fact that labour productivity had risen by 5.4 percent per year between 1925 and 1935 instead of the long-term average of 2.5 percent. This is much higher than van Zanden and Griffiths' estimate.

These calculations are not rooted in historical reality, and they are not part of a model that specifies the relationships between variables such as production, prices, wages, profits, and the elasticity of substitution between labour and capital. All that it indicates is that the high unemployment during the Depression cannot be explained simply by a decline in industrial output. In fact, the decline in production was limited mainly to 1931 and 1932, after which industrial production increased rapidly. However the demand for labour remained low after prices had been adjusted and the demand for industrial products had begun to rise.

What effect did this have on the demand for labour (and thus employment) in manufacturing? Is there, for example, a demonstrable connection between the decline in demand for labour and the substitution of capital for labour as a result of high real wages, as is suggested above? This confronts us with a rather complicated identification problem. We can begin with an analysis of the total factor productivity for 1925–1935, as presented in Table 8.3.

Table 8.3. Growth of real value added, labour- and capital inputs, and total factor productivity (TFP) in the sample industries, 1925–1935 (annual compound growth rates, relative weight of labour 0.6, weight of capital 0.4).

	Value added	Labour	Capital	TFP
1925–1935	4.24	−1.09 (0.60)	4.34 (Prim.)	3.2
			5.85 (Elect.)	2.6
			4.14 (Mach.)	3.2
			4.30 (Cap.)	3.2

Source: Appendix B, C and D.

This simple growth accounting framework demonstrates that between 1925–1935 there was strong growth in value added accompanied by a simultaneous decrease in employment. The capital indicators in this period also point to strong growth. However, only 25 percent of the growth can be explained by the combined factor inputs labour and capital. The growth in TFP in this period was exceptionally high. This is due statistically to the decline in the labour volume. Given the reasonably high growth in value added, the decline in employment is evidence that efficiency improved. The rise in real wages and under-utilisation of production capacity after 1929 led many companies to shift towards best-practice methods, which was achieved by scrapping older vintages and installing new capital goods. Furthermore industries were being restructured following the closing down of inefficient companies or production units. Three capital indicators, primary horsepower, number of machines and the real capital stock show about the same growth rates resulting in similar TFP growth. These indicators do not reveal any growth in the productivity of capital. Capital as a factor of production grew at the same rate as the volume of production, so the capital input per unit of output did not change. Since the quantity of labour used declined, this points to a process of 'capital deepening' and the substitution of capital for labour. The only capital indicator that points to an intensification of the amount of capital in comparison to production volumes is electrical power. Only by taking the growth in electrical power can we obtain a somewhat lower TFP. A correspondingly higher portion of the growth, i.e. 40 percent, is then explained. Even in this case, the proportion of the growth in production that is explained is quite small compared to the percentages that were found for the periods 1913–1921, 1921–1938 and 1938–1965, so the 'unexplained' (TFP) growth remains high.

The figures presented above reveal the effects of a development in manufacturing that was labelled by contemporary economists as 'mechanisation and rationalisation'.[29] This is a general term that includes all the technical and organisational changes that were undertaken to achieve greater efficiency in the production process. During the Depression, cost-saving was an important consideration for managements. The continual decline in prices during the 1920s led to declining profit levels. This was compensated for by cutting production costs, in part by substituting capital for labour and in part through extensive measures to raise efficiency, intended to yield savings in all factors of production (raw materials, labour and capital). These measures were linked to the introduction of Taylorism and the principles of scientific management, which had been steadily gaining ground in trade and industry in the Netherlands since the First World War.[30] In 1928 the Dutch pioneer in this field, Van der Waerden, drew a link between scientific management and rationalisation. He described the latter as forced development and reorganisation in the fields of technology, production, transport and distribution. In his view, 'rationalisation' embraced the introduction and improvement of labour-saving machinery (mechanisation), a far-reaching division of labour (planning), better work flows in factories (production lines, for example), fuel savings, the standardisation of raw materials, semi-manufactured products and final products, performance incentives in wages, collusion and cartelisation, and research and development.

Some observers saw rationalisation as a direct cause of the high unemployment. The most perceptive observer in this respect was Hulshoff Pol, who in his 1931 analysis of the crisis in the Netherlands said that the trend to rationalisation was also closely related to high wage rates in the Netherlands; Dutch wage levels were as an important reason

---

29 For example, De Graaff in his outline of industrial development during the inter-war period has pointed to accelerating mechanisation, due in part to the steady decline in prices (De Graaff, Industrie, 207). Keesing spoke of a process of mechanisation and rationalisation in the production process, which he says had begun during the 1920s (Keesing, *Conjuncturele*, 81–82, 176). Tinbergen draws a connection between capital formation and rationalisation in industry (Tinbergen, Kapitaalvorming, 14).

30 For productivity increasing measures in Dutch manufacturing see De Jong, *Nederlandse industrie*, 237–257. For a detailed treatment of Taylorism and 'scientific management' in the Netherlands, see Bloemen, *Scientific*. For the debates on such topics within the Dutch labour unions between the wars, see Laurier & Pot, Arbeidersbeweging, 71–154.

for managers to cut labour even further. He even predicted that productivity might rise further (which it did, in fact).[31] The process of further labour-saving rationalisation was accelerated by the Depression and the stickiness of money wages. This is also what we have seen from the comparison between real wages and real labour productivity in the previous chapter. During the 1930s both indicators rose simultaneously.

8.7. The impact of government policies in the 1930s

We can now turn to the pattern of industrial development in the Netherlands after 1932. The depreciation of the British pound in September 1931 and the introduction of the *General Tariff* on British imports in February 1932 worsened the Netherlands' export position still further.[32] The bilateralisation of trade with Germany only made things worse. The Netherlands not only lost important export markets, its domestic producers also faced competitive imports from countries whose currencies had been devalued. Although economic growth resumed again after 1932 in the United Kingdom, in Germany, and in Scandinavia, there was no such development in the Netherlands. In 1936 there were more than 600,000 unemployed, or 19 percent of the workforce, according to estimates by Den Bakker and Van Sorge. We repeat that the unemployment rate in manufacturing alone was more than 30 percent.[33] However price levels continued to decline until 1935. De Graaff therefore concluded (as Keesing had for the period 1920–1923) that the Netherlands suffered from a contraction in prices rather than a contraction of the volume of production, with the exception of some industries such as shipbuilding.[34]

It is striking that there was no rapid change in the volume of industrial production after 1936, the year in which the Netherlands abandoned the gold standard, resulting in a lower exchange rate of the guilder. While there was an increase in 1937, as compared to 1936, this had hardly any effect on the trend. The fall in the exchange rate and the resulting change in the Netherlands' international competitive position did not directly lead to higher growth in real output. However there was an increase in the price level: the rise in prices that had begun in 1936 accelerated in 1937. From De Graaff's survey of domestic and foreign sales by the industries in our sample, it appears that the increase in sales that occurred in 1937 and 1938 was mainly due to increased domestic demand. For example, domestic sales of machine-manufacturing increased from 32.4 to 72.2 million guilders between 1936 and 1938, while exports increased from 10 to 18.7 million guilders in the same period. In the cotton industry, overseas demand was still the most important factor. Domestic sales increased from 81.9 to 91.8 million between 1936 and 1938, and exports from 24.6 to 43.4 million guilders.[35]

---

31 Hulshoff Pol, Rationalisatie, 404–406.

32 Kitson & Solomou, *Economic*, 3.

33 Den Bakker & Van Sorge, Onbenut arbeidsvolume, 237–238.

34 De Graaff, Industrie, 27. He added that many people in the Netherlands were under the mistaken impression that the Netherlands had not surmounted the 1929 crisis, and had gone through the 1930s and as far as the Second World War in a permanent state of low economic activity.

35 De Graaff, Industrie, 15.

Dutch monetary policy during the Depression was focused on the gold standard, at least until September 1936. External balance was maintained through the constant gold parity of the guilder, so that export prices could only be adjusted to match lower price levels in other countries by reducing domestic prices. For Dutch industries, the 'fetters' of the gold standard meant that producers would have to cut the prices of their final products sharply if they were to remain competitive on domestic and international markets. This did happen to some extent, but not all prices fell with equal rapidity. Wholesale prices reached a low around 1935, when the price index for raw materials was just 42 percent of the 1929 level. However the index of output prices declined to only 67 percent of the 1929 level. The difference points to a certain degree of rigidity in the structure of production costs, including wages. The 'downward stickiness' of wages was in part due to a lag in the decline in the cost of living, which by 1935 had fallen by only 18 to 20 percent in comparison to 1929.[36] Important fixed costs such as house-rents did not change in this period, and taxes actually rose. Thus the adjustment of domestic prices, which the government advocated as a means of countering the effects of the strong currency, proved difficult to achieve in practice.[37] A system of legislation involving extensive intervention in the economy was gradually developed, in order to limit damage to sectors that were strongly dependent on international trade or that suffered from low price levels. This initial phase of government regulation was characterised by experimentation with a variety of policy instruments, the effects of which were sometimes contradictory. However specific sectors of industry did benefit.

The Wheat Act, adopted in 1931, proved to be the beginning of extensive legislation focusing on protecting the agricultural sector from the symptoms of the Depression in the Netherlands.[38] Because arable farming in the Netherlands was facing stiff competition from the import of cheap foreign grain, this law established a system of regulating prices and sales. The flour milling industry had to comply with a measure regulating the composition of inputs: 35 percent of the input had to consist of domestic grains. Imported grains were made more expensive by an import levy. This gave the flour milling industry a monopoly on the supply of flour within the Netherlands. Moreover, in June 1934 a manufacturers' agreement divided the domestic market into fixed shares, and overall production was determined by the government.[39] While part of the monopoly windfalls was passed on to agricultural producers, the high price levels and market agreements made this industry a very protected sector in the 1930s, so production increased rapidly in these years.[40] The margarine industry also had a stipulated composition of inputs, in this case of butter, as part of the support for dairy farming. From 1932, margarine had to contain 25 percent butter, and later 40 percent. Moreover there was an extra levy on

---

36 See CBS, *Zestig jaren*, 125; Schrage, Nijhoff & Wielsma, Inkomensontwikkeling, 384; Keesing, *Conjuncturele*, 111. See also Verdoorn, Verstarring.

37 Renaud, Prijsontwrichting, 937.

38 In 1933 all the emergency legislation relating to agriculture was consolidated in the Agricultural Emergency Act, which gave the government extensive powers, while eliminating much of parliamentary control.

39 Ammerlaan, Ordening, 832–833.

40 CBS, *Maandschrift 1934*, 1317–1321.

margarine, which raised its retail price. To prevent these measures being circumvented, the establishment of new factories and mixing plants was forbidden.[41]

The Agricultural Emergency Act of 1933 combined all the agricultural laws and regulations that had been developed up to that point. The Act gave the government many powers with regard to financial support and the regulation of production and trade, and it was intended to keep internal prices high enough to ensure the survival of farmers, by limiting supply, providing subsidies and levying import duties.[42] By doing this the government undermined its own policy of reducing domestic prices, not only by raising taxes but, in particular, also by direct intervention in the prices of food products.[43]

Secondly, the government protected Dutch industry by establishing a quota system for imports.[44] This policy was embodied in the Emergency Imports Act (*Crisisinvoerwet*) of 23 December 1931. The act restricted 'excessive imports' of particular goods by setting quotas for each product and exporting country, so that the necessary restructuring and adjustment of production could be implemented without too many casualties. In the course of time, quotas were established for pottery, clothing, leather, footwear, rubber tyres, wire products, bicycles, light bulbs, vacuum cleaners, paper, cotton and woollen cloth, machine-knitted products, carpets and a number of chemical products. The effect of these measures was that Dutch producers could sell an increasing portion of their output in the domestic market, strengthening a trend that had begun in the 1920s, i.e. for industry to focus more on the domestic market.[45]

Although it was thought that the necessary adjustment process would have to lead to further price decreases, the policy of protection had perverse effects.[46] In some cases the government even set maximum prices to force manufacturers to reduce their prices, as in the case of light bulb production. At first this was done by government directive, but in 1936 a Price Control Act was passed in association with the abandonment of the gold standard in that year.[47]

Moreover undesirable increases in production capacity and the unwanted role that outsiders could play in evading pricing agreements led to regulation laws. The most important were an act giving the government the right to sanction producer's agreements (1935) and the Industrial Licensing Act of 1938. The latter made it possible to

---

41 CBS, *Maandschrift 1934*, 724–728.

42 See Keesing, *Conjuncturele*, 186–189.

43 Keesing claims that this actually resulted in an eight to eleven percent increase in the cost of living for a family. Keesing, *Conjuncturele*, 187. For an estimation of price inertia in the U.S. during the same period see: Romer, Why did prices rise in the 1930s?

44 See Van Schaik, *Crisis*, for an extensive overview.

45 CBS, *Maandschrift 1939*, 11–12. De Graaff, Industrie, 15.

46 See 'Gevoerde contingenteeringspolitiek' ('The quota system as implemented'), in *Verslagen en mededelingen 1936*, no. 3.

47 The Act of 30 September, containing temporary measures to prevent the forcing up of prices (*Staatsblad 639 D*), was intended to annul the effects of the abandonment of the gold standard. The devaluation of the guilder would have the effect of driving up prices. However this Act was only actually applied in a few cases.

prohibit the entrance of new firms in a branche, thus enabling producers' agreements, import quotas, protective import levies and industrial regulation policies to be implemented.[48] The quota system, together with initiatives by the Ministry of Economic Affairs to support industry (f.i. the Employment Fund (*Werkfonds*) of 1934 and the Society for Industrial Finance in 1936), can be regarded as predecessors of the industrialisation policies that were implemented after the Second World War. The white papers on the import quota policy generally expressed satisfaction that the prices of quota products were not significantly higher than those of non-quota products.[49] Keesing, however, had pointed to the drawbacks of this policy with regard to the necessary downward adjustment of price-levels, but also he states that these measures had protected many industries from a worse fate.[50]

In addition to an increasing orientation to the domestic market and the driving up of relative prices, the quota system had the effect of enabling the government to pressure industries to organise, which favoured the formation of national and international producers' agreements. De Graaff points to this factor in observing that the continuation of the crisis after 1932 was due mainly to a domestic cause: adaptation to the new circumstances was too slow, as a result of producers' agreements on output volumes and prices.[51] There was an increasing trend towards collusion and concentration in Dutch industry. Several industries in the sample, such as the margarine, electrical engineering, wire and soap industries, had known producers' agreements and cartelisation long before 1929. De Hen locates the beginning of this first wave mainly during the crisis of 1921–1923, and mentions breweries, chemicals, matches, rubber, artificial silk, glass, paper and iron and steel. Although the Dutch government advocated economic liberalism, De Hen characterises the government's stance regarding these cartels as 'benevolent'.[52] In that sense, the organisation of industry during the 1930s was simply a continuation of a practice that had developed in the 1920s.

The quota system facilitated the growth of industries that would otherwise have been unlikely to become so big. The proliferation of the ready-made clothing and machine-knitting industry in the middle of the Depression is without doubt in this respect: in 1931 there were 660 and 98 companies, respectively, operating in the two industries, and in 1935 there were 914 and 155 companies.[53] Without the import restrictions, the growth would surely have been less rapid.

From analyses of the industrial policies of the Depression by De Hen and Van Schaik, it appears that there was no coherent policy.[54] The ad-hoc character of the sup-

48 Ibid. De Hen identifies the closure of the aluminium processing industry as the clearest example.

49 See 'Gevoerde contingenteeringspolitiek' (The quota system as implemented), in *Verslagen en mededelingen 1932*, no. 3, 33–34.

50 Keesing, *Conjuncturele*, 185.

51 De Graaff, Industrie, 30; Blaisse, Nederlandse, 392–396.

52 De Hen, *Actieve*, 30–33.

53 Ibid., 209.

54 See also Keesing, *Conjuncturele*, 194, 288–290. The measures taken were ineffective and insubstantial. Broadly speaking, the government lacked the means to implement a pro-active industrial or planning policy. Its responses were mainly defensive, focusing on import and export regula-

port, with some sectors receiving help and others (such as most of the metallurgical industries) getting no support, makes it difficult to clearly identify the effects of these measures for industry. The international trade regulations may have been important for some industries, but many industries, such as the shipbuilding industry, survived the Depression mainly through their own strength.

The emergency measures taken by the government created an economic climate in the Netherlands in the 1930s, in which the government, having proved unable to apply a coherent policy of external equilibrium and internal adjustment, approved and even required extensive agreements between producers. The expected benefits, in terms of job creation did not, at first, eventuate, because real wages were high. After a forced process of rationalisation between 1925 and 1935, employment began to rise again from about 1936 on. The question remains, whether the Netherlands developed an improper composition of industrial branches as a result, since additional employment was created in sectors that relied on the regulation of international trade, import quotas and other forms of protection. However this is a hypothetical question, since the Second World War and the German occupation prevent us seeing the possible 'natural' corrections to what may be supposed to be an inadequate industrial structure. In fact, the 1930s of regulatory and sometimes direct intervention by the state were followed by a decade characterised by German occupation measures and post-war reconstruction policies, in which government intervention in the economy was even more pervasive. For instance, during this period of the 1940s the metallurgical sector, which had had relatively moderate support in the 1930s, was granted exceptional opportunities for expansion. Once again, important parts of manufacturing industry were operating under exceptional circumstances.

8.8. Conclusions

Despite big differences between the fortunes of the various industries in the 1913–1938 period, some common trends can be identified. In general, the circumstances of the First World War and the global trend towards stronger official trade restrictions during the inter-war period (especially in the 1930s) led to a wave of industrialisation in the Netherlands.

Overall, there was a considerable increase in capacity during the First World War. Some industries had excess capacity in the 1920s. In other industries, the shortening of the working week led to new investments in labour-saving production techniques in response to higher labour costs. In the 1920s the increase in production capacity in industry was accompanied by growing employment. The increasing orientation of industry to the domestic market began as early as the 1920s, due not only to increasing domestic demand, but also to increasing international protection. The downturn in the international economy around 1930 led to extensive production cuts in large industries such as

tions and establishing a legal framework for planning measures to counter the negative effects of the crisis.

shipbuilding and the cotton industry, but the cuts are less pronounced if we compare production volumes to those of 1927 and 1928. Most industries had already recovered from the downturn in sales after 1930, long before the gold standard was abandoned. Adjustments were made by introducing new products and production methods. This process of adjustment was characterised especially by a marked decrease in employment. In some industries, such as the electrical engineering and margarine industries, employment opportunities were exported; in others there was a deliberate attempt to increase the efficiency of the production process. The much higher average labour productivity that had been achieved in the second half of the 1920s continued to increase at the same rate in the 1930s. Employment only began to grow significantly in 1936.

One conclusion that we can draw from the calculations of productivity is that the Depression revealed a strong underlying tendency to greater production efficiency in Dutch industry. The essential dynamic was already visible in the 1920s, with the first wave of mechanisation during and immediately after the First World War. Contemporaries were already pointing to the effects of shorter working hours and higher real wages, which would lead to the substitution of capital for labour.

The higher relative factor price of labour (another effect of shorter working hours) led to much greater capital intensity during the inter-war period. The exogenous decline in prices after 1929 amplified this. In the framework of disequilibrium theories, and distinguishing between vintages of capital goods with unequal levels of productivity, we can say that increasing labour costs implied that machines had a shorter economic life. This resulted in the retirement of older machinery and the application of more capital-intensive production techniques such as faster machines and better production processes.

The direct comparison between real wage costs and the user costs of capital in the previous chapter revealed a strong rising trend in relative labour costs. This process was further strengthened in the 1930s when lower profit margins prompted companies to undertake further restructuring. Producers discovered that the same volume of output could be manufactured with fewer workers and a constant capital intensity.[55] In the 1930s this led to massive job cuts, even in industries that were not suffering from a decline in demand and sales volumes.

The above provides a mainly structural explanation for the persistence of depression symptoms in Dutch industry. Supply-side effects had a great impact on manufacturing, because the underlying market mechanisms were inefficient, either because prices gave the wrong signals or adjusted unevenly (due in part to inconsistent economic policies) or because of institutional rigidities.[56]

---

55 Verdoorn, *Arbeidsduur*, 246.

56 For extensive overviews of other theories on the persistence of the Depression in the Netherlands, see Drukker, *Waarom*, Chapters 2, 3 and 4; Mulder, *Denken*, 14–17, 38–53, 199–206. More generally on the blurring of economic agents' perceptions of relative prices and the economic effects of regulations and bureaucratic hurdles see Harberger, Vision, 21–22.

Chapter 9: War, reconstruction and catching up between 1938 and 1965

9.1. Introduction

This chapter will consider the effects of the war and the German occupation on industrial production and production capacity in the Netherlands, and the nature of industrial development after the war.

The attempts of the government to protect industry from the harmful impact of the Depression were only a prelude to the regulation that took place just before and during the Second World War. During the war, state control increased rapidly, in the form of general wage and price controls, production quotas, rationing and the closure of branches of industry, to name just some of the measures. During the war many industries were forced to produce for the occupying German forces. In addition, the German authorities sought to control the governance of Dutch industry. However Van Zanden and Griffiths' overview has clearly shown that German attempts to merge large Dutch companies with German industry came to nothing. The reorganisation of the Dutch economy in accordance with the *Führerprinzip* also had few concrete effects in the end.[1]

After the reconstruction phase, between 1945 and 1950, all signs for the Dutch economy appeared to be good. Demand was growing, and the current account deficit was eliminated quite quickly, thanks in part to the Marshall Plan aid between 1948 and 1952. Levels of investment were high. Given the further liberalisation of international trade, and the low exchange rate of the guilder, Dutch products could easily find their way on foreign markets. The establishment of the European Economic Community in 1958 greatly increased the Netherlands' export potential. Despite rapid population growth, unemployment was low, in part because of the low rate of female participation in the labour market. Yet this low unemployment levels did not immediately lead to tension on the labour market and thus to higher wages, a fact that has been explained in the literature by referring to the consensus among the 'social partners' (government, employers and unions) about the objectives for wage-setting, investments and employment. Wages and prices were to be kept under control, and the resources made available by low wages invested, especially in industry, to create new jobs. This consensus is said to have been created by the government, at least in part, by means of a conscious policy of wage control and by stimulating industry through its industrialisation policy. These two pillars of the government's economic policy in the post-war period have been cited

1 Van Zanden & Griffiths, *Economische*, 166–169.

in numerous publications.[2] I will return to this point at the end of this chapter. Most of this chapter will be devoted to new findings, derived from the Statistics of Production.

9.2. Output and employment between 1938 and 1965

This section provides an overview of changes in value added and employment in industry between 1938 and 1965. As in Chapter 8, the figures used here are drawn from the Statistics of Production, and they are calculated in the same way: the total value of inputs has been subtracted from the total value of production in the industries included in the Statistics of Production. Then a time series in constant prices has been calculated, using the production price indexes listed in the appendices. Figure 9.1 provides an overview of the resulting real volume of net production and employment for the period 1938–1965.

Figure 9.1. Real value added and employment in the sample industries, 1938–1965 (1938 = 100)

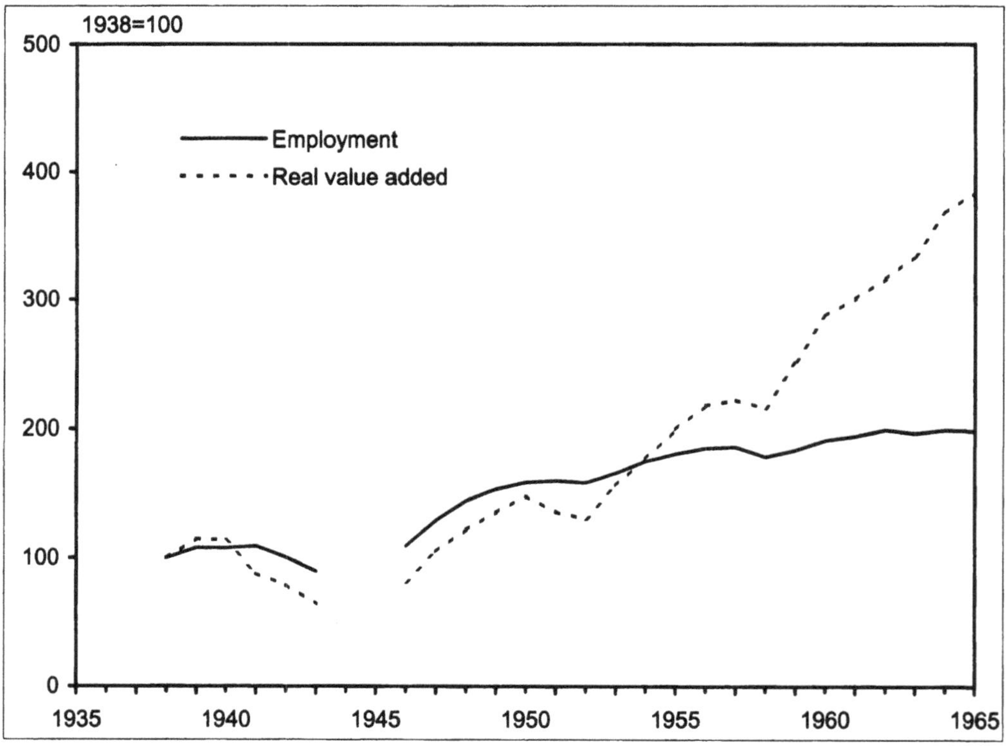

Source: Appendix C.

---

2 Weststrate, *Economic*; Dercksen, *Industrialisatiepolitiek*; Fase, *Vijfendertig*, Windmuller, De Galan and Van Zweeden, *Arbeidsverhoudingen*; Fortuyn, *Sociaal-economische*; Van Hulst, *Effectiviteit*.

Real production in manufacturing during 1939 and 1940 was higher than in 1938. The threat of war raised demand and led to exceptionally high industrial activity. Production rose by about 10 percent between 1938 and 1939. The increase was especially marked in the cocoa and soap industries, in several of the metallurgical industries such as steel furniture manufacturing, coachwork and wire production, and in the textiles and clothing sectors (see appendices).

During the first year of the German occupation, the level of production remained as high as in the previous year. Domestic demand was replaced with new demand generated by the war. However in the course of 1941, 1942 and 1943, the production index for all the industries in the Statistics of Production declined by more than 40 percent in comparison to 1940.

In 1946, industrial production was about 75 percent of the level of 1938. This percentage is based on exactly the same group of industries as in 1938. The rate of recovery was especially high in the metallurgical industries, with the exception of mechanical engineering and the bicycle industry. Total industrial production regained its 1938 level as early as 1947, and three years later it was 50 percent higher than in 1938. Once again, the most dynamic performances were in the metallurgical industries. If we exclude shipbuilding and mechanical engineering, production in all of the remaining metallurgical industries had more than doubled in comparison to 1938, and in most cases it actually tripled or quadrupled.

For several years after 1950, the economy was influenced by the exceptional demand conditions that the Korean War engendered in international trade. Steps taken by the Dutch government to restore the balance of payments (there was a deficit in the current account, and spending restraints were imposed) slowed down economic activity.[3] After 1950, the prices of raw materials rose very rapidly at first. Industry had to deal with higher input costs, with the result that increase in value added came to a halt in 1951.

There was a clear cyclical pattern during the 1950s.[4] In 1957 and 1958, production even declined. As in 1950–1952, there was a combination of international and national factors. The stagnation in 1957 can be attributed to spending restraints that the government had decided on in 1956 as a result of a balance of trade deficit. Public and private sector investments were limited.[5] However, the effects of these anti-cyclical Keynesian policies amplified the effects of the international recession of 1958. Looking to more structural characteristics of industrial production after 1955 one can observe that production growth in the textiles and clothing industries and in construction materials stagnated, while production in the 'newer' metallurgical industries (cars, electrical products and steel furniture) and in continuous-process industries such as paper, rubber and soapmaking, rose rapidly. Between 1956 and 1960 production in these rapidly growing industries increased by 50 percent or more. The automobile industry doubled its production:

3 Van Zanden & Griffiths, *Economische*, 238–239.

4 See also Van Duijn, *Lange golf*, 12ff. In the period dealt with here, 1949, 1952, 1958 and 1962/63 can be regarded as troughs, and 1951, 1956, 1960 and 1964/1965 as peaks.

5 Van Zanden and Griffiths, *Economische*, 239.

these were the early years of the Netherlands' first mass-produced car. In 1954 about 20,000 cars were produced; followed by 27,000 in 1956 and more than 58,000 in 1960.[6]

In the years 1960–1965, the production indexes for the 20 industries considered here begin to reveal greater variations. There was an absolute decline in the volume of production in five industries, including the cotton industry and shipbuilding, which had long distinguished Dutch industry. The production indexes of both industries peaked between 1960 and 1964. For the cotton industry, this was its absolute peak; in the rest of the 1960s and 1970s output and production capacity declined. The Netherlands' substantial shipbuilding industry, however, experienced a strong recovery later on in the 1970s, at least in terms of the tonnage produced.[7] During the 1960s consumer-goods industries such as the leather, soap, machine knitting, flour, margarine, footwear, wool and pottery industries exhibited below-average growth. Rapid growth can again be seen in the metallurgical industries: cars, wire production, electrical appliances, sheet-metal work, mechanical engineering and steel furniture. There was also high growth in the paper and ready-made clothing industries.

We can also note some features of the changes in employment levels during this period. The employment figures in the Statistics of Production are based on the same group of industries for which production figures are given. Since this is a sample of all industries, the absolute volume of employment reported is not the same as industrial employment as a whole. Nevertheless, the changes in the employment index for these industries are nearly identical to the pattern of the employment index for industry as a whole. The time series of employment levels points to an increase between 1938 and 1941, from 100 to about 110, respectively. From 1941 to 1943 the index declines to 90.[8] During the first three years of the war there was certainly not a "collapse of genuine employment opportunities in industry", as Griffiths has claimed.[9] On the contrary, jobs were being created.

No reliable data is available for 1944 and 1945. The index of employment for 1946, the first year following the war, is 109. Industrial employment was already higher than it had ever been, except for the peak in 1941. From 1946 to 1950, the index rises exceptionally rapidly. For 1950 it is more than 50 percent above the level of 1938. During the 1950s and early 1960s, industrial employment continued to grow; the index reaches about 200.

---

6 See CBS, *Statistics of Production (Carrosseriebouw)*, 1955 and 1960.

7 For developments after 1965, see for example CBS (1994), *Vijfennegentig jaren*, 78–84. The volume of production for shipbuilding is given in terms of an index of physical production. In the course of time, the value added per ton launched declined. While the construction of ever-larger tankers in the 1970s meant that the tonnage (carrying capacity) that was launched increased rapidly, the value added did not grow in proportion. The tonnage launched peaked in 1975, when more than one million gross registered tons of shipping capacity was produced. Two years later only 200,000 tons was launched.

8 This agrees reasonably well with figures for employment, based on the *Algemene Industrie Statistiek* (General industrial statistics): see CBS (1947), *Kroniek*, 18. However we will return to this point later in the chapter, in relation to an alternative calculation of the volume of production.

9 Griffiths, Exploitation, 119.

In retrospect we can see that 1965 was the year in which industrial employment, measured in terms of the number of job, reached the highest level of the century. A process of de-industrialisation began in the second half of the 1960s, and employment in industry declined. In this phase, less labour-intensive industries clearly grew faster than the labour-intensive industries.

9.3. Manufacturing industry during the Second World War

Within the framework of the present study, a description and analysis of the development of the industrial sector during the war and occupation must necessarily be concise.[10] Nevertheless, it will be given considerable weight: without a clear understanding of the developments during this period, the state of affairs in industry after the war could only be partially explained.

In 1939 the effects of the Depression could still be observed in the Dutch economy. Although the threat of war led to heightened economic activity in 1939, unemployment was still very high, at about 14 percent of the workforce.[11] Yet mobilisation and rising demand for labour led to a tight labour market. Low educational levels and lack of familiaritity with newer production methods made it difficult to reallocate older employees, in particular, within companies. Unemployed people were being trained in the metallurgical, textile and ready-made clothing industries to increase skills.[12]

When war broke out in September 1939, the Netherlands immediately felt the consequences of blockades by the belligerents. Exports were restricted, access to raw materials became more difficult, and the Dutch government imposed production ceilings on the chemicals and food and beverage industries. During the occupation, a state-controlled economy developed in the Netherlands. The government agencies that had been established before the war for each product group or industry were responsible for allocating raw materials and for designing and checking production requirements. This gave them wide authority over the inputs that industry used, and what was produced. Moreover from May 1940 there was an administrative system that set and monitored prices.

From the beginning of the occupation, the question of access to raw materials was central to industrial production. Overseas sources of raw materials were cut off. This had especially harmful effects on the food and beverage industry. Moreover the occupying German forces demanded much of the stocks of raw materials. Supplies of raw

10 For an extensive review of the fate of the various sectors of industry see the *Economische en sociale kroniek der oorlogsjaren 1940–1945* (Economic and social account of the war years, 1940–1945) published by the CBS (1947). This contains a summary of the detailed chapters on economic and social developments, which at that time were included as a supplement to the *Maandschriften*, and are our most important source of qualitative information on economic events and developments during the occupation. Recently Klemann finished a monograph on the Dutch economy between 1938 and 1948. Most of his conclusions underline what is said in the present study. See, Klemann, *Nederland 1938–1948*, also Klemann, niederländische Wirtschaft.

11 Den Bakker & Van Sorge, Arbeidsvolume, 237.

12 CBS (1947), *Kroniek*, 14 and *Onderzoek "blijvende werkloosheid"*.

materials declined by 56 percent between 1940 and 1943, while supplies of semi-manufactured products declined by 45 percent. The Netherlands received imports only from Germany, from other occupied countries on the continent and from neutral countries such as Sweden. Raw materials from domestic sources also became scarcer, in part as a result of a reduction in the number of livestock, which again had negative effects on the food and beverage industry.

Immediately after the invasion in 1940, industrial production temporarily slowed. The demand for goods on both the Dutch and German markets recovered quickly. The Dutch economy was subordinated to that of Germany as early as 1940. It was required to produce not only for the domestic, Dutch population but also for Germany. This led to direct German intervention in industry. The new demand consisted, on the one hand, of orders from the occupying forces and, on the other hand, of military and civilian orders for exports to Germany.[13] Orders also came in the form of *Verlagerungsaufträge*, i.e. 'transferred' orders for Dutch companies originating from German manufacturers, who provided the materials. Moreover selected industries were called on to assist with the reconstruction and expansion of the domestic infrastructure (bricks), supplying means of production (mechanical engineering, ships) and goods for military purposes (aircraft, coachwork, radio equipment) and to manufacture consumer goods for the occupation forces and for Germany (furniture, bicycles, footwear, textiles, food and beverages). During the occupation this production gradually increased from 21 percent of the total industrial output in the second half of 1941 to 35 percent in the first quarter of 1944.[14] However this probably under-estimates the actually amount, because many orders were placed indirectly, via Dutch customers.[15] L. de Jong reports that, according to figures produced by the *Zentralauftragsstelle* (the department responsible for the central administration and further treatment of German orders placed with Dutch firms), more than 4,000 million RM of goods were delivered. These were worth more than 3,000 million Dutch guilders.[16]

Although there was an overall decline of production due to the war, the production of some types of goods – including new ones – did increase. These ranged from ships for inland transport to packaging materials to stoves.[17] At the same time, production capacity for new products such as gas generators, methane gas, various metal alloys, mortar, wallboards, benzyl, bakelite, carbon paper, agricultural machines, medical instruments, imitation leather, batteries, photographic articles, lenses, office machines and vitamins was increased.[18] Production capacity also expanded in other areas, such as shipyards

13 For a detailed description of how this was organised, see L. de Jong, *Koninkrijk* part 7, 86ff.

14 CBS (1947), *Kroniek*, 15.

15 L. de Jong, *Koninkrijk*, part 7, 120, estimates that production for Germany amounted to 25% of turnover in 1941, more than 30% in 1942, and over 50% in 1944. For the regulations governing the filling of German orders by industry, see L. de Jong, *Koninkrijk*, part 4, 173–190, 201–206.

16 Griffiths has a lower estimate, at 2,300 million guilders, but several industrial sectors are not presented in his table. Griffiths, Exploitation, 122.

17 CBS, *Maandschrift mei/juni 1941*, k99.

18 Freseman Gratama, Herstel, 263–265. The author lists a total of 60 products and claims that the industrialisation process actually continued during the occupation.

(new construction and repairs), steel rolling mills, aircraft construction and the production of artificial fibres.[19]

In 1942 and 1943, industry suffered limitations in many fields. Fuel shortages increased, there was a lack of skilled personnel and there were transport difficulties due to the lack of local means of transport. This resulted in a further rise in unit costs, while output prices could not always rise at the same rate, because of the price controls.[20] During the occupation the average working hours were increased from 48 to 51 hours per week.[21] In early 1944, total employment in industry, measured in man-years, was about 90 percent of the level in 1938. In September 1941 it had been 110 percent. Thus employment measured in working hours early in 1944 was about the same as it had been when war broke out.

When the Netherlands once more saw direct military action, in September 1944, almost all industry came to a standstill. The causes were various. There was a lack of fuel, raw materials and transport (partly due to a rail strike), and the German army began to destroy means of production and plunder goods and property. The very serious food shortage in the west of the Netherlands during the winter of 1944–45 reduced economic activity drastically.

Labour relations were subjected to strong regulations. New regulations on the dismissal of workers were introduced at an early stage: on 11 June 1940. It was forbidden to stop work in a business, temporarily or permanently, without a permit, to shorten the working week to less than 36 hours per week, or to dismiss workers. To prevent unemployment, the Labour Inspectorate followed a policy of not allowing workers to be dismissed if it was possible to reduce working hours to 36 hours per week.

A second radical change during the occupation was the suspension of the existing system of organised consultation between employers and employees, and the intensification of government interference with conditions of employment. Wage increases and strikes were forbidden at the very beginning of the occupation, and wage cuts were also banned. In November 1940 all wage agreements in collective labour agreements had to be approved by the so-called Board of Mediators. The policy of the German authorities was that wage increases could only be implemented if they were unavoidable. Moreover, the level of Dutch wages had to be adjusted downward in relation to German wages, so that there would be a difference of about ten percent – to encourage work in Germany. There was also an effort to equalise the wages paid in different companies to prevent companies competing on the labour market. Finally, there was the widespread introduction of paid holidays. As a result of the initiatives taken by the Board, a large number of collective labour agreements and other binding regulations were established, extending also to industries in which they had previously been unthinkable because of poor labour relations. These included the dairy produce, textiles and chemicals industries. Between 1940 and the end of 1942, the number of employees working under a collective labour agreement rose from 350,000 to 1 million.[22]

---

19 See, for example, L. de Jong, *Koninkrijk*, dl.7, 124.

20 CBS, *Maandschrift* Febr./March 1943, k8.

21 CBS, *Maandschrift* March/April 1944, 102–105.

22 Ibid., 283.

The government also kept a tight grip on industry in the field of the pricing policies. The international political tensions of 1938 had already led to new legislation to prevent extraordinary price increases.[23] After the German invasion, legislation on price setting was reinforced.[24] The occupation soon gave rise to a scarcity of goods in the Netherlands. This was due initially to the loss of supplies of raw materials, other material inputs, machines and end products from countries that were at war with Germany. Later it was a result of the export of goods to Germany, without any compensatory increase in imports from Germany. In April 1941 the currency exchange restrictions between Germany and the Netherlands were abolished, which in practice meant that German residents were free to exchange Reichsmarks for guilders and to buy Dutch goods. Other factors also had a strong potential to force up prices: production for war purposes, the removal of raw materials and other production requirements, and later of machinery, forced labour in Germany and a decline in labour productivity. These led to an increasing scarcity of goods and an increase in the volume of money in circulation. The monetary overhang was to some extent neutralised through rationing for civilians, but this could not prevent the development of a black market.

Individual industries were obliged to provide information about the prices they charged, yet a wide range of prices and product types were permitted during the occupation, which led to a trend of persistent price rises.[25] It is therefore very likely that the official price indexes of the CBS for the years of occupation (which are based on wholesale prices) somewhat under-estimate the actual wholesale price movements, and they may strongly under-estimate the rise in retail prices.

9.4. Changes in labour productivity during the war years

The war and occupation led to a decline in industrial labour productivity.[26] Table 9.1 presents estimates of average labour productivity for the years 1938–1943, calculated

---

23 *Prijsopdrijvingswet* 1938, *Staatsblad 636*.

24 On the first day of the German invasion, 10 May 1940, an order was issued forbidding any increase in prices and rents above the level applying on 9 May 1940 (*Staatscourant* No. 92, 10 May 1940). This was known as the 'Stop' regulation. On 15 May and 19 May it was extended to cover the prices of services and wages and (on the instructions of the occupying forces) to include also exports to Germany. On 11 July an order known as the *Prijzenbeschikking 1940 No. 1* (First Pricing Order) was published. This provided basic rules binding the individual seller to limit the prices for products to no more than the prices of 9 May 1940. A year later, this order was extended in the *Prijsvormingsbesluit 1941* (1941 Price-setting Order), issued on 9 August. This was intended to implement more detailed regulations concerning the prices of new goods. The prices of goods that were classified as 'new', i.e. goods that had not been for sale previously, were to be determined using a pricing schedule. See Pruijt, *Prijsbeheersing*, 53.

25 Brouwers, Prijs- en loonpolitiek, 110.

26 In his conclusion to an examination of industry, L. de Jong reports that, on the basis of a general impression, his opinion is that most Dutch firms operated reasonably efficiently during the first

Table 9.1. Levels of labour productivity in manufacturing, 1938–1943 (1938 = 100)

	Real value added per worker
1938	100.0
1939	106.4
1940	105.8
1941	80.3
1942	78.4
1943	71.7

Source: See the text.

from the production and employment figures given above. The same group of industries are included in the figures throughout this period.

The time series in Table 9.1 shows that the average production per worker declined markedly after 1940. The productivity would be even lower if it was calculated in working hours, because the average working week increased during the occupation. The most striking feature is the rapid decline in productivity between 1940 and 1941, by more than one-quarter. This decline consists of a decline in the value of output, by about 25 percent, and rising employment levels. The productivity declined much less rapidly after 1941. In 1943 the index was still some 70 percent of the level of 1938.

The overview presented above has already listed several causes for the decline in productivity: shortages of raw materials and fuel, the necessity of using substitutes as inputs, transport problems, the deterioration of the production machinery, the ban on dismissing workers and a desire to protect employees against deportation by keeping them at work in the Netherlands. These obviously led to economically inefficient production processes in industry.

We can now use the estimate of the productivity of labour from the Statistics of Production to estimate the total industrial production for the period 1938–1943, on the assumption that the estimated index of productivity in the industries in the sample gives a representative picture of the whole industrial sector. By multiplying the index of production per worker by an index of the volume of total industrial employment (this is not the same as the index obtained from the Statistics of Production, because the latter covered only a sample of industries) we can compose a new estimate of the level of production in all manufacturing industries, year by year. This estimate in real terms can then be compared to an existing production index of the CBS, which is based on physical indicators. The following table shows changes in employment, productivity and total production for the period 1938–1943.

three years of the occupation. More than 84 percent of German orders placed between May 1940 and December 1943 were filled. In France the figure was 70 percent, and in Belgium it was about 75 percent. L. de Jong, *Koninkrijk*, part 7, 130.

Table 9.2. A new estimate of the volume of the industrial production, 1938–1943

	Labour Volume	Average Productivity	Output Volume	CBS Production index
1938	100.0	100.0	100	100
1939	106.0	106.4	113	113
1940	103.6	105.8	110	104
1941	109.7	80.3	88	81
1942	105.1	78.4	82	61
1943	94.5	71.7	68	53
1944				36
1945				27

Sources: Column 1: Ongevallenstatistiek Rijksverzekeringsbank (Accident Statistics of the National Insurance Bank. Column 2: CBS, *Statistics of Production*. Column 3: column (1) multiplied by column (2). Column 4: Estimate of production volume by the CBS; *Statistische en Econometrische Onderzoekingen* Vol. 1 (1946) p. 36, Vol. 2 (1947) p. 44; CBS, *Maandschrift* May–December 1944.

Column 1 is based on a data series for the volume of employment, calculated from the Accident Statistics. If we multiply this employment index by the index of labour productivity calculated from the Statistics of Production, we obtain successive production volumes of 88, 82 and 68 percent for the years 1941, 1942 and 1943, respectively. These are clearly higher than both the official estimates of the CBS, and the rather more recent figures of Van Zanden and Griffiths.[27] How can the difference be explained?

Detailed analysis reveals that the difference is mainly due to the fact that the CBS estimates of production volumes in the building materials, textiles and leather industries are systematically lower than our figures. The metallurgical industries also had a higher volume of production in 1943 than in the index calculated by the CBS. These industrial sectors account for more than 60 percent of all industrial production, so a difference in the production estimates for these industries will have a big influence on the total figure for industrial production.

We can best show that the CBS figures under-estimate actual production in this period through an example. Employment in the cotton and textile industry in 1943, as reported in the CBS' *Kroniek*, was about 70 percent of the level in 1938. At the same time, according to the CBS the index of production had declined to 27. This would mean that production per worker would have fallen to about 39 percent of the 1938 level. This is not in line with the productivity in the wool, cotton, machine knitting and ready-made clothing industries that we have calculated for that year from the Statistics of Production (see Appendix A). A similar exercise using the CBS figures for the metallurgical industries gives a supposed productivity in 1943 of 58 percent. This is only a plausible level for the machine-manufacturing industry: all the other metallurgical

---

27 Van Zanden & Griffiths, *Economische*, 177 and Griffiths, Exploitation, 122. See for another detailed analysis in which the present estimates are included: Klemann, niederländische Wirtschaft.

industries given in the Statistics of Production had higher levels of productivity.[28] The simple explanation for the differences in measurement is that the CBS index is based on fixed items (inputs and outputs) and does not allow for the new products and processes that were introduced during the war. These products, however, can be found in the Statistics of Production. Therefore the official index does not give an adequate representation of the actual levels of output during 1940–1945.

9.5. Explaining the low level of industrial labour productivity after the war

Figure 9.2 shows changes in productivity between 1938 and 1965. This figure is based on the data in Figure 9.1. The index of real value added has been divided by the employment index. The index shows that productivity levels recovered only slowly after the war,

Figure 9.2. Real labour productivity in the sample industries, 1938–1965 (1938 = 100)

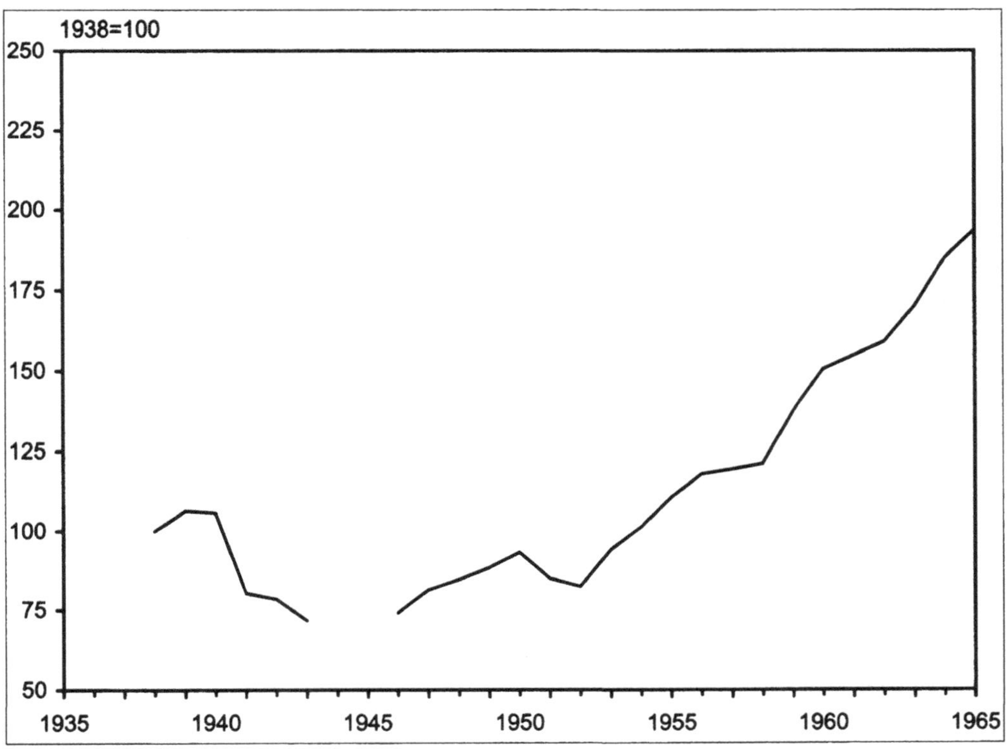

Source: Appendix C.

[28] See also, for example, Blanken (1997), *Geschiedenis*, 207. This states that the productivity at Philips 'during the war' was 60% of the 1939 level.

in contrast to the first few years following the First World War. In 1946, productivity was the same as it had been in 1943 and four years later it was still clearly below the level of the first year of the Second World War. Around 1950, at the time of the Korean War and the first cuts in government spending, the recovery process actually slowed, with the result that productivity did not return to 1938 levels until 1954.

The slow return to full productivity was also visible in the statistics available at the time, so many contemporaries were aware of the problem of low productivity in Dutch industry.[29] The Central Economic Plan of 1950 estimated that industrial productivity in 1949 was 88 percent of the 1938 level. The Netherlands and Germany were the two West European countries in which the recovery of industrial productivity was slowest. The comparative time series of productivity presented in Chapter 3 also shows that the Netherlands performed poorly compared to other countries. On the other hand, by 1949 the productivity indexes for the agricultural and services sector, and for the economy as a whole, stood at 121, 103 and 101, respectively. Thus the recovery of productivity in industry was clearly slower than in other sectors of the economy.

How are we to explain the lacklustre performance of industry? In the first place there is the damage that the industrial infrastructure had suffered during the Second World War. In addition to direct damage as a result of acts of war, there was overdue maintenance and the postponement of replacement investments. Particularly during the second half of the occupation, it seems that worn out or obsolete equipment was seldom replaced. And during the last year of the war, especially after September 1944, many goods were also stolen or destroyed by the German Army. L. de Jong has estimated the total damage as a result of this plunder to be 1.3 billion Dutch guilders, or six percent of the national assets.[30] Inventories were also seized. Immediately after the war the total war damage was estimated at about 8 billion guilders, in 1939 prices. The total national assets had fallen from 28 billion to less than 20 billion. To this we should also add the losses in foreign currency and investments, totalling 3 billion Guilders. According to this estimate, 40 percent of the national assets in 1939 had been lost.[31]

---

29 As early as 1946, P. J. Verdoorn expressed his concerns about the low levels of productivity following 1945 in a study that compared them to productivity levels following the First World War. He predicted that productivity would not return to 1938 levels until 1952 at the earliest. Verdoorn, Onbevredigend niveau, 503–506. A graph of the productivity of labour in industry, in the *Tweede Industrialisatienota* (i.e. the 'Second White Paper on Industrialisation', p. 135) shows that the pre-war levels were in fact equalled in 1952.

30 L. de Jong reports that 60,000 machines were stolen from 4,000 companies. De Jong, *Koninkrijk*, Volume10b, 77.

31 L. de Jong, *Koninkrijk*, Vol. 12, 269. A special study compiled to support the claim for reparations from Germany (*Memorandum of the Netherlands Government containing the claims of the Netherlands to reparations from Germany-Provisional Statement*) came to figures far exceeding these. In addition to the loss of national assets of eleven billion guilders, forced production for Germany was valued at six billion guilders, and there was a general loss of production of four billion guilders during the war and more than four billion following the war. The total came to more than 25 billion guilders, of which almost four billion was simply plunder. L. de Jong has suggested that, as the report was being compiled in haste, the estimates were made as high as possible to be on the safe side. See De Jong, *Koninkrijk*, Volume 12, 290. See also *Roof, restitutie en reparatie*,

All these estimates implicitly suppose that no investments were made during the war. Many analyses of economic developments during the 1950s, such as studies of the relationship between labour and capital, are based on this assumption. Therefore the 'paradoxical' rapid recovery of labour productivity in the Dutch economy as a whole after the war could only be explained by suggesting that there had been a lot of excess capacity in the pre-war years, so that labour productivity could rise rapidly after the war without requiring new investments on the same scale.[32]

Van Zanden and Griffiths later showed that the estimates of lost assets were very much exaggerated. They estimated the total loss of assets in the economy at 27 percent of the capital goods. Industry lost 17 percent of its fixed capital and 85 percent of its inventory.[33] The most recent figures, from Groote, Albers and de Jong, suggest that about seven percent of capital goods, excluding houses, were lost (in relation to 1938).[34]

So how substantial were the effects of the war for industry? After 1942, certain capital goods (mainly machines) were no longer permitted to be produced for the domestic market.[35] This undoubtedly delayed the replacement of machines and other capital goods. Nevertheless the figures in the Statistics of Production show that the process of mechanisation and especially of electrification continued unabated during the occupation. In 1946, more 'primary horsepower' was installed than in 1938 and 1943 (see section 7.7). It is not plausible that these power sources were being used to drive a much smaller stock of machinery.[36]

However, from the reports of damage we can see that the plunder and destruction by the Germans in the last year of the war must have caused large imbalances. While many industries came through unscathed, particular parts of the infrastructure were seriously affected, so that while there was sufficient production capacity in certain sectors of the economy and industry, there were also bottlenecks that limited production.[37] Not only had harbours been partly destroyed, but also many bridges and parts of the rail network.[38] The same unevenness can be seen in industry: some industries were scarcely

('Robbery, restitution and reparations') 206 ff. and Van Bochove & Van Sorge, Constant.

32 Brakel, *Industrialisatie*, 58; Witteveen, Vraagstuk, 161; Witteveen, *Structuur*, 96.

33 Van Zanden & Griffiths, *Economische*, 186.

34 Groote, Albers & De Jong, Standardised, 7–8. See also Section 7.7.

35 The ban affected machines of more than 100 kg, such as textile machinery, laundry machines, machinery for leatherwork and footwear manufacture, lifts, office machines, cocoa and chocolate machines and diesel locomotives. CBS (1947), *Kroniek*, 56.

36 On the other hand, Brakel claims that the arrears in replacement investments had not been made good, even by 1954. See Brakel, *Industrialisatie*, 143.

37 See for example *Roof, restitutie en reparatie*, 223–224 and De Jong, *Koninkrijk*, Volume 12, 307; see also Weisglas, *Nederlands*, 7.

38 In his inventory of the loss of railway locomotives and rolling stock, L. de Jong somewhat exaggerates the damage by including only some categories in his summary. It is true that the Germans commandeered a considerable number of locomotives, but the figure of 84% of steam locomotives is too high: it cannot have been more than 50%. The same applies for rolling stock. His figures for other steam-powered machinery are correct. The percentages for electrically powered and diesel-powered machinery (which he does not mention) are all lower than those for steam-powered machinery. See: *Roof, restitutie en reparatie*, 156–159.

affected, while others, especially the metallurgical industries, suffered more.[39] Many authors also mention the problem of the technical deterioration of machines, which resulted in frequent work stoppages.[40] This problem also required factories to hire extra engineers. And there is the related question of the composition of the stock of production machinery. While we have seen that the machinery that supplied power continued to expand in many companies during the war years, this does not tell us anything about what machines were being driven by the power sources. The lack of a few crucial machines in a plant could have had a strong negative effect on the whole production process.

Metallurgical industries can certainly be regarded as one of the principal victims of German destruction. However, appendix A shows that the metallurgical industries, with the exception of the machine-manufacturing industry, had by 1946 regained relatively high levels of production. Perhaps the levels of production would have been even higher had there been no destruction. Nevertheless we can conclude that war damage in itself is not an adequate explanation for the differences between the levels of production and productivity in various industries in 1946.

Low productivity levels after the war could also be caused by shortages of raw materials and by the variable quality of the raw materials that were available. Companies were very dependent on government authorisations for their supplies. The shortage of foreign exchange put the Netherlands in a difficult position regarding raw materials, and the government had addressed this with rationing and control systems, so that free production was limited. Domestic production of coal was slow to recover for various reasons (chiefly a shortage of labour), so that the allocation of coal for industry became a problem area.[41]

---

39 Some examples of the plunder and destruction (see for example *Roof, restitutie en reparatie*, 121–141 and L. de Jong, *Koninkrijk*, Volume 12, 290): General: 13,800 metalworking machines (drills, rollers, presses, welding equipment and lathes) and 18,000 electric motors. Machine-manufacturing: the entire equipment of 30 factories, and part of the equipment of 120 factories, 2,100 machines. Metallurgical industries: the entire equipment of 9 plants, including the Hoogovens plate rolling mill. Shipbuilding: 2,500 machines, 12,000 tons of tools, and the destruction of docks and cranes. Electrical engineering industry: 8,000 machines. Chemicals industry: a total of 120 plants for soap making, paint, artificial fertiliser and sulphuric acid. Rubber industry: the entire equipment of 3 complete factories. 2,700 machines from the textile industry, including 2,400 sewing machines. Some of the stolen goods were returned: 15,000 of the 55,000 machines, significant portions of the nitrogen binding plant from Sluiskil, the Hoogovens heavy plate rolling plant, rolling stock belonging to the railways and to municipal tram companies, and 70% of the shipping that had been stolen or seized.

40 Nederhorst, Arbeidsproductiviteit, 564–568.

41 The low levels of productivity can also be regarded as a measurement problem: in the years following 1945 there was both a considerable demand for consumer goods and a shortage of raw materials. One effect was that many firms tried to add as much value as possible to the scarce raw materials they could obtain (by producing labour-intensive goods). In addition, the poor quality of the raw materials meant that they required more workers. The result was that the level of productivity was under-estimated. Moreover, the extensive repairs required in the industries that manufacture the means of production may well be under-represented in the index of production. In short, the structure of production in this period was abnormal. Nijhuis, Indexcijfer, 700–701.

The third factor to consider is the defective market mechanism of the early post-war years. Market dynamics suffered considerably from price-setting regulations, limited competition and continual inflation. These meant that many marginally competitive companies could remain in the market, making it possible to continue the excessively high staffing levels that had arisen between 1940 and 1945. Several studies of individual industries have shown that extensive government interference in production and price setting continued after the war. During the occupation, levels of domestic prices had diverged from international prices. Moreover, in 1944 the Dutch government had devalued the guilder by between 15 percent and 30 percent in comparison to other currencies, including those of its European trading partners. It was not until the end of 1945 that the government had a more or less complete picture of international price levels. Tentative steps were then taken to achieve a price level appropriate to the new situation. These initiatives were preceded by monetary reform, under the leadership of Minister of Finance Lieftinck, to prevent the monetary overhang leading to uncontrollable inflation.[42] To support the price-control policy, many products continued to be rationed until 1948. However even after the monetary reform there was strong inflationary pressure: the aim of the price-control polices was to keep this pressure under control as much as possible, while also moving toward a competitive level of prices in comparison to the Netherlands' trading partners. Prices in the United Kingdom were taken as the target level. In addition to this, the relationship between wages and prices and between prices and profits was to be maintained.[43] Regulations were particularly strict in the food and beverages sector. One result was that raw materials were allocated to individual companies on the basis of their production in the base year, which was often the year 1939. This meant that scarce raw materials did not always go to the most efficient producer.[44] The liberalisation of the Dutch economy began in 1949. Rationing, distribution and price controls were in principle abolished, although there were still some direct pricing regulations for wheat, bread, milk, sugar, energy, construction materials and rents and leases.

The fourth factor explaining the low levels of productivity is the negative effect that these strong regulations had on the functioning of the labour market. Contemporaries complained about a shortage of well-trained workers as a result of bad selection and *mismatch*. It was said that wage differentials had become too small during the occupation, leading to a lack of mobility. Since there had been a ban on increasing or reducing wages during the war, the wage system that had been developed before 1940 was not operating.[45] The new wages system that was developed by the Foundation of Labour

---

42 Barendregt, *Money purge*. During the occupation the quantity of money (in notes and coins and in bank accounts) had increased by a factor of 3, while the stock of goods had declined sharply.

43 Brouwers, Prijs- en loonpolitiek, 104. Price controls did not mean that prices did not rise, but that they rose in line with increasing wages. The price increases were partly due to increasing costs for raw materials and other inputs. The CBS price index for raw materials rose by 57 percent between 1946 and 1950, while the index for final products rose by 24 percent.

44 Brouwers, Prijs- en loonpolitiek, 113.

45 For example, piece rates were used extensively in the metal industry, so that part of the wages depended on individual work performance. Wage regulations were evaded during the war by

and others after the occupation recognized only three categories of labour: skilled, medium-skilled, and unskilled. This institutionalised the lack of differentiation of labour, with the result that at the beginning of the 1950s the Netherlands, along with Sweden, had the smallest wage differentials of all the countries in North-West Europe. Greater wage differentiation was suggested as a solution, and the introduction of piece-rate wages was regarded as a suitable means of increasing the productivity of labour.[46] However the government feared uncontrolled wage increases, and maintained a policy of wage freezes and wage controls. Those who advocated an end to the wage freezes thought that this would have the additional advantage of disciplining company behaviour, since companies would be aware that not all wage increases could simply be passed on in the form of higher prices. Moreover greater wage differentiation was expected to stimulate employees to undertake better and higher professional training.[47]

What theoretical explanation can we give for the initially very low levels of productivity after the war and the rapid rise in productivity after 1950? Simple equilibrium theory supposes that as capital becomes scarcer the relative price and productivity of this factor of production will rise, and *vice versa*. The price and productivity of labour will move in the opposite direction to the price and productivity of capital. When there is a change in the relative scarcity of the factors, a new equilibrium will be achieved by changes in the relative prices of the factors of production.[48] However there may also be a substitution response: the relatively cheaper factor of production becomes more attractive to the entrepreneur, which leads to a process of substitution within industries. If the relative price of labour increases, production techniques will be adapted in favour of more capital-intensive production methods, for instance by using faster machines. This need not entail more modern production methods, but would generally lead to

---

employers who gave their staff the income levels they had had before 1940, without a corresponding level of productivity, simply by recording fictitious hours of work. They wanted to keep their workers out of the hands of the *Arbeitseinsatz*. See Berger, Prae-advies.

46 In this connection, Berenschot has distinguished between technical changes and organisational change. He proposed that organisational changes require smaller investments, since they may often result in capital savings. Berenschot, Prae-advies, 8.

47 Ibid., 18.

48 Witteveen has described the mechanism by which equilibrium is achieved as follows: suppose a situation of gradually declining capital scarcity in an economy. In this situation the quantity of capital increases faster than the available units of labour. The demand for investment funds will then be less than the actual volume of new savings. The change in the equilibrium on the capital market will lead to falling interest rates. If wages and prices remain the same, this will mean greater potential profits for firms entering the market. This leads to new business entrance, but also to falling prices, increased competition and a reduction in the average volume of production for all firms. Real wages then increase as a result of the decline in prices (supposing that wage rates remain the same), which changes the relationship between capital and labour. Capital intensity will increase, and the prices of final products will be adjusted accordingly. As capital becomes less scarce, those products requiring a great deal of capital input will become relatively cheaper. The demand for these products will then rise in comparative terms. The net effect of lower interest rates is an increase in the demand for capital, so that the demand for investments rises to match new savings. See Witteveen, *Vraagstuk*, 114ff.

technical progress or modernisation, because new investments often embody new technologies.

Immediately after the Second World War, the relative cost of labour was high, but Figure 7.4 shows a strong decline over the second half of the 1940s and in the 1950s. How was the relationship between the total quantity of labour and total quantity of capital changing during this period? The interpretation of the 1940s and 1950s is made more difficult by the fact that is difficult to ascertain the 'true' size of the stock of capital outlays. However we can say that the loss of production capacity and the continual increase in the working population during the 1940s led to a situation of capital scarcity. Although there were no free markets immediately after the war, the key indicators all point in the direction that we would expect if there were a shortage of capital. We know interest rates were kept artificially low, under Minister of Finance Lieftinck's 'cheap money' policy. But we also know that company investments had to be approved by the Ministry of Economic Affairs. Initially this limitation had the same effect as high interest rates. Therefore the growth in capital equipment lagged behind growth in demand. Prices rose continually (even after the monetary reform) as the capital goods were used more intensively. Real wages declined, while less capital was used per unit of labour. Product prices in the more labour-intensive industries rose less rapidly, which led to a shift in favour of the less capital-intensive industries.

The substitution mechanism now worked in the opposite direction compared to the inter-war period. The decline in real wages prompted a technology adjustment in the direction of less capital-intensive methods of production, because the relatively low labour costs delayed the economic obsolescence of the capital outlays. Thus we can identify a direct relation between a low level of real wages, the delayed economic obsolescence of installed machinery, the under-utilisation of labour as a factor of production, and the very low post-war levels of industrial labour productivity. Even during the war there had been a certain adjustment in the direction of a less capital-intensive production. In this period, the long-term trend for increasing mechanisation was not evident, which led to a further decline in the productivity of labour. The deterioration of the capital stock was thus counterbalanced, as it were, by a temporary pause in mechanisation. This was possible because the technical life expectancy of capital goods is considerably higher than their economic life. While real wages were in decline, it was possible to keep pre-war production systems functioning alongside newer systems for a long time. Thus post-war replacement investments had a capital broadening effect and even led to capacity expansion.[49]

9.6. Post-war industrialisation and the impact of government policies

Although in general industrial activity in the Netherlands declined during the years of war and occupation, the metallurgical industries had full order books until well into

49 Witteveen, *Vraagstuk*, 162. Brakel, *Industrialisatie*, 56.

1944. Part of the plunder and destruction of the occupying forces in that year was aimed at this sector. Yet the production figures show that the metallurgical industries very quickly surpassed their pre-war levels of output and employment. Many other industries also had rapidly rising employment. Between 1946 and 1950 industrial employment increased by 50 percent, and by another 25 percent between 1950 and 1965. The volume of production initially increased less rapidly than employment. To what extent can these characteristics of post-war industrialisation be attributed to the government policies of the time? We will consider the possible effects on industrialisation of the guided wages policy, Marshall Plan aid and government industrialisation policies.

The policy of guided wages

The legal basis of wage control was the Special Ministerial Decision on Labour Relations of 1945. While this law began as an emergency measure to guarantee each worker a minimum wage level, it continued to serve as the basis of post-war labour relations. Wage controls had been introduced early during the occupation, and the law of 1945 also prevented the unions and employers agreeing on wages and other conditions of employment that were not approved by the Board of Mediators, which had been established by the government. Thus the government could in practice intervene directly in agreements between unions and employers. The wages policy that the government implemented after the war was aimed primarily at restraining production costs to improve competitiveness and to free up funds for investments that would create employment.[50] This centrally controlled instrument was used in various ways in the post-war period. Between 1945 and 1953 the permitted rise in wages was linked to the cost of living index, so that real wages measured in consumer prices remained stable. Between 1954 and 1959, under pressure from the union movement, there were wage increases, aimed at the improvement of real incomes of wage earners. From 1959 to 1963 the principle of central co-ordination was somewhat relaxed, to allow wage differentials between sectors. Permitted increases were based on the productivity principle that specific changes in productivity in a sector should determine the amount of flexibility in wage negotiations. However it was quickly found that under this system wages in 'weak' sectors rose just as rapidly as those in 'strong' sectors. Dutch labour relations were characterised by a strong centralisation of wage negotiations, and this continued after the end of the guided wages policy in the 1960s.[51]

To determine the effect of wage policy on industrial development, we will first have to consider how low wage levels can influence the industrial structure, and then ask whether these effects should be regarded as positive or negative. Finally, one has to ask whether the guided wages policy did in fact produce low wage levels in Dutch industry.

---

50 Windmuller et al. points to the usefulness of wage co-ordination as a policy instrument because wages are the most important cost factor in the production process. In this period the highest priority was put on goals other than higher wages, such as industrialisation, full employment and international competitiveness. Windmuller c.s., *Arbeidsverhoudingen*, 205.

51 Ibid., 172ff.

As for the first question, there appears to be a reasonable consensus among economists who wrote on this topic: there is a clear relation between low wages and industrial expansion. Windmuller's opinion may be considered typical: "there is little room for doubt ... the low wage level in the Netherlands favoured exports and thus raised turnover, kept profits – considered as both the motive and the source of investments – high, created a favourable business climate and stimulated capital broadening investments."[52] In this view, low wages strengthened the supply side of the economy by keeping costs low and through investments in the production infrastructure. This stimulated growth of industrial employment. It made it possible for labour-intensive activities to be continued or expanded, and the increase in profits made possible above normal investments. In my opinion, the effects of these factors on the structure of industry can be seen in two characteristics of industry in the 1950s: first, small-scale companies remained viable for longer; and, second, labour-intensive industries such as clothing and metal working were stimulated more than less labour-intensive industries.

Not only were wages relatively low, there was also very little differentiation of wages. Low differentials were a conscious goal, under the slogan of equal pay for equal work. The goal was apparently achieved. This study has shown not only that the differences in wage levels between industries in the 1950s were relatively slight, but also that changes in wages were very similar in the sample industries. Dutch inter-industry wage differentials were also small in comparison to those in other countries.[53] What was the effect of this 'double' levelling of wages? Small wage differences across industries may reinforce the rigidity of the industrial structure, because expansionary companies and industries have no instruments to compete on the labour market. Seen in this way wage compression can be counterproductive to structural change and the dynamic of the industrial development. Lack of vertical mobility for labour can have the same effect. Vertical mobility was sacrificed after the war when the wages of skilled and unskilled labour tended to converge, which is said to have limited any qualitative increase in the supply of labour, because workers had fewer incentives to qualify for better jobs.[54] However others have presented more subtle interpretations. In the first place, we have already demonstrated that wage differences between industries can be explained mainly by the composition of the workforce, which is linked in turn to the specific production process in an industry. Moreover, Weststrate has suggested that companies occasionally were able to offer higher wages, even within the legal framework (and not in the form of 'black' wages, which also was the case). He concludes, "*If* wage policy 'froze' the distribution of the labour force between branches and firms, and thereby impeded economically justified expansions and contractions, it can only have been to a very slight extent." He also suggests that wage differentiation would have been limited even without wage controls, because of the centralised system of wage negotiations in the Netherlands.[55] Both the international comparisons and the comparisons of wage spread over time, presented in previous chap-

52 Ibid., 181, 210–211.
53 Dercksen, *Industrialisatiepolitiek*, 66.
54 See the previous section in this chapter, and Brakel, *Industrialisatie*, 125.
55 Weststrate, *Economic*, 180–182.

ters, have shown that the situation of Dutch industry in the 1950s was not exceptional or abnormal. Thus we can regard the low wage differentials not as a consequence of the wage policy, but as the natural effect of a reasonably unified labour market.

The final question is, whether the low industrial wages were actually the outcome of a deliberate wages policy or maybe the effect of market forces or other circumstances. Brakel regarded the guided wages policy as the main reason for the success of industrialisation.[56] This supposes that there was causality between wage policies and low wage levels in the years following the war. Van Hulst has tried to determine to what extent the wages policy produced changes in the nominal wage rate in conformity with market forces. He used an econometric approach – by estimating wage equations – but was not able to identify any effects.[57] Dercksen and Woltjer have recalculated Van Hulst's estimates and concluded that it is not possible to identify any effects of the wages policy on the long-term pattern of wage levels. They do, however, suggest that the wages policy had short-term effects: in the 1950s, wages reflected changes in the productivity of labour more accurately.[58] On the other hand, Van Ark and De Jong have pointed out that average industrial wages in the Netherlands increased just as rapidly after 1950 as in other countries.[59] Any special effects due to wage policies in general must therefore be sought in the period before 1950. This is in accordance with what we have seen in Chapter 6.

From what has been said above, we can conclude that the direct measures taken by the government during and immediately after the war created a gap between levels of labour costs and labour productivity in such a way that profit margins in industries became indeed higher. After 1950, wage policies were no longer successful in keeping wage increases below productivity increases. But that was also unnecessary. The merit of these policies was that the difference between average wages and average production per worker that had been created before 1950 was perpetuated. The initially very low productivity level was the price paid for this. After the war Dutch policy makers followed a prescription of low wages, a low exchange rate and low output prices, to support investments and exports, so that the employment could grow. Welfare and efficient production had to wait.

Marshall Plan aid and the industrialisation policy

Although parts of manufacturing were supported throughout the 1930s, a systematic policy in relation to industry and industrial expansion was only developed after 1945. Did this policy actually affect the speed and direction of industrialisation? In 1949 industrial policy was officially recognised as a means of offering the Netherlands better prospects for the future, especially since the country had had to recognise the independence of Indonesia in the same year, thus losing its political and economic position as a

---

[56] Brakel, *Industrialisatie*, 147.

[57] Van Hulst, *Effectiviteit*, 1984.

[58] Dercksen, *Industrialisatiepolitiek*, 73–78. Van Zanden, Geleide, 464–477.

[59] Van Ark & De Jong, Accounting, 219.

colonial power. Industrialisation was necessary to provide work for the growing working population and to export products, and so reduce the balance of trade deficit.[60] In 1949 the first 'White Paper on Industrialisation in the Netherlands' (*Nota inzake de Industrialisatie van Nederland*) was issued by the Minister of Economic Affairs, Van den Brink. This highlighted the need for industrialisation. For as long as he was the Minister, a similar white paper was published every year. The most important objective was to create 120,000 new jobs from new investments in the 1948–1952 period. If we are to form an accurate estimate of the effect of these policies on actual industrial development, it is important that we have a clear picture of the sequence of development of the policies and of the actual industrial development.

How new were the ideas in the first White Paper on Industrialisation? Kohnstamm had written a dissertation on industrial policy in 1948. The first white paper on industrialisation had been preceded by memoranda and reports on industrial development, including the planning estimates of the Central Planning Bureau (CPB, which actually developed into a forecasting agency), a proposal for the use of Marshall Plan funds (1948) and a loan request submitted to the World Bank (1948). These had already set out the central ideas and purposes of industrialisation in the Netherlands. Griffiths has pointed out that the first white paper on industrialisation was not published until the developments it predicted were already under way. In fact the white papers followed the facts. He goes further, characterising the system of investment calculations in the later white papers as "... a book-keeping exercise, in which the final goals were modified to match changes in the investment equilibrium that had already been felt in industry."[61] There is little room in his interpretation for economic policies to play any independent role in the expansion of Dutch industry during the 1950s. Likewise, De Hen has said that from the very beginning there was scarcely any consistent policy of stimulation.[62]

A total of eight white papers on industrialisation were to be published, with indicative plans concerning investments per sector, an overall investment policy and, in the later papers, with focused policies for regional development. We will briefly examine what demonstrable effects can be traced back to these policies. But since the first measures under the Marshall Plan preceded these industrialisation policies, we will first identify the measurable effects for industry of this aid.

The Netherlands received a total of 1,127 million U.S. dollars in Marshall Plan aid, most of it in the form of gifts. From an overview of the Marshall Plan imports between 1948 and 1950 we can see that while almost 60 percent of the aid was destined for industrial purposes, much of this was used to import raw materials (cotton, tobacco, ores, oil). The machinery and equipment bought with Marshall Plan funds accounts for about 35 percent of the total aid. Between 1948 and 1950 an average of 50 percent of imports from North and South America were funded by Marshall Plan aid, but this accounted for about 10 percent of total Dutch imports during the aid period.[63] Van der Eng has

---

60 G. A. Kohnstamm, Tien jaren, 416–421.

61 Griffiths, Enkele, 111–115.

62 De Hen, *Actieve*, Chapter 6.

63 Van der Eng, *Marshall-hulp*, 172–183. Dercksen, *Industrialisatiepolitiek*, 126.

shown that a large part of the aid was directed to the cotton and food and beverage industries (especially raw materials), and to a lesser extent to the metallurgical and chemical industries. Small companies profited to a large extent, and big concerns were aided less. A company such as Philips, for example, could finance 60 percent of its need for dollars in the aid period with Marshall Plan funds, but this still accounted for no more than 2 percent of the company's total foreign purchases. The most noteworthy component of the direct help in these years was a new steel rolling mill at the Hoogovens company that was established with money from the Marshall Plan and the Dutch government.[64] All in all, direct investments from Marshall Plan aid played only a moderate role in the recovery period. The same can be said of spending from the 'currency exchange account', which contained the accumulated payments, in Dutch guilders, which Dutch importers made to the *Nederlandsche Bank* for their Marshall Plan imports. The money could only be spent with the agreement of the Americans. They insisted that these moneys should be spent on promoting internal monetary and financial stability, and on expanding production capacity. Only a modest proportion, some 300 million Dutch guilders (ten percent of the currency exchange account), was used to directly benefit industry and for building and repairing the infrastructure. About 70 percent of the funds in the currency exchange account were spent on debt repayments, military projects, the great floods of 1953 and on repairing war damage to houses and buildings. Although we can conclude on the basis of this data that the Marshall Plan gave scarcely any recognizable impulse to further industrialisation in the Netherlands, we must be careful with excessively easy generalisations. While the recovery had already clearly begun in the years before 1948 (see the overviews of production in Appendix A), that process had laid a heavy claim on the Netherlands's foreign exchange reserves. Shortage of reserves therefore threatened the recovery process, because imports would have had to be limited. The Marshall Plan meant that the Netherlands was able to initiate a path of long-term growth earlier than would otherwise have been the case.[65]

Dercksen has made a systematic attempt to identify the demonstrable effects, if any, of the industrialisation policy on the process of industrialisation. As we have seen, much of the policy was rather general, which makes it more difficult to trace any direct causal relationships. In his analysis, Dercksen distinguished between the possible effects of the industrialisation policy in the fields of taxation and investment regulations, promoting

---

64 Van der Eng, *Marshall-hulp*, 180–181. Dercksen, *Industrialisatiepolitiek*, 149–150.

65 Van der Eng, *Marshall-hulp*, 201. For a general discussion of the effect of Marshall Plan aid on the Dutch economy, see also: Inklaar, *Amerika*, Chapter 1. Eichengreen & Uzan have shown that the Marshall Plan benefited European economies not so much in terms of increased investments in production capacity and infrastructure, as is often said, but rather by promoting financial stability and economic liberalisation: "... Europe was suffering a 'marketing crisis', in which producers refused to bring goods to the market, and workers and managers limited the effort they devoted to market activity. Political instability, shortages of consumer goods and fears of financial chaos led them to hoard commodities and withhold effort. The Marshall Plan facilitated the restoration of financial stability and the liberalisation of production and prices; this was its crucial role." Eichengreen & Uzan, Marshall Plan, 15.

higher productivity, and stimulating technology, and regional policy.[66] We will confine ourselves here to the first two of these: taxation and investment regulations; and promoting higher productivity.

The fiscal policies consisted of an investment deduction and an allowance to depreciate capital goods faster, which resulted in lower taxation levels. These measures were intended to enable firms to finance their investments internally. In fact, Dercksen says, they supported the existing production infrastructure rather than risk-bearing investments in new businesses, i.e. they did not really stimulate the capital market.[67] Brakel has also observed that the high rate of internal financing made it difficult for new businesses, and for companies whose expansion plans were more ambitious, to find the required funds. The capital market for risk-bearing capital was very tight.[68] On the other hand, the investment deduction benefited mainly the capital-intensive sectors of the economy, which to some extent counterbalanced the shift in favour of more labour-intensive industries, a result of the low-wage strategy.

In the field of investment and financing, there were policies that were directly effective, and others that provided a stimulus. The government was involved in industrial investments through institutions such as the *Herstelbank* (Reconstruction Bank), the *Nederlandse Participatiemaatschappij* (a government share-holding company) and the Export Finance Corporation. It had direct participations in public utility companies (22 percent), the Dutch State Mines (2 percent), and in the Hoogovens and Dutch Soda Industry companies. Dercksen has estimated government involvement between 1950 and 1965 at 30 percent of all industrial investments, but of this, 24 percent went to the utility companies and mines, so that government participation in manufacturing can have been no more than 6 percent of all investments, of which less than 1 percent of this was direct investment.[69] Thus the government's influence on financing industrial development was felt mainly through its policies on wages and its tax policies.

In short, the government's direct industrialisation activities were slight and limited to a few exceptional cases. Given the instruments available, especially in the first four years (1948–1952), and the broad aims of the programme, the goals could not be achieved in the short term. Brakel observes: "From this it necessarily follows that the close agreement between the plans set out in the white papers on industrialisation and the industrial expansion achieved in the Marshall period must be a matter of chance."[70] From Griffiths' conclusions and the findings mentioned above, we now know that it was not a

66 Government investments in R & D, which amounted to 20 percent of total R & D expenditures in the Netherlands, could be said to have served as a stimulus, although the technology policy had its origins in the pre-war period, with initiatives such as the Patents Act, and the foundation of tertiary technical institutes and the Dutch Organisation for Applied Scientific Research (TNO). However it is not possible to quantify the effects of the government's R & D expenditures on industrial development. The regional development policy is less relevant for our present purposes, because it focused on the geographical distribution of employment.

67 Dercksen, *Industrialisatiepolitiek*, 112–113.

68 Brakel, *Industrialisatie*, 146.

69 Dercksen, *Industrialisatiepolitiek*, 151.

70 Brakel, *Industrialisatie*, 96.

coincidence, but that the causality between economic policies and economic results should be reversed in this case. The economic results were already there, before the policies were formulated and implemented.

So what does explain the rapid growth of industrial production and productivity after 1950? Van Zanden and Griffiths have put a great deal of weight on increased liberalisation after 1949, and I am inclined to concur. Many government measures that had been instituted before, during or just after the war were abolished from 1949. These include controls on investments, the distribution of raw materials and manufactured goods, the liberalisation of the pricing policy, the abolition of import quotas and the abolition of governmental distribution agencies (*Rijksbureaus*). A major factor was the opening up of the German market, which for the first four years after the war had been strongly regulated by the occupying powers. This greater international openness proved to be a success factor for Dutch industry, especially after a second devaluation in 1949 (following the first in 1944) lowered the prices of Dutch exports. The growth in exports was the main driving force behind the economic and industrial growth that followed the recovery period, and this was made possible by low unit costs.[71] The fact that this was coupled with an exceptional rise in average labour productivity in industry can be largely explained by the exceptionally low level of productivity in the first post-war years. From this low, a rapid *catching up* process was possible.

9.7. Conclusions

Industrial production fell sharply during the Second World War, but the official CBS index of physical production under-estimated the actual levels of production during the occupation. This can be explained by the fact that substitute raw materials and substitute product sales were under-recorded. My estimates, which are based on the recorded values of production and of inputs, do account for these factors.[72] Production circumstances differed markedly between industries, depending on the availability of raw materials and whether the occupying forces considered the sector important.

It can be seen from the statistical data that many companies increased the 'primary horsepower' of the sources of power used in their factories during the occupation. Thus developments in this field certainly did not come to a halt. As early as 1946, many industries had more powered machinery than in 1938. Moreover, two large industrial sectors, food products and textiles (which in 1938 accounted for 52 percent of the gross value added in manufacturing) came through the war virtually unscathed. Further, many industries were able to rapidly approach or even surpass their 1938 level of production once the occupation had ended. This would not have been possible if the condition of industry after the war was as bad as has been suggested in many studies. It is sometimes

---

71 Van Zanden & Griffiths, *Economische*, 200–201, 210–211.

72 The figures for industrial production calculated here are broadly in line with Klemann's conclusion (Nederlandse, 38–40) that production and employment continued at close to normal levels during the war, until well into 1943.

claimed, rather too easily, that the Dutch economy was in ruins in 1945. That is certainly not the case for industry: it is partly myth – a much-cherished story – but that does not make it true.[73]

Since many companies continued to work during the occupation, but had less opportunity to make replacement investments, some machines were not replaced and were kept in operation through more intensive maintenance. Thus deterioration and obsolescence were partly offset by employing more workers. This helps to explain the high level of employment during and immediately after the war. Other factors such as regulation (many office staff, the ban on firing workers, desire to protect workers from the *Arbeitseinsatz*) and transport problems also contributed to high employment. In the first ten years following the war we can see rapid growth in both average labour productivity and employment. The growth in productivity was substantial, but the initial level in 1946 was exceptionally low (even compared to other countries at that time). Productivity did not return to pre-war levels until after 1953. This was coupled with the gradual improvement of production methods and a trend to allow business organisations to work more efficiently. Nevertheless, in those first years the incentives were not strong, considering the high degree of regulation in the economy, low wages, high inflation and the absence of competition. Apparently the rise in the productivity of labour immediately after 1945 had little influence on the shedding of workers. At first the rise in labour productivity was not linked to any marked increase in capital intensity, but rather with the increasing productivity of capital.

Industrial development during the 1950s was in broad lines a continuation of the pattern of development that had emerged before and during the Second World War. Industries that had grown up under the quota system could continue their import substitution production after the war (e.g. clothing and footwear), and the metallurgical industries that had expanded during the occupation were among the first to return to pre-war levels of production after the liberation.

All in all, the period of strong government regulation and intervention (1931–1949) coincided with a deterioration of the Netherlands' international trade position, a long-term decline in real product wages (the wages adjusted for changes in the prices of industrial products) after 1935, and very rapid growth in industrial employment. From this perspective I observe a large degree of continuity in the developments of the 1930s and 1940s. Import quotas, wage and price controls and regulations controlling initiatives such as the establishment of new firms characterized these decades. Regulations introduced during the occupation and the early post-war years reinforced this situation. Many textbooks on Dutch economic history have described the post-1945 period as an era in which the government strengthened its control over the economy. Van Zanden even regards the government's stronger leading role following the Second World War as a major force in the long-term development of the Dutch economy.[74] However in the

---

73 Messing, *Nederlandse*, 42–44; De Vries, *Nederlandse*, 87; Klein, *Foundations*, 6–7; Dercksen, *Industrialisatiepolitiek*, 45 and, for a much more sophisticated view, Van Zanden & Griffiths, *Klein land*, 185–186. Windmuller et al, *Arbeidsverhoudingen*, 163, 204.

74 Van Zanden, *Klein land*, 16–17.

Netherlands (and not only there) direct government control had been very strong during the trans-war period from 1930 to 1950. After 1950 government control became much looser.

Many studies refer to the salutary effects of the wages policy and industrialisation policy, which are supposed to be characteristic of the economic policy of the 1950s. The guided wages policy produced its biggest effects in terms of wage restraint in the 1940s, but it must be conceded that it also ensured stability in the 1950s. Furthermore, the exceptional combination of ten successive years of growing employment and growth in productivity was not the result of a well thought-out industrialisation policy. The programme set out in the industrialisation policy was not suitable to promote rapid mechanisation in industry, since the low wage strategy did not favour the substitution of capital for labour. In fact, the industrialisation policy served no practical purpose, it was first overtaken by events, and then trailed behind them.

Chapter 10: Conclusions

Between 1913 and 1965, the growth of Dutch manufacturing was higher than that of the Dutch economy as a whole. The effects of the two world wars and of the depression of the 1930s go some way towards explaining this process of industrial growth. The reduced opportunities for international trade, and the absence of foreign competition, led to import substitution, giving industrial companies an opportunity to expand. The process widened the industrial base in the Netherlands, but this was not always accompanied by a better economic performance.

A comparison between Dutch industrial productivity and that of surrounding countries reveals differences per period, but also per sector. In 1913, productivity in Dutch industry was much lower than in British and German industry. The difference was substantially reduced during the First World War and in the post-war years. In the 1930s, Dutch industry attained higher levels of productivity than British and German industries. Dutch industry even shows up better in comparison to Belgian industry. During the 1930s, industrial productivity in the Netherlands was about 30 percent higher than in Belgium. After the Second World War, comparative productivity in the Netherlands was very low. It did not equal the British level until about 1960, and German productivity has been higher than the Dutch level until at least 1965. Our view of patterns of international convergence or divergence in industrial productivity is severely hampered by the effects of the wars. But even if we take a longer period, from 1913 to 1992, we can certainly not observe a pattern of convergence between levels of industrial productivity in these countries. However there is convergence of productivity in the economies as a whole. This points to specialisation processes within the industries of the four countries considered here.

Dutch comparative productivity was high in the food and beverage, paper and several of the metallurgical industries such as shipbuilding. A comparison with German industry during the 1930s confirms established ideas about the specialisation in the two countries: at that time the Netherlands had a significant advantage in the food and beverage industry, and Germany had an advantage in metallurgical industries. Comparisons with the United Kingdom and Belgium reveal a different picture: Dutch industry had a small productivity advantage in the food and beverage industry, but a bigger advantage in the metallurgical industries.

Differences in comparative productivity at the industry level cannot be explained by differences in the machine intensity, if we take primary horsepower of the installed machinery per worker as a measure. However machines are only part of the stock of capital goods. A more refined indicator, such as the extent of electrification, does point to a relationship, at any rate in the case of Germany and the Netherlands. The higher the comparative level of electrification, the higher the productivity. In this context, the degree of electrification is a good indicator of the modernity of production processes in specific industries.

In addition, we have observed a positive relationship between comparative wage levels and the comparative labour productivity per industry, both in the comparisons between the Netherlands and Germany and between the Netherlands and Belgium. In these cases, the quality of labour, as a factor of production, has a positive influence on the average value added per worker. The same may be said for demand factors such as the size of the market: the bigger the market, the higher the productivity.

Comparison between the United Kingdom and the Netherlands revealed a correlation coefficient between wage levels and productivity with a negative sign. More than half of the difference in general wage levels between these countries can be explained by the higher rate of labour market participation of women (earning lower standard wages than males) in the United Kingdom. Factory size only had an influence in the British food and beverage industry: British production was concentrated in larger production units than in the Netherlands, and they were also more productive.

In the process of industrial development in the Netherlands, the industries that grew fastest also had the most rapid rise in productivity. However newer industries had no higher productivity levels than existing industries from the outset. Shifts in employment between industries made hardly any contribution to the overall growth in productivity. The rise in productivity between 1913 and 1965 is mainly an intra-sectoral phenomenon. Therefore for this period, the distinction between old and new industries and their respective contributions to manufacturing output contributes little to the analysis.

In the long term, the index of average wage rates for industry as a whole moves in line with the index for average labour productivity. However, at a lower level of aggregation there is no connection between the two variables. In the sample industries rapid growth in labour productivity does not cause higher wage rises. This points to a unified national labour market and/or centralised wage bargaining. During the 1913–1965 period there is no clear increase or decrease in the wage differences between industries. Differences in wage levels between industries are chiefly determined by the composition of employment: industries with many female and younger employees have low average wage levels, and those with many male and well-trained workers have higher average wages.

The different rates of productivity growth in the sample industries cannot be explained by differences in changes in machine intensity. Industries in which productivity grew rapidly were not marked by a higher than average substitution of capital for labour. It is difficult to demonstrate factor substitution at the level of industries. While an increase in capital intensity can be observed for industry as a whole, the general picture is one of simultaneous savings on labour and capital. Scale economies played an important role in this, expansion leading to new investments and the use of new technologies.

In comparison with the surrounding countries, three exceptional periods for the development of Dutch productivity can be highlighted: 1913–1921, 1925–1935 and 1946–1950. In the first two periods, comparative productivity in the Netherlands was high. In the last period it was low.

From 1913 until 1921 Dutch industry grew rapidly. The underlying forces that can be identified are rapid electrification, import substitution, and a supply shock as a result of the shortening of the working week while keeping weekly wages constant. Industrial electrification in the Netherlands occurred at the same time and at the same speed as in the United States.

During the depression of the 1930s, productivity rose very rapidly. This can be regarded as an expression of the potential efficiency that had in part been achieved in the 1920s, for instance through the electrification of industries. Declining profits and high real wages accelerated productivity increases, but also job losses. In this way one can speak of a true 'productivity paradox', with productivity growth lagging behind technological advance. In this period, average wage levels in Dutch industry were high even in comparison to other countries. Although the Depression caused a decline in demand, in the course of time supply factors became more important. A large part of the industrial unemployment of the 1930s can be attributed to structural developments. Expensive labour was one factor contributing to the introduction of a whole range of production techniques that required less labour.

In the 1930s and 1940s government regulation became predominant in the Dutch economy. During the twentieth century, state intervention in the economy was never so extensive as in this period. Not only was there emergency legislation. The government also introduced restrictive social and economic legislation in response to the Depression, in response to the circumstances of the war, and later on as repression related to the occupation and finally by way of protecting the economy from the post-war chaos. Thus we can see these two decades as one continuous period of unusually strong government intervention. At the same time, there was a long-term decline in real wages (measured in product prices) from 1935 to 1951. This gave a further stimulus to industrial growth, backed by capital broadening investments. Under emergency measures such as import quotas, and also because of the steadily increasing population, large sectors of industry were able to expand their production further. These included the footwear, wool, machine knitting, ready-made clothing, rubber, and soap and food products industries. However the reduction in real wages and the tight regulations had a negative effect on the growth in productivity in the long term. This helps to explain the absence of structural effects in the process of productivity growth.

The capital stock in industry increased in the first years of the Second World War. During this period growth occurred mainly in the metallurgical industries. While the Dutch production infrastructure did suffer from the circumstances of war and occupation, the popular idea that the country was in ruins after the war is misleading, to put it mildly. In overall terms, by 1948 the production capacity had been restored to the level of 1938. In 1947, industrial production had already attained the level of 1938. Once again, it was mainly the metallurgical industries that grew rapidly in this period. Employment levels in this sector witnessed extraordinary growth.

Productivity performance remained low not only because of the initially strong regulation but also because policy makers had chosen a strategy of low levels of wages and prices. The Dutch guilder devalued in 1944 and 1949. For industry as a whole this strategy provided no stimulus for technological development and capital deepening. Between 1946 and 1960 the relative price of labour declined in comparison to the user cost of capital. Machine intensity in manufacturing declined during the first post-war years.

In some industries there was capital deepening. These are sometimes to be found concealed among replacement investments, as in the cotton industry, and sometimes among the expansion of capital outlays, as for example in the chemicals and in the electrical engineering and automobile industries. Nevertheless many companies in the other metallurgical sectors were characterised by small-scale operations and by scant progress in manufacturing techniques.

The centrepieces of the government's post-war industrial policy – the policy of wage moderation and the industrialisation policy – generally have been labelled as manifestations of increasing government intervention in the economy. In the present study they have been interpreted mainly in the light of declining government intervention. The industrialisation policy of the 1950s was mainly a policy of liberalisation, coinciding with the abolition or alteration of regulations and socio-economic legislation that had been put in place in the 1940s. The policy of wage moderation was most effective during and immediately after the war. Wage restraints were so effective that by about 1950 wage increases had fallen a long way behind the increases in average productivity. During the 1950s real wages grew at the same rate as labour productivity. The perpetuation of the gap between wage and productivity levels that had been established before 1950 meant that businesses enjoyed exceptionally large profit margins during the post-war period, and thus had plentiful resources to invest. The wage-productivity gap was also one reason for the 'reversed' process of factor substitution, as mentioned above. Thus the negative social experience of the 1930s with high unemployment due in part to high real wages shaped the specific relationships of the 1950s, with full employment and low real wages. This helps to explain why there was no strong increase in industrial labour productivity directly after the Second World War, to match the strong productivity increase following the First World War.

Appendices

Appendix A consists of the main quantitative characteristics of the 24 industrial branches in the Dutch production statistics that are central in this book. The time series are expressed as indexnumbers with the year 1938 as the central reference year (= 100). The first row in all tables presents the actual values of respectively the number of companies in the census, the money value of inputs and outputs (in guilders), the number of persons employed, the powered machinery (in horsepower). Multiplication of the current value of 1938 with any index value in the same column results in the actual value of the chosen year.

The last four columns in each table present my own calculations of indices of input prices and output prices and of single deflated real value added and real labour productivity. Indices of input- and output prices were calculated by allowing for the changing structure of inputs and outputs in the industries. Deflation of net output using the output price series results in real value added. Finally, the real labour productivity series was calculated by dividing the real value added with the employment index. (Sources: CBS, *Productie statistiek*, and De Jong, *Nederlandse industrie*)

Appendix B presents weighted price indices based on the 80 products of the industries involved in the Dutch production statistics. Sub-periods of five years were constructed to allow for changing value added weights of the different industries and were linked at the overlapping years. For a description and analysis of the methods involved see De Jong, *Measuring*, 213–242. The comparison input- and output price indices were taken from the CBS.

Appendix C presents output and productivity estimates for total manufacturing in the production statistics.
Total net output in current prices was deflated by applying the weighted price indices in appendix B. Total employment was taken from the same source. For the years 1944 and 1945 no information was available. A very important characteristic of the series is that the sample of industries is consistent over the war -years, which guarantees consistency in the time series, not only concerning output and employment, but also concerning the industry-specific price indices. See De Jong, *Nederlandse industrie*, 339–394.

Appendix D contains weighted series of the annual money wage per worker, primary power and real user costs of capital for total manufacturing, calculated mainly from the production statistics. For a description see De Jong, *Nederlandse industrie*, 202–204 and 462–466.

Appendix A. Bicycles

	Number of companies in census	Value of inputs mln. gld.	Value of gross output mln. gld.	Number of workers	Primary power in h.p.	Index input prices	Index output prices	Index real value added	Index real labour productivity
	Absolute numbers								
1938	31	4.3	8.2	1738	2982				
Index 1938 = 100									
1921	77	109	107	99	38	234	331	31	32
1922	74	91	90	86	41	202	256	35	41
1923	87	83	84	83	45	177	219	38	46
1924	97	82	84	92	45	177	198	42	46
1925	100	106	108	119	48	157	178	61	51
1926	113	128	130	124	51	152	175	74	60
1927	123	130	137	132	56	141	158	87	66
1928	119	145	155	138	62	138	155	100	73
1929	113	141	160	135	65	130	152	106	78
1930	116	138	152	134	74	127	146	104	77
1931	113	110	126	111	81	119	137	92	82
1932	113	91	96	94	83	111	117	82	88
1933	110	89	95	103	84	99	92	103	100
1934	113	87	95	100	87	92	87	109	109
1935	113	75	86	97	87	85	81	107	111
1936	110	76	89	101	91	80	78	115	114
1937	100	98	106	109	91	84	89	119	109
1938	100	100	100	100	100	100	100	100	100
1939	106	121	120	114	100	94	100	120	106
1940	103	164	160	141	107	104	119	134	95
1941	110	177	169	132	108	138	139	114	86
1942	90	70	69	75	99	135	134	51	68
1943	68	33	35	50	89	143	129	29	59
1944									
1945									
1946	68	58	61	81	96	215	273	23	28
1947	100	210	189	126	114	230	282	59	47
1948	123	427	361	170	149	253	287	101	60
1949	142	692	578	214	184	259	302	150	70
1950	81	914	747	224	174	265	293	193	86
1951	81	1156	885	201	178	341	309	191	95
1952	81	1294	964	224	191	331	312	194	87
1953	81	1439	1098	224	198	329	323	226	101
1954	77	1469	1158	236	205	322	340	242	102
1955	81	1891	1449	247	218	329	357	272	110
1956	74	2087	1583	230	228	333	362	287	125
1957	71	1949	1492	219	238	310	357	279	128
1958	61	1555	1235	190	231	314	358	249	131
1959	68	2010	1592	224	238	288	342	333	149
1960	68	2397	1891	244	252	282	345	389	159
1961	65	2478	1941	222		295	366	371	167
1962	61	2220	1769	210		295	360	356	169
1963	61	1975	1556	194		302	351	314	161
1964	61	2320	1903	194		295	368	395	203
1965	58	2220	1823	178		298	373	374	210

Brick

	Number of companies in census	Value of inputs mln. gld.	Value of gross output mln. gld.	Number of workers	Primary power in h.p.	Index input prices	Index output prices	Index real value added	Index real labour productivity
	Absolute numbers								
1938	250	3.0	18.5	13813	41449				
Index 1938 = 100									
1921									
1922									
1923									
1924									
1925									
1926									
1927									
1928									
1929									
1930									
1931									
1932									
1933									
1934					106				
1935	102				101				
1936	83	76	68	85	97	91	87	77	90
1937	84	90	79	91	96	105	94	82	91
1938	100	100	100	100	100	100	100	100	100
1939	96	110	114	106	110	106	105	109	103
1940	94	117	112	91	109				
1941	94			113					
1942	93			62					
1943	92			41					
1944				37					
1945									
1946	79	174	163	74	105	246	305	53	71
1947	82	251	246	85	109	308	342	72	85
1948	81	294	329	91	111	317	356	94	103
1949	83	395	398	95	112	393	378	106	111
1950	64	438	431	89	103	423	396	109	122
1951	64	555	496	89	106	512	436	111	125
1952	65	656	517	87	110	591	447	110	126
1953	66	642	530	86	113	585	456	111	129
1954	66	649	601	85	116	571	492	120	141
1955	71	732	715	90	133	571	540	132	147
1956	72	833	778	88	138	620	575	134	151
1957	60	1007	826	80	135	737	620	128	160
1958	60	896	696	75	138	657	562	117	155
1959	60	789	723	74	141	572	571	124	169
1960	61	763	816	73	145	501	613	135	184
1961	60	950	874	70		469	673	128	182
1962	38	823	779	59		531	723	107	182
1963	38	883	793	58		550	678	114	198
1964	38	1043	947	57		532	743	125	219
1965	37	1084	1011	56		505	766	130	231

Calcium silicate

	Number of companies in census	Value of inputs mln. gld.	Value of gross output mln. gld.	Number of workers	Primary power in h.p.	Index input prices	Index output prices	Index real value added	Index real labour productivity
	Absolute numbers								
1938	17	1.5	3.5	1014	6788				
Index 1938 = 100									
1921									
1922									
1923									
1924									
1925									
1926									
1927									
1928									
1929									
1930									
1931									
1932									
1933									
1934	112	86	109	113	100	73	114	111	98
1935	112	61	68	96	98	65	86	86	90
1936	100	48	48	75	93	69	84	59	78
1937	94	74	73	95	95	85	90	81	85
1938	100	100	100	100	100	100	100	100	100
1939	100	93	95	89	104	101	109	89	100
1940	100	53	58	77	108	120	141	43	56
1941	100	120	127	87	114	163	169	79	91
1942	100	47	49	53	115	187	212	24	46
1943	100	53	46	42	111	207	217	19	45
1944	94			42					
1945	94			22					
1946	94	80	78	45	112	292	363	21	47
1947	88	167	168	70	112	335	390	43	62
1948	88	313	312	100	117	343	397	79	78
1949	88	326	379	104	121	362	408	103	99
1950	82	400	515	133	129	379	435	139	105
1951	82	493	581	138	134	428	469	138	100
1952	88	506	575	128	153	493	479	131	102
1953	88	520	639	128	156	457	485	151	118
1954	88	560	709	138	178	467	513	161	116
1955	94	573	729	138	197	488	532	159	115
1956	94	680	850	148	202	516	555	177	120
1957	94	853	992	148	205	577	585	188	127
1958	94	666	792	138	208	544	578	154	111
1959	94	640	772	128	211	539	565	155	121
1960	94	700	853	128	211	514	572	170	132
1961	100	753	937	138		515	584	184	134
1962	100	819	1056	138		543	625	198	143
1963	112	879	1087	138		566	651	192	139
1964	112	1146	1443	138		579	664	252	182
1965	118	1166	1533	128		604	703	258	201

Cars and coachwork

	Number of companies in census	Value of inputs mln. gld.	Value of gross output mln. gld.	Number of workers	Primary power in h.p.	Index input prices	Index output prices	Index real value added	Index real labour productivity
	Absolute numbers								
1938	57	1.8	4.0	1535	1738				
Index 1938 = 100									
1921									
1922									
1923									
1924									
1925									
1926									
1927									
1928									
1929									
1930									
1931									
1932									
1933									
1934	108	51	58	72		59	89	73	101
1935	96	48	51	61	83	58	82	67	110
1936	75	46	52	58	83	70	83	71	122
1937	89	76	77	84	92	100	93	84	100
1938	100	100	100	100	100	100	100	100	100
1939	121	149	149	125	132	100	111	134	108
1940									
1941									
1942									
1943									
1944									
1945									
1946	143	685	725	366	496	235	269	286	78
1947	204	1373	1379	472	640	254	363	382	81
1948	187	1556	1492	457	683	260	446	319	70
1949	209	2239	1990	452	720	267	460	375	83
1950	66	2354	1860	285	501	280	447	299	105
1951	62	2439	1971	271	518	375	483	306	113
1952	66	2458	1894	276	587	424	605	214	78
1953	66	3268	2568	313	713	346	611	299	96
1954	72	5013	4041	383	725	384	692	436	114
1955	79	6157	4991	421	817	410	699	538	128
1956	83	7186	5677	463	938	397	745	547	118
1957	81	5974	4840	421	1076	416	730	499	119
1958	79	4734	3643	383	1191	405	657	379	99
1959	74	6456	5280	453	1392	408	536	753	166
1960	79	9915	7626	575	1456	439	497	1046	182
1961	79	9464	7657	533		445	525	1094	205
1962	92	9961	8077	584		435	492	1237	212
1963	89	10367	8488	579		438	488	1331	230
1964	91	12523	10254	621		466	468	1676	270
1965	92	12785	10715	607		476	474	1796	296

Cocoa and chocolate

	Number of companies in census	Value of inputs mln. gld.	Value of gross output mln. gld.	Number of workers	Primary power in h.p.	Index input prices	Index output prices	Index real value added	Index real labour productivity
	Absolute numbers								
1938	41	27.9	41.8	1784	24811				
Index 1938 = 100									
1921	122	124	132	128	57	207	209	71	55
1922	122	116	128	115	65	184	189	80	69
1923	124	115	122	107	66	174	163	82	77
1924	120	122	128	116	70	162	153	92	79
1925	117	144	143	124	73	176	186	76	61
1926	112	148	146	117	74	184	195	72	61
1927	112	159	149	107	78	243	244	53	50
1928	105	176	160	110	79	233	223	57	52
1929	107	161	158	115	82	187	190	79	69
1930	107	144	146	118	93	157	162	93	78
1931	107	115	121	113	91	117	124	107	95
1932	107	82	89	93	100	96	104	99	106
1933	117	83	88	104	104	91	90	110	106
1934	120	77	82	104	103	79	78	120	115
1935	115	78	84	98	101	75	74	129	132
1936	110	91	94	102	100	85	89	112	110
1937	107	105	100	100	101	115	111	81	81
1938	100	100	100	100	100	100	100	100	100
1939	98	94	100	100	104	88	86	131	131
1940	95	90	111	95	108	99	108	140	148
1941	93	71	107	105	107	137			
1942	90	56	79	87	106	147			
1943	88	27	43	54	119	125			
1944									
1945									
1946	105	162	219	97	127	223	286	116	120
1947	107	305	349	113	133	371	474	92	82
1948	110	346	345	116	132	557	716	48	41
1949	115	430	476	124	146	457	476	120	96
1950	115	745	736	141	153	629	666	108	76
1951	122	888	756	139	169	832	755	65	47
1952	120	819	694	136	171	816	725	61	45
1953	115	969	829	136	177	739	708	77	57
1954	107	1072	894	131	185	1081	937	57	44
1955	107	1097	922	131	177	977	856	67	51
1956	112	976	896	128	182	683	665	111	87
1957	105	1047	967	132	189	637	676	120	90
1958	100	1208	1064	127	195	947	840	92	73
1959	102	1291	1100	125	202	852	744	96	77
1960	102	1297	1136	127	205	719	650	125	99
1961	98	1105	1077	127		566	589	173	136
1962	93	1163	1111	132		538	568	177	134
1963	88	1189	1146	124		561	585	182	146
1964	88	1248	1176	120		586	592	174	146
1965	85	1180	1161	113		493	555	203	179

Cotton spinning and weaving

	Number of companies in census	Value of inputs mln. gld.	Value of gross output mln. gld.	Number of workers	Primary power in h.p.	Index input prices	Index output prices	Index real value added	Index real labour productivity
	Absolute numbers								
1938	99	82.3	136.6	36434	167645				
Index 1938 = 100									
1921	93	152	146	87	53	249	231	59	68
1922	101	161	156	92	58	238	202	73	79
1923	102	159	142	89	61	271	205	57	64
1924	101	160	140	96	67	301	223	49	51
1925	104	214	187	100	69	274	226	65	65
1926	107	168	154	105	74	215	196	68	64
1927	111	165	164	111	77	185	180	90	81
1928	106	192	180	114	85	210	188	86	75
1929	106	194	179	116	87	208	181	87	75
1930	103	154	138	107	90	172	158	72	67
1931	90	101	99	97	93	121	123	77	79
1932	90	64	65	76	94	93	105	65	85
1933	101	61	64	77	96	85	94	72	93
1934	102	61	64	78	96	86	89	76	97
1935	100	64	66	79	96	87	86	80	101
1936	101	74	78	88	98	89	89	95	108
1937	100	119	114	109	96	115	109	99	91
1938	100	100	100	100	100	100	100	100	100
1939	101	108	114	106	102	96	99	124	117
1940	110	113	127	104	105	119	127	116	111
1941	120	89	110	91	112	173	205	69	76
1942	117	72	89	75	116	209	259	44	59
1943	110	70	89	63	119	225	287	41	65
1944									
1945									
1946	114	173	200	89	121	338	415	58	65
1947	118	328	364	107	125	422	534	78	73
1948	121	430	472	122	127	447	549	98	80
1949	125	522	569	136	105	471	542	118	87
1950	125	691	730	146	110	573	604	131	89
1951	123	932	875	147	122	773	752	105	72
1952	120	786	687	138	125	733	648	83	60
1953	119	785	737	148	135	608	593	112	76
1954	119	810	782	152	130	609	588	126	83
1955	115	813	785	146	126	597	590	126	86
1956	83	784	773	140	142	574	597	127	90
1957	86	822	821	144	132	565	610	134	93
1958	85	731	732	134	135	539	600	122	91
1959	85	734	767	134	132	486	559	146	109
1960	84	842	882	138	137	501	579	163	118
1961	81	869	894	138		511	622	150	108
1962	93	878	869	135		491	587	146	108
1963	93	930	923	131		486	592	154	118
1964	89	989	1002	126		490	596	171	136
1965	82	961	958	117		486	601	159	136

Electrical engineering

	Number of companies in census	Value of inputs mln. gld.	Value of gross output mln. gld.	Number of workers	Primary power in h.p.	Index input prices	Index output prices	Index real value added	Index real labour productivity
	Absolute numbers								
1938	46	27.9	83.9	23105	35286				
Index 1938 = 100									
1921	74	32	40	44	38	206	365	11	24
1922	67	29	35	41	39	155	272	13	32
1923	65	36	41	48	42	138	217	20	42
1924	65	39	45	55	44	132	189	26	47
1925	63	46	57	61	51	127	187	32	54
1926	61	47	56	63	57	124	199	31	50
1927	70	56	73	67	55	112	190	42	62
1928	70	80	91	95	58	106	185	50	52
1929	78	114	155	130	67	112	180	93	72
1930	78	115	157	127	72	114	178	95	75
1931	76	59	88	94	81	93	158	64	68
1932	80	32	66	70	81	77	101	71	101
1933	78	33	59	71	78	64	103	67	94
1934	89	35	65	83	84	62	85	93	111
1935	100	31	68	81	87	59	105	78	96
1936	89	35	61	78	87	64	98	79	101
1937	100	62	86	96	91	88	99	102	107
1938	100	100	100	100	100	100	100	100	100
1939	115	119	96	104	111	96	93	97	93
1940	130	136	105	103	120	122	111	84	81
1941	143	181	138	127	147	136	145	89	71
1942	143	192	160	139	152	140	175	83	60
1943	137	162	149	138	153	153	153	87	63
1944									
1945									
1946	217	250	267	185	237	168	230	116	63
1947	250	446	472	212	276	213	248	190	89
1948	285	673	647	228	300	248	251	245	108
1949	280	766	679	227	336	243	244	253	111
1950	152	945	843	248	374	252	252	305	123
1951	159	1355	1168	271	377	380	384	272	100
1952	154	1406	1100	263	403	439	361	254	97
1953	159	1300	1133	274	425	354	321	317	116
1954	163	1551	1426	313	462	339	315	420	134
1955	170	1935	1728	344	516	390	350	451	131
1956	176	2203	2017	363	516	438	373	501	138
1957	178	2658	2178	361	525	367	355	529	147
1958	178	2816	2225	367	567	319	304	617	168
1959	172	3194	2638	389	597	334	309	740	190
1960	165	3671	3180	419	665	359	309	920	220
1961	163	4584	3602	440		347	309	976	222
1962	176	5105	3879	466		326	309	1024	220
1963	180	5098	3949	452		323	304	1078	238
1964	187	6117	4872	479		353	321	1284	268
1965	200	6927	5422	498		365	338	1340	269

Flour

	Number of companies in census	Value of inputs mln. gld.	Value of gross output mln. gld.	Number of workers	Primary power in h.p.	Index input prices	Index output prices	Index real value added	Index real labour productivity
	Absolute numbers								
1938	19	93.7	105.1	2006	23717				
Index 1938 = 100									
1921	132	138	131	114	72	187	186	39	34
1922	116	95	94	112	82	128	128	61	55
1923	116	87	87	106	82	115	118	72	68
1924	126	103	108	104	84	121	129	111	107
1925	105	120	119	103	80	149	153	73	72
1926	100	106	103	95	80	140	144	59	62
1927	105	100	100	92	82	134	137	70	76
1928	121	95	97	97	85	124	126	86	88
1929	100	91	91	96	84	110	111	88	92
1930	95	79	81	98	85	92	99	93	95
1931	100	53	60	95	84	64	74	157	165
1932	95	66	66	98	86	68	71	101	103
1933	84	69	71	97	91	74	82	104	107
1934	100	77	77	91	91	80	84	91	100
1935	105	81	84	95	96	82	88	115	121
1936	105	88	90	96	97	91	97	113	118
1937	105	106	108	101	100	104	108	116	115
1938	100	100	100	100	100	100	100	100	100
1939	100	88	91	102	102	90	91	121	119
1940	95	104	104	107	105	107	103	102	95
1941	95	116	114	112	105	123	114	84	76
1942	95	106	104	107	110	140	125	70	65
1943	95	106	103	103	108	147	127	60	58
1944									
1945									
1946	95	202	198	111	116	195	179	92	83
1947	116	206	200	116	113	208	188	81	70
1948	147	198	191	120	125	215	192	70	59
1949	126	230	221	121	110	229	214	69	58
1950	137	240	230	122	120	229	215	71	58
1951	142	274	266	119	126	258	238	83	70
1952	163	345	333	120	130	300	274	85	71
1953	153	356	342	120	134	292	267	84	70
1954	153	337	328	120	135	276	261	95	80
1955	142	317	311	115	132	259	244	108	94
1956	132	313	307	113	140	254	238	110	97
1957	132	309	304	110	141	256	248	106	96
1958	126	298	297	99	116	247	242	117	119
1959	121	301	291	94	114	254	234	90	95
1960	111	309	308	93	130	265	254	118	127
1961	100	307	313	91		265	264	135	148
1962	100	325	330	92		288	274	136	147
1963	95	358	367	93		304	299	149	160
1964	100	367	379	94		314	309	153	163
1965	100	379	394	91		311	317	164	180

Footwear

	Number of companies in census	Value of inputs mln. gld.	Value of gross output mln. gld.	Number of workers	Primary power in h.p.	Index input prices	Index output prices	Index real value added	Index real labour productivity
	Absolute numbers								
1938	119	12.7	28.6	11600	7269				
Index 1938 = 100									
1921	156	131	134	74	65	254	380	36	49
1922	137	89	94	50	63	215	314	31	62
1923	143	84	79	59	69	184	253	30	50
1924	170	127	118	77	70	181	233	48	62
1925	164	123	114	75	69	186	232	46	62
1926	171	135	127	80	72	181	230	52	66
1927	168	149	134	83	73	188	228	54	64
1928	176	184	154	89	74	218	236	55	62
1929	171	169	152	88	76	202	232	59	67
1930	171	157	147	90	85	179	217	64	71
1931	171	122	120	88	90	144	183	65	74
1932	176	91	100	85	82	102	134	80	95
1933	103	84	96	88	82	90	114	93	106
1934	109	83	92	92	93	87	105	95	103
1935	112	87	95	99	106	80	96	106	106
1936	105	86	92	97	100	86	95	103	106
1937	103	106	104	100	99	109	102	100	99
1938	100	100	100	100	100	100	100	100	100
1939	92	130	136	106	98	100	112	125	118
1940	94	170	165	103	108	143	155	103	100
1941	93	184	161	100	112	179	193	74	74
1942	52	136	124	68	92	202	186	62	91
1943	56	189	159	69	91	221	172	79	114
1944									
1945									
1946	91	363	279	86	110	332	358	59	68
1947	97	588	419	100	122	422	388	73	73
1948	108	769	540	116	133	460	411	87	75
1949	115	789	559	119	140	491	419	90	75
1950	115	869	609	124	147	520	445	90	73
1951	112	1082	724	124	144	616	539	81	65
1952	109	924	659	130	154	477	470	95	73
1953	107	934	693	129	153	488	438	114	88
1954	112	1000	752	135	169	477	453	122	90
1955	116	1045	820	138	175	460	478	134	97
1956	120	1107	880	141	176	472	476	147	104
1957	122	1137	915	145	182	488	501	147	102
1958	120	1037	860	141	187	470	476	151	107
1959	122	1189	972	142	193	509	486	164	116
1960	120	1090	926	128	180	527	495	160	125
1961	87	1060	898	119		531	491	157	132
1962	83	1006	871	115		519	491	156	136
1963	82	1066	938	111		519	495	169	152
1964	81	1180	1061	109		512	510	189	173
1965	78	1204	1092	107		527	514	195	182

Leather

	Number of companies in census	Value of inputs mln. gld.	Value of gross output mln. gld.	Number of workers	Primary power in h.p.	Index input prices	Index output prices	Index real value added	Index real labour productivity
	Absolute numbers								
1938	89	16.9	24.1	3355	15780				
Index 1938 = 100									
1921									
1922									
1923									
1924									
1925									
1926									
1927									
1928	133	231	202	96	76	255	187	72	75
1929	135	197	178	95	77	194	166	80	84
1930	135	170	165	96	84	160	150	101	106
1931	113	125	125	91	86	120	123	102	112
1932	109	72	82	86	87	68	89	117	136
1933	106	75	85	89	91	75	86	126	141
1934	104	68	75	82	89	71	79	114	139
1935	109	72	77	86	91	73	77	116	134
1936	84	81	86	83	89	87	94	105	127
1937	93	124	113	95	95	126	115	75	79
1938	100	100	100	100	100	100	100	100	100
1939	101	106	134	109	103	101	116	172	158
1940	100	116	148	105	109	120	153	146	139
1941	100	100	128	105	122	113	177	110	105
1942	94	87	100	72	116	107	191	69	96
1943	69	82	103	66	99	107	204	76	115
1944									
1945									
1946	85	197	214	106	110	236	285	89	84
1947	103	376	401	126	126	319	352	131	103
1948	106	487	512	136	134	385	386	148	108
1949	107	585	561	129	156	473	415	121	94
1950	107	640	650	132	166	498	473	143	108
1951	108	743	681	121	172	670	560	95	79
1952	104	509	474	125	178	426	404	97	77
1953	100	587	569	131	182	435	389	135	103
1954	101	595	581	140	184	393	381	144	103
1955	102	534	559	137	192	359	350	177	129
1956	102	566	608	134	201	371	376	188	140
1957	98	572	600	131	206	374	379	176	134
1958	97	515	546	119	202	368	367	169	141
1959	92	631	682	122	207	467	413	195	159
1960	88	602	631	113	214	468	424	165	146
1961	66	572	613	104		443	426	167	160
1962	62	540	587	104		395	417	168	161
1963	60	499	574	98		361	398	188	191
1964	60	549	623	98		423	401	199	202
1965	60	560	618	89		461	411	184	206

Machine knitting

	Number of companies in census	Value of inputs mln. gld.	Value of gross output mln. gld.	Number of workers	Primary power in h.p.	Index input prices	Index output prices	Index real value added	Index real labour productivity
	Absolute numbers								
1938	68	13.0	26.8	10939	5848				
Index 1938 = 100									
1921	43	43	47	35	23	189	291	18	49
1922	44	56	61	41	26	184	219	30	72
1923	40	39	39	32	25	181	179	22	67
1924	35	53	47	34	32	215	178	23	67
1925	37	54	47	34	32	204	174	24	69
1926	37	51	48	37	35	178	162	28	74
1927	40	55	55	43	39	154	143	38	89
1928	41	67	61	46	42	173	150	37	81
1929	41	70	65	49	46	173	145	42	86
1930	60	88	84	67	59	149	142	56	84
1931	59	64	65	62	62	115	121	55	89
1932	71	62	65	68	66	94	87	79	116
1933	69	69	74	77	75	89	91	86	111
1934	88	77	82	85	89	91	82	105	124
1935	93	72	79	88	91	85	80	106	121
1936	99	85	89	97	95	85	80	116	120
1937	103	106	100	98	103	106	96	99	101
1938	100	100	100	100	100	100	100	100	100
1939	116	127	136	126	108	93	112	129	102
1940	122	155	174	124	115	107	142	134	108
1941	122	136	147	109	124	119	186	85	78
1942	118	133	142	97	126	108	189	79	82
1943	101	103	117	83	128	140	207	63	77
1944									
1945									
1946	104	174	174	84	139	248	307	57	68
1947	113	337	306	107	144	312	371	75	69
1948	126	467	412	125	156	344	386	93	75
1949	134	618	545	140	151	384	398	120	86
1950	140	838	722	155	177	453	450	136	88
1951	131	994	776	142	182	589	449	127	90
1952	124	767	625	137	178	591	389	127	92
1953	118	912	766	148	183	561	391	161	109
1954	122	1021	853	153	207	575	408	171	112
1955	124	1041	919	147	217	575	432	186	127
1956	124	1220	1015	154	226	596	424	194	126
1957	119	1345	1098	156	243	620	435	199	127
1958	132	1163	971	146	239	590	391	202	138
1959	132	1190	1033	154	256	561	386	229	149
1960	129	1312	1135	159	291	563	394	246	155
1961	112	1351	1180	154		575	397	257	167
1962	110	1498	1270	153		572	397	266	174
1963	113	1756	1475	152		607	407	298	196
1964	112	2052	1700	152		620	418	328	216
1965	109	1952	1662	147		594	432	322	219

Mechanical engineering

	Number of companies in census	Value of inputs mln. gld.	Value of gross output mln. gld.	Number of workers	Primary power in h.p.	Index input prices	Index output prices	Index real value added	Index real labour productivity
	Absolute numbers								
1938	149	57.5	126.3	29492	110437				
Index 1938 = 100									
1921	94	93	103	82	42	214	255	43	53
1922	77	51	66	68	43	123	148	53	78
1923	74	48	53	65	44	114	142	40	62
1924	77	57	63	74	47	108	142	47	64
1925	75	64	68	77	50	96	142	50	66
1926	71	69	72	78	52	92	148	51	65
1927	71	81	82	83	56	96	150	56	67
1928	82	107	106	102	65	93	168	63	62
1929	89	129	124	118	74	89	142	85	72
1930	95	107	112	108	78	86	116	101	93
1931	87	64	70	82	78	72	96	78	95
1932	68	42	44	57	78	57	94	48	84
1933	64	47	46	64	77	53	89	50	78
1934	68	46	49	64	79	58	82	63	99
1935	68	41	44	60	82	59	72	64	106
1936	74	51	51	68	83	62	71	72	107
1937	87	84	80	91	91	88	104	74	82
1938	100	100	100	100	100	100	100	100	100
1939	101	112	108	104	107	96	104	100	97
1940	115	106	110	112	114	122	125	90	81
1941	177	123	122	128	125	141	183	66	52
1942	171	110	127	130	127	134	183	77	60
1943	160	94	117	126	129	132	202	67	54
1944									
1945									
1946	199	149	181	140	119	237	289	72	51
1947	253	265	291	167	135	278	282	111	67
1948	287	383	403	196	145	291	249	169	86
1949	296	446	463	208	159	292	306	156	75
1950	187	467	497	204	162	297	294	178	87
1951	184	704	666	215	175	392	334	190	88
1952	170	829	771	218	188	464	365	198	91
1953	181	929	852	229	204	421	365	216	95
1954	189	990	932	241	214	370	365	242	101
1955	205	1130	1063	257	225	409	375	269	105
1956	212	1314	1249	267	240	436	385	310	116
1957	221	1369	1270	269	252	467	395	300	112
1958	224	1301	1195	250	261	459	395	280	112
1959	225	1431	1310	259	262	430	375	322	125
1960	238	1672	1520	273	277	449	385	362	133
1961	244	1790	1637	286		463	395	382	134
1962	260	1855	1727	294		461	405	400	136
1963	260	1764	1740	290		458	405	424	146
1964	264	2005	2016	294		463	425	476	162
1965	262	2327	2333	307		471	446	525	171

Paper

	Number of companies in census	Value of inputs mln. gld.	Value of gross output mln. gld.	Number of workers	Primary power in h.p.	Index input prices	Index output prices	Index real value added	Index real labour productivity
	Absolute numbers								
1938	28	19.6	37.8	6296	137526				
Index 1938 = 100									
1921	79	102	78	70	42	281	235	22	31
1922	82	76	75	72	43	157	170	43	60
1923	86	78	72	73	44	167	160	41	56
1924	86	85	80	77	47	158	151	50	64
1925	89	95	93	80	47	148	155	60	74
1926	93	99	101	84	50	149	156	67	79
1927	89	105	103	88	62	145	145	70	79
1928	93	112	112	96	65	138	141	79	83
1929	93	121	119	101	78	138	139	84	83
1930	93	123	116	101	83	139	133	81	80
1931	93	109	102	100	84	120	115	83	82
1932	89	81	78	91	84	94	90	81	89
1933	86	71	69	93	84	78	76	87	94
1934	93	64	65	87	84	70	70	94	108
1935	93	62	65	89	85	62	67	102	115
1936	96	66	71	94	89	62	69	112	119
1937	100	98	107	105	92	83	90	129	123
1938	100	100	100	100	100	100	100	100	100
1939	104	107	113	99	107	92	91	131	133
1940	100	118	136	105	109	124	123	126	120
1941	100	108	123	100	109	149	152	91	91
1942	100	73	76	85	109	173	164	49	57
1943	96	64	65	69	110	181	167	40	58
1944									
1945									
1946	93	207	206	82	87	284	293	70	85
1947	93	341	274	91	87	431	323	62	68
1948	96	561	425	100	88	524	380	73	73
1949	100	505	418	95	94	441	361	90	94
1950	107	541	507	101	99	417	388	121	120
1951	107	1150	973	112	105	876	672	116	104
1952	114	1051	742	108	110	873	567	72	67
1953	114	823	726	113	116	528	475	131	116
1954	118	940	845	114	122	569	503	148	129
1955	118	1020	916	130	174	608	531	151	116
1956	121	1131	959	135	172	637	524	148	109
1957	121	1265	1078	141	180	629	539	163	115
1958	121	1165	1005	141	179	595	510	163	115
1959	121	1218	1098	146	184	557	497	195	133
1960	121	1348	1233	154	213	565	493	226	146
1961	125	1476	1336	156		552	498	241	154
1962	125	1398	1321	162		527	493	257	159
1963	129	1613	1518	183		527	498	294	161
1964	129	1948	1738	183		540	523	316	173
1965	129	2134	1901	189		578	533	347	183

Pottery

	Number of companies in census	Value of inputs mln. gld.	Value of gross output mln. gld.	Number of workers	Primary power in h.p.	Index input prices	Index output prices	Index real value added	Index real labour productivity
	Absolute figures								
1938	50	2.7	10.6	5207	9600				
Index 1938 = 100									
1921									
1922									
1923									
1924									
1925									
1926									
1927									
1928									
1929									
1930									
1931									
1932									
1933									
1934									
1935							78		
1936							81		
1937	96	95	88	100	95	100	88	97	97
1938	100	100	100	100	100	100	100	100	100
1939	96	119	113	111	100	105	106	105	94
1940	102	119	115	104	107	117	109	104	100
1941	128	115	187	137	142	139	143	148	108
1942	134	78	145	115	143	142	152	111	96
1943	128	67	144	93	142	135	154	111	119
1944									
1945									
1946	128	233	256	106	163	234	251	105	99
1947	156	352	381	133	223	242	269	145	109
1948	186	478	509	160	259	233	283	184	115
1949	190	574	561	176	232	262	294	189	108
1950	130	622	628	182	225	278	303	208	114
1951	130	600	606	174	240	321	354	172	99
1952	128	774	720	180	250	326	371	189	105
1953	128	841	702	176	272	320	422	155	88
1954	124	822	733	175	330	314	439	160	91
1955	116	878	815	177	267	378	447	177	100
1956	114	933	851	171	265	414	459	179	105
1957	108	1037	912	167	278	417	476	183	109
1958	106	1126	964	174	293	417	479	190	109
1959	102	1070	931	169	300	418	481	184	109
1960	100	1141	1000	171	311	431	487	195	114
1961	100	1185	1136	168		453	498	225	134
1962	76	1174	1156	168		442	518	222	132
1963	72	1196	1165	163		443	527	219	135
1964	62	1178	1236	161		504	555	226	141
1965	64	1130	1281	142		560	572	233	164

Preserved food

	Number of companies in census	Value of inputs mln. gld.	Value of gross output mln. gld.	Number of workers	Primary power in h.p.	Index input prices	Index output prices	Index real value added	Index real labour productivity
	Absolute numbers								
1938	82	16.9	24.0	4782	5383				
Index 1938 = 100									
1921									
1922									
1923									
1924									
1925									
1926									
1927									
1928									
1929									
1930									
1931									
1932									
1933									
1934									
1935									
1936									
1937	93	92	94	90	97				
1938	100	100	100	100	100	100	100	100	100
1939	98	129	132	116	104	77	95	147	127
1940	105	174	202	134	138	94	131	205	154
1941	109	199	223	148	177				
1942	110	204	242	159	200	126	169	197	124
1943	111	195	236	128	185	135	207	162	126
1944									
1945									
1946	112	420	499	168	235	264	363	189	113
1947	120	418	517	183	279	225	314	239	131
1948	129	473	558	178	314	256	343	221	124
1949	128	562	619	184	326	248	299	252	137
1950	134	530	613	177	336	223	302	268	151
1951	122	628	666	159	358	332	389	194	122
1952	122	533	574	148	366	240	328	205	138
1953	133	696	748	178	373	253	327	267	150
1954	133	848	917	197	385	287	361	300	152
1955	130	947	1026	192	394	315	336	361	188
1956	134	1063	1150	199	418	314	350	388	195
1957	132	1071	1142	188	416	377	374	351	186
1958	133	1170	1275	209	435	287	351	434	208
1959	134	1209	1300	211	479	326	381	398	188
1960	130	1357	1470	220	496	273	333	522	238
1961	127	1466	1634	236		327	352	578	245
1962	116	1751	1993	253		347	380	677	268
1963	115	1764	2026	251		321	348	762	304
1964	120	1762	2055	243		309	367	750	309
1965	113	1786	2190	215		374	407	775	360

Ready-made clothing

	Number of companies in census	Value of inputs mln. gld.	Value of gross output mln. gld.	Number of workers	Primary power in h.p.	Index input prices	Index output prices	Index real value added	Index real labour productivity
	Absolute numbers								
1938	210	55.2	85.6	26642	5094				
Index 1938 = 100									
1921									
1922									
1923									
1924									
1925									
1926									
1927									
1928									
1929									
1930									
1931									
1932									
1933	85	74	78	85	76	95			
1934	92	71	75	85	80	91	59	143	168
1935	90	72	76	89	86	79	60	140	157
1936	93	77	81	91	90	81	68	131	144
1937	99	90	92	96	90	94	78	124	129
1938	100	100	100	100	100	100	100	100	100
1939	107	130	130	114	117	96	115	114	99
1940	106	152	159	111	116	120	125	139	125
1941	104	107	130	102	126	179	167	104	101
1942	78	89	117	93	118	224	169	99	106
1943	75	88	114	82	118	239	185	87	105
1944									
1945									
1946	87	182	197	78	111	413	297	75	97
1947	111	327	326	100	132	448	336	97	97
1948	121	412	413	115	154	468	350	119	103
1949	127	519	516	134	165	506	371	138	103
1950	136	684	649	147	209	571	394	149	101
1951	114	722	639	128	211	673	428	114	89
1952	111	610	551	128	206	580	379	117	92
1953	121	662	622	139	220	573	391	140	101
1954	129	744	712	146	236	568	399	164	112
1955	133	827	812	149	257	568	401	196	131
1956	140	873	868	164	293	544	412	209	128
1957	139	895	889	163	296	556	439	200	122
1958	130	789	780	150	310	538	423	180	120
1959	133	851	851	158	332	516	422	201	127
1960	136	947	948	166	351	529	436	218	131
1961	142	1096	1099	176		529	450	246	140
1962	144	1098	1129	182		529	458	258	142
1963	150	1258	1283	189		539	472	282	149
1964	149	1397	1444	191		557	493	310	162
1965	153	1405	1473	188		565	504	316	168

Roofing tiles

	Number of companies in census	Value of inputs mln. gld.	Value of gross output mln. gld.	Number of workers	Primary power in h.p.	Index input prices	Index output prices	Index real value added	Index real labour productivity
	Absolute numbers								
1938	49	0.8	3.9	2282	5357				
Index 1938 = 100									
1921									
1922									
1923									
1924									
1925									
1926									
1927									
1928									
1929									
1930									
1931									
1932									
1933									
1934									
1935									
1936									
1937	76	93	75	93	102	95	92	77	83
1938	100	100	100	100	100	100	100	100	100
1939	98	113	108	103	116	100	102	105	102
1940	92	88	82	86	116	119	137	59	69
1941	84		103	98	121		144	90	92
1942	82		69	85	121		147	59	70
1943	82		90	79	127		153	74	93
1944	82		59	77			146	51	66
1945	84		56	53			230	31	59
1946	82	150	197	79	120	220	233	90	114
1947	82	175	223	80	119	253	253	93	116
1948	71	225	279	85	121	280	259	113	133
1949	78	313	349	99	123	340	275	130	131
1950	45	338	385	90	115	373	294	135	149
1951	45	450	423	94	126	467	306	136	145
1952	45	500	428	92	131	511	321	127	139
1953	41	525	474	88	129	538	351	131	150
1954	45	575	554	88	138	537	376	146	167
1955	45	600	549	88	159	560	382	140	160
1956	45	663	615	88	162	568	406	149	170
1957	45	750	690	88	164	615	431	156	178
1958	41	688	618	79	161	622	440	136	173
1959	41	675	677	83	172	599	452	150	180
1960	41	675	672	79	174	564	463	145	184
1961	49	825	721	79		471	500	139	176
1962	45	863	751	74		533	537	135	181
1963	43	938	803	74		553	577	133	179
1964	43	1038	990	79		535	647	151	192
1965	41	1038	1031	74		507	688	150	201

Rubber

	Number of companies in census	Value of inputs mln. gld.	Value of gross output mln. gld.	Number of workers	Primary power in h.p.	Index input prices	Index output prices	Index real value added	Index real labour productivity
	Absolute numbers								
1938	17	4.9	10.2	3039	14307				
Index 1938 = 100									
1921	76	63	62	49	42	252	405	15	31
1922	71	53	53	38	41	176	339	16	41
1923	65	59	54	47	41	229	296	16	35
1924	59	60	59	44	36	218	257	23	52
1925	53	83	74	52	38	402	263	25	47
1926	53	75	67	49	38	447	245	25	50
1927	59	69	65	53	39	341	205	30	56
1928	59	67	66	58	40	223	182	36	63
1929	59	70	72	60	41	184	170	43	72
1930	59	71	69	56	43	160	165	41	73
1931	59	52	59	55	44	89	138	48	86
1932	59	39	47	60	45	45	105	52	86
1933	71	42	54	71	49	39	97	67	94
1934	100	49	55	68	72	56	92	65	96
1935	100	60	62	74	85	68	92	68	92
1936	100	68	71	77	92	75	90	81	105
1937	106	106	96	93	100	122	107	81	88
1938	100	100	100	100	100	100	100	100	100
1939	129	140	133	114	115	112	106	118	104
1940	129	122	136	93	118	138	143	104	111
1941	124	71	91	83	117	166	212	51	62
1942	118	79	97	85	125	272	226	50	59
1943	112	124	121	91	126	292	298	40	44
1944									
1945									
1946	112	340	308	112	116	311	351	79	71
1947	118	604	510	153	162	242	319	133	87
1948	124	895	762	175	177	225	291	220	125
1949	153	879	750	171	192	219	341	185	109
1950	147	1318	1067	196	197	340	392	213	109
1951	153	2130	1480	192	217	734	528	167	87
1952	153	1729	1334	211	236	484	480	202	96
1953	171	1774	1560	240	249	335	411	332	138
1954	200	1943	1684	270	289	289	401	360	134
1955	224	2527	2043	280	312	423	408	391	140
1956	218	2678	2174	280	337	442	431	397	142
1957	218	2690	2192	276	351	411	409	424	153
1958	218	2368	2028	265	372	354	394	435	164
1959	218	2983	2486	291	377	419	395	514	176
1960	218	3554	2998	352	392	500	406	613	174
1961	182	3231	2944	352		396	385	695	197
1962	159	3095	2968	369		360	372	767	208
1963	147	3107	2953	362		337	386	729	201
1964	147	3398	3358	375		324	407	816	217
1965	165	3530	3545	378		316	413	862	228

Sheet-metal work

	Number of companies in census	Value of inputs mln. gld.	Value of gross output mln. gld.	Number of workers	Primary power in h.p.	Index input prices	Index output prices	Index real value added	Index real labour productivity
	Absolute numbers								
1938	72	17.7	29.9	7426	13638				
Index 1938 = 100									
1921	89	74	87	89	57	146	200	53	59
1922	78	65	77	77	58	132	122	78	101
1923	79	77	80	76	57	141	116	73	96
1924	79	92	92	81	57	125	116	79	98
1925	85	104	103	89	56	125	116	87	98
1926	81	109	106	92	58	119	123	83	91
1927	82	101	102	90	61	119	115	90	100
1928	89	115	119	103	71	122	115	108	105
1929	94	131	133	118	75	124	116	118	100
1930	100	109	119	109	81	104	114	118	109
1931	90	81	90	90	83	86	108	95	105
1932	78	54	64	75	83	65	95	84	112
1933	82	62	72	82	83	63	88	97	119
1934	81	59	68	79	85	61	86	93	117
1935	86	60	65	77	91	63	83	87	112
1936	90	66	73	83	95	73	80	102	122
1937	94	108	103	99	102	119	99	96	97
1938	100	100	100	100	100	100	100	100	100
1939	107	113	116	107	106	103	102	118	110
1940	110	121	122	108	114	141	123	102	94
1941					99		130		
1942					104		130		
1943					104		131		
1944									
1945									
1946	99	196	301	186	184	209	246	185	99
1947	132	346	500	246	240	242	282	257	104
1948	160	546	723	305	272	261	293	335	110
1949	165	727	891	338	325	279	314	360	106
1950	176	961	1150	377	378	309	343	414	110
1951	176	1317	1500	403	432	388	364	485	121
1952	167	1368	1416	364	444	479	351	423	116
1953	172	1374	1515	389	468	428	391	440	113
1954	172	1586	1782	411	499	396	418	495	120
1955	197	1943	2152	436	557	436	454	541	124
1956	208	2302	2477	448	584	460	431	634	141
1957	206	2370	2591	451	576	452	506	575	127
1958	206	2143	2347	407	583	445	514	514	126
1959	194	2439	2685	420	601	429	539	564	134
1960	200	2841	3092	446	622	436	561	616	138
1961	186	2673	3039	440		426	588	607	138
1962	193	2627	3166	463		426	618	639	138
1963	197	2857	3538	489		415	648	698	143
1964	204	3436	4227	520		441	653	823	158
1965	211	3870	4780	533		462	583	1046	196

Shipbuilding

	Number of companies in census	Value of inputs mln. gld.	Value of gross output mln. gld.	Number of workers	Primary power in h.p.	Index input prices	Index output prices	Index real value added	Index real labour productivity
	Absolute numbers								
1938	78	87.5	157.5	34458	112519				
Index 1938 = 100									
1921	138	111	129	109	51	241	174	88	81
1922	118	81	95	76	54	208	174	65	85
1923	126	45	55	65	65	159	164	42	64
1924	131	55	65	79	65	125	144	54	68
1925	127	58	74	91	70	110	128	74	81
1926	132	68	82	94	71	99	120	83	89
1927	132	80	88	102	80	93	126	77	75
1928	137	97	104	111	83	92	119	94	85
1929	153	95	104	120	97	93	128	90	75
1930	159	102	108	109	102	90	127	90	83
1931	127	58	67	60	102	82	127	62	103
1932	73	21	25	34	99	71	106	29	84
1933	73	18	23	35	94	62	91	33	93
1934	73	24	27	40	94	61	76	40	99
1935	71	20	25	38	93	63	66	46	119
1936	77	34	38	56	95	72	62	68	122
1937	95	65	70	83	99	86	79	97	116
1938	100	100	100	100	100	100	100	100	100
1939	108	108	111	84	107	115	118	99	117
1940	104	77	81	82	108	118	123	70	84
1941									
1942									
1943									
1944									
1945									
1946	145	97	158	113	140	265	254	92	82
1947	158	189	233	122	147	287	272	106	87
1948	174	262	299	128	150	317	341	101	79
1949	178	306	333	131	166	330	356	103	79
1950	174	322	367	133	177	369	397	106	80
1951	110	414	452	135	183	446	400	125	92
1952	113	563	547	142	192	526	422	125	88
1953	117	656	613	145	199	535	435	129	89
1954	117	690	656	146	216	506	457	135	92
1955	131	759	761	148	224	489	459	166	112
1956	138	826	832	151	232	517	472	178	118
1957	142	970	945	155	250	547	471	194	125
1958	137	893	894	156	259	557	508	176	113
1959	129	904	911	150	264	545	507	181	121
1960	128	978	956	145	280	524	504	184	127
1961	128	873	869	143		506	484	178	125
1962	126	880	879	142		496	457	192	135
1963	121	751	827	134		488	482	191	143
1964	121	783	836	129		495	557	162	125
1965	117	790	888	126		496	623	162	128

Soap

	Number of companies in census	Value of inputs mln. gld.	Value of gross output mln. gld.	Number of workers	Primary power in h.p.	Index input prices	Index output prices	Index real value added	Index real labour productivity
	Absolute numbers								
1938	46	13.7	24.0	2923	5830				
Index 1938 = 100									
1921	133	123	112	76	36	243	239	41	54
1922	137	121	113	73	39	248	218	47	64
1923	126	134	118	74	45	266	211	46	62
1924	122	138	120	74	49	277	208	45	62
1925	126	147	126	77	51	293	213	46	60
1926	137	145	130	78	53	256	198	55	70
1927	133	151	132	82	56	242	183	59	72
1928	135	151	133	85	59	233	175	62	73
1929	135	149	132	84	60	232	176	62	73
1930	128	139	128	85	59	211	166	68	80
1931	124	108	110	88	62	136	141	81	92
1932	135	90	97	82	66	96	118	90	110
1933	122	85	94	92	70	89	117	92	100
1934	122	73	87	95	80	73	105	101	106
1935	100	82	95	95	89	81	104	107	113
1936	104	88	96	97	93	95	102	104	107
1937	100	110	106	97	102	125	107	94	96
1938	98	100	100	100	100	100	100	100	100
1939	96	115	124	97	110	100	109	125	129
1940	98	139	145	98	114	182	166	92	94
1941	96	92	110	98	117	208	228	59	60
1942	109	255	240	96	117				
1943	35	112	125	72	89				
1944									
1945									
1946	174	165	196	101	129	381	386	61	61
1947	189	306	299	120	140	506	386	75	62
1948	174	436	375	124	149	563	381	77	62
1949	148	479	402	125	160	714	429	70	56
1950	174	612	542	155	172	660	432	104	67
1951	165	636	544	144	180	767	455	92	64
1952	152	539	470	137	189	678	404	94	69
1953	150	560	533	140	202	642	412	121	86
1954	150	626	603	137	209	668	443	129	94
1955	141	635	612	137	223	675	451	129	94
1956	139	633	642	137	223	627	449	146	107
1957	135	641	621	133	230	634	454	131	98
1958	130	639	651	127	204	651	487	137	108
1959	128	676	722	127	206	643	527	149	117
1960	72	812	920	168	206	662	523	204	121
1961	76	846	998	174		620	547	219	126
1962	83	951	1124	185		592	572	237	128
1963	87	985	1207	188		626	601	250	133
1964	89	1194	1435	195		703	639	275	141
1965	96	1375	1615	205		823	732	264	129

Steel furniture

	Number of companies in census	Value of inputs mln. gld.	Value of gross output mln. gld.	Number of workers	Primary power in h.p.	Index input prices	Index output prices	Index real value added	Index real labour productivity
	Absolute numbers								
1938	28	2.7	5.7	1947	2657				
Index 1938 = 100									
1921									
1922									
1923									
1924									
1925									
1926									
1927									
1928									
1929									
1930									
1931									
1932									
1933	136	65	75	81	71	55	88	96	120
1934	150	71	80	86	81	56	86	102	119
1935	168	74	82	91	100	57	83	107	118
1936	118	77	81	87	89	58	80	105	121
1937	100	91	93	93	88	82	99	95	103
1938	100	100	100	100	100	100	100	100	100
1939	125	140	139	127	109	92	100	139	109
1940	132	162	174	127	119	124	124	150	118
1941	139	173	181	122	130	155	180	105	86
1942	114	114	136	95	132	163	215	72	76
1943	93	81	116	89	120	159	211	70	79
1944									
1945									
1946	146	284	322	133	148	281	390	92	69
1947	171	409	447	145	182	298	416	116	80
1948	200	590	618	184	218	336	416	155	84
1949	193	660	655	187	211	354	387	168	90
1950	75	535	542	158	179	354	351	157	99
1951	82	734	722	159	189	434	381	187	118
1952	79	870	796	164	207	493	389	187	114
1953	89	907	857	180	241	448	387	210	117
1954	96	1073	1042	205	271	407	411	247	120
1955	100	1195	1206	216	294	422	447	272	126
1956	104	1442	1423	236	316	448	436	323	137
1957	111	1656	1632	247	354	468	457	352	143
1958	111	1482	1408	221	354	469	452	296	134
1959	118	1755	1711	241	403	449	440	380	157
1960	121	2035	2009	257	437	459	424	468	182
1961	125	2060	2156	290		463	424	529	182
1962	121	2118	2317	290		447	427	585	202
1963	118	2209	2363	280		438	427	586	209
1964	121	2438	2745	286		433	448	676	236
1965	125	2595	3022	292		427	462	738	253

Wire

	Number of companies in census	Value of inputs mln. gld.	Value of gross output mln. gld.	Number of workers	Primary power in h.p.	Index input prices	Index output prices	Index real value added	Index real labour productivity
	Absolute numbers								
1938	20	6.8	10.5	2042	9998	(period 1921–1938)			
1938	44	8.0	12.9	2677	11022	(period 1938–1965)			
Index 1938 = 100									
1921	95	116	99	93	67	112	143	47	51
1922	100	57	72	87	67	98	104	96	110
1923	110	66	81	91	67	99	114	95	104
1924	105	78	82	99	71	95	98	92	93
1925	100	82	93	118	69	83	85	133	113
1926	90	91	97	116	69	78	76	143	124
1927	105	114	119	137	73	80	90	144	105
1928	110	130	141	154	73	82	85	189	123
1929	115	145	147	150	82	88	91	165	110
1930	115	117	123	125	83	84	87	152	122
1931	120	82	89	107	85	70	78	128	120
1932	105	54	59	90	84	61	74	92	102
1933	110	46	54	93	93	64	88	80	86
1934	100	46	55	89	96	64	80	91	103
1935	100	40	50	81	95	61	74	91	113
1936	110	51	63	88	103	60	72	116	132
1937	105	93	100	92	94	89	100	113	123
1938	100	100	100	100	100	100	100	100	100
1939	105	111	118	102	98	92	102	127	124
1940	114	119	129	107	104	131	147	99	92
1941	139	129	140	108	121	159	143	111	102
1942	141	118	128	105	123	150	130	110	105
1943	141	131	141	107	125	142	132	120	112
1944									
1945									
1946	148	268	301	147	131	316	243	146	99
1947	157	508	541	177	149	364	310	192	108
1948	184	686	723	208	169	391	338	232	111
1949	164	754	767	217	194	385	307	257	118
1950	68	700	731	205	206	331	279	280	137
1951	66	1279	1207	216	227	522	407	268	124
1952	66	1290	1139	204	240	602	458	196	96
1953	64	1077	977	207	246	479	392	208	100
1954	61	1096	1052	223	236	438	355	277	124
1955	66	1326	1258	228	279	499	401	287	126
1956	61	1513	1424	234	310	552	450	284	121
1957	68	1620	1525	246	317	583	464	296	120
1958	68	1392	1346	232	332	554	390	326	141
1959	68	1593	1620	257	353	540	396	420	163
1960	68	1793	1786	259	371	583	429	414	160
1961	66	1638	1697	256		557	436	411	161
1962	77	1806	1888	285		528	429	471	166
1963	77	1735	1876	281		504	434	484	172
1964	80	1974	2215	300		503	452	576	192
1965	80	2169	2443	297		526	477	605	204

Wool spinning and weaving

	Number of companies in census	Value of inputs mln. gld.	Value of gross output mln. gld.	Number of workers	Primary power in h.p.	Index input prices	Index output prices	Index real value added	Index real labour productivity
	Absolute numbers								
1938	92	31.4	50.5	13940	39616				
Index 1938 = 100									
1921	89	98	111	74	67	166	174	77	103
1922	91	96	114	77	70	155	136	106	138
1923	89	96	103	73	70	177	135	86	117
1924	89	125	120	77	71	246	144	78	102
1925	89	112	110	73	71	249	179	60	82
1926	89	105	109	75	72	209	170	67	89
1927	87	125	128	80	74	207	167	79	98
1928	84	141	138	83	77	223	172	77	93
1929	85	140	136	85	82	210	163	79	94
1930	86	114	121	85	85	159	148	89	105
1931	85	83	96	82	88	115	125	94	115
1932	88	67	81	82	90	90	107	96	117
1933	91	75	86	89	90	84	94	111	125
1934	96	74	82	83	93	87	95	99	119
1935	103	71	79	87	99	81	83	110	126
1936	104	80	90	88	102	81	84	125	142
1937	103	102	104	91	99	105	97	111	121
1938	100	100	100	100	100	100	100	100	100
1939	99	129	145	110	104	92	103	164	149
1940	98	142	178	103	109	119	126	188	183
1941	91	131	165	95	117	166	109	201	211
1942	90	110	134	82	125	181	115	152	185
1943	64	91	109	56	102	185	141	99	175
1944									
1945									
1946	91	260	295	97	132	284	369	95	98
1947	95	434	462	114	135	329	406	125	110
1948	97	578	597	125	134	393	390	161	129
1949	98	732	745	136	131	453	401	191	141
1950	97	950	956	138	143	584	500	193	140
1951	92	1081	944	128	147	892	609	118	92
1952	90	896	766	134	156	706	464	119	89
1953	90	948	870	138	160	669	465	160	116
1954	91	993	909	139	156	672	470	164	118
1955	92	1012	932	140	174	635	449	179	128
1956	85	985	909	131	175	607	443	177	136
1957	87	1089	970	136	181	664	468	166	121
1958	85	895	807	129	161	585	440	150	116
1959	85	961	936	132	163	497	396	226	171
1960	85	990	961	129	170	538	418	219	169
1961	86	1059	1047	131		509	417	246	188
1962	86	979	984	130		488	399	249	192
1963	83	1080	1062	126		513	405	254	201
1964	83	1142	1115	117		572	442	242	207
1965	75	1044	1039	105		526	425	243	232

Appendix B. Prices in Dutch Manufacturing 1921–1965 (index 1938 = 100)

	Input prices Production Statistics	Output prices Production Statistics	Raw materials prices CBS	Industry products prices CBS
1921	210	210	220	203
1922	169	167	200	159
1923	167	158	210	148
1924	174	160	210	156
1925	177	168	202	156
1926	157	159	181	141
1927	153	157	184	135
1928	155	157	186	133
1929	146	148	178	131
1930	127	134	149	124
1931	98	115	109	111
1932	80	97	81	96
1933	76	90	77	93
1934	76	83	75	90
1935	76	78	76	88
1936	81	82	88	89
1937	104	98	122	104
1938	100	100	100	100
1939	96	103	109	103
1940	117	125	158	125
1941	155	166	171	147
1942	175	180	168	152
1943	184	211	168	157
1944			171	161
1945			184	182
1946	278	301	270	258
1947	328	343	316	273
1948	363	370	329	280
1949	380	376	355	290
1950	425	409	421	321
1951	575	493	563	397
1952	568	463	546	377
1953	509	447	513	367
1954	509	459	510	372
1955	518	467	527	382
1956	522	477	556	382
1957	527	483	583	392
1958	512	467	566	387
1959	497	456	553	387
1960	506	460	550	387
1961	496	465	536	387
1962	486	461	527	392
1963	485	465	533	397
1964	503	490	563	418
1965	510	510	573	433

Sources:
Columns 1 and 2: De Jong, *Nederlandse industrie*, 445
Columns 3 and 4: CBS, *Statistical Yearbook of the Netherlands.*

Appendix C. Real Value Added, Employment and Real Labour Productivity for Total Manufacturing 1921–1965
Index 1938=100

	Real value added Single deflation	Real value added Double deflation	Labour volume Number of Workers	Real labour productivity Single defl.	Real labour productivity Double defl.
1921	50	50	80	63	63
1922	56	58	71	79	82
1923	47	52	69	69	75
1924	51	58	76	67	76
1925	56	60	81	69	74
1926	59	59	84	71	70
1927	66	63	88	74	71
1928	73	72	99	74	73
1929	88	87	108	82	81
1930	92	85	103	89	83
1931	80	66	83	96	79
1932	66	51	66	100	78
1933	71	56	70	101	80
1934	79	71	73	108	97
1935	84	81	73	116	112
1936	88	87	80	111	109
1937	95	101	96	99	106
1938	100	100	100	100	100
1939	115	104	108	106	96
1940	114	105	108	106	97
1941	88	81	109	80	74
1942	79	76	101	78	76
1943	64	55	90	72	61
1944					
1945					
1946	81	74	109	74	67
1947	105	99	129	81	76
1948	122	118	144	85	82
1949	135	135	153	88	88
1950	148	152	159	93	96
1951	136	162	160	85	101
1952	130	166	158	82	105
1953	156	181	166	94	109
1954	177	198	175	101	113
1955	200	223	181	111	123
1956	219	239	185	118	129
1957	222	243	186	119	130
1958	216	237	179	121	133
1959	253	275	184	137	149
1960	288	317	192	150	165
1961	301	320	195	155	164
1962	317	331	200	159	166
1963	334	346	197	170	176
1964	368	374	199	185	188
1965	385	379	199	194	191

Source: De Jong, *Nederlandse industrie*, 446.

Appendix D. Average Money Wages, Installed Machinery and Real User Costs of Capital for Total Manufacturing 1921–1965

	Money wage per worker in guilders per year	Primary power of installed machinery 1938 = 100	Real user costs of capital 1938 = 100
1921	1306	49	807
1922	1263	51	680
1923	1196	55	499
1924	1165	58	379
1925	1160	60	247
1926	1165	62	199
1927	1190	67	194
1928	1200	73	207
1929	1220	79	226
1930	1232	84	244
1931	1225	86	232
1932	1196	86	220
1933	1138	86	191
1934	1096	89	167
1935	1059	92	136
1936	1022	94	135
1937	1022	96	119
1938	1037	100	100
1939	1051	107	
1940	1102	111	
1941	1217	110	
1942	1301	111	
1943	1439	111	
1944			
1945			
1946	1911	133	126
1947	2166	148	150
1948	2279	159	174
1949	2352	163	197
1950	2498	173	220
1951	2825	183	243
1952	2949	191	266
1953	3007	201	289
1954	3320	212	314
1955	3641	226	326
1956	4061	238	357
1957	4464	244	394
1958	4712	251	441
1959	4815	259	468
1960	5235	275	458
1961	5684		414
1962	6056		377
1963	6406		379
1964	7252		382
1965	8245		364

Source: De Jong, *Nederlandse industrie*, 462, 471.

References

Abramovitz, M. (1986). Catching Up, Forging Ahead, and Falling Behind. *The Journal of Economic History 46*, pp. 385–406.

Abramowitz, M. (1993). The Search for the Sources of Growth: Areas of Ignorance, Old and New. *The Journal of Economic History 53*, pp. 217–243.

Albers, R. M. A. (1998) *Machinery investment and economic growth: the dynamics of Dutch development 1800–1913.* Dissertation University of Groningen.

Aldcroft, D. H. (1969). Economic Growth in Britain in the Inter-War Years: A Reassessment. In D. H. Aldcroft & P. Fearon (eds.), *Economic Growth in 20th Century Britain*. London: Macmillan, pp. 34–54.

Allen, R. G. D. (1975). Indexnumbers in Theory and Practice. London: Macmillan.

Ammerlaan, B. (1935). Een jaar ordening in de Nederlandsche meelindustrie. *Economisch-Statistische Berichten 1030*, pp. 832–833.

Ark, B. van (1990). Comparative Levels of Labour Productivity in Dutch and British Manufacturing. *National Institute Economic Review 131*, pp. 71–85.

Ark, B. van (1993). *International Comparisons of Output and Productivity: Manufacturing Productivity Performance of Ten Countries from 1950 to 1990*. Groningen Growth and Development Centre Monograph Series, no. 1.

Ark, B. van (1996). Sectoral Growth Accounts and Structural Change in Post-War Europe. In B. Van Ark & N. F. R. Crafts (eds.), *Quantitative Aspects of Post-War European Economic Growth*. CEPR/Cambridge University Press, pp.84–164.

Ark, B. van, J. de Haan & H. J. de Jong (1996). Characteristics of Economic Growth in the Netherlands During the Postwar Period. In N. F. R. Crafts & G. Toniolo (eds.). *Economic Growth in Europe Since 1945*. Centre for Economic Policy Research. Cambridge: Cambridge University Press, pp. 290–328.

Ark, B. van & H. J. de Jong (1996). Accounting for Economic Growth in the Netherlands Since 1913. *Economic and Social History in the Netherlands 7*, pp. 199–242.

Van Ark, B & M. Timmer (2002). Industry Productivity Comparisons. *De Economist* 150, pp. 95–109.

Arnold, A. J. (1999) Profitability and capital accumulation in British industry during the transwar period, 1913–1924. *Economic History Review, LII*, 1, pp. 45–68.

Bakker, G. P. den (1991). The Choice of Index Number Formulae and Weights in the National Accounts. CBS National Accounts Occasional Paper, nr. 44, Voorburg.

Bakker, G. P. den (1992). Beroepscategorieën in de beroepsbevolking, 1930 en 1938. *Supplement sociaal economische maandstatistiek*, pp. 10–16.

Bakker, G. P. den, C.A. van Bochove & Th. A. Huitker (1987). *Macro-economische ontwikkelingen, 1921–1939 en 1969–1985*. 's-Gravenhage: Staatsuitgeverij.

Bakker, G. P. den & J. de Gijt (1994). Labour Force Data in a National Accounting Framework. *Paper presented to the IARIW 23rd General Conference*. New Brunswick, Canada.

Bakker, G. P. den, J. de Gijt & S. J. Keuning (1994). An Historical Social Accounting Matrix for the Netherlands. *Review of Income and Wealth 40*, no. 2, pp. 175–190.

Bakker, G. P. den & W. van Sorge (1991). Het onbenut arbeidsvolume in het interbellum. *Economisch- en Sociaal-Historisch Jaarboek 54*, pp. 212–240.

Barendregt, J. (1993). *The Dutch Money Purge*. Amsterdam: Vrije Universiteit.

Baumol, W. J. (1986). Productivity Growth, Convergence and Welfare: What the Long-Run Data Show. *American Economic Review 76*, pp. 1072–1085.

Berenschot, B. W. m.m.v. T. J. Bezemer (1951). Prae advies over de vraag: *Welke maatregelen dienen te worden genomen ter verhoging van de productiviteit?* 's-Gravenhage, Martinus Nijhoff.

Berger, J. A. (1951), *Ibid.*

Bie, R. J. van der (1995). *Een doorlopende groote roes. De economische ontwikkeling van Nederland, 1913–1921*. Amsterdam: Thesis Publishers.

Blanken, I. J. (1992). *Geschiedenis van Philips Electronics N. V. III (1922–1934)*. Leiden: Martinus Nijhoff.

Blanken, I. J. (1997). *Geschiedenis van Philips Electronics N. V. IV (1935–1950)*. Zaltbommel: Europese Bibliotheek.

Bloemen, E. S. A. (1988). *Scientific Management in Nederland 1900–1930*. Amsterdam: NEHA.

Bloemen, E. S. A., J. Kok & J.L. van Zanden (1993). *De top 100 van industriële bedrijven in Nederland 1913–1990*. Den Haag: Adviesraad voor het Wetenschaps- en Technologiebeleid.

Blomme, J. (1986). Changes in Labour Productivity and their Consequences for the Per Capita Income Levels in Belgium and the Netherlands, 1880–1980. In P. O'Brien (ed.), *International Productivity Comparisons and Problems of Measurement, 1750–1939*.

Bochove, C. A. van & Th. A. Huitker (1987). Main National Accounting Series 1900–1986. *Occasional Paper nr. NA-017*. Voorburg: CBS.

Bochove, C. A. van & W. van Sorge (1989). Constant Wealth National Income: Accounting for War Damage with an Application to the Netherlands, 1940–1945. *Review of Income and Wealth, series 35, 2*, pp. 187–208.

Boff, R. B. Du (1966). Electrification and Capital Productivity: A Suggested Approach. *The Review of Economics and Statistics XXXVIII*, pp. 426–431.

Bölger, B. (1930). De beteekenis van de loongegevens der Rijksverzekeringsbank van de algemeene loonstatistiek. *Economisch-Statistische Berichten 736*, pp. 122–124.

Bonebakker, J. W. (1936). *De scheepsbouwnijverheid in Nederland*. Haarlem: Bohn.

Brakel, L. (1962). A Comparison of Productivity and Recent Productivity Trends in Various Countries. *The Review of Economics and Statistics XLIV*, pp. 121–133.

Brakel, W. (1954). De industrialisatie in Nederland na 1945. Leiden: Stenfert Kroese.

Brandes de Roos, R. (1927). *Die Industrie, der Kapitalmarkt und die industriellen Effekten in Holland*. Den Haag.

Broadberry, S. N. (1986). *The British Economy Between the Wars: A Macroeconomic Survey*. Oxford: Blackwell.

Broadberry, S. N. (1993). Manufacturing and the Convergence Hypothesis: What the Long-Run Data Show. *The Journal of Economic History 53*, pp. 772–795.

Broadberry, S. N. (1994). Technological Leadership and Productivity Leadership in Manufacturing Since the Industrial Revolution: Implications for the Convergence Debate. *The Economic Journal 104*, pp. 291–302.

Broadberry, S. N. (1997). *The Productivity-Race*. Cambridge: Cambridge University Press.

Broadberry, S. N. & N. F. R. Crafts (1990). Explaining Anglo-American Productivity Differences in the Mid-Twentieth Century. *Oxford Bulletin of Economics and Statistics 52*, pp. 375–402.

Broadberry, S. N. & N. F. R. Crafts (1990). The Impact of the Depression of the 1930's on Productive Potential in the U. K. *European Economic Review 34*, pp. 599–607.

Broadberry, S. N. & N. F. R. Crafts (1992). Britain's Productivity Gap in the 1930s: Some Neglected Factors. *The Journal of Economic History vol. 52*, pp. 531–558.

Broadberry, S. N. & R. R. Fremdling (1990). Comparative Productivity in British and German Industry 1907–37. *Oxford Bulletin of Economics and Statistics 52*, pp. 403–421.

Broadberry, S. N. & A. O. Ritschl (1995). Real Wages, Productivity, and Unemployment in Britain and Germany during the 1920s. *Explorations in Economic History 32*, pp. 327–349.

Broadberry, S. N. & H. J. de Jong, (2000), 'Technology and Productivity in Historical Perspective', *European Review of Economic History*, Vol. 4, Part 2. (Cambridge University Press), pp. 115–121.

Broer, D. P. & W. J. Jansen (1989), Employment, schooling and productivity growth. *De Economist 137*, nr. 4, pp. 425–453.

Brouwers, G. (1941). De industrialisatie in Nederland gedurende de afgelopen vijfentwintig jaar. *Economisch-Statistische Berichten 1302*, pp. 11–16.

Brouwers, G. (1946). Prijs- en loonpolitiek. In M. Weisglas, *Nederlands economisch herstel*. Amsterdam: Elsevier, pp. 103–113.

Brown, B. C. (1954). Industrial production in 1935 and 1948. *London and Cambridge Economic Bulletin, new series 12*, pp. v–vii.

Brown, M., (1966). *On the Theory and Measurement of Technological Change*. Cambridge: Cambridge University Press.

Brugmans, I. J. (1969). *Paardenkracht en mensenmacht. Sociaal-economische geschiedenis van Nederland 1795–1940*. 's-Gravenhage: Martinus Nijhoff.

Burger, A. (1994). A five-country comparison of industrial labour productivity 1850–1990. *Paper for seminar on Comparative Historical National Accounts for Europe in the 19th and 20th centuries*, 10–11 June 1994 at the University of Groningen.

Byatt, I. C. R. (1979). *The British Electrical Industry, 1875–1914: The Economic Returns of a New Technology*. Oxford: Oxford University Press.

Caron, F. (1979). *An Economic History of Modern France*. New York: Columbia University Press.

Carter, C. F., W. B. Reddaway & R. Stone (1948). *The Measurement of Production Movements*. Cambridge: Cambridge University Press.

Cassiers, I. (1989). *Croissance, crise et régulation en économie ouverte. La Belgique entre les deux guerres*. Bruxelles: De Boeck Université.

Cassiers, I. & P. M. Solar (1990). Wages and Productivity in Belgium, 1910–1960. *Oxford Bulletin of Economics and Statistics 52*, no. 4, pp. 437–449.

CBS, *Jaarcijfers voor Nederland*, Various volumes.

CBS, *Maandschrift van het Centraal Bureau voor de Statistiek*, Various volumes.

CBS, *Nationale Rekeningen*, Various volumes.

CBS, *Prijzen en kosten van levensonderhoud*, Various volumes.

CBS, *Productiestatistieken van de Nederlandse nijverheid* (Production Statistics). Various volumes.

CBS, *Statistical Yearbook of the Netherlands*, Various volumes.

CBS, *Statistiek van de investeringen in de nijverheid*. (1951–1975). 's-Gravenhage.

CBS, *Statistiek der lonen in de nijverheid*, Various volumes.

CBS (1920). Statistiek van de voortbrenging en het verbruik der Nederlandsche Nijverheid in 1913 en 1916. *Bijdragen tot de Statistiek van Nederland*, no. 292. 's-Gravenhage.

CBS (1921). Statistiek van de voortbrenging en het verbruik van een aantal takken der Nederlandsche Nijverheid in 1919. *Bijdragen tot de Statistiek van Nederland*, no. 322. 's-Gravenhage.

CBS (1933–1937). *Onderzoek naar den invloed van het arbeidsloon op den kostprijs der producten*, (vier delen). 's-Gravenhage:

CBS (1935–1937). *Bedrijfstelling 31 december 1930*. Drie dln. 's-Gravenhage: Algemene Landsdrukkerij.

CBS (1936). Indexcijfers van de productie per arbeider. *De Nederlandsche Conjunctuur 7*, afl. 4, pp. 16–18.

CBS (1939). *De Nederlandsche volkshuishouding 1914–1918. Een economisch-statistische schets*. 's-Gravenhage.

CBS (1939). *Onderzoek naar het verloop der arbeidsproductiviteit*. 's-Gravenhage.

CBS (1941). Berekeningen over het nationale inkomen van Nederland voor de periode 1900–1920. *De Nederlandsche conjunctuur. Speciale Onderzoekingen no. 4*. 's-Gravenhage.

CBS (1946). Indices van de industriële productie van Nederland. *Statistische en Econometrische Onderzoekingen, 1*, nr. 3, pp. 34–36.

CBS (1947). *Economische en sociale kroniek der oorlogsjaren 1940–1945*. Utrecht.

CBS (1948). Het nationale inkomen van Nederland 1921–1939. *No. 7 der Monografieën van de Nederlandsche Conjunctuur*, Utrecht.

CBS (1949). *Statistische gegevens over de Nederlandse melk- en zuivelproductie 1933–1948*. 's-Gravenhage.

CBS (1950). De Nationale Jaarrekeningen: doeleinden, problemen, resultaten. *No. 8 der Monografieën van de Nederlandsche Conjunctuur.* Utrecht.

CBS (1955). Herziening van de hoeveelheidsindexcijfers van de produktie in de nijverheid. *Statistische en Econometrische Onderzoekingen*, 13, no. 1, pp. 5–18.

CBS (1955). De Nederlandse volkshuishouding in de periode 1945–1955. *Maandschrift CBS 50*, pp. 288–335.

CBS (1958). Ontwikkeling van de produktie per werknemer in enkele bedrijfsgroepen. *Statistische en Econometrische Onderzoekingen, 13*, no. 4, pp. 181–192.

CBS (1959). *Zestig jaren statistiek in tijdreeksen*. Zeist.

CBS (1962). Econometric Analysis of Cost and Productivity Measurement at Plant Level in the Netherlands. *Statistical Studies*, no. 12. Zeist.

CBS (1966). Hoeveelheidscijfers van de industriële produktie. *Statistische en Econometrische Onderzoekingen, 21*, no. 5. Hilversum.

CBS (1966). *Uitkomsten van de 13e algemene volkstelling 31 mei 1960*. Hilversum.

CBS (1967). *Arbeidsvolume en geregistreerde arbeidsreserve 1947–1966*. 's-Gravenhage:

CBS (1984). *Vijfentachtig jaren statistiek in tijdreeksen*. 's-Gravenhage.

CBS (1984). *De produktiestructuur van de Nederlandse Volkshuishouding, deel XII*.

CBS (1994). *Vijfennegentig jaren statistiek in tijdreeksen*. 's-Gravenhage.

CBS, Enkele kenmerken van de ontwikkeling der Nederlandsche nijverheid sedert 1921. *Maandschrift CBS 1936*, pp. 1333–1337.

Chandler, A.D. (1990). *Scale and Scope: The Dynamics of Industrial Capitalism*. Cambridge: Harvard University Press.

Chapman, A.L. (1953). *Wages and Salaries in the United Kingdom, 1920–1938*. Cambridge: Cambridge University Press.

Clark, C. (1937). *National Income and Outlay.*

Clark, C. (1951). *The Conditions of Economic Progress.* London: Macmillan.

Clark, C. (1958). *International Comparisons of Productivity Trends*, (reprint). Chicago: University of Chicago.

Collins, W.J. & J.G. Williamson (2001). Capital-Goods Prices and Investment, 1870–1950. *The Journal of Economic History, vol. 61*, nr. 1, pp. 59–94.

CPB, *Centraal Economisch Plan*, (various volumes).

CPB, (1970). *De Nederlandse economie in 1973*, deel I en II. 's-Gravenhage: Staatsuitgeverij.

CPB, (1976). *De Nederlandse economie in 1980*. 's-Gravenhage: Staatsuitgeverij.

Crafts, N.F.R. & M.F. Thomas (1986). Comparative Advantage in UK Manufacturing Trade, 1910–1935. *Economic Journal 96*, pp. 629–645.

Crafts, N.F.R. (1992). Productivity Growth Reconsidered. *Economic Policy 15*, pp. 388–426.

Cramer, J.S. (1956). Loonverschillen tussen industriële bedrijfstakken (1920–1939 en 1947–1953). *Economisch-Statistische Berichten 2012*, pp. 31–33.

Dahmén (1970). *Entrepreneurial Activity and the Development of Swedish Industry 1919–1939.* Irwin, Homewood.

David, P.A. (1966). Measuring Real Net Output. A proposed index. *The Review of Economics and Statistics XLVIII*, pp. 419–425.

David, P.A. (1975). *Technical Choice, Innovation and Economic Growth. Essays on American and British Experience in the Nineteenth Century*. Cambridge University Press, Cambridge and New York.

David, P.A. (1990). The Dynamo and the Computer: An Historical Perspective on the Modern Productivity Paradox. *Economic History of Technology 2*, pp. 355–361.

DeMonchy, E.P. (1928). Commerce and navigation. *The Netherlands and the World War vol. II*, pp. 115–162. New Haven.

Denison, E.F. (1967). *Why Growth Rates Differ. Postwar Experience in Nine Western Countries.* Washington, D.C.: The Brookings Institution.

Denison, E.F. (1972). Classification of Sources of Growth. *The Review of Income and Wealth.* Series 18, no. 1, pp. 1–25.

Dercksen, W.J. (1986). *Industrialisatiepolitiek rondom de jaren vijftig*. Assen/Maastricht: Van Gorcum.

Devine, W.D. Jr. (1990). Electrified Mechanical Drive: The Historical Power Distribution Revolution. In S. Schurr e.a., *Electricity in the American Economy*. New York: Greenwood Press, pp. 21–42.

Die deutsche Industrie. Gesamtergebnisse der amtlichen Produktionsstatistik (1939). Schriftenreihe des Reichsamts für wehrwirtschaftliche Planung, Heft 1. Berlin: Verlag für Sozialpolitik, Wirtschaft und Statistik.

Dierendonck, J.E. van. (1948). Het niveau der arbeidsproductiviteit in Engeland. *Economisch-Statistische Berichten 1641*, pp. 828–829.

Dierendonck, J.E. van. (1948). Het industriële loonpeil in Nederland. *Economisch-Statistische Berichten 1645*, pp. 906–909.

Dijk, J.J. van (1985). *Consistente tijdreeksen voor bedrijfsklassen van de Nederlandse industrie 1951–1981.* Institute for economic research. 8515/G. Rotterdam, EUR.

Dimsdale, N.H., S.J. Nickell & N. Horsewood (1989). Real Wages and Unemployment in Britain During the 1930s. *Economic Journal 99*, pp. 271–292.

Dorp, E.C. (1920). Handel en nijverheid. In H. Brugmans (red.), *Nederland in den oorlogstijd*, pp. 191–249. Amsterdam: Elsevier.

Dowie, J.R. (1968). Growth in the Interwar Period: Some more Arithmetic. *Economic History Review 21*, pp. 93–112.

Dowie, J.R. (1975). 1919–20 is in Need of Attention. *The Economic History Review 28*, pp. 429–450.

Drukker, J.W. (1990). *Waarom de crisis hier langer duurde. Over de Nederlandse economische ontwikkeling in de jaren dertig*. Amsterdam: NEHA.

Duijn J.J. van (1979). *De lange golf in de economie*. Assen: Van Gorcum.

Dumke, R.H. (1990). Reassessing the *Wirtschaftswunder*: Reconstruction and Postwar Growth in West Germany in an International Context. *Oxford Bulletin of Economics and Statistics 52*, no. 4, pp. 451–491.

Economic Commission for Europe (1950). *Economic Survey of Europe since the war.*

Eichengreen, G. & M. Uzan (1992). The Marshall Plan: economic effects and implications for Eastern Europe and the former USSR. *Economic Policy 14*, pp. 14–75.

Eichengreen, B. (1996). Institutions and Economic Growth: Europe After World War II, in N.F.R. Crafts & G. Toniolo (eds.), *Economic Growth in Europe Since 1945*. Cambridge: Cambridge University Press, pp. 38–72.

Elbaum, B. & W. Lazonick (eds.), (1986). *The Decline of the British Economy*. Oxford: Oxford University Press.

Eng, P. van der (1987). *De Marshall-hulp*. Houten: De Haan.

Etemad, B. & J. Luciani (1991). *World Energy Production 1800–1985*. Genève: Droz.

Fabricant, S. (1940). *The Output of Manufacturing Industries 1899–1937.* New York: National Bureau of Economic Research.

Fabricant, S. (1942). *Employment in Manufacturing 1899–1939. An Analysis of its Relation to the Volume of Production.* New York: N.B.E.R.

Fase, W.L.P.M. (1980). *Vijfendertig jaar loonbeleid in Nederland. Terugblik en perspectief.* Alphen a/d Rijn.

Feinstein, C.H. (1972). *National Income, Expenditure and Output of the United Kingdom 1855–1965*. Cambridge: Cambridge University Press.

Feinstein, C.H. (1972). *Statistical Tables of National Income, Expenditure and Output of the United Kingdom, 1855–1965*. Cambridge: Cambridge University Press.

Feinstein, C.H., P. Temin & G. Toniolo (1997). *The European Economy between the Wars*. Oxford; Oxford University Press.

Field, A.J. (1985). On the Unimportance of Machinery. *Explorations in Economic History 22*, pp. 378–401.

Final Report on the Fifth Census of Production and the Import Duties Act Inquiry (1935), Parts I–IV. Board of Trade.

Frankel, M. (1955). Obsolescence and Technological Change in a Maturing Economy. *The American Economic Review 45*, 296–319.

Frankel, M. (1957). *British and American Manufacturing, Productivity*. Urbana: University of Illinois Press.

Fremdling, R.R. (1988). German National Accounts for the 19th and Early 20th Century. A Critical Assessment. *Vierteljahrschrift für Sozial- und Wirtschaftsgeschichte, 75*, Band, Heft 3. Stuttgart: Franz Steiner Verlag.

Fremdling, R.R. (1990). *Van voorsprong en achterstand naar divergentie en convergentie. Denkbeelden in de economische geschiedenis*. Oratie. Groningen: Rijksuniversiteit.

Fremdling, R.R. (1991). Productivity Comparison between Great Britain and Germany, 1855–1913. *Scandinavian Economic History Review XXXIX*, pp. 28–42.

Fremdling, R.R. (1995). German National Income, Product and Expenditure, 1816–1939: A Review of the Evidence. *Economies et Sociétés. Histoire quantitative de l'économie française*, série A.F. no. 21, pp. 25–55.

Fremdling, R.R. (1997). Die niederländischen Eisenbahnen und ihr deutsches Hinterland 1853–1938. In H.-J. Gerhard (ed.) Struktur und Dimension. Stuttgart: Frans Steiner Verlag, pp. 50–72.

Fremdling, R., H.J. de Jong & J.P. Smits (2001), 'Die niederländische Wirtschaft während des zwanzigsten Jahrhunderts', *Jahrbuch für Wirtschaftsgeschichte* 2001/1. (Akademie Verlag, Berlin), pp. 13–33.

Freseman Gratama, J.A. (1946). Het herstel en de ontwikkelingsmogelijkheden van onze industrie. *Economisch-Statistische Berichten 1511*, pp. 263–265.

Frey, M. (1998). *Der Erste Weltkrieg und die Niederlande: ein neutraler Land in politischen und wirtschaftlichen Kalkül der Kriegsgegner*. Berlin : Akademie Verlag.

Gales, B.P.A. (1993). Mijnbouw. In H.W. Lintsen e.a. (red.), *Geschiedenis van de techniek in Nederland. De wording van een moderne samenleving 1800–1890*, Deel IV. Zutphen: Walburg, pp. 13–35.

Geary, R.C. (1944). The Concept of Net Volume of Output, with Special Reference to Irish Data. *Journal of the Royal Statistical Society, Parts III–IV*, pp. 251–261 en pp. 290–292 (Rejoinder).

A General View of Trade and Industry in The Netherlands. Composed by the Commercial Department of The Netherlands Ministry of Agriculture, Industry and Commerce. The Hague (s.a.) dl. I–XX.

Gerschenkron, A. (1962). *Economic Backwardness in Historical Perspective*. Cambridge, MA: Harvard University Press.

Gilbert, M. & I.B. Kravis (1954). *An International Comparison of National Products and the Purchasing Power of Currencies*. Paris: Organisation for European Economic Cooperation.

Goldin, C & L.W. Katz (1996), The Origins of Technology-Skill Complementarity. NBER Working Paper Series, nr. 5657. NBER, Cambridge Ma.

Graaff, A. de (1952). De industrie. In P.B. Kreukniet (red.), *De Nederlandse volkshuishouding tussen twee wereldoorlogen, deel VIII*. Utrecht: Het Spectrum.

Griffiths, R.T. (1986). Enkele kanttekeningen bij de eerste industrialisatienota's van J.R.M. van den Brink. *Bijdragen en mededelingen betreffende de geschiedenis der Nederlanden 101*, pp. 110–117.

Griffiths, R. T. (1996). The Dutch Economic Miracle, in J. L. van Zanden (red.), *The Economic Development of the Netherlands Since 1870*. Cheltenham: Edward Elgar, pp. 173–186.

Griliches, Z. (1988). Hedonic price indexes and the measurement of capital and productivity: Some historical reflections. *NBER Working paper no. 2634*. Cambridge Mass. (NBER).

Griliches, Z. (1994). Productivity, R & D and the Data Constraint. *American Economic Review 84*, pp. 1–23.

Groot, G. de (1995). Foreign Technology and the Gender Division of Labour in a Dutch Cotton Spinning Mill. In G. de Groot & M. Schrover (eds.), *Women Workers and Technological Change in Europe in the Nineteenth and Twentieth Centuries*. London: Taylor & Francis, pp. 52–66.

Groote, P., R. M. Albers & H. J. de Jong (1996). A standardised time series of the stock of fixed capital in the Netherlands. *Research Memorandum GD-25*. Groningen: Groningen Growth and Development Centre.

Habbakuk, H. J. (1962). *American and British Technology in the Nineteenth Century*. Cambridge: Cambridge University Press.

Harberger, A. C. (1998). A Vision of the Growth Process. *American Economic Review*, vol. 88, no. 1, pp. 1–32.

Hartog, H. den & H. S. Tjan (1974). Investeringen, lonen, prijzen en arbeidsplaatsen. *CPB Occasional paper*, nr. 2. 's-Gravenhage.

Hebbink, G. E. (1991). Employment by level of education and production factor substitutability. *De Economist 139*, nr. 3, pp. 379–399.

Heerma van Voss, A. E. (1994). *De doodsklok voor den goeden ouden tijd. De achturendag in de jaren twintig*. Amsterdam.

Hen, P. E. de. (1980). *Actieve en re-actieve industriepolitiek in Nederland*. Amsterdam: Arbeiderspers.

Herrigel, G. (1996). *Industrial Constructions. The sources of German industrial power.* Cambridge: Cambridge University Press.

Hiscox, M. J. (2002). Interindustry Factor Mobility and Technological Change: Evidence on Wage and Profit Dispersion Across U. S. Industries, 1820–1990. *The Journal of Economic History, vol. 62*, no.2, pp. 383–416.

Hjerppe, R. (1994). Productivity of Industry in Denmark, Finland and Sweden, 1905–1937. *Paper for seminar on Comparative Historical National Accounts for Europe in the 19th and 20th centuries*, 10–11 June 1994 at the University of Groningen.

Hoffmann, W. G. (1958). Zur Vorausschätzbarkeit von Produktivitätsveränderungen im Wachstumsprozess. *Zeitschrift für die gesamte Staatswissenschaft*, pp. 66–98.

Hoffmann, W. G. (1959). Die Produktivitätsstruktur der Industrie in verschiedenen Entwicklungsstadien. *Zeitschrift für die gesamte Staatswissenschaft*, pp. 536–557.

Hoffmann, W. G. (1965). *Das Wachstum der deutschen Wirtschaft seit der Mitte des 19. Jahrhunderts*. Berlin: Springer-Verlag.

Hogg. R. L. (1986). *Structural rigidities and policy inertia in interwar Belgium*. AWLSK, nr. 118, Brussel.

Hulshoff Pol, D. J. (1931). Rationalisatie en werkloosheid. *Economisch Statistische Berichten 800*, pp. 404–406.

Hulst, N. van (1984). *De effectiviteit van de geleide loonpolitiek in theorie en praktijk*. Groningen: Wolters Noordhoff.

Inklaar F. (1997). *Van Amerika geleerd. Marshall-hulp en kennisimport in Nederland*. Den Haag: Sdu Uitgevers.

Jackson, R. U. (1992). Rates of Industrial Growth During the Industrial Revolution. *Economic History Review XLV*, nr. 1, pp. 1–23.

Jerome, H. (1934). *Mechanization in Industry*. New York: N.B.E.R.

Jong, H. J. de (1993). Measuring Real Output and Productivity in Dutch Manufacturing 1921–1960. *Economic and Social History in the Netherlands, vol. 5*, pp. 213–242.

Jong, H. J. (1999). *De Nederlandse industrie 1913–1965. Een vergelijkende analyse op basis van de productiestatistieken*. Amsterdam: NEHA.

Jong, H. J. de (2001), 'Dutch manufacturing performance in comparative perspective 1913–1965', *Jahrbuch für Wirtschaftsgeschichte* 2001/1. (Akademie Verlag, Berlin), pp. 35–52.

Jong, H. J. de & R. B. M. Oude Vrielink (1993). Produktie en arbeidsproduktiviteit in de voedingsmiddelenindustrie 1918–1939. *Economisch en Sociaal Historisch Jaarboek 56*, pp. 289–339.

Jong, H. J. de & R. M. Albers (1994). Industriële groei in Nederland, 1913–1929: een verkenning. In *NEHA-jaarboek voor economische, bedrijfs- en techniekgeschiedenis 54*, pp. 444–490.

Jong, H. J. de & R. M. Albers (1994). Industrial Output and Labour Productivity in the Netherlands, 1913–1929: Some Neglected Issues. *Research Memorandum GD-13*. Groningen: Groningen Growth and Development Centre.

Jong, H. J. de & A. Soete (1997). Comparative Productivity and Structural Change in Belgian and Dutch Manufacturing, 1937–1987. *Research Memorandum GD-36*. Groningen: Groningen Growth and Development Centre.

Jong, H. J. de & A. Soete (1998). Comparative Levels of Labour Productivity and Labour Costs in Manufacturing in Belgium and The Netherlands, 1921–1990. In C. E. Núnez ed., *Historical Benchmark Comparisons of Output and Productivity*. Madrid: Fundación fomento de la historia economicá, pp. 73–91.

Jong, H. J. de & S.N. Broadberry (ed.) (2000). *European Review of Economic History Special Issue on Technology and Productivity in Historical Perspective*, Vol. 4, Part 2. (Cambridge University Press).

Jong, L. de. *Het Koninkrijk der Nederlanden in de Tweede Wereldoorlog (1970–1988)*. 's-Gravenhage: Martinus Nijhoff.

Jonge, J. A. de (1976). *De industrialisatie in Nederland tussen 1850 en 1914*. Nijmegen: SUN Reprint.

Karsten, L. (1989). *De achturendag. Arbeidstijdverkorting in historisch perspectief 1817–1919*. Groningen: Universiteitsdrukkerij.

Keesing, F. A. G. (1978). *De conjuncturele ontwikkeling van Nederland en de evolutie van de economische overheidspolitiek 1918–1939*. Nijmegen: SUN Reprint

Kendrick, J. W. (1961). *Productivity trends in the United States*. Princeton: National Bureau of Economic Research.

Kendrick, J. W. (1973). *Postwar Productivity Trends in the United States, 1948–1969*. New York: National Bureau of Economic Research.

Kendrick, J. W. & B. N. Vaccara (1980). *New Developments in Productivity Measurement Analysis*. Chicago: National Bureau of Economic Research.

Kindleberger, Ch. P. (1973). *The World in Depression*. London.

Kinghorn, J. R. & J. V. Nye (1996). The Scale of Production in Western Economic Development: A Comparison of Official Industry Statistics in the United States, Britain, France, and Germany, 1905–1913. *The Journal of Economic History 56*, pp. 90–112.

Kitson, M. & S. Solomou (1990). *Protectionism and Economic Revival. The British Interwar Economy*. Cambridge: Cambridge University Press.

Klein, P. W. (1973). Depressie en beleid tijdens de jaren dertig. Kanttekeningen bij de ontwikkeling van de Nederlandse volkshuishouding in de jaren dertig. In J. van Herwaarden (red.). *Lof der Historie*, pp. 289–336. Rotterdam: Universitaire Pers.

Klein, P. W. (1980). The foundations of Dutch prosperity. In R.T. Griffiths (ed.), *The Economy and Politics of the Netherlands since 1945*. The Hague: Martinus Nijhoff, pp. 1–12.

Klemann, H. A. M. (1990). *Tussen Reich en Empire. De economische betrekkingen van Nederland met zijn belangrijkste handelspartners: Duitsland, Groot-Brittannië en België en de Nederlandse handelspolitiek, 1929–1936*. Amsterdam: NEHA.

Klemann, H. A. M. (1997). De Nederlandse economie tijdens de Tweede Wereldoorlog. *Tijdschrift voor geschiedenis 110*, pp. 3–40.

Klemann, H. A. M. (2001) die niederländische Wirtschaft von 1938 bis 1948 im Griff von Krieg und Besatzung. *Jahrbuch für Wirtschaftsgeschichte* 2001/1. (Akademie Verlag, Berlin),

Klemann, H. A. M. (2002). Nederland 1938–1948. *Economie en samenleving in jaren van oorlog en bezetting*. Boom, Amsterdam.

Klundert, Th. van de (1997). *Groei en Instituties: over de oorzaken van economische ontwikkeling*. Tilburg: Tilburg University Press.

Knibbe, M. (1993). *Agriculture in the Netherlands 1851–1950*. Amsterdam: NEHA.

Kohnstamm, G. A. (1948). *De toekomst van de Nederlandse industriële ontwikkeling*. 's-Gravenhage.

Kohnstamm, G. A. (1955). Tien jaren van industriële groei. *Economisch-Statistische Berichten 1977*, pp. 416–42.

Kooij, P. (1972). De eerste verbruikers van electriciteit in de gemeente Groningen (1895–1912). *Economisch- en Sociaal-Historisch Jaarboek 35*, pp. 274–302.

Kravis, I. B. (1976). A Survey of International Comparisons of Productivity. *The Economic Journal 86*, pp. 1–44.

Kravis, I. B., A. Heston, & R. Summers (1982). *World Product and Income. International Comparisons of Real Gross Product*. Baltimore: Johns Hopkins University Press.

Krijnse Locker, H. & M. D. Faerber (1984). Space and Time Comparisons of Purchasing Power Parity and Real Values. *Review of Income and Wealth 30*, pp. 53–83.

Kuipers, S. K. (1977). *Over structurele en conjuncturele ontwikkelingen binnen de Nederlandse economie sinds de eerste wereldoorlog*. Amsterdam: Noord-Hollàndsche Uitgeversmaatschappij.

Kuipers, S. K. (1991). *Marktwerking en werkloosheid in Nederland in de jaren dertig en tachtig*. Amsterdam: K. N. A. W.

Kuipers, S. K. & G. H. Kuper (1996). Wage Formation, Investment and Growth in the Netherlands in the Postwar Period: a Cross-Section Analysis. *De Economist 144, no. 3*, pp. 487–495.

Kuypers, I. (2002). *In de schaduw van de Grote Oorlog. De Nederlandse arbeidersbeweging en de overheid, 1914–1920*. Amsterdam.

Lamfalussy, A. (1961). *Investment and Growth in Mature Economies*. London: Macmillan.

Lange, P. W. de (1933). De productiviteit van den arbeid in de nijverheid. *De Nederlandsche Conjunctuur 4*, afl. 4, pp. 10–15.

Larssen, H. K. & C. A. Nilsson (1992) Some Remarks on the Use of Prices when Constructing Volume Series. *Scandinavian Economic History Review XL*, pp. 28–39.

Leak, H. & A. Maizels (1945). The Structure of British Industry. *Journal of the Royal Statistical Society*, Series A, 108, pp. 142–207.

Lebergott, S. (1947). Wages Structures. *The Review of Economics and Statistics 29*. pp. 280–292.

Lebergott, S. (1960). Labor Force and Employment, 1800–1960. In D. S. Brady (ed.), *Output, Employment and Productivity in the United States After 1800, Vol. 30, Studies in Income and Wealth*. New York: National Bureau of Economic Research, pp. 117–204.

Lindlar, L. (1997). *Das missverstandene Wirtschaftswunder: Westdeutschland und die westeuropäische Nachkriegsprosperität*. Tübingen: Mohr Siebeck.

Ljungberg, J. (1991). Prices and Industrial Transformation. *Scandinavian Economic History Review XXXIX*, no. 2, pp. 49–63.

Lomax, K. S. (1959). Production and Productivity Movements in the United Kingdom Since 1900. *Journal of the Royal Statistical Society, Series A, 122*, pp. 185–210.

Lomax, K. S. (1969). Growth and Productivity in the United Kingdom. In D.H. Aldcroft & P. Fearon (eds.), *Economic Growth in 20th Century Britain*. London: Macmillan, pp. 10–33.

Lorenz, E. H. (1984), The Labour Process in British and French shipbuilding from 1880 to 1930. *Journal of European Economic History 13*.

Maddison, A. (1982). *Phases of Capitalist Development*. Oxford: Oxford University Press.

Maddison, A. (1987). Growth and Slowdown in Advanced Capitalist Economies: Techniques of Quantitative Assessment. *Journal of Economic Literature 25*, pp. 649–698.

Maddison, A. (1991). *Dynamic Forces in Capitalist Development*. Oxford: Oxford University Press.

Maddison, A. (1993). Standardised Estimates of Fixed Capital Stock: A Six Country Comparison. *Innovazione e Materie Prime*, pp. 1–29.

Maddison, A. (1995). *Monitoring the World Economy 1820–1992*. Paris: Organisation for Economic Cooperation and Development.

Maddison, A. & B. van Ark (1994), The International Comparison of Real Product and Productivity, *Research Memorandum GD-6*, Groningen: Groningen Growth and Development Centre.

Maizels, A. (1958). Comparative Productivity in Manufacturing Industry: a Case Study of Australia and Canada. *The Economic Record 4*, pp. 67–89.

Mankiw, G., D. Romer & D. Weil (1992). A contribution to the empirics of economic growth. *Quarterly Journal of Economics 107*, pp. 407–437.

Matthews, R.C.O., C.H. Feinstein & J.C. Odling-Smee (1982). *British Economic Growth, 1856–1973*. Oxford: Oxford University Press.

Melman, S. (1956). *Dynamic Factors in Industrial Productivity*. Oxford: Blackwell.

Mensink, G.J.A. (1966). Comparisons of labour productivity in the United Kingdom and the Netherlands, 1958. *Statistical Studies* no. 18, CBS, Den Haag.

Messing, F. (1981). *De Nederlandse Economie 1945–1980. Herstel, Groei, Stagnatie*. Haarlem: Fibula-Van Dishoeck.

Methorst, H.W. (1928). The Cost of Living, Prices and Wages. *The Netherlands and the World War vol. II*. New Haven, pp. 303–361.

Ministerie van Economische Zaken, *Economische en Sociale Telling van 27 februari 1937*. Brussels.

Mitchell, B.R. (1975). *European Historical Statistics 1750–1950*. London: Macmillan.

Moore, B.F. (1919). *Economic Aspects of the Commerce and Industry of the Netherlands, 1912–1918*. Washington: Government Printing Office.

Mulder, A.M. (1994). *Denken over beleid: De Nederlandse economische politiek in het interbellum*. Delft: Eburon.

Nordvik, H.W. & O.H. Grytten (1994). The Labour Market, Unemployment and Economic Growth in Norway, 1920–1939. *Scandinavian Economic History Review XLII*, pp. 125–144.

Nota inzake de industrialisatie in Nederland (1949). Den Haag.

O'Brien, P. (1986). *International Productivity Comparisons and Problems of Measurement 1750–1939*. Bern.

O'Brien, P. (1993). Introduction: Modern Conceptions of the Industrial Revolution. In P. O'Brien, & R. Quinault (eds.). *The Industrial Revolution and British Society*. Cambridge: Cambridge University Press.

OECD, (1964). *Industrial Statistics 1900–1961*. Paris: OECD.

Onderzoek naar de "blijvende werkloosheid" en haar bestrijding. (1939). *Rapport van de commissie ingesteld bij beschikking van den voorzitter van den Hoogen Raad van Arbeid dd. 18 december 1936*. 's-Gravenhage: Rijksuitgeverij.

Oortwijn Botjes, J. (1936). Het peil der loonen in de West-Europeesche landen. *Economische-Statistische Berichten 1054*, pp. 185–186.

Oude Vrielink, R.B.M. (1992). *Arbeidsproduktiviteit in de Nederlandse voedings- en genotmiddelenindustrie, 1918–1939*. Unpublished master thesis University of Groningen.

Oulton, N. & M. O'Mahony (1994). *Productivity and Growth: A Study of British Industry, 1954–1986*. Cambridge: Cambridge University Press.

Paige, D. & G. Bombach (1959). *A Comparison of National Output and Productivity of the United Kingdom and the United States*. Paris: Organisation for European Economic Cooperation.

Phelps Brown, E.H. (1973). Levels and Movements of Industrial Productivity and Real Wages Internationally Compared, 1860–1970. *The Economic Journal 83*, pp. 58–71.

Pollard, S. (1983). *The Development of the British Economy 1914–1980*, London.

Porter, M.E. (1990). *The Competitive Advantage of Nations*. London: Macmillan.

Pruijt, B. (1948)., *De prijsbeheersingspolitiek tijdens de bezetting 1940–1945*. Leiden: Stenfert Kroese.

Renaud, A. W. J. (1937). Prijsontwrichting en monetaire aanpassingspolitiek. *Economisch-Statistische Berichten 1147*, pp. 935–937.

Richardson H. W. (1967). *Economic Recovery in Britain 1932–1939*. London: Weidenfeld & Nicolson.

Rijken van Olst, H. (1950). Over de meting van de arbeidsproduktiviteit. *Economisch-Statistische Berichten*, 1729, pp. 519–521.

Ritschl, A. O. (1994). On the origins and course of the Great Depression in Germany: A quantitative assessment of industrial production and aggregate output data, 1925–1938. Paper presented at the *11th International Economic History Congress* in Milan, 12–16 September 1994.

Ritschl, A. O. (1996). An exercise in futility: East German economic growth and decline, 1945–1989, in N. F. R. Crafts & G. Toniolo (eds.), *Economic Growth in Europe Since 1945*. Cambridge: Cambridge University Press, pp. 498–540.

Romer, C. D. (1999). Why Did Prices Rise in the 1930s? *The Journal of Economic History vol. 59*. no. 1, pp. 167–199.

Romer, D. (1996). *Advanced Macroeconomics*. McGraw Hill.

Roof, Restitutie, Reparatie (1947). 's-Gravenhage: Staatsdrukkerij- en Uitgeverijbedrijf.

Roos, F. de & W. J.. Wieringa (1953). *Een halve eeuw rente in Nederland*. Schiedam: Levensverzekeringsmaatschappij HAV Bank.

Rosenberg, N. (1982). *Inside the Black Box*. Cambridge: Cambridge University Press.

Rosenberg, N. (1994). *Exploring the Black Box. Technology, Economics and History*. Cambridge: Cambridge University Press.

Rostas, L. (1943). Industrial Production, Productivity and Distribution in Britain, Germany and the United States, 1935–37. *The Economic Journal 53*, pp. 39–54.

Rostas, L. (1948). *Comparative Productivity in British and American Industry*. Cambridge: Cambridge University Press.

Rostas, L. (1948). *Productivity, Prices and Distribution in Selected British Industries*. Cambridge: Cambridge University Press.

Rostow, W. W., (1971). *The Stages of Economic Growth*, 2nd ed. Cambridge, Cambridge University Press.

Rijksverzekeringsbank. *Ongevallenstatistiek 1903–1963*. (National Insurance Bank. Accident Statistics 1903–1963).

Saalfeld, K. (1927). *Die niederländische Metallindustrie in ihren volks- und weltwirtschaftlichen Zusammenhängen*. Rostock: Carl Hinstorffs Verlag.

Salter, W. E. G. (1960). *Productivity and Technical Change* (2nd ed. 1966). Cambridge: Cambridge University Press.

Sandee, J. (1947). Over de meting van de arbeidsproduktiviteit. *Economisch-Statistische Berichten 1590*, pp. 863–864.

Saunders, C. T. (1952). Consumption of Raw Materials in the United Kingdom: 1851–1950. *Journal of the Royal Statistical Society, Series A (General), Part III*, pp. 313–346.

Schaik, A. van (1986). *Crisis en protectie onder Colijn*. Alblasserdam: Kanters.

Schalk, F. C. J. van der (1938). *De wiskundig-statistische analyse van de arbeidsproductiviteit en haar practische toepassing op eenige bedrijfstakken en ondernemingen in Nederland*. Haarlem: Bohn.

Schippers, J. J. & J. J. Siegers (1991). Labour market inequality between men and women: allocational differences versus wage rate differences. *De Economist 139*, Nr. 3, pp. 401–427.

Schön, L. (1988). *Industri och hantverk 1800–1980*. Lund: Ekonomisk-historika föreningen.

Schot, J. W. et. al. (1998–2002). *Techniek in Nederland in de twintigste eeuw* (7 Vol.). Eindhoven: Stichting Historie der Techniek. Zutphen Walburg Pers.

Schrage, P., E. Nijhoff & P. Wielsma (1989). Inkomensontwikkeling van werkenden en werklozen in Nederland, 1913–1939. *Tijdschrift voor Sociale Geschiedenis, vol. 15*, pp. 347–394.

Schrover, M. (1995). Cooking up Women's Work: Women Workers in the Dutch Food Industries 1889–1960. In G. de Groot & M. Schrover (eds.), *Women Workers and Technological Change in Europe in the Nineteenth and Twentieth Centuries*. London: Taylor & Francis, pp. 170–192.

Schumpeter, J. A. (1962). *The Theory of Economic Development*, 2nd ed. New York, Oxford University Press.

Schumpeter, J. A. (1976). *Capitalism, Socialism & Democracy*, 5th ed. London: Allen & Unwin.

Schurr, S. & B. C. Netschert (1960). *Energy in the American Economy. An Economic Study of its History and Prospects*. Baltimore: Johns Hopkins.

Seegers, J. J. (1986). *Het indexcijfer van de industriële produktie in Nederland gedurende het interbellum: inventarisatie en nieuwe berekeningen. Research-memorandum 8601*. Amsterdam: University of Amsterdam.

Seegers, J. J. (1987). Produktie en concurrentievermogen van de Nederlandse industrie in het interbellum. *Economisch en Sociaal Historisch Jaarboek 50*, pp. 186–211.

Sims, C. A. (1969). Theoretical basis for a double deflated index of real value added. *Review of Economics and Statistics, Vol. 51*, no. 4, pp. 470–471.

Sleifer, J. A. (2003). *Falling Behind: The East German Economy in Comparison with West Germany 1936–2002*. Groningen Growth and Development Centre. Monograph Series, no. 6.

Sluyterman, K. E. & H. J. M. Winkelman (1993). The Dutch Family Firm confronted with Chandler's Dynamics of Industrial Capitalism, 1890–1940. *Business History 35*, pp. 152–183.

Smidt, M. de & E. Wever (1990). *De Nederlandse industrie*. Assen/Maastricht: Van Gorcum.

Smissaert, J. H. (1913). *Die niederländische Industrie*. Haag: Mouton & Co.

Smits, J. P., H. J. de Jong & B. van Ark (1999), 'Three Phases of Dutch Economic Growth and Technological Change, 1815–1997', *Research Memorandum* GD-42, Groningen Growth and Development Centre, 24 p.

Smits, J. P., E.. Horlings & J. L. van Zanden (2000). *Dutch GNP and its Components, 1800–1913*. Groningen Growth and Development Centre. Monograph Series, no. 5.

Smith, A. D., D. M. W. N. Hitchens & S. W. Davies (1982). *International Industrial Productivity: A Comparison of Britain, America and Germany*. Cambridge: Cambridge University Press.

Soete, A. (1994). *The Evolution of the Competitiveness of the Belgian Manufacturing Industry in the Long Run, 1880–1990*. Paper presented at the Economics Department of the Catholic University Leuven.

Solar, P. M. & H. J. de Jong (1998). The Benelux countries. In Bernard J. Foley (ed.), *European Economies since the Second World War*. London: Macmillan Press Ltd, pp. 102–123.

Solow, R. M. (1957). Technical Change and the Aggregate Production Function. *Review of Economics and Statistics 39*, pp. 313–320.

Sonenblum, S. (1990). Electrification and Productivity Growth in Manufacturing. In S. H. Schurr e.a., *Electricity in the American Economy*. New York: Greenwood Press, pp. 277–324.

Sonenblum, S. & S. Schurr (1990). Electricity Use and Energy Conservation. In S. Schurr e.a., *Electricity in the American Economy*. New York: Greenwood Press, pp. 325–339.

Statistischen Reichsamt, *Vierteljahrshefte zur Statistik des Deutschen Reichs*. Div. jrg. Berlin: Verlag für Sozialpolitik, Wirtschaft und Statistik.

Statistischen Reichsamt, *Wirtschaft und Statistik*. Div. jrg. Berlin: Verlag für Sozialpolitik, Wirtschaft und Statistik.

Statistisches Handbuch von Deutschland, 1928–1944 (Länderrat des amerikanischen Besatzungsgebiets, München, 1949).

Stone, R. (1956). *Quantity and Price Indices in National Accounts*. Paris: Organisation for European Economic Cooperation.

Stuyvenberg, J. H. van. (1969). Aspects of Government Intervention, in J.H. van Stuyvenberg (ed.), *Margarine: An Economic, Social and Scientific History, 1869–1969*. Liverpool: Liverpool University Press, pp. 281–327.

Svennilson, I. (1954). *Growth and Stagnation in the European Economy*. Geneva: United Nations.

Szilagyi, G. (1984). Procedures for Updating the Results of International Comparisons. *Review of Income and Wealth 30*, pp. 207–262.

Temin, P. (1966). Labor Scarcity and the Problem of American Industrial Efficiency in the 1850s. *Journal of Economic History, 26*, pp. 361–379.

Thorp, W. (1929). Horsepower Statistics for Manufacturing. *Journal of the American Statistical Association*, pp. 376–388.

Tinbergen, J. (1932). Kapitaalvorming en conjunctuur in Nederland 1880–1930. *De Nederlandsche Conjunctuur 3*, no. 1, pp. 8–16.

Tinbergen, J. (1934). De invloed van de conjunctuur op de arbeidsproductiviteit. *De Nederlandsche Conjunctuur 5*, no. 2, pp. 13–20.

Tinbergen, J. (1936). Prijsdispariteit en handelsbeweging. *De Nederlandsche Conjunctuur 6*, pp. 10–20.

Tinbergen, J. & A. L. G. M. Rombouts (1939). De samenhang tusschen de prijzen van ingevoerde grondstoffen en die van afgewerkte producten in Nederland. *De Nederlandsche Conjunctuur 10*, pp. 150–165.

Trienekens, G. M. T. (1985). *Tussen ons volk en de honger. De voedselvoorziening 1940–1945*. Utrecht: Matrijs.

Tunzelmann, G. N. von. (1982). Structural Change and Leading Sectors in British Manufacturing, 1907–1968. In C. P. Kindleberger & G. di Tella (eds.), *Economics in the Long View, Vol. 3: Applications and Cases, Part II*, pp. 1–49. London: Macmillan.

Tunzelmann, G. N. von. (1995). *Technology and Industrial Progress*, Aldershot: Edward Elgar.

Tweede Nota inzake de industrialisatie van in Nederland (1950). Den Haag.

Veen, D. J. van der & J. L. van Zanden (1989). Real Wage Trends and Consumption Patterns in the Netherlands (c. 1870–1940). In P. Scholliers (red.), *Real Wages in 19th and 20th century Europe*. New York: Berg, pp. 205–228.

Verdoorn, P. J. (1943). De verstarring der productiekosten. *Nederlandsch Economisch Instituut nr. 33*. Haarlem: Bohn.

Verdoorn, P. J. (1946). Het onbevredigend niveau onzer arbeidsproductiviteit. *Economisch-Statistische Berichten 1526*, pp. 503–506.

Verdoorn, P. J. (1947). *Arbeidsduur en welvaartspeil*. Leiden: Stenfert Kroese.

Verdoorn, P. J. (1951). On an Empirical Law Governing the Productivity of Labour. *Econometrica 19*, no. 2, p. 209.

Vierde Nota inzake de industrialisatie van Nederland (1953). Den Haag.

Volks-, Berufs- und Betriebszählung vom 16. Juni 1925, gewerbliche Betriebszählung (1929). *Die gewerblichen Betriebe und Unternehmungen im Deutschen Reiche, Teil III, die technischen Betriebseinheiten im Deutschen Reiche*. Berlin.

Volks-, Berufs- und Betriebszählung vom 1933 (1935). *Das Personal der gewerblichen Niederlassungen nach der Stellung im Betrieb und die Verwendung von Kraftmaschinen*. Berlin.

Vries, Joh. de (1983). *De Nederlandse economie tijdens de 20e eeuw*. Bussum: Fibula-Van Dishoek.

Vries, Joh. de (1983). Het economisch leven in Nederland 1918–1940. In D. P. Blok et. al. *Algemene Geschiedenis der Nederlanden deel XX*. Haarlem: Fibula-Van Dishoeck, pp. 103–145.

Waerden, Th. van der (1929). *Over rationalisatie en werkloosheid*. Amsterdam: N.V. "Ontwikkeling".

Waerden, Th. van der (1933). Prae-advies over de vraag: *Leidt het streven naar arbeidsbesparing in het huidige productie-proces tot een duurzame of een tijdelijke vermeerdering van werkloosheid?* 's-Gravenhage: Martinus Nijhoff.

Wagenführ, R. (1933). "Die Industriewirtschaft. Entwicklungstendenzen der Deutschen und internationalen Industrieproduktion 1860 bis 1932". *Vierteljahreshefte zur Konjunkturforschung*, Sonderheft 31, 3–70.

Weisglas, M. (1946). *Nederlands economisch herstel*. Amsterdam/Brussel: Elsevier.

Weisglas, M. (1952). *De Nederlandse industrie sinds 1945. Een wereld van groei*. Leiden: Sijthoff N.V.

Weststrate, C. (1959). *Economic Policy in Practice: the Netherlands 1950/1957*. Leiden: Stenfert Kroese.

Wilson, Ch. (1954). *Geschiedenis van Unilever. Een beeld van economische groei en maatschappelijke verandering*. Den Haag: Martinus Nijhoff.

Windmuller, J. P., C. de Galan & A. F. van Zweeden (1979^3). *Arbeidsverhoudingen in Nederland*, Utrecht/Antwerpen: Aula.

Witteveen, H. J. (1950). Prae-advies over de vraag: *Het vraagstuk der kapitaalschaarste in Nederland, meer in het bijzonder de schaarste aan risicodragend kapitaal*. 's-Gravenhage: Martinus Nijhoff.

Witteveen, H.J. (1956). *Structuur en conjunctuur. Het vraagstuk der kapitaalschaarste en de huidige ontwikkeling der conjunctuurtheorie.* Haarlem: Bohn.

Woestijne, W. J. van de (1969). De goede jaren die aan de depressie vooraf gingen. *Tijdschrijft voor Geschiedenis 82*, pp. 359–382.

Wonnacott, T. H. & R. J. Wonnacott, R. J. (1985). *Introductory Statistics* (4th edn.). New York: Wiley.

Woolf, A. G. (1980). *Energy and Technology in American Manufacturing: 1900–1929*. Ann Arbor.

Zaalberg, C. J. P. (1928). The manufacturing industry. *The Netherlands and the World War. Studies in the War history of a neutral, vol. II*. New Haven: Yale University Press, pp. 3–111.

Zanden, J. L. van. (1988). *De dans om de gouden standaard. Economische beleid in de depressie van de jaren dertig*. Oratie VU. Amsterdam.

Zanden, J. L. van. (1988). Geleide loonpolitiek en de internationale concurrentiepositie van Nederland 1948–1962. *Maandschrift Economie 52*, pp. 464–477.

Zanden, J. L. van (1997). *Een klein land in de 20e eeuw. Economische geschiedenis van Nederland 1914–1995*. Utrecht: Het Spectrum.

Zanden, J. L. van (1997). *The economic history of the Netherlands, 1914–1995: a small open economy in the 'long' twentieth century*. London: Routledge.

Zanden, J. L. van & R. T. Griffiths (1989). *Economische geschiedenis van Nederland in de 20e eeuw*. Utrecht: Het Spectrum.

Index

Z

www.ingramcontent.com/pod-product-compliance
Lightning Source LLC
Chambersburg PA
CBHW080938240926
51849CB00004BA/493
* 9 7 8 3 0 5 0 0 3 6 9 7 7 *